THE RENAISSANCE OF LETTERS

The Renaissance of Letters traces the multiplication of letter-writing practices between the fourteenth and seventeenth centuries in the Italian peninsula and beyond to explore the importance of letters as a crucial document for understanding the Italian Renaissance.

This edited collection contains case studies, ranging from the late medieval re-emergence of letter-writing to the mid-seventeenth century, that offer a comprehensive analysis of the different dimensions of late medieval and Renaissance letters—literary, commercial, political, religious, cultural, social, and military—which transformed them into powerful early modern tools. The Renaissance was an era that put letters into the hands of many kinds of people, inspiring them to see reading, writing, receiving, and sending letters as an essential feature of their identity. The authors take a fresh look at the correspondence of some of the most important figures of the Italian Renaissance, including Niccolò Machiavelli and Isabella d'Este, and consider the use of letters for others such as merchants and physicians.

This book is essential reading for scholars and students of Late Medieval and Early Modern History and Literature, Early Modern History, Renaissance Studies, and Italian Studies. The engagement with essential primary sources renders this book an indispensable tool for those teaching seminars on Renaissance history and literature.

Paula Findlen is Ubaldo Pierotti Professor of Italian History at Stanford University, USA. She is the author of *Possessing Nature: Museums, Collecting and Scientific Culture in Early Modern Italy* (1994) and many other publications on Renaissance/early modern Italy and the history of science. Professor Findlen is the 2016 recipient of the Premio Galileo for her contributions to understanding Italian culture.

Suzanne Sutherland is an Associate Professor of Early Modern European History at Middle Tennessee State University, USA. She is finishing a book on early modern military entrepreneurs and has worked on Stanford's Mapping the Republic of Letters interdisciplinary digital humanities project since 2008.

THE RENAISSANCE OF LETTERS

Knowledge and Community in Italy, 1300–1650

Edited by Paula Findlen and
Suzanne Sutherland

Routledge
Taylor & Francis Group

LONDON AND NEW YORK

First published 2020
by Routledge
2 Park Square, Milton Park, Abingdon, Oxon, OX14 4RN

and by Routledge
52 Vanderbilt Avenue, New York, NY 10017

Routledge is an imprint of the Taylor & Francis Group, an informa business

Library of Congress Cataloging-in-Publication Data
Names: Sutherland, Suzanne, (Professor of history), editor. |
Findlen, Paula, editor.
Title: The Renaissance of letters : knowledge and community in Italy,
1300-1650 / edited by Suzanne Sutherland, Paula Findlen.
Description: New York, NY : Routledge, 2019. | Includes
bibliographical references and index. |
Identifiers: LCCN 2019029783 (print) | LCCN 2019029784 (ebook) |
ISBN 9781138367494 (hardback) | ISBN 9781138367500 (paperback) |
ISBN 9780429429774 (ebook)
Subjects: LCSH: Italian letters–Early modern, 1500-1700–History and
criticism. | Letter writing, Italian–history.
Classification: LCC PQ4183.L4 R46 2019 (print) | LCC PQ4183.L4
(ebook) | DDC 856/.2–dc23
LC record available at https://lccn.loc.gov/2019029783
LC ebook record available at https://lccn.loc.gov/2019029784

ISBN: 978-1-138-36749-4 (hbk)
ISBN: 978-1-138-36750-0 (pbk)
ISBN: 978-0-429-42977-4 (ebk)

Typeset in Bembo
by Swales & Willis, Exeter, Devon, UK

In memory of Mark Kennett, who always wanted to write history, and Mabelle Avery Findlen, who loved to write and receive letters.

CONTENTS

4 Isabella d'Este's Employee Relations   93
Deanna Shemek

5 Letters as sources for studying Jewish conversion: the case of
Salomone da Sesso/Ercole de' Fedeli   104
Tamar Herzig

PART III
Humanism, diplomacy, and empire   **123**

6 Writing a letter in 1507: the fortunes of Francesco Vettori's
correspondence and the Florentine Republic   125
Christopher Bacich

7 Minding gaps: connecting the worlds of Erasmus and
Machiavelli   146
William J. Connell

8 The Cardinal's Dearest Son and the pirate: Venetian empire and
the letters of Giovan Matteo Bembo   164
Demetrius C. Loufas

PART IV
Science and travel   **185**

9 The literary lives of health workers in late Renaissance Venice   187
Sarah Gwyneth Ross

10 A Florentine humanist in India: Filippo Sassetti, Medici agent by
annual letter   208
Brian Brege

11 "*La verità delle stelle*": Margherita Sarrocchi's letters to Galileo   227
Meredith K. Ray

PART V
Information, politics, and war   **253**

12 Publishing the Baroque post: the postal itinerary and the
mailbag novel   255
Rachel Midura

FIGURES

CONTRIBUTORS

Christopher Bacich, Stanford University

Brian Brege, Syracuse University

William J. Connell, Seton Hall University

Filippo de Vivo, Birkbeck, University of London

Paula Findlen, Stanford University

Tamar Herzig, Tel Aviv University

Demetrius C. Loufas, Stanford University

Rachel Midura, Stanford University

Jeffrey Miner, Western Kentucky University

Monique O'Connell, Wake Forest University

Meredith K. Ray, University of Delaware

Diana Robin, The Newberry Library

Sarah Gwyneth Ross, Boston College

Deanna Shemek, University of California, Irvine

Suzanne Sutherland, Middle Tennessee State University

Lynn Lara Westwater, The George Washington University

ACKNOWLEDGMENTS

This project began with a question—what was there before the Republic of Letters? From such discussions, the idea of a project that might focus on earlier Italian contributions to letter-writing practices, communication systems, and even postal services was born. We received a great deal of assistance along the way that we gratefully acknowledge.

Most of the essays in this volume were originally presented at a May 2016 workshop entitled "The Renaissance of Letters: Knowledge and Community in Italy, 1300–1650," which was co-sponsored by Stanford University and Middle Tennessee State University and hosted by the Stanford Humanities Center. This project was partly inspired by our work with a group of faculty, staff, and students on *Mapping the Republic of Letters* and we thank Dan Edelstein, Caroline Winterer, Giovanna Ceserani, Nicole Coleman, Iva Lelková, Molly Taylor-Poleskey, Hannah Marcus, and the rest of the MRofL team for their collaboration. We thank Rosemary Rogers for her marvelous administrative support of the workshop and the History Department and Suppes Center for the History and Philosophy of Science and Technology for providing material support in other ways. We also received funding from Stanford's UPS Endowment Fund that proved crucial to seeing the final stages of this publication through.

At Routledge, Laura Pilsworth, Lydia Cruz, Morwenna Scott, Zoe Forbes, and Sally Evans-Darby handled all our queries with good will, put up with the inevitable unanticipated delays, and cheered this book to the finish line. Their care in production has made it a better book.

Finally, we owe a debt to our families who have lived with *The Renaissance of Letters* for a few years. Suzanne would like to thank Karel, Lukas, and Veronika, as well as her happy network of family, friends, and neighbors in Tennessee and beyond, all of whom make community truly meaningful. Back in California, Paula gratefully acknowledges the joy with which Jeff, Natalie, and their dog

Coco whisked her away to Colorado for a year where she completed most of the research and editing with Suzanne before returning to Stanford for the final push. At the Cantor Arts Center, Susan Dackerman and Tammy Fortin generously allowed her to finish in a quiet corner of the museum.

The "renaissance of letters" is of course an ideal as much as lived experience of this particular past. Our collaborators, many of whom participated in a roundtable on this volume at the 2019 Renaissance Society of America, have embodied the very spirit of this book. To them especially we offer our heartfelt thanks and appreciation.

Paula Findlen and Suzanne Sutherland

INTRODUCTION

With a letter in hand: writing, communication, and representation in Renaissance Italy*

Paula Findlen

In 1449–50, the recently appointed Venetian consul in London and future doge Marco Barbarigo (1413–86) had his portrait painted, probably by a Flemish follower of Jan van Eyck. Recent scholarship has identified this painting as one of the first portraits to incorporate "a hand in a way that was not to become common in Venetian portraiture for another half century" (Figure 0.1).[1]

The letter that Barbarigo holds in his hand turns out to be equally interesting. The artist carefully inscribed the names of the sender and recipient and its destination on the outside of the folded letter in an effort to represent the look and feel of inked paper communicating Venetian interests abroad. It brings to mind frequent discussions of the material culture of communication in Renaissance correspondence: "But I shall fold the letter, since the courier is in a hurry," the Florentine humanist Angelo Poliziano (1454–94) hastily wrote at the end of a letter.[2] In this portrait, Barbarigo has already broken the seal, and probably read the contents. The painting captures him in the midst of contemplating his plan of action and response. This fifteenth-century painting of an ambassador is both a portrait of a person and a letter – a tangible representation of the continuous cycle of writing, reading, and communication that became important by the mid-fifteenth century. It may well be the first portrait of the Renaissance letter.

Long before the emergence of an early modern "Republic of Letters," there was a *renaissance of letters* – a self-conscious rebirth of the meaning and purpose of correspondence. Barbarigo's portrait bears witness to a transformation that began in the fourteenth century. *Nota hic bonam litteram*, "Take note of this good letter," scribbled an English clerk in 1390 in the margins of a letter from the Florentine republic's chancellor Coluccio Salutati (1331–1406). The duke of Milan, Gian Galeazzo Visconti, allegedly declared: "one letter of Salutati was worth a troop of horses."[3] In the century that followed, western Europe completed the long transition from using vellum (animal hides scraped clean to

FIGURE 0.1   Follower of Van Eyck, *Marco Barbarigo* (ca. 1449–50), oil on oak, 24.2 ×
16 cm, bought 1862 (NG696).
© National Gallery of Art, London/Art Resource ART374460

produce a thin, durable writing surface) to writing on rag linen paper which
became more plentiful and affordable in the late thirteenth century. The letter,
already an object of great antiquity, now emerged as "a modern, agile, and
multiform instrument" of communication.[4] Written in different scripts and
languages for public and private purposes, the letter became a way of bridging
distance, conveying information and instructions, establishing and maintaining
relationships. Fundamentally, letters were remade. They became objects whose
specific materiality attracted a great deal of commentary and interest, inspiring
experiments in how to represent them.

In light of the singular fame of the most celebrated humanist letters, Barbarigo's letter seems rather ordinary – born of the pragmatic necessity to establish and maintain a network of foreign relations. At the same time, it is far from banal because it is diplomatic correspondence. By contrast, Petrarch's rediscovery of Cicero's *Letters to Atticus* in Verona in 1345, the subsequent discovery of his *Familiar Letters* by the next generation, and numerous printings of these works before 1500 closely associated the eloquence of Latin letters with humanist oratory, rhetoric, and friendship.[5] Even as Petrarch polished his *Letter to Posterity* (ca. 1350–61) and gathered his *Familiar Letters* before undertaking *Letters in Old Age*, he found himself dealing with the practicalities of communication at a distance that far less exalted minds also contemplated. He used virtually every means of delivering mail in the fourteenth century – papal, royal, and imperial couriers, Florentine runners, friends, servants; even a former soldier turned monk named Bolanus working as a private messenger. Petrarch may have been crowned poet laureate in 1341, but this did not exempt him from dealing with impatient couriers, delayed mail, and lost letters. The concrete nature of human communication and its numerous practical difficulties has not been a focal point for studies of Renaissance correspondence, though a new kind of diplomatic, intellectual, and religious history concerned with how people overcame distance is now engaging these issues.[6] Writing to Boccaccio, Petrarch knew that leaving letters unsealed increased the chances of a safe arrival across the borders of hostile states.[7]

This harsh reality of corresponding at a distance connects Petrarch's letters to the Renaissance diplomatic pouch and the vibrant commercial networks linking the Mediterranean to northern Europe. Without the commercial necessity of correspondence, neither the diplomat nor the humanist secretary would have known how to send and receive letters.[8] Their letters traveled the same routes, forging connections between cities and constantly seeking to expand the sphere of influence. Barbarigo's portrait is an artifact of how Italian states coped with political uncertainty by establishing permanent embassies in strategic locations, securing the image of the ambassador as the resident man of letters. The Venetian consul may still have been writing his own letters, as was common practice before the sixteenth century, or he could have employed a secretary to write on his behalf.[9] This portrait invites us to consider the ways in which Renaissance artists captured the epistolary practices of their time with great attentiveness and verisimilitude, once letters became visible markers of identity.

Portrait of a Renaissance letter

During the fifteenth century, letters began to penetrate the consciousness of many different kinds of people. Writing to the learned humanist educator Guarino da Verona in 1436, Laura Cereta (1418–66) presented herself as "a beginner in the world of letters," yet within a decade or two, she was renowned for her "letters now collected in a volume."[10] The erudite and witty Aeneas Silvius Piccolomini (1405–64), a curial secretary and diplomat before becoming Pius II, composed his *Historia de duobis amantibus* (1444), a Latin romance containing ten imaginary letters between a young man and woman. Printed twenty times by 1500 and widely translated, it was a bestselling Renaissance epistolary novella.[11]

Renaissance artists not only painted portraits with letters but also cultivated their own correspondence. Leonardo da Vinci (1452–1519) was sufficiently concerned about how to write a good letter that he owned three letter-writing manuals – Gian Mario Filelfo's *Epistolarium novum sive Ars scribendi epistolas* (1481), his father Francesco Filelfo's *Exercitatiunculae latinae* (1483), and Cristoforo Landino's *Formulario de epistole vulgare* (1485).[12] Albrecht Dürer (1471–1528) sent letters home to Germany from Italy, observing and drawing couriers in transit between relay stations, while also experimenting with how to bring writing in various forms into his art. Michelangelo Buonarotti (1475–1564) cultivated a beautiful cursive and distinctive signature to demonstrate how artful letter writing could be.[13]

Well before Quentin Massys portrayed Peter Gillis in 1517, holding a letter recognizably simulating Thomas More's handwriting as a gift to accompany his painting of Erasmus for More, correspondence became a signature artifact in Renaissance portraits.[14] The materiality of correspondence mattered. More than fifty surviving portraits done before 1600 by Italian artists depict people with letters. The earliest ones portrayed ambassadors, princes, and merchants who self-consciously projected their identities through letters. Scholars, secretaries, clerics, literate women, and occasionally artisans came to see the letter as equally revealing of their status and learning.

Thus, the Italian Renaissance portrait provides us with a trail of letters to follow. Such portraits need to be considered in relationship to northern European portraits, for instance Hans Holbein the Younger's 1532 depiction of the Danzig merchant George Giese in London on the eve of his marriage, opening his brother's letter with a penknife. The many letters, writing implements, seals, stamps, and wax scattered throughout the painting underscore Giese's role in the family business at the hub of a prosperous Hanseatic commercial network. Later Dutch portraits such as Johannes Vermeer's *Girl Reading a Letter at an Open Window* (ca. 1657–59) represent a second take on a well-established theme.[15]

Painted letters hint at the stories contained inside folded slips of paper. What might their contents reveal? Poggio Bracciolini (1380–1459), who worked as an apostolic secretary to various popes from 1403 until 1453 and spent five years in London corresponding regularly with the Florentine antiquarian Niccolò Niccoli (1364–1437), exhibited great self-consciousness about how writing filled the page. "But farewell; my poor scrap of paper has run out, for I took only a small sheet thinking I would not find anything to write. But in the course of talking the flow began," he wrote in 1420.[16] Each page harbored the potential to become a portrait in words. People measured the quality of their relations by the quantity and frequency of letters. When Margherita Bandini (1360–1425) discovered that Francesco di Marco Datini (1335–1410) was writing letters of "three or four pages" to a Florentine business partner, she chided her husband for "unburdening your mind with him" more than with her.[17]

During the 1450s, shortly after Barbarigo's portrait commemorated his London embassy, the Marquis of Mantua, Ludovico Gonzaga (1412–78), decided to remodel and redecorate a fourteenth-century audience chamber in his palace. In spring 1465, Andrea Mantegna (1431–1506) began to paint the ceiling and walls of the Camera Picta, an important space for receiving visitors, completing the task in summer 1474. Mantegna's representation of the Gonzaga court starts with the north wall. Ludovico, Barbara of Brandenburg, and their court await the arrival of visitors, but the duke has already received and opened a letter (Figure 0.2). One interpretation suggests that it is a letter from Bianca Maria Visconti in Milan, requesting his presence right away as military commander of the ailing Duke Francesco Sforza. A man leans in to converse with Ludovico Gonzaga who holds the missive with both hands to underscore its importance and potential urgency. Possibly he was the courier, or more likely the Marquis's secretary Marsilio Andreasi.[18]

Letters were still on Mantegna's mind as he completed the West Wall shortly before 1474. In this scene, the Marquis encounters his sons Federico and Francesco, made a cardinal in December 1461 at age seventeen, at Bozzolo, just beyond the city on the road to Milan (Figure 0.3). Cardinal Francesco Gonzaga carries a folded but open letter, with another possibly tucked in his cap. It is tempting to see Ludovico's departure as a continuation of the narrative begun with the arrival of a letter from Milan, setting the scene at the beginning of 1462 as he responded to Bianca Maria Visconti's command to defend the Sforza interests. Keith Christiansen convincingly argues that the portraits of Ludovico's two sons and presence of so many of Federico's offspring suggest a much later date for this encounter. This fresco may instead commemorate the 1472 arrival of Cardinal Francesco in Mantua from Bologna with his retinue.[19] Either way, he came bearing letters.

On the other side of the doorframe are portraits of two members of the Gonzaga retinue with the famous Gonzaga dogs. The attendant dressed in white holds a barely visible folded letter; his companion carries documents in his red hatband. Mantegna's Camera Picta contains multiple portraits of Renaissance letters read, delivered, and transported. The letter is a skein unwinding across different scenes of encounter, binding them together. Ultimately, it becomes a place to declare, in tiny cursive on the letter in cardinal Francesco's right hand: "Andrea painted me" (A[ndrea] me pi[nxit]).[20] Mantegna's almost invisible signature tells two fundamental truths – he indeed painted the entire room, floor to ceiling, and he also painted this letter.

As the goals of Renaissance portraiture evolved, representations of letters attempted to capture the full range of human activity and emotion that they indicated.[21] Hans Memling's *Portrait of a Man with a Letter* (1485–89) probably depicts a Tuscan merchant resident in Bruges who commissioned the German painter, popular with Italians, to paint his portrait. The left hand of this unknown Renaissance man grasps another tightly folded letter, less rich in detail than Barbarigo's missive from Venice, let alone the profusion of letters in

FIGURE 0.2 *The Meeting Scene*: detail of Ludovico II Gonzaga and his second son, Cardinal Francesco. Fresco. 1465–74. Andrea Mantegna, *The Court of Mantua* (1465–74), fresco, 805 × 807 cm, Camera degli Sposi (West Wall)

Palazzo Ducale, Mantua. Courtesy Scala/Art Resource ART126772

FIGURE 0.3 Ludovico II Gonzaga in conversation with his secretary Marsilio Andreasi after opening a letter. Andrea Mantegna, *The Court of Mantua* (1465–74), fresco, 805 × 807 cm, Camera degli Sposi (North Wall)

Palazzo Ducale, Mantua. Courtesy Scala/Art Resource ART76803

Holbein's portrait of Giese, yet unmistakably an artifact of commercial correspondence. Memling's portrait subtly captured the essence of the Renaissance
merchant, a prosperous, confident man of business in the midst of transactions
conducted on paper. Rather than depict a merchant with his money, Memling
indicates currency by other means. It could be a letter of credit, a bill of
exchange, a contractual agreement between partners, personal correspondence,
or instructions from a distant employer to an agent acting on his behalf.

The fourteenth-century Tuscan grain merchant Paolo da Certaldo advised
that when the courier arrived:

> If you are merchant, and letters for you arrive along with other letters,
> always remember to read your own letter first before giving the other let-
> ters to the people to whom they are addressed. And if your letters should
> advise you to buy or sell some merchandise for your own advantage, call
> immediately for your agent, and do what the letters say, and then hand
> over the other letters that came with yours. But don't give them over
> until you have concluded your transactions because those other letters
> might say things that could ruin your own dealings, and the service that
> you would have done to your friend or neighbour or some stranger
> would turn into a great evil.[22]

The act of holding a letter anchors the self-assured gaze of this Italian Renaissance man abroad, connecting him to different parts of the world. "It befits
a merchant always to have ink-stained hands," wrote Leon Battista Alberti,
describing the ideal Florentine man of affairs.[23] The sheet of paper in Memling's portrait – probably folded three times, closed with a cord, sealed with
wax, and stamped with the merchant's insignia, if he was attentive to standard
practices of transforming the written page into a letter[24] – conveys many
unspoken possibilities.

Letters did not escape the attention of Jacob Burckhardt, arguably the Renaissance's greatest historian. In *The Civilization of the Renaissance in Italy* (1860),
Burckhardt described how humanists became indispensable servants "for the official correspondence of the state." He connected the emergence of the office of
secretary, a professional writer known for his Latin eloquence and fine hand, to
the growth of the Renaissance chanceries and bureaucracies. He reflected on the
diffusion of these practices, including the increase in letter-writing manuals.
Ultimately, Burckhardt noted the transformation of humanist epistolary practices
with the emergence of a new vernacular style of letter writing, which Burckhardt proclaimed "wholly modern, and deliberately kept free from Latin influence, and yet its spirit is thoroughly penetrated and possessed by the ideas of
antiquity."[25]

These allusive remarks have generated a considerable scholarship on the
renaissance of letters, starting with the pioneering work of Cecil Clough and
Amadeo Quondam.[26] What was a public letter in relation to private

correspondence? How did printing transform the very meaning of a letter, from a communication between two parties, potentially shared with and copied by others, into a public document? Describing it as an "epistolary revolution" that needs to be studied as carefully as the so-called printing revolution, Jean Boutier, Sandro Lando, and Olivier Rouchon highlight the "rapid diversification of the uses and kinds of letters" as a key development in the fourteenth through sixteenth centuries.[27]

The emergence of vernacular letter collections, starting with Pietro Aretino's (1492–1556) six volumes of letters, published 1538–57, has received considerable attention.[28] Aretino recognized that a letter was ideally suited to small portable books. In December 1537, he wrote to Sebastiano Fanto describing his plan "to reduce ... in a half sheet" his publishable letters.[29] This compact genre placed thousands and thousands of letters in the hands of Renaissance readers. In 1580, Michel de Montaigne reported that there were over one hundred printed collections of *libri di lettere* during his trip to Italy, while Quondam identified an impressive 540 volumes of letters from this era.[30] The profusion of letters increased the ardor for communicating via correspondence. A good letter was "the most natural portrait of things," Alessandro Mola declared to Lorenzo Poggioulo in February 1562, and "a most lucid mirror."[31] Letters not only became an essential component of the Italian Renaissance portrait, but they were also portraits by other means. A good letter is "between nature and art," declared Stefano Guazzo in 1590, further underscoring how a well-constructed correspondence shared many characteristics with the Renaissance portrait.[32]

Writing, reading, and friendship

At the beginning of the sixteenth century, portraits of diplomats and their secretaries began to appear. Shortly after arriving in Rome, Sebastiano del Piombo created a *Portrait of Ferry Carondelet with His Secretaries* (1510–12), depicting the Flemish diplomat and confessor to Margaret of Austria at the beginning of his appointment as papal nuncio to Maximilian I's court in Innsbruck (Figure 0.4). Carondolet's principal secretary records the ambassador's words, with another figure less visible in the background. This is a painting filled with letters demarcating the shifting terms of the relationship between pope and emperor. It is a Roman curial portrait of men of letters at the nexus of an active correspondence, highlighting the relationship between ambassadors and secretaries.[33] The secretary is the instrument of communication, the man who holds the pen in hand, hovering above a half-inscribed sheet of paper, awaiting the next words to record. Carondolet seems to have just emerged from the correspondence scattered in front of him, his right hand tightly grasping a Latin letter, address visible. His reading of other letters precipitates what is about to be written, though it is the secretary who presumably gives it the final polish. In this portrait, Piombo captures the role of the secretary at the height of the Renaissance papacy.

FIGURE 0.4 Sebastiano del Piombo, *Portrait of Ferry Carondolet with His Secretaries* (ca. 1510–12), oil on panel, 112.5 × 87 cm, Inv. No. 369 (1934.20).
Courtesy of Museo Nacional Thyssen-Bornemisza, Madrid/Scala/Art Resource ART445806

Years later, Titian drew inspiration from Piombo's portrait, transforming the ingredients into his own *Cardinal Georges d'Armagnac, Ambassador to Venice, and His Secretary Guillaume Philandrier* (1538) (Figure 0.5). Here, as Douglas Biow observes, Titian has emphasized the mutual dependence of the ambassador and his secretary. Letters are a shared task. The folded letters lie before Philandrier,

FIGURE 0.5 Titian, *The Cardinal Georges d'Armagnac, Ambassador to Venice, and His Secretary Guillaume Philandrier* (1538), oil on canvas, 102 × 116 cm. MNR959.
Photo: Gérard Blo. Courtesy of the Louvre/Art Resource. © RMN-Grand Palais/Art Resource, NY ART148756

potentially indicating that he more than the French ambassador is in charge of their correspondence.[34] Perhaps the most interesting feature of this other portrait of an ambassador and his secretary, however, regards its posthumous misidentification. As early as the seventeenth century, Titian's painting became known as a portrait of "the Duke of Florence dictating to Machiavel his secretary." Some thought it might be a portrait of a Sforza duke, or even a Borgia cardinal, but Machiavelli was uniformly proclaimed to be Titian's model secretary.[35] Thus, a famous painting of two men with letters became a spurious portrait of one of the most important letter-writers of the Italian Renaissance. "Fortune has determined that, not knowing how to talk either about the silk business or the wool business or about profits and losses, I must talk about politics," declared Machiavelli in a famous letter to Piero Vettori on 9 April 1513, "and I must either take a vow of silence or talk about that."[36]

Some months later, Machiavelli advised another correspondent "to use a clear style with those whom you do business with so that whenever they get one of your letters they think, because your way of writing is so detailed, that you are there."[37] What exactly did it mean to establish presence? The more vivid and precise one's prose, the truer one's intent. Renaissance portraits began to represent writing as well as receiving letters. The *Portrait of an Olivetan Monk* (ca. 1515) attributed to Baldassare Peruzzi (Figure 0.6) pays careful attention to

FIGURE 0.6 Baldassare Peruzzi, attr., *Portrait of an Olivetan Monk* (ca. 1515), oil on canvas, 38 ¼ × 28 ⅝ in. (97.2 × 72.7 cm).
Courtesy of the Metropolitan Museum of Art, New York 1986.339.1

writing instruments – quill, penknife, red wax, and seal – and meticulously depicts a bundled packet of papers. Tied with string, addressed and ready for a courier to pick up, the documents reveal how pages filled with writing become letters to deliver. This portrait moves beyond the worlds of commerce and diplomacy to begin to imagine other possible functions of letter writing.

The act of receiving a letter soon captured the attention of Renaissance artists. Sixteenth-century portraits explored the affective response of readers to the written page. Rosso Fiorentino's *Young Man Holding a Letter* (1518) (Figure 0.7) is not the first extant portrait of an opened letter, which may belong to Mantegna's Camera Picta. Nonetheless, its depiction of a young man reading reminds us how frequently letters were a motif of Florentine portraits, as Jodi Cranston observes.[38] Interrupted, the young man gazes directly at us while the fully opened letter bends in his hand, its creases visible, its writing nearly legible, enough to make us want to read it even though there is nothing to read. Not very many years later, the *Portrait of a Young Man* (ca. 1530) by a follower of Dosso Dossi further tantalizes the viewer, playing with the desire to read the letter by making random words legible.

Taking the desire to decipher letters one step further, Lorenzo Lotto's *A Nobleman on a Balcony* (ca. 1525) (Figure 0.8) presents correspondence as a meeting of hearts and souls. Lotto's nobleman attempts to cover with his hand the contents of what is presumably a love letter in light of the flowers scattered nearby. Letters indeed might contain secrets; perhaps even a portrait of the soul stripped bare. Letters between a state and its representatives, patrons and clients, merchants and agents, letters expressing love and most importantly friendship begin to define a spectrum of relations at a distance facilitated by correspondence. If painting, as Alberti famously remarked, was capable of making the absent present, then it paralleled the ability of letters also to create a double of a different kind: portraits in words rather than images.[39]

As Machiavelli's correspondence with Vettori famously reveals, letters between friends became a highly symbolic and meaningful form of correspondence.[40] Letters are "the fruits of friendship," wrote the Sicilian humanist Giovanni Aurispa to Lorenzo Valla in 1443.[41] Jacopo da Pontormo's *Two Men with a Passage from Cicero's On Friendship* (ca. 1524) (Figure 0.9) is an especially fascinating example of this genre. Pontormo portrays two men – one or both sons-in-law of the glass-maker Becuccio Bicchieraio – joined by a letter. One man holds a letter while the other points to its content – a transcription of a key passage from Cicero's *De amicitia* painted in a recognizable chancellery hand. This striking portrait of humanist friendship, including Pontormo's relationship to these two men, reveals the penetration of these values among learned artisans.[42] In a matter of decades, the letter had migrated from centers of commerce, faith, and power to the home and the workshop. Portraits such as Giovanni Battista Moroni's late sixteenth-century depiction of a Neapolitan lawyer (Figure 0.10) refined the use of the letter as a *cartellino* upon which to inscribe words identifying the sitter or the artist, but also demonstrated how the possession of a letter, a sign of professional activity and competence, became utterly ordinary in the course of a century.

FIGURE 0.7 Rosso Fiorentino, *Portrait of a Young Man Holding a Letter* (1518), oil on wood, 85.5 × 66.5 cm. Bought with the generous support of the George Beaumont Group and a legacy from Mrs. Olive Brazdzionis, 2000 (NG6584).
© National Gallery of Art, London/Art Resource ART375402

Women also wrote and received letters; indeed it is one of the primary measures of the growth of female literacy and the uses to which it was put. Since the 1990s, a considerable amount of scholarship has appeared on women's letters.[43] Individually rich correspondences such as the letters of St. Catherine of Siena

FIGURE 0.8   Lorenzo Lotto, *A Nobleman on a Balcony* (ca. 1525).
Courtesy of the Cleveland Museum of Art

(1347–80), Margherita Bandini Datini, and Alessandra Macinghi Strozzi (ca. 1406–71) are well studied; the voluminous correspondence of Isabella d'Este (1474–1539) is being edited, analyzed, and digitized.[44] St. Catherine's letters were in print by 1500, and their publication by the Aldine Press indicates how appealing they were to an audience of Renaissance readers, just as Vittoria Colonna's spiritual letters would become for later generations with their publication in 1544.[45] The many collections of letters edited and translated in the Other Voice series have greatly increased access to women's correspondence. They provide an important point of departure for understanding what letters meant to women and how they helped to define the uses of literacy in family, business, scholarship, and profession.

FIGURE 0.9 Jacopo Pontormo, *Portrait of Two Friends* (ca. 1524)
Courtesy of the Collezione Vittorio Cini, WGA18109

FIGURE 0.10   Giovanni Battista Moroni, *Portrait of a Man Holding a Letter ("L'Avvocato")*, ca. 1570. Oil on canvas, 89 × 72.5 cm. Bought 1865 (NG742).
© National Gallery, London/Art Resource ART374731

By the late sixteenth century, a handful of portraits of women reading and writing letters began to appear. Women's portraits with letters barely scratch the surface of what is out there – thousands of letters await rediscovery in the archives. Nonetheless, the idea of a woman in command of a network defined by correspondence indicates the appeal of letter writing to ambitious and talented women. St. Catherine was said to compose letters quickly and fluidly, at times dictating multiple letters simultaneously to different scribes. When nuns could not act as scribes, she asked her confessor.[46] More typically women delighted in the acquisition and refinement of their own literacy. What did letters really mean to them? How did they function in their lives?

The Bolognese artist Lavinia Fontana (1552–1604) was well known for her detailed, attentive portraits of learned men in this university town, including friendship portraits exchanged between male scholars in correspondence. Not surprisingly,

FIGURE 0.11   Lavinia Fontana, attr., *Portrait of Laura Gonzaga in Green* (1580), oil on canvas, 34 ⅝ × 44 1/16 in. (88 × 112 cm), private collection.
Courtesy of Galerie Canasso, Paris and the owner

FIGURE 0.12 Lavinia Fontana, *Portrait of Antoinetta Gonzalez* (ca. 1594–95), oil on canvas, 57 × 46 cm.

Photo: Michèle Bellot. Courtesy of Chateau Blois, France © RMN-Grand Palais/Art Resource, NY ART175028

she had a special interest in depicting female literacy. Her *Self-Portrait in a Studio* (1579) portrays her with brush and paper. Solicited by Alonso Chacon in Rome, along with some of her portraits of learned men, most notably Carlo Sigonio, it is in dialogue with these images. Fontana envisions her pose in relation to the image of the learned church historian Sigonio, seated at his desk with a meticulously illustrated letter he has just received and opened as one of Bologna's most distinguished professors. She is poised to paint yet in a position that suggests she can equally write if she chooses. In fact, Fontana *has* written a letter to accompany her self-portrait, which she sent to Rome on 3 May 1579.[47] The painting and the letter together create the portrait. One wonders if she was aware of the exchange between the Venetian painter Jacopo Tintoretto (1518–94) and the famed Venetian courtesan Veronica Franco (1546–91). Upon receiving Tintoretto's *Portrait of a Lady* (ca. 1575), potentially her own portrait, Franco responded with a written portrait of the artist in words.[48]

Fontana's *Portrait of a Woman in Green* (mid-1580s), provisionally identified as Laura Gonzaga, depicts a woman whose arm rests comfortably near a loosely folded letter (Figure 0.11). We can almost make out the words inscribed on the exterior. There is virtually no self-consciousness about this portrait of a lady with a letter. Indeed, Fontana underscores the very ordinariness of this pose. By contrast, Fontana's *Portrait of Antonietta Gonzalez* (ca. 1595) is a bold, jarring presentation of the uses of literacy in a detailed *cartellino*. Gonzalez, the famously hairy woman from the Canary Islands, holds a sheet of paper, an *avviso* or newssheet describing how she came to live in proximity to the Farnese court in Parma (Figure 0.12).[49] These portable words – curious writing about her rather than by her – animate Fontana's portrait of this young woman. She grasps her own portrait in her hands.

A letter was a portrait of an individual by other means. In the early sixteenth century, Giovanni Pico della Mirandola famously compared a portrait unfavorably to a letter because "the former represents the body and the latter the mind."[50] Letters conveyed thoughts and passions, desires and commands, through the living hand. There was a magic to writing things down that animated letters: portraits in words to challenge those rendered in image. Letters belonged in Renaissance portraits not simply as accoutrements of human action and behavior, but also because they, too, were objects that lived and breathed from the moment pen touched paper.[51] If Renaissance artists rose to the challenge of painting a letter, it was because they understood very well that each page was already a portrait, both *paragone* and provocation.

An epistolary guide to the volume

This brief discussion of Renaissance portraits with letters, by no means designed to be comprehensive, is a prolegomenon to the general subject of this volume, namely the many different ways in which letters became symbolic capital in Renaissance Italy. In our own fashion, we inevitably sketch portraits from letters, perceiving them as an exceptional resource for penetrating the *zeitgeist* of the Renaissance world.

The Renaissance was an era that multiplied epistolary practices, putting letters into the hands of many different people. Reading, writing, receiving, and sending letters became essential to their identity. This volume explores the importance of letters in the Italian peninsula, and beyond, through a series of case studies regarding the use and meaning of letters. *The Renaissance of Letters* emerged from our recent experience working on the Stanford-based digital humanities project, *Mapping the Republic of Letters*, including the development of *Palladio*, a correspondence visualization tool designed to facilitate working with historical correspondence to map relations between people in time and space in order to explore with greater precision the evolution of human networks. The essays in this volume are not all products of digital scholarship, but many approach their subjects in light of the revelations of digital humanists, contributing to an energetic conversation that encompasses digital tools and archival research. Most importantly, *The Renaissance of Letters* is a collective reflection on the importance of letters as a crucial document for understanding the Italian Renaissance. It emerged from the experience of working with fragmentary and often dispersed correspondence.

In the past few decades the early modern "Republic of Letters" has become the subject of a sophisticated interdisciplinary scholarship focusing primarily on the ideals and realities of scholarly communities in the seventeenth and eighteenth centuries, the role of correspondence for intellectual brokers, and the ways in which letters reflected the evolution of knowledge and communication. Letters have a much longer history that precedes these developments, indeed helped make them possible. The origins of letter-writing practices did not begin with the Republic of Letters but in the late medieval and early Renaissance worlds of commerce, diplomacy, faith, and friendship. To return to the basic premise of this book: before there was a *republic* of letters, there was a *renaissance* of letters.

The first known mention of the term "Republic of Letters" – *Respublica litteraria* – occurred during the Italian Renaissance when Francesco Barbaro thanked Poggio Bracciolini for sending a list of manuscripts he discovered during his travels in Germany in 1417.[52] This often-repeated fact deserves a broader context. The quantity of early humanist letters, for example, pales in comparison to the profusion of commercial letters. Petrarch's carefully curated letters, real and imagined, look sparse in comparison to the massive business archive of the fourteenth-century Prato merchant Francesco Datini. The growth of political, religious, and diplomatic letters in the fifteenth and sixteenth centuries far outpaced the steady increase in scholarly correspondence – or at least the classic examples of scholarly correspondence that have long dominated the study of letters. How should we compare the correspondence of Machiavelli and his contemporaries to Isabella d'Este's thousands of letters, carefully studied by Deanna Shemek, or the letters that Ignatius of Loyola wrote from Rome that became the warp and woof of the Society of

Jesus as a global missionary order? What role do the letters of those who set out on the incredible journeys of the age play when we look at them with fresh eyes? Columbus wrote publishable letters about his voyages, inspiring Amerigo Vespucci to write letters to Florence, not only about the voyages to the New World he took but also voyages he probably never took. Vespucci recognized that if he put them in a letter, they would exist – and bolster his claims to even greater discoveries.

The dramatic increase in letter writing between 1300 and 1650 accompanied a period in which people, goods, and ideas traveled much further and faster than ever before. Late medieval and early modern letters testify to a world in communication. Trade routes and credit networks expanded, scientific and literary communities grew, battlefields multiplied, colonial and missionary outposts emerged, and the political machinations at distant courts seemed suddenly relevant to politics at home. Letters played a key role in expanding horizons. They conveyed crucial information between distant parties and were the medium through which actors extended and developed relationships that gave meaning to new commercial, political, and cultural arteries. Correspondence allowed Europeans to engage with an enlarged world characterized by the dissemination of humanism and the new science, the confessional strife of the Reformation, the foundation and consolidation of global empires, and a steady drumbeat of war.

The Italian Renaissance states tackled the problem of delivering the mail with greater speed and efficiency with gusto. They dealt with the logistical problems of transportation in an age of frequent warfare and uneasy relations between different states. By the end of the sixteenth century the Italian postal systems were the envy of many other parts of Europe. So too were their archives. Collecting, storing, and publishing letters is another legacy of Renaissance Italy. *The Renaissance of Letters* offers an interdisciplinary analysis of the literary, commercial, political, religious, cultural, social, and military functions of letters that transformed them into powerful tools.

None of these developments belonged exclusively to the Italian peninsula; indeed some began elsewhere before arriving in this part of the world. Others were a product of the kind of practical literacy, innovative commercial practices, diplomatic exchange, and long-distance travel in which various Italian city-states and the papacy played a central role. The relatively urban polycentric nature of late medieval and Renaissance Italy encouraged greater literacy as well as self-consciousness about their special relationship to the legacy of ancient Rome. It gave birth to institutions such as the university and the learned academies that facilitated knowledge-making communities. The early adaption and transformation of the printing press in cities such as Venice ensured that letters became a publishable genre.

The goal of this research is not to claim Italy's precedence in some absolute sense, but to reflect on the importance of the Italian peninsula as the location of many early initiatives that contributed to the renaissance of letters. This is a perspective that Erasmus, one of the sixteenth century's greatest letter-writers, knew and understood well from his own interactions with scholars and printers in Renaissance Italy. The idea of a dynamic scholarly network based on letter exchange, an early modern "Republic of Letters," could only occur in a world already shaped by travel and letter writing. As missionary, mercantile, scholarly, and imperial networks thickened and grew, letters increased in importance; news circulated in correspondence and by courier inspired printed newspapers in the seventeenth century. There was indeed "too much to know," and the ways in which recipients understood and responded to letters (or failed to do so) are key to understanding the conversation and its impact.[53]

In the Italian peninsula, humanists such as Barbaro were among the first to perceive and articulate the power of letters. Letters became the tools of many different kinds of social actors: scholars but also merchants, diplomats, physicians, soldiers, and literate women. Finally, the Italian peninsula is an especially important location for documenting how letters traveled with the development of the post, and how they were received and ultimately processed with the evolution of archival systems. Letters are a terrific way to observe the local, regional, and global features of the Italian Renaissance. Italian merchants relayed goods between Mediterranean ports, providing a bridge between eastern and western commercial networks, while some ventured beyond the Mediterranean as both traders and explorers, most notably Columbus and Vespucci. The global traveler was often a global letter writer.

Letters are fascinating and unique documents for studying these changes in part because of the ways they transcend the boundaries of discipline and field. Not only were they written by multi-dimensional individuals whose careers took them across spheres of early modern life – family, court, university, battle-field – ordinarily studied separately by scholars, but they also often contain information about the dynamic factors at play in an individual's life at the moment of writing. A single letter may discuss a writer's health, economic circumstances, marriage prospects, intellectual interests, artistic and antiquarian pursuits, and political maneuvers, allowing modern scholars to perceive how letters indeed offered richly varied portraits of the lived experience of men and women. The letter was a portrait of this world. This is why we began this volume with a brief account of the role of letters in Renaissance portraits. It is not designed to be exhaustive, let alone comprehensive, but hopefully will whet your appetite for more.

The fifteen chapters in this volume bring together many of the current approaches to correspondence. Some revisit classic episodes, whereas others break new ground by studying a less familiar correspondence. Several chapters take advantage of digital humanities techniques to map and analyze correspondence. All of our contributors emphasize the importance of digging deeply into the archives and developing a methodologically sophisticated reading of letters as a peculiar kind of artifact, paying attention to their contents, style and scripts, and means of conveyance.

Writing to her father Francesco, duke of Milan, in July 1453 at the tender age of eight, Ippolita Maria Sforza (1445–88) explained:

> Since I have returned to Pavia, having extra time during these long days, I have learned how to write a little, which I do so with the greatest pleasure so that I can speak with your most illustrious Lordship in my frequent letters and receive pleasing letters from you in return. And because I am not able to be there with you as I wish, I will make up for my absence with letters.[54]

This sentiment expresses the eagerness with which many Renaissance men and women, endowed with the opportunities to become literate, consciously participated in the shaping of an epistolary culture. No single volume can capture the renaissance of letters in its entirety, but it is our fond hope that our contributions will stimulate further scholarship on this subject.

Notes

* Thanks to Babette Bohn, Maria Loh, Lorenzo Pericolo, and Mary Sauer for their suggestions and the University of Warwick Renaissance seminar for giving me the opportunity to present these ideas. Ken Gouwens commented on a preliminary draft; Suzanne Sutherland read it more than once and made it better. The entire group who participated in this workshop made me think about letters in new ways.

1 Peter Humfrey, "The Portrait in Fifteenth-Century Venice," in *The Renaissance Portrait: From Donatello to Bellini*, ed. Patricia Lee Rubin (New Haven, CT: The Metropolitan Museum of Art, with Yale University Press, 2011), 50.

2 Angelo Poliziano, *Letters*, ed. and trans. Shane Butler (Cambridge, MA: Harvard University Press/I Tatti Renaissance Library, 2006), 183.

3 Ronald G. Witt, *Coluccio Salutati and His Public Letters* (Geneva: Librairie Droz, 1976), 5, 4.

4 Armando Petrucci, *Scrivere lettere. Una storia plurimillenaria* (Rome: Laterza, 2008), 53; idem, "Du brouillon à l'original: la lettre missive au Moyen-Âge," *Genesis* 9 (1996): 67–70. See also Giles Constable, *Letters and Letter-Collections* (Turnhout: Brepols, 1976); Ronald G. Witt, "Medieval 'Ars Dictaminis' and the Beginnings of Humanism: A New Construction of an Old Problem," *Renaissance Quarterly* 35 (1982): 1–35; and Malcolm Richardson, "The *Ars dictaminis*, the Formulary, and Medieval Epistolary Practice," in *Letter-Writing Manuals and Instruction from Antiquity to the Present*, ed. Carol Poster and Linda C. Mitchell (Columbia, SC: University of South Carolina Press, 2007), 52–67.

5 Cecil H. Clough, "The Cult of Antiquity: Letters and Letter Collections," in *Cultural Aspects of the Italian Renaissance: Essays in Honour of Paul Oskar Kristeller* (Manchester, UK: Manchester University Press/New York: Alfred Zambelli, 1976), 36, 43.

6 Jean Delumeau, *Vie économique et sociale de Rome dans la seconde moitié du XVIe siècle* (Paris: E. De Boccard, 1957), vol. 1, 37–79; Fernand Braudel, *The Mediterranean and the Mediterranean World in the Age of Philip II*, trans. Siân Reynolds (New York: Harper & Row, 1972), vol. 1, 276–352. On postal networks, see for instance Eric R. Dursteler, "Power and Information: The Venetian Postal System in the Early Modern Mediterranean," in *From Florence to the Mediterranean: Studies in Honor of Anthony Molho*, ed. Diogo Ramada Curto, Eric R. Dursteler, Julius Kirshner, and Francesca Trivellato (Florence: Olschki, 2009), 601–623.

7 Ernest H. Wilkins, "On the Evolution of Petrarch's Letter to Posterity," *Speculum* 39 (1964): 304–308; idem, "On the Carriage of Petrarch's Letters," *Speculum* 35 (1960): 214–223.

8 Francesca Trivellato, "A Republic of Merchants?" in *Finding Europe: Discourses on Margins, Communities, Images ca. 13th ‾ ca. 18th Centuries*, ed. Anthony Molho, Diogo Ramada Curto, and Niki Koniordos (New York: Berghahn, 2007), 133–158.

9 Filippo de Vivo, "Archival Intelligence, Diplomatic Correspondence, Information Overload, and Information Management in Italy, 1450–1650," in *Archives and Information in the Early Modern World*, ed. Liesbeth Corens, Kate Peters, and Alexandra Walsham (Oxford: The British Academy/Oxford University Press, 2018), 54–58, 61; and Isabella Lazzarini, *Communication and Conflict: Italian Diplomacy in the Early Renaissance, 1350–1520* (Oxford: Oxford University Press, 2015).

10 Isotta Nogarola, *Complete Writings*, ed. and trans. Margaret L. King and Diana Robin (Chicago, IL: University of Chicago Press, 2004), 45, 107.

11 Enea Silvio Piccolomini, *Storia di due amanti* (Palermo: Sellerio, 1985). Discussed in Claudio Guillen, "Notes Towards the Study of the Renaissance Letter," in *Renaissance Genres: Essays on Theory, History, and Interpretation*, ed. Barbara Kiefer Lewalski (Cambridge, MA: Harvard University Press, 1986), 74, 95; and Clough, "The Cult of Antiquity," 45.

12 Paula Findlen, *Leonardo's Library: The World of a Renaissance Reader* (Stanford, CA: Stanford University Press, 2019), 14–15.

13 Shira Brisman, *Albrecht Dürer and the Epistolary Mode of Address* (Chicago, IL: University of Chicago Press, 2016); and Deborah Parker, *Michelangelo and the Art of the Letter* (Cambridge, UK: Cambridge University Press, 2010).

14 John Pope-Hennessy, *The Portrait in the Renaissance* (New York: Bollingen Foundation/Pantheon Books, 1966), 92–96; Lorne Campbell, Miguel Falomir, Jennifer Fletcher, and Luke Syson, eds., *Renaissance Faces* (London: National Gallery/Yale University Press, 2008), 168–169; Lisa Jardine, *Erasmus Man of Letters: The Construction of Charisma in Print* (Princeton, NJ: Princeton University Press, 1993), 27–33. I thank Rachel Midura for bringing my attention to Clemente Fedele, "Ritratti e lettere," *Cronaca filatelica* n. 370 (March 2010): 82–88.

15 Thomas S. Holman, "Holbein's Portraits of the Steelyard Merchants: An Investigation," *Metropolitan Museum Journal* 14 (1980): 139–158. See also Alain Buisine, "La lettre peinte," in *L''Épistolarité a travers les siècles. Geste de communication et/ou d'écriture*, ed. Mireille Bossis and Charles A. Porter (Stuttgart: Franz Steiner Verlag, 1990), 68–79.

16 Phyllis Walter Goodhart Gordon, ed. and trans., *Two Renaissance Book Hunters: The Letters of Poggius Bracciolini to Nicolaus De Niccolis* (New York: Columbia University Press, 1991; 1974), 35 (London, 29 January [1420]).

17 As quoted in Ann Crabb, *The Merchant of Prato's Wife: Margherita Datini and Her World, 1360–1425* (Ann Arbor, MI: University of Michigan Press, 2015), 29–30.

18 Michele Cordaro, ed., *Mantegna's Camera degli Sposi* (Milan: Electa, 1993), 71; Keith Christiansen, *Andrea Mantegna: Padua and Mantua* (New York: George Braziller, 1994), 73–74, 78. See Rodolfo Signorini, "Per una diversa interpretazione degli affreschi della cosiddetta 'Camera degli Sposi' di Andrea Mantegna," in *Mantova e i Gonzaga nella civiltà del Rinascimento* (Segrate: Edigraf, 1978), 217–240; Ronald Lightbown, *Mantegna* (Oxford: Phaidon, 1986); and Randolph Starn and Loren Partridge, eds., *Arts of Power: Three Halls of State in Italy, 1300–1600* (Berkeley, CA: University of California Press, 1992), 81–148.

19 Christiansen, *Andrea Mantegna*, 82; Cordaro, ed., *Mantegna's Camera degli Sposi*, 127.

20 Signorini, "Il Mantegna firmò la sua camera," *Gazzetta di Mantua* (3 September 1972): 3; Starn and Partridge, *Arts of Power*, 106.

21 Here I paraphrase Rubin, "Understanding Renaissance Portraiture," in Rubin, ed., *The Renaissance Portrait*, 9.

22 Paolo da Certaldo, "Book of Good Practices," in *Merchant Writers: Florentine Memoirs from the Middle Ages and the Renaissance*, ed. Vittore Branca, trans. Murtha Baca (Toronto: University of Toronto Press, 2015), 66.

23 As quoted in Iris Origo, *The Merchant of Prato: Francesco di Marco Datini 1335–1410* (New York: Knopf, 1957), 97. See Trivellato, "A Republic of Merchants?".

24 Origo, *The Merchant of Prato*, 98–99.

25 Jacob Burckhardt, *The Civilization of the Renaissance in Italy*, trans. S.G.C. Middlemore (London: Phaidon, 1960), 137–138.

26 Clough, "The Cult of Antiquity," 33–67; and Amadeo Quondam, ed., *Le "carte messaggiere." Retorica e modelli di comunicazione epistolare per un indice dei libri di lettere nel Cinquecento* (Rome: Bulzoni, 1981). Recent studies include Claudio Griggio, ed., "Dalla lettera al epistolario. Aspetti rettorico-formali dell'epistolografia umanistica," in *Alla lettera. Teorie e pratiche epistolari dai Greci al Novecento*, ed. Adriana Chemello (Milan: Guerini, 1998), 83–108; Maria Luisa Doglio, *L'arte delle lettere. Idea e pratica delle scritura epistolare tra Quattro e Seicento* (Bologna: Il Mulino, 2000); and Luc Vaillancourt, *La lettre familière au XVIe siecle. Rhétorique humaniste de l'épistolaire* (Paris: Honoré Champion 2003); and more specifically, Nancy Siraisi, *Communities of Learned Experience: Epistolary Medicine in the Renaissance* (Baltimore, MD: Johns Hopkins University Press, 2013).

27 Jean Boutier, Sandro Landi, and Olivier Rouchon, eds., *Politique par correspondance. Les usages politiques de la lettre en Italie (XIVe–XVIIIe siècle)* (Rennes: Presses Universitaires de Rennes, 2009), 9, 11.

28 Jeannine Basso, *Le genre épistolaire en langue italienne, 1538–1662: Répertoire chronologique et analytique* (Rome: Bulzoni, 1990); Laura Fortini, Giuseppe Izzi, and Concetta Ranieri, eds., *Scrivere lettere nel Cinquecento. Corrispondenze in prose e in versi* (Rome: Edizioni di Storia e Letteratura, 2016); Claudia Ortner-Buchberger, *Briefe schreiben im 16. Jahrhundert. Formen und Funktionen des epistolaren Diskurses in den italienischen libri di lettere* (Munich: Wilhelm Fink, 2003); Gianluca Genovese, *La lettere oltre il genere. Il libro di lettere dall'Aretino al Doni, e le origini dell'autobiografia moderna* (Rome: Antenore, 2009); Lodovico Braida, *Libri di lettere. Le raccolte epistolari del Cinquecento tra inquietudine religiose e "buon volgare"* (Rome: Laterza, 2009); Gennaro Tallini, *Il volgar modo. Lingua volgare, antiquaria e intrattenimeno cortigiano nella scrittura epistolare dal Cinquecento al primo Seicento* (Verona: QuiEdit, 2014).

29 Paolo Procaccioli, "Aretino e la primogenitura epistolare," in *Scrivere lettere nel Cinquecento*, eds. Fortini, Izzi, and Ranieri, 14n29.

30 Michel de Montaigne, *Essais* I.XI, as quoted in Quondam, *Le "carte messaggiere,"* 13, 30. See also Petrucci, *Scrivere lettere*, 91.

31 Stefano Guazzo, *Lettere volgari di diversi gentilhuomini del Monferrato* (Brescia, 1565), 16v, as quoted in Doglio, *L'arte delle lettere*, 131.

32 Ibid., 137.

33 Pope-Hennessy, *Portrait*, 117; Douglas Biow, *Doctors, Ambassadors, Secretaries: Humanism and Professions in Renaissance Italy* (Chicago, IL: University of Chicago Press, 2003), 155–158; De Vivo, "Archival Intelligence," 61–62.

34 Biow, *Doctors, Ambassadors, Secretaries*, 158.

35 Michael Jaffé, "The Picture of the Secretary of Titian," *The Burlington Magazine* 108, n. 756 (March 1966): 112, 114–127.

36 Quoted in Najemy, *Between Friends*, 4.

37 James B. Atkinson and David Sices, ed. and trans., *Machiavelli and His Friends* (DeKalb, IL: Northern Illinois University Press, 1996), xxii (Machiavelli to Giovanni Vernacci, Florence, 4 August 1513).

38 Jodi Cranston, *The Poetics of Portraiture in the Italian Renaissance* (Cambridge, UK: Cambridge University Press, 2000), 79.

39 Ibid., 62–65.

40 John Najemy, *Between Friends: Discourses of Power and Desire in the Machiavelli-Vettori Letters of 1513–1515* (Princeton, NJ: Princeton University Press, 1993).

41 Lorenzo Valla, *Correspondence*, ed. and trans. Brendan Cook (Cambridge, MA: Harvard University Press/The I Tatti Renaissance Library, 2013), 151.

42 Elizabeth Cropper, "Pontormo and Bronzino in Philadelphia: A Double Portrait," in *Pontormo, Bronzino and the Medici*, ed. Carl Strehlke and Elizabeth Cropper (University Park and Philadelphia, PA: The Pennsylvania State University Press/Philadelphia Museum of Art, 2004), esp. 17–19; and Campbell, Falomir, Fletcher, and Syson, *Renaissance Faces*, 172–173.

43 See especially Gabriella Zarri, ed., *Per lettera. La scrittura epistolare femminile tra archivio e tipografia secoli XV–XVII* (Rome: Viella, 1999); Maria Luisa Doglio, "Letter Writing, 1350–1650," trans. Jennifer Lorch, in *A History of Women's Writing in Italy*, ed. Letizia Panizza and Sharon Wood (Cambridge, UK: Cambridge University Press, 2000), 13–24; Maria Grazia Nico Ottaviani, *"Me son missa a scriver questa lettera … " Lettere e altre scritture femminili tra Umbria, Toscana e Marche nei secoli XV–XVI* (Naples: Liguori, 2006); and Meredith K. Ray, *Writing Gender in Women's Letter Collections of the Italian Renaissance* (Toronto: University of Toronto Press, 2009).

44 Karen Scott, "'Io Caterina': Ecclesiastical Politics and Oral Culture in the Letters of Catherine of Siena," in *Dear Sister: Medieval Women and the Epistolary Genre*, ed. Karen Cherewatuk and Ulrike Wiethaus (Philadelphia, PA: University of Pennsylvania Press, 1993), 87–121; Crabb, *The Merchant of Prato's Wife*; idem, "How to Influence Your Children: Persuasion and Form in Alessandra Macinghi Strozzi's Letters to Her Sons," in *Women's Letters Across Europe, 1400–1700*, ed. Jane Couchman and Ann Crabb (Aldershot, Hampshire, UK: Ashgate, 2005), 21–41. On Isabella d'Este, see Deanna Shemek, "Isabella d'Este and the Properties of Persuasion," in *Women's Letters*, ed. Couchman and Crabb, 123–140; Sarah Cockram, "Epistolary Masks: Self-Presentation and Dissimulation in the Letters of Isabella d'Este," *Italian Studies* 64 (2009): 20–37; and IDEA (*Isabella d'Este Archive*) devoted to her: http://isabelladeste.web.unc.edu.

45 Doglio, "Letter Writing," 15–16, 18.

46 Scott, "'Io Catarina.'"

47 Maria Teresa Cantaro, *Lavinia Fontana bolognese "pittore singolare" 1552–1614* (Milan: Jandi Sapi, 1989), 86–87. Also Babette Bohn, "Female Self Portraiture in Early Modern Bologna," *Renaissance Studies* 18 (2004): 239–286; and idem, *Women Artists, Their Patrons, and Their Publics in Early Modern Bologna* (forthcoming).

48 Veronica Franco, *Poems and Selected Letters*, ed. and trans. Ann Rosalind Jones and Margaret F. Rosenthal (Chicago, IL: University of Chicago Press, 1998), 35–37.

49 Caroline P. Murphy, *Lavinia Fontana: A Painter and Her Patrons in Sixteenth-Century Bologna* (New Haven, CT: Yale University Press, 1993), esp. 73–77, 162–165; and Merry Weisner-Hanks, *The Marvelous Hairy Girls: The Gonzales Sisters and Their Worlds* (New Haven, CT: Yale University Press, 2009).

50 In Cropper, "Pontormo and Bronzino," 18.

51 Frederika H. Jacobs, *The Living Image in Renaissance Art* (Cambridge, UK: Cambridge University Press, 2005).

52 Françoise Waquet, "Qu'est-ce que la République des Lettres? Essai de sémantique historique," in *Bibliothèque de l'École des chartes* 147 (1989): 475. Most recently, see Marc Fumaroli, *The Republic of Letters*, trans. Lara Vergnaud (New Haven, CT: Yale University Press, 2018); and Dan Edelstein, Paula Findlen, Giovanna Ceserani, Caroline Winterer, and Nicole Coleman, "Historical Research in the Digital Age: Reflections from the Mapping the Republic of Letters Project," *American Historical Review* 122 (2017): 400–424.

53 Ann Blair, *Too Much to Know: Managing Scholarly Information Before the Modern Age* (New Haven, CT: Yale University Press, 2010).

54 Ippolita Maria Sforza, *Duchess and Hostage in Renaissance Naples: Letters and Orations*, ed. and trans. Diana Robin and Lynn Lara Westwater (Toronto: ITER, 2017), 62.

PART I

Late medieval commerce and scholarship

1

LETTERS, NETWORKS, AND REPUTATION AMONG FRANCESCO DI MARCO DATINI AND HIS CORRESPONDENTS

Jeffrey Miner

In December 1401, Francesco di Marco Datini of Prato (ca. 1335–1410) wrote a letter from Florence to Giovanni da Pessano, a long-time acquaintance in Milan. He opened by acknowledging Giovanni as "dearest like a brother," apologizing that he had received four letters from his Milanese associate to which he could not reply as he would have liked, owing to "the many things that occupy me, because of my accounts in the nineteen years and more since I left Avignon." Francesco's letter dealt with a variety of subjects, and closed, "Because I have much to write to many places, I cannot say more to you here. Christ protect you, from Francesco di Marco da Prato in Florence, at your pleasure always," reiterating both his affection for da Pessano as well as how busy he was.[1]

In this moment, Datini was a mature merchant near the peak of his fortunes, having been engaged in business for around half a century. Orphaned by the plague in 1348, Francesco had been taken in by another couple and sent to Avignon in 1350 to begin work as an office boy in a Florentine merchant firm there.[2] During his time in Avignon, he worked his way up from an office boy and errand runner to a junior partner in larger Florentine firms, until in 1373 he was operating independently as a merchant in his own right. In 1376, aged around 40, he married Margherita Bandini, then about 16, the daughter of an exiled and dispossessed Florentine aristocrat. The couple returned home to Prato in 1378, and it is at this point that Francesco's commercial network truly began to take off. Though he never gave up on Avignon as a significant market and incubator of talent, Francesco spent the years after his departure building a much more extensive web of relationships from his home base in Tuscany.

Personal ties mentioned in the 1401 letter give a hint as to how Francesco succeeded in trade despite some initial disadvantages. As the son of a tavern-keeper, Datini lacked the inherited family connections that more established Florentine families could provide for their sons as an entrée into commercial life.[3] Nevertheless, he built a dynamic enterprise by cultivating capable employees and allowing them to progress as he had, from errand runners to factors and, in some cases, eventually partners. Writing to Milan, Francesco complained that,

> because of the burdens that accost me every day, which are not few, I cannot put my hand to my mouth and so I have told Bindo Piaciti, who is like a son to me and moreover is my wife's brother, that he should go to you and do what you see fit concerning cottons and every other thing and that I will be responsible for everything with you.[4]

He enumerated at length his expectations about what business Piaciti might do with Pessina, offering that he would consider everything the Milanese did with Piaciti to be "well done because I have faith in him and you as in my own person." He went on to reference Pessina's "good reputation," suggesting that the Milanese should "account me like a dear brother and I will do the same for you." Datini also mentioned the good opinion his long-time employee, Tommaso di ser Giovanni, had of Pessina. Francesco never refused to employ his own relations or those of his associates, which is why he was putting Piaciti forward. Nevertheless, he did not found or run a family firm.[5]

Writing from Florence, Datini's letter mentioned a number of different places and goods, suggesting opportunities for trade between Avignon and Milan, recommending a taffeta-worker in Bologna, discussing the demand for cotton in Avignon, and updating Giovanni on the status of a bundle of velvet and other cloths from Tuscany that had been delayed in reaching Milan. The recipient, Giovanni da Pessina, was the latest in a series of Francesco's business associates in Milan. Although it was never the permanent home of a Datini-run business, Milan had been an important point of reference for Francesco from his earliest days as a merchant. Datini's early success was largely due to investment in bringing arms to Avignon, a business that also involved him in trading in raw metals and required him to cultivate links with Milanese arms makers, reputed to be the best in the world. As his wealth and range had grown, Francesco also came to invest heavily in the cloth trade, importing wool from northern Europe and the east, while exporting finished cloth from various points in northern Italy. Datini did not specialize, however, and traded in nearly everything that could be bought and sold, ranging from silks to salt and art to alum in addition to arms and clothing.[6] At its peak, the Datini enterprise comprised trading companies run wholly by Francesco in Florence and Prato, as well as individual partnerships between Francesco and trusted associates in Avignon, Florence, Genoa, Pisa, and Barcelona, with companies dependent on Barcelona located in Valencia and Palma. Francesco also operated a bank in Florence and controlled workshops devoted to wool-working and dyeing in Prato. Though Datini never established permanent partnerships in places like Milan and Venice, he also enjoyed a broader network of trusted factors and agents who worked on his and his companies' behalf.

Francesco was not exaggerating when he wrote to Giovanni in 1401 that he had many letters to write. Activities over long distances required coordination, though it bears remembering that the Datini enterprise did not duplicate the extreme geographic range of the most spectacular early or mid-fourteenth-century Florentine firms.[7] Francesco was a prolific writer and reader of letters, and his archive contains a massive amount of written material, including letters from 4,384 distinct individual correspondents in 267 different towns and cities.[8] This represents only a fraction of the paper Datini's enterprise produced, for the archive was formed out of papers saved by the different partnerships, meaning that it is missing letters sent outside the Datini group. The papers saved by the Avignon partnership, too, seem to have been mostly lost in the aftermath of Francesco's death. Pope Urban VII would later laud Nicolas-Claude Fabri de Peiresc (1580–1637) as the "general attorney" of the republic of letters in honor of his friend's extensive correspondence, yet the 10,000 letters to 500 people Peiresc wrote in his lifetime pale in comparison to the scale of merchant letter-writing.[9] In 1399 alone, the Datini archive indicates that at least 1,376 letters passed through Francesco's hands, counting only those within his circle of his partners and employees.[10] The geographic range of letters received is broad, stretching from Bristol, Nuremberg, and Cologne in the north to Lisbon and Safi in the west, and as far east as Mecca, Tana, Varna, and Ragusa. The scale of this correspondence is truly exceptional, representing a massive investment of time, materials, and labor in creating and maintaining written communication.

Francesco lived during an important period in the history of letter-writing, especially for commercial letters.[11] As the economic circuits of European and Mediterranean exchange were becoming more routinized and stable, merchants increasingly turned to employing resident agents or factors in important towns, instead of traveling themselves.[12] Because of the need to manage relationships between associates at a distance, letter-writing became a much more important part of merchant practice. This routinization led to the development of a roughly similar template for medieval merchant letters. Because this period also saw the flourishing of humanist letters generally, merchant letters have been read as a sub-type of this broader literary phenomenon and employed as a site for investigating humanist interest in concepts like fortune.[13] The development of a consistent language of correspondence among Italian merchants, as well as their encounters with different linguistic traditions abroad, may also have played an important role in the development of the Italian language itself.[14]

Since the discovery of medieval merchant letters in the late nineteenth century, their use in economic history has evolved. Previous generations of economic historians interested in trade looked most intensely at the formal organization of commerce and the internal legal and economic patterns of firms: forms of partnership, capital structure, and contractual forms of insurance and risk management.[15] The sheer mass of internal documentation, not only the letters, conserved by the Datini archive has made it particularly fertile terrain for quantitative studies of prices and commodities.[16] Recently, however, the influence of institutional economics has led scholars to read merchant letters in new ways. In the past, the fourteenth-century transition to more sedentary merchants, smaller companies, and more routinized circuits of exchange was interpreted by some as a "loss of nerve" by European merchants.[17] Yet institutional economists' focus on conditions that enabled trade has helped prod scholars to look beyond the internal and contractual framework of merchant companies to examine more closely the informal structures and patterns that enabled commerce, the social and cultural framework that helped make long-distance exchange possible.[18] Much of this research has focused on religious diaspora communities – the so-called Maghribi traders (Jews operating in the eastern Mediterranean in the eleventh century) and the Armenians of New Julfa in the sixteenth century, and the well-known Sephardic diaspora centered on Livorno in the seventeenth century.[19] These studies have keyed in on the importance of reputation to long-distance commerce, and on how the circulation of information about and among merchants served to promote trust and successful commercial partnerships. Readers of these merchant correspondences have found relatively frequent "relationship grooming" as a major feature of their letters: commentary on the behavior of others; invocations of words about reputation (honor, faith, trust). These studies have expanded our sense of merchant letters' economic function beyond a simple vehicle for giving orders and conveying market information. Rather, they argue that letters communicated information about people, helping merchants to monitor who was a good business partner and who was not. The mass of documents in the Datini archive circa 1400 has been cited as evidence of this same kind of trust-based mercantile practice, a medieval tradition that continued on into the early modern period.[20] According to these studies across multiple periods, places, and mercantile enterprises, it seems that letter-writing was essential to trade because of its ability to communicate information about partners, both current and potential.

The size of the Datini archive precludes any individual from reading and consuming all of its contents. However, an increasingly large sample of the network's letters has become available in modern scholarly editions.[21] This chapter focuses on a few hundred letters from the 1390s, split roughly evenly between three sets: those between Francesco in Florence and Margherita, his wife in Prato, letters written from Milan to other Datini partnerships, and those received from North Africa, an important source of goods for Datini enterprises, but not home to any actual Datini agents.[22] This sample has the advantage of being coherent in time and covering the Datini network from multiple geographic and personal perspectives. This allows consideration of the roles played by different members of the epistolary network of a late medieval merchant, including employees, his wife, long-time partners, and mere acquaintances.

Doing business in Italy

Letters from Milan provide a useful entry point into the importance of letter-writing and reputation in the Datini network. Milan had been an important point of reference for Datini economically since his days in Avignon, yet it was never home to a permanent company and was most often a place where Datini employed factors to handle his business, rather than a partner.[23] At the same time, Milan was an important enough market and source for goods that Frances-co's partners and employees did occasionally visit the city to settle accounts, conduct business, and check on local factors. Thus, letters from Milan offer an opportunity to examine epistolary exchange among merchants from the perspec-tive of multiple letter-writers operating in key sectors of the Datini economic network, both inside and outside his companies proper.

The dominant figure in the Milan correspondence is Tommaso di ser Giovanni, who, like many of Francesco's other close associates, was a Tuscan whose early mer-chant training took place while he was an employee of the Avignon company. Hired as a young man to sell goods and manage correspondence in 1392, he even-tually earned enough of Francesco's trust to be made a partner in the Avignon com-pany in 1397, replacing one of Francesco's deceased long-time collaborators there. As such, he was an ideal person to periodically stop in Milan to oversee Datini interests there, and many of the surviving Milanese letters consist of Tommaso's reports to other partners as well as coordination with Andrea di Bonanno di ser Berizo, the Datini partner resident in Genoa.[24] Because of the impermanent nature of Tommaso's stay, however, there is also a reasonable amount of discussion of other merchants and correspondence received from non-Datini agents.

The Milanese letters in the Datini correspondence are broadly representative of the format of late medieval merchant letters as a whole. Though scholars disagree about exactly how far merchant letters diverged from non-mercantile letters and differ on how standardized they were formally, merchant letters are nevertheless recognized as a distinctive genre whose particular elements were closely related to their social and economic function.[25] Letters almost always opened by summariz-ing the recent correspondence – how many, if any, letters had been received and from whom.[26] If they had not received anything recently, it was not uncommon to say, "we haven't had one of yours and there's nothing new to say."[27] After this, there followed a mostly undifferentiated list of different subjects, including discussions of goods, debts, accounting, money transmitted via bills of exchange, local market conditions, news of ships entering or leaving nearby ports, political news, specific instructions, comments on the health of associates or acquaintances, and news of other merchants. This list varied in length widely, and terminated with a closing of some kind and the name of the sender. Closings, too, varied. Some were an abrupt full stop; others ended with commonplace religious invoca-tions such as "Christ be with you."[28] Frequently, but not always, the closing included an update on exchange rates between different major currencies or prices of key goods such as fustian cloth.

One of the most important aspects of the overall exchange of letters, one with major effects on the form and contents, is that individual missives were often writ-ten and sent out before new correspondence was received. A good merchant in the Datini orbit did not wait to receive a letter in reply before writing another of his own. On three consecutive days in March 1397, for example, Tommaso di ser Giovanni wrote twice to Barcelona then once to Florence. These letters began, "I have written you today what is needed and I have no [letters] of yours and now there is nothing to say," "The last letter I sent yesterday through Avignon and with it more [letters] of our friends, and I have none of yours," and "We have written you what is needed recently and now there is little to say."[29] Among the Datini correspondents, writing was predicated on a continual stream of back-and-forth writing, not a one-for-one exchange of letters, and the form was designed to facilitate that process.

Given the emphasis of current scholarship on the role letter-writing played in creating and maintaining a merchant's reputation in premodern trade, it is remarkable how little overt commentary on merchants' reputations and behavior can be found in Datini's Milan correspondence. There are inevitable exceptions in such a large correspondence, as with the letter of 1401 previously cited. Yet in the vast majority of the Milan letters, the interpersonal commentary that was so essential to other merchant correspondences is far from common. This is particularly surprising given the supposedly sensitive or reactive nature of merchant letters to news, events, and other information peripheral to strictly economic matters.[30] In place of commentary about other merchants, the vast majority of letters concern goods sent and accounts updated: "I write to say that I sent some merchandise marked with our sign to Venice. Put it on the Avignon account."[31] Where disputes are referenced between different correspondents, these seem to concern accounting matters more than decision-making or trust.[32] In one case, Tommaso di ser Giovanni wrote several letters to other Datini companies, trying to clarify that an alleged problem with the accounting was due, among other things, to the difference between Milan and other Italian cities over how bills of exchange were employed. Tommaso wrote to Florence,

> You have the accounts and you say there are many errors, but I do not know how, as they are correct and I will clarify for you a few parts. First, you say that there are 208 florins drawn for you on Marchesino and that I put 209 florins. That is correct because for all letters of payment that come here they pay the net value and not the written, and on the net they have 2 denarii per florin and they put ½ a percent. Thus, remitting you your money you have the same advantage, because that is the practice for every letter of exchange that comes from outside to pay here. You can be certain that no one is trying to cheat you or do anything other than what is right as far as we know it.[33]

He went on to explain away discrepancies in the accounting of a variety of transactions, including other bills of exchange as well as a quantity of wool damaged in transport to a merchant in Monza, north of Milan. This letter clearly failed to settle the issue, for Tommaso wrote to Florence again a few days later, commenting that "about the entries in the accounts sent you, I see what you have said and as I have already said they are correct, record them as was explained to you and again about this I will clarify briefly," before going on to reiterate in abbreviated form his previous instructions.[34] His frustration is clear, but explicitly negative comments are restricted to things like complaints by the Datini factor in Milan about "negligence" in keeping accounts by an employee in Florence.[35]

Confusion about accounts, the movement of goods, and other commercial business was far from uncommon. Even at only five or six days of remove from Genoa, the company's primary agent in Milan occasionally struggled to get relatively straightforward orders conveyed in time to make adequate use of them. The period from the 1380s through the first decade of the fifteenth century was one of frequent warfare between Milan and Florence, as well as civil disruption in Genoa itself.[36] At times, warfare gave rise to rumors that Florentines might be expelled from Milan altogether.[37] Both distance and political instability meant that even routine tasks, like sending money from one place to another, could become the subject of three or four successive letters. Tommaso di ser Giovanni wrote from Milan to Florence in February 1397 that,

> It has been a while and I hear nothing from Boni and Marchexino, and I've written to them. It is true that I've written to Boni asking him to send the money to Venice to Zanobi, I don't know if they've done it as I have had no reply.[38]

This kind of writing confirms that agents were still required to make independent judgments and decisions. The administrative tone of the letters should not blind us to the fact that even within Italy, trading relationships necessitated flexibility as well as a significant amount of trust between business partners. Yet although the Datini enterprise thrived on the scope of action enabled by trust between partners and tested factors, the correspondence itself shows less explicit discourse on reputation than one might expect. The absence is not absolute. In the 1401 letter cited above, Francesco felt comfortable writing to Giovanni da Pessina that "although I have not met you personally in person, I do know your good reputation."[39] In recommending a Bolognese associate, Datini put him forward as "a dear Lucchese friend who is a good person and experienced in taffeta and silk drapery."[40] Other scholars have noted a burst of commentary and judgment among network members after the death of an important factor.[41] None of this, however, is enough to conclude that letters were the Datini enterprise's dominant means of creating or maintaining relationships of trust or cultivating individual reputations.

Concerns about reputation seem to surface especially at the margins of the Datini enterprise directed toward its center. They do not seem to have been an internal preoccupation. One common way merchants claimed trustworthiness in letters was by openly stating that they were at the recipient's disposal, ready and willing to do what he asks. When this occurs in the Milan letters, it does not come in letters from Tommaso di ser Giovanni, the most common author of letters from Milan, written to Andrea di Bonanno, Francesco's partner in Genoa and the most frequent recipient of Milanese letters. Instead, offers of service appear in letters by more peripheral figures; for example, from a relatively unknown Francesco Tanso who wrote in March 1397 to Genoa that "if we can do anything for you, write it and we will do it willingly."[42] The next month, the same individual wrote to ask a favor. In this case, he needed some help in prodding a third party to help him find a house in Genoa, writing:

> I wrote to Michellozzo to look for a house for me, and not too big. I don't think he is searching, so I am asking you: please ask him, if you would, to look for a good house for me. I don't care if it's near the Banchi, only that it is good. And beautiful. And not too big. Near Porta di la Vacho or in le Vigne … Ask him to search, or make a search. Please respond.[43]

Likewise, in a very brief notice from another marginal figure to Andrea di Bonanno in Genoa, "I have nothing else to say to you except that I am always at your service, and I pray God to keep you in a good state."[44] These kinds of rhetorical flourishes and requests are far more likely to occur in letters making unusual requests or introducing less-familiar actors. In 1399, Giovanni di Lando da Caseria wrote to Genoa asking for arrangements to be made concerning a shipment of iron:

> I sent [the goods] to you so they would not bear the expense of shipping overland, that is through Pisa, and when you have them I pray you send them to Rome by ship to my [partners], that is Domenico di Sandro and Giovanni di Lando and tell them what you should have [for the service] which they will give to Giuliano di Giovanni or whomever else you name.[45]

This kind of favor among merchants was not uncommon, but it was also not routine and di Lando went on to state that if "Andrea [di Bonanno] were there, who knows me, he would act well for me and thus I am sure you will do, because Francesco di Marco was my teacher and here I received his letter of recommendation."[46] By invoking his association with Datini's partner in Genoa, di Lando hoped his letter could leverage his reputation to receive a service that was out of the ordinary, rather than the typical business of the Datini companies.

If the amount of commentary on reputations and trust among the Datini correspondents differs substantially from that among the Armenian merchants of New Julfa or the Sephardic network centered on Livorno, then the question is both why reputational discourse is less frequent and why it occurs in the particular moments and places in which it can be found. The answer is likely to be in the social structure of the network itself, which was neither even nor uniform. For those who were already formally incorporated into the network through legal forms of partnership and capital investment, their reputation was already solid and only needed to be maintained by frequent correspondence. The constant and frenetic passing along of information itself constituted a proven merchant's reputation, without needing it explicitly stated. Not all participants in the network had the same privilege to comment on the behavior of others. For example, Francesco complained about the handwriting of a factor by mocking some of his other partners, "You write me such that it makes me crazy. You would do well to learn to write so that I can understand better. Your writing is worse than Stoldo [di Lorenzo] or Manno [d'Albizo]!"[47] This, then, represents the privileged talk and gentle mockery allowed for those who had the status and capital to make judgments about others. The uneven distribution of reputational talk in the Datini letters is itself an important fact to be explained and reveals the critical importance of social position in conditioning the contents of merchant correspondence.

Beyond the Datini enterprise: letters from North Africa

Comparing letters received from Milan with those from North Africa reinforces the impression that explicit invocations of reputation are associated with weaker interpersonal bonds and more peripheral figures, rather than central ones. For Tuscan merchants around 1400, North Africa was an important source for raw materials as well as a market for the export of finished cloth.[48] Tuscan merchants were interested both in regional North African products like wool, leather, skins, and wax, as well as products that had come via trans-Saharan trade networks, especially dyestuffs and copper.[49] Although Datini himself never sent a partner or factor to trade directly with North Africa, he and his associates leaned on a variety of other Tuscans as intermediaries to obtain goods they otherwise would not have been able to access.

The Muslim ports of North Africa were highly important to Mediterranean commerce, but they were not the kind of locations in which it was easy for a smaller-time merchant like Datini to operate. Religious tensions, differences in language, and political instability all contributed to a general air of insecurity. As a result, the letters Datini and his associates received from North Africa were very different in tone and contents. Far more than letters within Italy itself, Tunisian letters mention challenges in maintaining connections between merchants. So in 1400, Giovanni di Bartolo Carocci, a Pisan in Tunis, complained to Manno d'Albizi, Francesco's partner in Florence, that because of frequent corsairing,

> few ships are coming here, and those few that do are from Catalonia, or Cagliari in Sardinia. From Genoa none come, from Pisa it is over a year that no ship has come, from Venice it is 9 months that none has come, and from Sicily 4 months no one has come, and there is no news about anyone who should arrive.[50]

In another letter from the same period, he begged an acquaintance in Barcelona, "if there is any news there about our country, I pray you write it to me, as from Pisa it is nearly a year since any ship came."[51] In addition to the updates about the prices of goods, local demand, and exchange rates, these letters show much greater struggles to receive secure news, challenges locating ships that could carry letters, problems with corsairs, the absence of ships arriving with merchandise, and a major interest in redeeming Christians who had been captured and enslaved. As will be made clearer below, the epistolary and personal distance between Tuscany and North Africa came with social costs as well as trading opportunities, leading to strains that left their mark on these letters.

Explicit invocations of reputation are noticeably more concerted and repeated in this segment of Datini's correspondence. For example, a Catalan in Tunis who wrote to Mallorca to strike up a relationship with the Datini introduced himself by saying, "my cousin sent me to Tunis, he is a great friend of Lucca di Sera."[52] The Catalan merchant, Fillel Benxarvit, hoped that Datini would accept his offer to do business with Mallorca "for love of him," knowing that Lucca di Sera was one of Francesco's longest-serving employees, having worked as a factor for Datini in Genoa and Florence. As opposed to Milan, where associations seem relatively stable, Tunisian letters frequently recommend one merchant to another.[53] There are also frequent offers of service, in which one individual proclaims his willingness to enter into a relationship if a potential partner will reciprocate.[54]

The most dramatic example of this behavior occurs in the series of letters Giovanni di Bartolo Carocci sent in 1384, attempting to leverage his personal connections to have himself redeemed from slavery.[55] The unfortunate victim sent a letter through a Genoese agent, Imperiale Gentile, whom he recommended to his correspondents as a "discreet man," known by "long acquaintance," who will come "in my service by his courtesy."[56] In his desperation, Giovanni pleaded with Francesco di Marco himself, first evoking the arbitrary nature of his fate: "You see what point I have come to. Not one year ago I was rich, now I've lost everything and am in such misery."[57] He went on, flattering Francesco and pleading: "in this miserable state I run to you, because of the friendship and acquaintance we had with you when I was in Genoa, and then in Avignon."[58] He closed, "I commend myself to you, to our other friends, and anyone who will aid me. It is my intention to satisfy everyone. If it pleases God! Giovanni Carocci God watch over you! in Bône, a slave."

Whether real or feigned, Giovanni's posture of desperation clearly intended to appeal to Francesco's sympathies, simultaneously playing up the extent of his fall and encouraging Francesco to see himself as someone who could step in as a savior to an old associate. Captives, like Iacopo di Giovanni Franceschi, who could not call on specific individuals instead made generalized appeals, in this latter case addressing a letter generically, "to you, Florentine merchants," asking them to write to one of his acquaintances in Pisa to have him redeemed from "the worst khan of Barbary."[59] Praising another merchant's reputation, appeals to shared history and a supplicatory posture were emotional levers that were needed in letters written at the margins of the social and geographic network of Tuscan merchants abroad.

This distance left its mark on the rhetorical tone of the letters as well, where frequent supplications to God and invocations of his aid appear. For example, Salello de Malandrino da Lerba, a Pisan, wrote in a letter requesting news from Cristofano di Bartolo Carocci in Maiorca, "God guard you always! I commend you to God always!"[60] In another letter, awaiting ships from the Latin world, the author interjected, "May God make things as they ought to be!"[61] Invocations of the divine and explicit claims on reputations appear more often from subordinates writing to Datini or correspondents supplicating him for a favor for good reason. In a network that was not egalitarian, in which access to influence and capital was unequal, demonstrating a submissive attitude to God simultaneously showed one's own piety and pantomimed a submissive attitude to a letter's recipient.[62] Invoking ethical norms and affective ties could put additional weight behind a marginal figure's plea for assistance, support, or exchange. If we conceive of the network as a social space, it makes sense that overt appeals to reputation would appear more often at the periphery than at the core. Datini's correspondence helps to illuminate this pattern with greater clarity.

Household and network between Prato and Florence

The Datini archive is exceptional not only in the volume of letters it preserves, but also in the type of correspondence. Because Francesco had important business and personal interests in both Florence and Prato, there were several periods in which he lived separately from his wife, leaving Margherita to manage the household in Florence while he traveled to Prato, or vice versa.[63] This was clearly an exceptional arrangement rather than one typical for all merchants or traders, but the occasional distance between Francesco and Margherita forced them temporarily into a marriage by correspondence. This, then, makes it possible to see inside the conjugal unit to consider more fully Margherita's role in Francesco's business. By paying close attention to Margherita's role in creating and maintaining significant relationships for Francesco, we can revise upward our understanding of a wife's impact on commercial exchange, a space traditionally conceived of as exclusively male. Margherita's importance as a capable household manager and domestic figure is well known, but closer attention to the mercantile implications of honor and reputation allows us to see her significance to her husband's broader commercial life and activity more clearly.[64]

Over the course of their periodic separations, Margherita invested serious time and effort in learning to write in her own hand, rather than dictating.[65] As with letters between business partners, there were practical advantages to be had in writing one's own letters. A wife, like a business partner, might wish to communicate sensitive information or opinions to her husband without having them dictated to a third party. Additionally, by developing her ability to write well, Margherita was also making a claim to authority. Formally, the letters between

Margherita and Francesco keep to the same structure as the others, opening with a summary of correspondence received, listing various matters, and finishing with a brief closing.[66] The tone of these letters was initially not much more personal than those between merchant partners, a situation that only changed over time as Margherita became progressively better able to write her own letters, rather than dictating them to a scribe. Margherita, 24 years younger than Francesco, was treated like a factor whose opinion was sometimes valued but was definitely subordinate, someone who could be expected to take charge of administrative and managerial duties during Francesco's long absences.

The form of Margherita's letters mimics those of Francesco's partners, partly as a simple consequence of how Margherita was trained in writing. Nevertheless, just as merchants paid attention to the quality of their commercial associates' writing, Margherita's successful use of the proper conventions and writing in her own hand demonstrated to Francesco her competence as a manager, partner, and judge of character. Sustaining dependable commercial partnerships required cultivating important partners and employees, projecting a solid public persona, and maintaining a good household. In each of these capacities, Margherita frequently commented on the capacities and activities of Francesco's associates. She wrote Francesco in Florence that some bread she had paid for did not come out well. "It was the fault of that wretch who came from Florence," she complained, "he is exactly the sort of assistant you needed!"[67] In the same letter she groused that someone from Montepulciano who had been sent to her in Prato via Florence brought a lice infestation with him. She also offered comment on Francesco's commercial associates, writing that "I think that Bellozzo and Stoldo are spoiling you so much that you won't be inclined to come home. I think Bellozzo is probably much more capable than Stoldo."[68] Given the close links between an established merchant's household and his economic relationships, Margherita was in an ideal position to observe and comment on the behavior both of Francesco's employees and associates. Francesco's partners and employees were spread among a variety of western Mediterranean cities, yet his closest associates were exclusively Tuscan and were often recruited into the business only after a period of formation and training in Tuscany. At times, it even seems that Francesco hired people as much for the advantage he could gain in Florence or Prato as in his activities abroad.[69] As a result, while Margherita's presence is invisible in the letters from Milan, her activities in Prato and Florence were indispensable to the functioning of the broader Datini enterprises.

Margherita had a critical role in maintaining Francesco's public persona, keeping him properly connected to important figures in Prato and Florence. This was not always a duty she relished. There are clear examples in the correspondence where she was sometimes reluctant to do this, as in a dispute over whether she would call on the wife of the *podestà* of Prato as Francesco wanted.[70] Eagerly or otherwise, Margherita was intimately involved in mediating Francesco's relationships with influential people. This mediation was anything but abstract, and depended on Margherita's ability to manage household resources. In one case,

Francesco ordered Margherita to provide bread he could serve when making peace between two acquaintances, while in another he had her outfit and lend a pair of horses to two Florentine ambassadors heading to Genoa.[71] In other cases, Margherita was perfectly capable of acting on her own initiative, as when she decided to send some Corsican wine to the Magistracy of the Eight Defenders in Prato after hearing that one of them had a taste for it through a mutual acquaintance.[72] She also cultivated less direct connections, as when she invited the wife of Guelfo di Simone Pugliese, a Pratese magnate, to stay with her through some upcoming feast days.[73] Even if Francesco seems at times to have wanted Margherita kept on a short leash, she was an active participant in creating and maintaining Francesco's public persona.

A reputation for wealth and success was extremely useful for Francesco, as it meant he would attract employees whom he could groom into associates or partners. Yet a reputation for wealth and success could also cause serious problems for his wife and household in Prato. Without Francesco present to do so directly, Margherita was forced to try and curate the reputation of her absentee husband as best she could. In April 1397, officials from the Abbondanza came to the Datini home, searching for hidden grain, "because someone told them that there is a great deal of grain hidden here."[74] Three days later, they returned and fined the absent Francesco 25 florins for taking 30 *moggia* of wheat to Florence, and hoarding grain for speculation rather than putting it on the market.[75] Margherita did the best she could to deal with these nosy officials, but these kinds of damaging and incendiary rumors were an inevitable byproduct of Francesco's reputation for prosperity. Francesco needed to be known as prosperous, yet the appearance of wealth inevitably led to jealousy and suspicion.

Keeping a vigilant ear for what people were saying about Francesco was an important preoccupation of Margherita's, her protests that she did not like to pass on gossip notwithstanding. In one case, Margherita wrote to Francesco after learning that Nofri degli Strozzi, one of his acquaintances, was spreading outlandish tales of his wealth in advance of a communal tax assessment. She apologized for gossiping, yet added,

> I do this to inform you, because I think that you had greater trust in Nofri than anyone. But I excuse him somewhat because he has to pay up, and he is considered a bit of a miser. If you were to behave that way, you would confirm their suspicions.[76]

Here we can clearly see Margherita's ability to provide both dense and current commentary on the social fabric of Prato and Florence in ways that could impact Francesco's reputation, cautioning him about Nofri degli Strozzi's rash words and encouraging her husband to be mindful of how others perceived his behavior. This situation is a marked contrast to the situation of Giovanni Carocci discussed earlier. If Carocci's protests that no ship had come to Tunis from Pisa for a year are to be believed, his connection to his city of origin must have become seriously attenuated. It might be commercially useful to operate out of a port like Tunis for a time, yet this sort of move also put a merchant far away from the living social world on which his broader ambitions depended. Letters might compensate for this lack somewhat, but the epistolary community could only supplement rather than substitute for the kind of dense social monitoring that Margherita could provide as Francesco's eyes and ears around the household and civic community.

Margherita worked diligently in her management of Francesco's public persona, trying to demonstrate in whatever ways she could that he recirculated his wealth, rather than hoarding it.[77] Certainly, this is something Francesco did on his own behalf on many occasions, as when he provided dowries for daughters of his partners, female servants, or kin.[78] Francesco could utilize Margherita directly, as when he demanded she spread the word about what kind of creditor he was – that he was interested in collecting debts from the rich, and not from those who could not pay: "I do not want them [collected] from those who cannot pay, but I want anyone who is rich to pay. Say so to everyone."[79] In other cases, Margherita was asked to provide charity for those who had fallen on hard times, especially if the recipients were connected to the Datini family in some way, as when she sent bread and flour to the wife of one of the family's agricultural laborers. Here, too, Margherita acted on her own initiative, in this case encouraging Francesco explicitly, "If you are agreeable, I think he should be helped to some extent, considering that he also clearly loves you and this is something that should never be forgotten."[80]

For trusted associates, Margherita could broker additional services, as when she was asked to find a wet-nurse who could work for the uncle of Francesco's partner in Pisa, even going so far as to offer to have both wet-nurse and baby stay at the Datini house in Prato.[81] Thus, Margherita played a critical role in creating the trust in Francesco he needed to keep his companies together and functioning, a role that is revealed in the letters, though not performed through them. On the one hand, she maintained ties to important individuals and projected a strong public face – an essential part of keeping the confidence of Francesco's partners. On the other, she helped deepen and maintain closer affective ties with the most important of the company's human assets. Although reputation in this context functioned differently than that used to cultivate cross-cultural trading ties, it nevertheless fulfilled a critical economic role.

The household and circle of acquaintances around it served both as an incubator of talent and as a source of new employees, factors, and partners for the future. Francesco's tutor, Piero di Gunta del Rosso, worked in Datini's wool and dying workshops in Prato, before he was joined there by his son, Niccolò di Piero. After Piero's death, his grandson, Agnolo di Niccolò, worked there too, about whom Margherita wrote, "I have always considered him not just a relative but my own son, and he has always respected me as a mother."[82] Without the affective bonds that could be cultivated in an extended household, the longer-distance and longer-term collaborations that facilitated Francesco's commercial enterprises would not have been possible in the same way.

Commercial letters, networks, and hierarchies

The move to consider informal factors such as trust, reputation, and personal networks in enabling trade has lent new impetus to studying mercantile letters as a source for economic history. This study comparing different segments of the Datini correspondence offers two preliminary conclusions on which to build in the future. First, the Datini archive, because of the density and diversity of letters it conserves, allows us to consider more carefully where and why reputation mattered in a mercantile correspondence, both physically and socially. At the margins of Francesco's network of contacts, lively and visible invocations of people's reputations were relatively plentiful. In correspondence between core members of Datini's companies, however, the vast majority of letters in the archive deal much less directly and obviously with the creation and maintenance of trust. This feature of the epistolary network may allow us to think with more precision about the role of letter-writing in economic networks that are not as thoroughly documented.

The unequal distribution of conversations about reputation in the Datini correspondence is also important because it reveals both the limits and strengths of the network concept for historical analysis.[83] In economic history, the concept of the network was adopted as a complement to or replacement for studies of economic association that focused on firms – explicitly hierarchical and vertically integrated units. As a result, theorizing about networks tends to treat the network as a non-hierarchical form of organization, explicitly opposing them to formally hierarchical forms of associations like firms or companies.[84] However, correspondence from the Datini archive suggests that differences in status, in knowledge, and in access to resources were actually critical to making a large and heterogeneous network function. Among the Datini correspondents, invocations of reputation functioned as ways for outsiders and marginal figures to gain attention at least as much as an opportunity to police the behavior of insiders. Ultimately, this investigation suggests that, even within a single social grouping, not all merchant letters functioned in the same way. Trust and reputation were not generated in the abstract, but by actors whose specific position in particular hierarchies and formal organizations had a lot to do with what kinds of reputational commentary they were allowed to make.

Second, the varied and uneven invocations of reputation among Francesco's correspondents abroad contrast with the relative frequency with which reputation was a subject of discussion in letters between Datini and his wife. The lucky accident of Margherita's marriage by correspondence, combined with a new emphasis on networks and informal forms of economic association, allows us to pay even more attention to her role in his commercial activities, not to mention his reputation at home. To the extent that informal or social factors like trust and reputation affected commerce, Margherita's correspondence demonstrates that wives could play a critical, if indirect and often invisible, role in creating and sustaining trading relationships. From the perspective of Francesco's correspondents in Milan or North Africa, Margherita was completely invisible. Yet from her letters we can see the way she, too, played an important role in Francesco's businesses at the very heart of this enterprise. She helped create his public persona and policed his reputation, an indispensable activity for maintaining a network that was simultaneously widely dispersed and physically grounded in Tuscany. In a similar vein, she actively contributed to the life cycle of Francesco's partnerships by monitoring, commenting on, and promoting those whom she observed and encountered while running the Datini household. The formal partnership arrangements, technical skills, and commercial techniques that structured the day-to-day trading activities of Francesco and his associates were obviously indispensable to his commercial ambitions. At the same time, however, they would have been insufficient if not tightly embedded in the broader fabric of Francesco and Margherita's shared social world.

Notes

1 Luciana Frangioni, *Milano fine trecento: Il carteggio Milanese dell'Archivio Datini di Prato* (Firenze: Opus Libri Edizioni, 1994), vol. 2, Appendices n.23, pp. 598–599.
2 For an accessible introduction to the economic activities of Datini and his companies as well as his person and possessions, see Giampiero Nigro, ed. *Francesco di Marco Datini: The Man the Merchant* (Firenze: Firenze University Press, 2010) as well as Paolo Nanni, *Ragionare tra mercanti: Per una rilettura della personalità di Francesco di Marco Datini (1335–ca. 1410)* (Pisa: Pacini, 2010). For a biographical study of Francesco, see the lively and humane treatment in Iris Origo, *The Merchant of Prato* (London: The Folio Society, 1963). See also the many studies of Federigo Melis, including *Aspetti della vita economica medievale. Studi nell'Archivio Datini di Prato* (Siena: Monte dei paschi di Siena, 1962).
3 Ingrid Houssaye Michienzi, *Datini, Majorque et le Maghreb (14e–15e siècles): Réseaux, espaces méditerranéens et strategies marchandes* (Leiden: Brill, 2013), 43–59.
4 Frangioni, *Milano fine trecento*, vol. 2, Appendices n.23, p. 598.
5 Jérôme Hayez, "Les correspondances Datini: un apport à l'étude des réseaux marchands toscans vers 1400," in *Les échanges en Méditerranée médiévale. Marqueurs, réseaux, circulations, contacts*, ed. Élisabeth Malamut and Mohammed Ouerfelli (Aix en Provence: Presses Universitaires de Provence, 2012), 173–182.
6 For a brief survey of the range of goods, see Origo, *Merchant*, 26–33, 59–70, 90–95.
7 Edwin S. Hunt. *The Medieval Super-Companies: A Study of the Peruzzi Company of Florence* (Cambridge: Cambridge University Press, 1994).
8 Angela Orlandi. "Networks and Commercial Penetration Models in the Late Medieval Mediterranean: Revisiting the Datini," in *Commercial Networks and European Cities, 1400–1800*, ed. Andrea Carcausi and Christof Jeggle (London: Pickering & Chatto, 2014), 83.
9 Francisco Bethencourt and Florike Egmond. "Introduction," in *Cultural Exchange in Early Modern Europe: Vol. III. Correspondence and Cultural Exchange in Europe, 1400–1700* (Cambridge: Cambridge University Press, 2007), 1–2. On Pereisc, see Peter N. Miller, *Pereisc's Europe: Learning and Virtue in the Seventeenth Century* (New Haven, CT: Yale University Press, 2000).
10 Orlandi, "Networks and Commercial Penetration Models," 91.
11 For a recent survey of letter writing practices more generally, see Armando Petrucci, *Scrivere lettere. Una storia plurimillenaria* (Roma: Laterza, 2008). For a sampling of different genres and approaches, see the 2009 issue of *Reti medievali rivista*, and especially the Introduction by Isabella Lazzarini, 1–9.
12 See the summary and bibliography in Giagnacovo, *Mercanto toscani*, 23–43.
13 For a much-debated thesis on the relationship between letter-writing and humanism, see Ronald Witt, "Medieval 'Ars dictaminis' and the Beginnings of Humanism:

A New Construction of the Problem," *Renaissance Quarterly* 35:1 (1982): 1–35. For an English perspective on the *Ars dictaminis* tradition and merchant letters, see Malcolm Richardson, "The Fading Influence of the Medieval *Ars Dictaminis* in England After 1400," *Rhetorica: A Journal of the History of Rhetoric* 19:2 (2001): 225–247. For humanism among merchant writers, Christian Bec, *Marchands écrivains, affaires et humanisme à Florence (1375–1434)* (Paris: Mouton, 1967); Christian Bec, "Au début d XVe siècle: Mentalité et vocabulaire des marchands florentins," *Annales Histoire, Sciences sociales* 22:6 (1967): 1206–1226.

14 Josh Brown, "Multilingual Merchants: The Trade Network of the Fourteenth Century Tuscan Merchant Francesco di Marco Datini," in *Merchants of Innovation: The Languages of Traders*, ed. Wagner, Beinhoff, and Outhwaite (Berlin: De Gruyter, 2017), 235–251.

15 For a recent historiographic summary, see Jérôme Hayez, "Les correspondances Datini," 155–173. See also Mario del Treppo, "Federigo Melis and the Renaissance Economy," *Journal of European Economic History* 10:3 (1981): 709–742. For classic studies, see Raymond De Roover, *The Rise and the Decline of the Medici Bank, 1397–1494* (Cambridge, MA: Harvard University Press, 1963). Using the Datini archive itself, see Melis, *Aspetti*.

16 For two exemplary studies that emphasize the quantitative possibilities, see Maria Giagnacovo, *Mercanti a tavola: Prezzi e consume alimentari dell'azienda datiniana di Pisa (1383–1390)* (Firenze: Opus Libri Edizioni, 2002); Maria Giagnacovo, *Mercanti toscani a Genova: Traffici, merci e prezzi nel XIV secolo* (Roma: Edizioni Scientifiche Italiane, 2005).

17 See, for example, Benjamin Z. Kedar, *Merchants in Crisis: Genoese and Venetian Men of Affairs and the Fourteenth-Century Depression* (New Haven, CT: Yale University Press, 1976).

18 Much of this work has taken the form of responses to the work of Avner Greif from the 1990s. For a compendium of his articles, slightly revised for publication as a single volume, see Avner Greif, *Institutions and the Path to the Modern Economy: Lessons from Medieval Trade* (Cambridge: Cambridge University Press, 2006). While historians have been rightly skeptical of some of the details of Greif's analysis as well as its ability to explain the long-run divergences between the Muslim and Latin Christian worlds, the issues of trust his work focused on have retained their interest. For a theoretical critique, see Francesco Boldizzoni, *The Poverty of Clio: Resurrecting Economic History* (Princeton, NJ: Princeton University Press, 2011). For a response to Greif as well as an attempt to map changes in contractual relations onto changing informal networks of interaction among merchants, see Quentin Van Dooseelaere, *Commercial Agreements and Social Dynamics in Medieval Genoa* (Cambridge: Cambridge University Press, 2009).

19 For three exemplary studies, all of whom engage with Greif in productive ways, see Francesca Trivellato, *The Familiarity of Strangers: The Sephardic Diaspora, Livorno, and Cross-Cultural Trade in the Early Modern Period* (New Haven, CT: Yale University Press, 2009); Jessica Goldberg, *Trade and Institutions in the Medieval Mediterranean: The Geniza Merchants and their Business World* (Oxford: Oxford Unviersity Press, 2012); Sebouh David Aslanian, *From the Indian Ocean to the Mediterranean: The Global Trade Networks of Armenian Merchants from New Julfa* (Berkeley, CA: University of California Press, 2011).

20 Francesca Trivellato, "Merchants' Letters Across Geographical and Social Boundaries," in *Correspondence and Cultural Exchange in Europe, 1400–1700*, ed. Egmond et al., 80–103.

21 For editions devoted to correspondence from particular fondachi, see, among others, J. Ruis I Cornadó, "Documentació catalana a l'arxiu Datini: la correspondència del mercader barceloní Lleonard de Johan," *Acta mediaevalia* 1 (1980): 127–132; Luciana Frangioni, "'In capo del mondo.' Sei lettere mercantile da Bergamo alla fine del

Trecento," in *L'età dei Visconti. Il dominio di Milano fra XVIII e XV secolo*, ed. L. Chiappa Mauri, L. De Angelis Cappabianca, and P. Mainoni (Milan: La storia, 1993); Luciana Frangioni, *Milano fine Trecento*. 2 vols. Elena Cecchi Aste, *Il carteggio di Gaeta nell'Archivio del mercante pratese Francesco di Marco Datini, 1387–1405* (Gaeta: Comune di Gaeta, 1997); Angela Orlandi, *Mercanzie e denaro: la corrispondenza datiniana tra Valenza e Maiorca (1395–1398)* (Valencia: Universitat de Valencia, 2008); Giampiero Nigro, *Mercanti in Maiorca. Il carteggio datiniano dall'Isola, 1387–1396* (Firenze: Le Monnier, 2003). A partial selection of the correspondence from the Genoa *fondaco* is in Renato Piattoli, *Lettere di Piero Benintendi, mercante del trecento* (Genova: Società ligure di storia patria, 1932). Datini's merchant manual has also been published as Cesare Ciano, *La "pratica di mercatura" datiniana (secolo XIV)* (Milano: Giuffrè, 1964).

22 For Margherita's letters, see Carolyn James and Antonio Pagliaro, trans. *Margherita Datini: Letters to Francesco Datini* (Toronto: Iter Inc., 2012). For Francesco's letters to Margherita, Elena Cecchi, ed. *Le lettere di Francesco Datini alla moglie Margherita (1385–1410)* (Prato: Società pratese di storia patria, 1990). For the Milan correspondence, Frangioni, *Milano fine Trecento*, vol. 2. For the North African correspondence, see the documentary appendix to Michienzi, *Datini, Majorque et le Maghreb*.

23 Luciana Frangioni, "Milano 'is a good land and the basis of our trade,'" in *Francesco di Marco Datini: The Man the Merchant* ed. Giampiero Nigro (Firenze: Firenze University Press, 2010), 419–431.

24 For a brief history of the Datini *fondaco* in Genoa and its personnel, see Giagnacovo, *Mercanti toscani a Genova*, 50–78.

25 Frangioni "Il carteggio commerciale" takes the less-structured view, against Jérôme Hayez, "Io non so scrivere a l'amicho per siloscismi: Jalons pour une lecture de la lettre marchande toscane de la fin du Moyen Age," *I Tatti Studies in the Italian Renaissance* 7 (1997): 37–79.

26 Hayez, "Io non so scrivere."

27 Frangioni, *Milano fine trecento*, n.658 p. 478, e.g. On 24 March 1397, for example, "Abianvi detto il bisogno in questi dì e vostre lettere non abiamo poi e ora nonn è a dire."

28 Frangioni, *Milano fine trecento*, n.657 p. 478, e.g. On 24 March 1397, Manno d'Albizo closed with "Né altro per ora. So a' vostri piaceri. Cristo vi guardi."

29 Frangioni, *Milano fine trecento*, n.660–662 p. 480.

30 Maria Giagnacovo, "Guerre, epidemie e privato: il contenuto extra-economico del carteggio commerciale," *Reti medievali rivista* X (2009): 163–199.

31 Frangioni, *Milano fine trecento*, n.627 p. 460.

32 This marks a major contrast with the Maghribi traders discussed by Goldberg, for whom prices, local market conditions, and exchange rates are not as much of a concern. The Datini company does seem to have imagined that it could take advantage of brief fluctuations in market conditions. See Giagnacovo, "Guerre, epidemie e privato."

33 Frangioni, *Milano fine trecento*, n.634 pp. 464–465.

34 Frangioni, *Milano fine trecento*, n.641 p. 468.

35 Frangioni, *Milano fine trecento*, n.610 p. 449.

36 On the political struggle between Florence and Milan, see Hans Baron, *The Crisis of the Early Italian Renaissance* (Princeton, NJ: Princeton University Press, 1966), 12–46. On the same conflict in a later period, see also the contributions by Riccardo Fubini and Vincent Ilardi to *Florence and Milan: Comparisons and Relations*, vol. 2 (Florence: La Nuova Italia Editrice, 1989).

37 Frangioni, "Milano 'is a good land … ,'" 421–422.

38 Frangioni, *Milano fine trecento*, n.646 p. 472.

39 Frangioni, *Milano fine trecento*, n.23 p. 599. "chome che io non abia auta chon voi istretta dimesticheza nella presenza di voi e di me, io l'òe cho lla vostra buona fama."

40 Ibid. "anchora v'òe uno charo amicho luchese ch'è una buona persona ed è praticho di tafettà e di draperia di seta."

41 Giagnacovo, "Guerre, epidemie," 194–195.

42 Frangioni, *Milano fine trecento*, n.651 p. 474, 3 March 1397.

43 Frangioni, *Milano fine trecento*, n.666 p. 483, 6 April 1397.

44 Frangioni, *Milano fine trecento*, n.645 p. 471.

45 Frangioni, *Milano fine trecento*, n. 722 pp. 512–513.

46 Frangioni, *Milano fine trecento*, n.722 pp. 512–513. "Se Andrea fosse costà, che mi conoscie, mi servirebe bene e chosì sono certo farete voi perché Francescho di Marcho fu mio maestro e qua rechai sua lettera di racomandigia."

47 Melis, *Aspetti*, 26.

48 Michienzi, *Datini, Majorque et le Maghreb*.

49 For the Datini archive as a source for much larger circuits of exchange linking Africa and Europe, see Martin Malcolm Elbl, "From Venice to the Tuat: Trans-Saharan Copper Trade and Francesco di Marco Datini," in *Money Markets and Trade in Late Medieval Europe: Essays in Honour of John H.A. Munro* ed. Lawrin Armstrong, Ivana Elbl, and Martin M. Elbl (Leiden: Brill, 2007), 411–459. For issues of trust in the trans-Saharan trade itself, see Ghislaine Lydon, *On Trans-Saharan Trails: Islamic Law, Trade Networks and Cross-Cultural Exchange in Nineteenth-Century Western Africa* (Cambridge: Cambridge Unviersity Press, 2009).

50 Michienzi, n.26 p. 605.

51 Michienzi, n.27 p. 607.

52 Michienzi, n.3 p. 559.

53 Michienzi, *Datini, Majorque*, n.8–9 pp. 566–567.

54 Michienzi, *Datini, Majorque*, n.10 p. 568.

55 Domenico Ventura, "Cronaca di un riscatto. Dalle lettere di Giovanni Carocci, mercante pisano 'schiavo' in Tunisi (1384–1387)," *Ricerche storiche* 22 (1992): 3–20.

56 Michienzi, *Datini, Majorque*, n.5 p. 562.

57 Michienzi, *Datini, Majorque*, n.6 p. 563.

58 Ibid.

59 Michienzi, *Datini, Majorque*, n.9 p. 567.

60 Michienzi, *Datini, Majorque*, n.7 p. 565.

61 Ibid., n.26 p. 605.

62 The rhetorical flourishes in these letters bear more similarities to letters seeking patronage than other letters from the Datini archive examined here. For recommendation letters as a means of pursuing patronage, see Paul McLean, *The Art of the Network: Strategic Interaction and Patronage in Renaissance Florence* (Durham, NC: Duke University Press, 2007).

63 For an introduction to Margherita's writing, see James, *Letters*, 18–25.

64 Ann Crabb, "Gaining Honor as Husband's Deputy: Margherita Datini at Work, 1381–1410," *Early Modern Women: An Interdisciplinary Journal* 3 (2008): 225–231.

65 Ann Crabb, "'If I Could Write': Margherita Datini and Letter Writing, 1384–1410," *Renaissance Quarterly* 60 (2007): 1170–1206. On the late medieval trend toward autograph rather than dictated letters, see Armando Petrucci, *Writers and Readers in Medieval Italy: Studies in the History of Writing*, Charles M. Radding, trans. (New Haven, CT: Yale University Press, 1995), especially 145–168.

66 See also Joseph P. Byrne and Eleanor A. Congdon, "Mothering in the Casa Datini," *Journal of Medieval History* 25:1 (1999): 35–56. Jerôme Hayez, "Le rire du marchand. Francesco Datini, sa femme Margherita et les 'gran maestri' florentins," in *Les femmes et le quotidian (XIVe–XVIIIe siècle): Textes offerts à Christiane Klapisch-Zuber*, ed. Chabot, Lett, and Hayez (Paris: Publications de la Sorbonne, 2006), 407–458. Carolyn James, "A Woman's Work in a Man's World: The Letters of Margherita Datini (1384–1410)," in *Francesco di Marco Datini: The Man the Merchant* ed. Nigro, 53–74.

67 James, *Letters*, n.107 p. 194.

68 Ibid., p. 195.
69 Hayez, "Les correspondances Datini," 178–179.
70 James, *Letters*, n.117 p. 201, n.128 p. 224. See also n.136 p. 231.
71 Cecchi, *Le lettere*, n.77 p. 152, n. 28–29 pp. 74–77.
72 James, *Letters*, n.32 pp. 87–88.
73 James, *Letters*, n.136 p. 231.
74 James, *Letters*, n.124 p. 220.
75 James, *Letters*, n.126 p. 222.
76 James, *Letters*, n.27 p. 79.
77 On the importance of recycling one's wealth productively in the late Middle Ages, see Giacomo Todeschini, *I mercanti e il tempio. La società Cristiana e il circolo virtuoso della ricchezza fra Medioevo ed Età Moderna* (Bologna: Il Mulino, 2002).
78 Origo, *Merchant*, 180.
79 Cecchi, *Le lettere*, n. 81 p. 161. "Io no volglo da chi non puote, ma chi e riccho volglo che nmi paghi: chosi fa dire a tutti."
80 James, *Letters*, n.113 p. 203. See also a similar arrangement in which Margherita gave a bushel of flour to the wife of one of the family's laborers. Ibid., n.116 p. 210.
81 Ibid., n.120 p. 213, n.121 p. 216.
82 James, *Letters*, n.206 p. 331.
83 For a discussion of the limits of network analysis, see Chapter 2 of this volume.
84 See Mike Burkhardt, "Networks as Social Structures in Late Medieval and Early Modern Towns: A Theoretical Approach to Historical Network Analysis," in *Commercial Networks and European Cities*, ed. Carcausi and Jeggle, 15.

2

CIRIACO D'ANCONA AND THE LIMITS OF THE NETWORK

Monique O'Connell

In the 1440s, Ciriaco de Pizzicolli (1391–1452), also known as Ciriaco d'Ancona, composed a letter to the archbishop of Ragusa, Giacomo Veneri de Racaneto. Ciriaco recounted his exploration of the small Northern Italian town of Vercelli, examining the ruins of the Roman amphitheater, aqueduct, and tombs and documenting its ancient inscriptions. When a local priest approached him and asked what he was doing, Ciriaco boldly announced, "It is my profession to wake the dead!"[1] Ciriaco's passion for resurrecting the ancient world through attention to its material remains, particularly his interest in recording and preserving Greek and Roman inscriptions, has earned him the title "Father of Archeology." From one perspective, the incident in Vercelli offers clear evidence of Ciriaco's industrious search for any fragment from the classical past. From a different perspective, the account highlights the importance of correspondence in the way Ciriaco framed and publicized his self-appointed mission as the savior of ruined cities and reused marbles. The letter communicates Ciriaco's sense of divine calling, saying that he had learned the art of waking the dead from Pythia, the Delphic oracle. While best known for his copies of over a thousand ancient inscriptions, Ciriaco's letters formed an important part of how he circulated knowledge about his discoveries and influenced his reputation for humanist learning and antiquarian expertise.

Ciriaco's activities as a merchant, antiquarian, diplomat, and humanist crusader brought him into contact with people, events, and places across the Mediterranean. As a merchant, he bought, transported, and sold nuts, wax, and wood as well as manuscripts, gems, and luxury textiles. When his friend and patron Cardinal Gabriele Condulmer was elected Pope Eugenius IV, he involved himself in diplomatic relations between the Ottoman sultan, the Byzantine emperor, and the pope. Racanati is only one of many clerics, rulers, and merchants who exchanged letters with Ciriaco, writing about their shared antiquarian interests but also trading information about military movements, peace negotiations, and commercial activities. Ciriaco's letters offer evidence not only of the way he reported his discoveries and represented his interest in antiquity but also how he tried to influence others through his writings.

Just as Ciriaco's varied pursuits make it difficult to categorize his profession, his letters upend expectations about correspondence. Renaissance "familiar" letters directly communicated personal thoughts and experiences, representing the mind of the sender and bridging the distance between two individuals.[2] There are certainly differences between genres of correspondence: merchant letters, diplomatic letters, and humanist letters all took on their own particular forms and stylistic conventions.[3] Ciriaco's correspondence, like his lived experience, does not fit neatly into any single genre. In fact, Ciriaco might be considered a sort of epistolary go-between, acting as an intermediary between the Renaissance worlds of commerce, humanist culture, and diplomacy.[4] This essay explores how Ciriaco's letters move between different types of epistolary exchange, arguing that while the sources allow us to observe the communication practices of a complex and unique individual, they do not lend themselves to network analysis, a tool scholars have commonly applied to correspondence collections. While network analysis has proven useful in a variety of instances, this contribution argues that it would not capture the importance of Ciriaco's correspondence, demonstrating the limits of the network when it comes to Renaissance letters.

In general, correspondence seems to embody the idea of direct communication: the letter-writer is transferring information about his or her actions, observations, thoughts, or feelings to a recipient. Ciriaco's correspondence overturns this expectation as well: while it is clear that Ciriaco wrote and received many letters, our knowledge of almost all that correspondence is indirect. Ciriaco bequeathed his papers to the municipal archive in Ancona, where fire destroyed them in 1532.[5] Ciriaco also had notebooks called the *Commentaria*, in which he kept a diary of his travels, detailed descriptions and sketches of the ancient monuments he visited, copies of ancient inscriptions, and his interspersed commentary and interpretations.[6] By the end of his life, these *Commentaria* expanded to six volumes, and Ciriaco himself as well as others copied and circulated pieces of the notebooks.[7] A 1514 fire that eviscerated the Sforza library at Pesaro destroyed the original notebooks, leaving scholars to reconstruct their contents based on surviving fragments and copies.[8] The main source for our knowledge of Ciriaco's early life through 1435 is a biography written by his friend and fellow humanist Francesco Scalamonti, who drew his information from Ciriaco, from his mother and other relatives, and the now-lost notebooks.[9] The letters thus need to be gathered from widely scattered copies, later editions, and interpolations in other sources, raising questions about the direct nature of the original communication.

Merchant by necessity, humanist by aspiration

Ciriaco worked as a merchant, and yet his correspondence is not comparable to the Florentine merchant Francesco Datini, whose letters survived nearly complete under the staircase in his house in Prato.[10] Ciriaco also worked as a diplomat on behalf of Pope Eugenius IV, and yet his letters do not fit within the mountains of diplomatic correspondence preserved in fifteenth-century Italian archives.[11] While Ciriaco was a humanist, he did not follow Petrarch's model and collect his correspondence into *Familiar Letters* designed to show his erudition and connections among other Italian humanists.[12] Instead, his correspondence is woven through the fragments of other sources that form the shattered mosaic of his life and works. The action in Scalamonti's *Life* is punctuated by references to sending and receiving of letters, and his biographer includes some of his letters.[13] Ciriaco himself mined his notebooks for material he repeated in his letters, and the Renaissance scholars, artists, and armchair travelers interested in Ciriaco's material copied selections from his letters and notebooks indiscriminately. The dispersion of Ciriaco's letters in the historical record certainly represents a type of knowledge circulation, but it takes a different form than a network of correspondence that demonstrates the deliberate choices of sender and recipient.[14]

The scholarship on Ciriaco has largely focused on reassembling the scattered evidence of his life and interests. The late classicist Edward J. Bodnar dedicated his career to editing and translating Ciriaco's corpus, including Scalamonti's *Life*, Ciriaco's early letters (1423–1438) and his later travels (1443–1449), in addition to many interpretative books and articles.[15] A 1992 conference in Ancona illustrates the wide range of specialized subfields relevant to Ciriacan studies, with sections on archeology, epigraphy, humanism, and antiquarianism.[16] The French scholar Jean Colin compiled a trove of material in order to demonstrate Ciriaco's foundational position as the Father of Archeology but its posthumous publication lacks narrative coherence.[17] A more recent biography of Ciriaco aimed at a popular audience, Belozerskaya's *To Wake the Dead*, gives readers a sense of Ciriaco's world.[18]

When looking at Ciriaco's life, scholars typically point to the breadth of his travels (Figure 2.1) and the diversity of the social networks and friendships he developed. In the first part of his life, he trained as a merchant, became prominent in local politics, and began his enduring interest in the classical past.[19] According to Scalamonti, his merchant career was a practical way of making a living, but "his noble spirit drove him to see the world" and travel widely.[20] His biographer uses his early voyages to show his passion for discovery and his evolution over time, from a child excited at his first sighting of lions to a young man amazed by "new peoples with their strange garments and accents."[21] While he was involved in the reconstruction of the harbor of Ancona, Ciriaco was seized by curiosity about the Roman arch of Trajan there; Scalamonti wrote that it was this arch that inspired Ciriaco "to search out and examine all other noble memorials of antiquity in the world."[22]

From 1424–1434, Ciriaco laid the groundwork for the combination of interests that would characterize the rest of his life. Over the course of the decade, he studied Latin and Greek at the same time he continued his commercial career, consolidated his political position in Ancona, and undertook his first major antiquarian

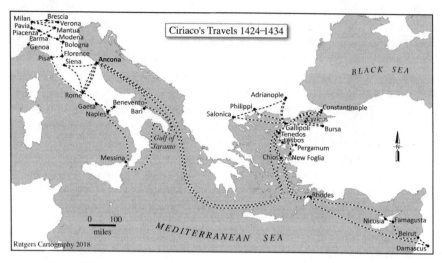

FIGURE 2.1   Ciriaco's travels 1424–1434; locations from Scalamonti's *Life*, travel routes are approximations.

Courtesy of Rutgers Cartography Lab

investigations. In December 1424, he went to Rome as Cardinal Condulmer's guest, where he inspected the Roman ruins and realized "the stones themselves afforded to modern spectators much more trustworthy information about [the Romans'] splendid history than was to be found in books."[23] He returned briefly to Ancona and was elected to a government position, but when the Venetian Zaccaria Contarini needed a commercial representative to oversee his business interests in Cyprus, Ciriaco began his second major trip of the decade. From 1428–1429, Ciriaco traveled from Ancona to Cyprus by way of Constantinople, where in addition to inspecting that city's antiquities he began to learn Greek. During this trip, Ciriaco met and became friends with Andreolo Giustiniani-Banca. Andreolo belonged to the Genoese *maona*, the company of merchants with monopolies on the alum mines of Foglia as well as the mastic production on Chios. Andreolo's intellectual interests manifested themselves in the construction of his villa, near the so-called "School of Homer" in a pine grove on the island, as well as in his library of more than 2,000 manuscripts.[24] Ciriaco continued on to Rhodes, Beirut, and Damascus before eventually reaching Cyprus.

On Cyprus, Ciriaco managed Contarini's business interests and forged a friendship with the Cypriot king Janus, accompanying him on panther-hunts.[25] There he also located copies of Homer's *Iliad* and *Odyssey*, and other Greek texts. After about a year, Ciriaco left Cyprus and headed home, stopping to visit Andreolo on Chios and wintering in the western Ottoman capital of Adrianople. Ciriaco shipped his merchandise to Ancona but remained in the region to investigate the local antiquities; he was near Gallipoli when he received the news that his friend and patron Gabriele Condulmer had been elected pope. After writing to friends in Italy and Dalmatia, Ciriaco set out to collect information and view antiquities in Anatolia before briefly returning to Ancona. He remained at home only a few days before leaving on his third major trip of the decade, this one a looping itinerary through Italy. It was on this trip that Ciriaco toured the classical ruins of Rome with emperor-elect Sigismund of Luxemborg, visited the dome of the cathedral in Florence with its architect Filippo Brunelleschi, and admired the manuscripts and artworks in the collections of the learned men in Cosimo de Medici's circle.[26] Ciriaco's adventures continued after 1434, but this overview of his activities in a single decade is enough to show the combined commercial and cultural nature of his travels and the reach of the relationships and connections he established as he moved through the Eastern Mediterranean.

Just as Ciriaco's experiences and activities demonstrate his overlapping interests in intellectual and political spheres, his correspondence shows his engagement with humanist and diplomatic worlds. In the early fifteenth century, the humanist community of scholars found cohesion through epistolary exchange: humanists used letters to share discoveries of ancient texts and information on patrons and positions, and to assert social status, friendships, and common tastes.[27] By 1430, Ciriaco had begun to assert his interests in the classical world and his claims to expertise and knowledge through correspondence with others in the humanist world.[28] One of Ciriaco's humanist correspondents was Francesco Filelfo (1398–1481).[29] The two men's lives overlapped in many ways: Filelfo was born in Tolentino, about 40 miles from Ancona, he also learned Greek in Constantinople in the 1420s, and he was also involved in Byzantine–Ottoman diplomatic circles of the era.[30] It is not clear where the two men met, and Ciriaco's correspondence to Filelfo does not survive, but Filelfo's letters to and about Ciriaco are highly complimentary and reinforce the image of Ciriaco as a passionate revivifier of the classical past. "Apply yourself, then, as you have been doing, in this liberal and laudable task of renewing, or rather resurrecting antiquity," instructed Filelfo in one letter; in another he addresses him saying, "you, who bring the dead back to life."[31] In yet another letter to the Sicilian humanist Antonio Beccadelli (1394–1471), known as Panormita, Filelfo wrote: "You will be aware of the extraordinary zeal of Cyriac of Ancona in calling the dead back to life."[32]

Filelfo's letters show how humanists could create reputations for learning and expertise for one another; they could also do so for themselves in their own writings, which is what Ciriaco did in a surviving exchange with Leonardo Bruni, chancellor of Florence and one of the most renowned literary stylists of the day. In the first set of letters, which Bodnar dates to 1432–1433, Ciriaco inquires of Bruni whether the title of king or emperor was more honorable, referencing the newly crowned Holy Roman Emperor Sigismund's decision to take the title of emperor.[33] Bruni responded that the title of king was superior to that of emperor, pointing to a set of examples from Roman history to support his position and by extension expressing his preference for classical Latin usage over contemporary linguistic practice.[34] Ciriaco again wrote to Bruni in 1436 in order to intervene in the polemic between Poggio Bracciolini and Guarino Guarini over interpretations of the Roman past, specifically the relative merits of Scipio Africanus and Julius Caesar.[35] In spring 1435, Poggio wrote a letter arguing that while Caesar destroyed the Roman Republic, Scipio was a zealous defender of republican values; in response, Guarino defended Caesar's admirable qualities and praised his foundation of the Roman Empire.[36] Poggio's response in autumn 1435 attacked Caesar's character and achievements, defending republican values over monarchical or princely rule. In a 1436 letter addressed to Bruni, Ciriaco took aim at Poggio's position, citing his "mad and highly unfair opinion, which I heard recently, regarding our divine Caesar."[37] By offering his opinion in a major intellectual controversy between some of Italy's most prominent humanists, Ciriaco boldly claimed a place in the highest intellectual circles.

Ciriaco may have chosen to address his letter to Bruni not only because of their prior acquaintance, but also because of Bruni's reputation as one of the foremost Greek scholars of the day. Ciriaco's own experience in the Greek-speaking world of the Eastern Mediterranean and his expertise in Greek material culture had been his point of entry into Medicean Florence, and his affinity for things Greek also framed his defense of Caesar against Poggio.[38] Ciriaco's letter begins as he arrives in the Dalmatian city of Zadar as the guest of the humanist Giorgio Begna; when news arrives of Poggio's claims, the group of Dalmatian humanists decide "they should be passed over in total silence and suppressed by everyone."[39] Instead of doing so, Ciriaco launches into a lengthy defense of Caesar framed as a dream conversation with the Greek Muses Polyhymnia and Calliope and then by impersonating the god Mercury, who is firmly in favor of Caesar. Schadee's study of this text argues that Ciriaco's letter not only advances the pro-Caesarian position, it also defends the value of poetry and maintains Greek culture as the equal of the Latin classical heritage.[40]

Poggio, one of the most talented and vicious wielders of invective in Italy, was not one to let such a challenge pass without remark.[41] Rather than engage directly with Ciriaco, he addressed his response to Bruni.[42] Poggio did not engage with the substance of Ciriaco's pro-Caesarian position but instead took the opportunity to attack the self-taught Ciriaco's Latin. He wrote:

> I laughed at first quite a bit that such a frivolous, tasteless, and capricious man had stuck together so absurdly such a pile of verbosity that neither the writer nor his readers could understand what he wrote, unless they wanted to guess: a lot of Greek mixed with Latin, words improperly used, bad Latin, awkward constructions, no sense, so that really they seem to be the unintelligible responses of Apollo or the words of the Sphinx, which no one but the Sibyl could understand.[43]

While Poggio's harsh judgment of Ciriaco's literary abilities did not create a permanent rupture between the two men, the negative opinion of Ciriaco's Latin style did shape subsequent scholarship.[44] Ciriaco certainly did not conform to the imperatives of Ciceronian style, but both Schadee and Parroni have argued that Ciriaco's idiosyncratic language arose from choice rather than ignorance.[45] Ciriaco took great pride in being a philhellene, and his language showed the influence of the Greek world, giving him an original way of expressing himself that he was able to adjust according to his correspondent and his intentions. In Schadee's words, there was "an element of choice in Ciriaco's language, which may be informed by a vain belief that he expressed himself in an original and brilliant fashion."[46]

Like many humanists, Ciriaco exchanged letters with others interested in antiquity to demonstrate his own erudition; his idiosyncratic incorporation of Greek language, culture, and poetry set him apart from others. He took an equally individual approach when he engaged with diplomatic networks of exchange in the Eastern Mediterranean. Scholars have disagreed on the extent to which we might consider Ciriaco as a diplomat.[47] There is no question he was involved in the high politics of his day, particularly after the 1431 election of Condulmer as Pope Eugenius IV. According to Scalamonti's *Life*, as soon as Ciriaco heard the news he canceled his proposed trip to Persia and instead headed to Ottoman territory, stopping in Bursa, Constantinople, Lesbos, Mytilene, and Smyrna (see Figure 2.1).[48] The *Life* is clear on Ciriaco's plan:

> having collected all the intelligence he could concerning a Union with the Greeks and the whole Eastern Church and on an effective crusade against the Turks, to hasten home to Italy and to visit the pope in Rome in order, both orally and by written report, to lay before him whatever of importance in his view he had discovered on these matters.[49]

Over the next decade, Ciriaco tried without success to get an official diplomatic assignment from Eugenius that would have given him ambassadorial status and at the same time finance his antiquarian travels.[50]

An occasional diplomat and passionate antiquarian

In the late 1430s and early 1440s, the conventions and practices of Italian and Mediterranean diplomacy were in a developmental phase. Lazzarini's work on Italian diplomacy shows that the Councils of Constance (1414–1418), Basle (1431–1438), and Ferrara/Florence (1435–1439) helped to develop a "national" network of political interaction and diplomatic representation; the individuals who performed diplomatic work had a wide variety of social and educational backgrounds.[51] Lazzarini also identifies a composite group of occasional diplomats, "all the different men and women who performed some diplomatic interaction, more or less regularly, with or without a specific purpose, and without and explicit mandate or formal credentials but still with a certain degree of legitimacy."[52] Ciriaco's activities leading up to and during the Council of Florence fall into this category of "occasional" diplomacy. He had no formal mandate or credentials from the pope, but correspondence demonstrates that he nonetheless played an important role at the Council. A 1442 letter from Jacopo Zeno to Ciriaco credits him with persuading the Byzantine emperor John VII Palaeologus to attend the Council of Florence, and he was part of the Emperor's entourage while the Council was happening.[53] After the Council agreed on Union, Ciriaco wrote to the pope, Francesco Sforza, and Filippo Maria Visconti calling for peace in Italy in order to pursue a Crusade against the Ottomans.[54]

In late 1443, Ciriaco began a five-year trip to the Eastern Mediterranean that combined his diplomatic work on behalf of an anti-Ottoman Crusade with his search for Greek and Roman ruins and inscriptions. While Francesco Pall saw Ciriaco's post-1441 travels as private and unauthorized, other scholars have argued that such a long and expensive trip must have been supported or sponsored in some way, especially given the paucity of commercial or mercantile activity during the trip.[55] Bodnar, the principal editor of the 53 letters and diary excerpts that survive from this voyage, argues convincingly that Ciriaco most likely traveled as a semi-official representative of the pope, charged with keeping lines of communication open with potential allies and ensuring their cooperation for the crusading navy. Ciriaco's correspondence from 1444 circulates news of peace agreements, military movements, and fortification strength (Figure 2.2).[56]

The particular blend of humanist and diplomatic concerns Ciriaco brought to his work on behalf of the Crusade can be seen in a set of letters from June 1444, when Ciriaco was at the Ottoman capital of Adrianople during peace negotiations

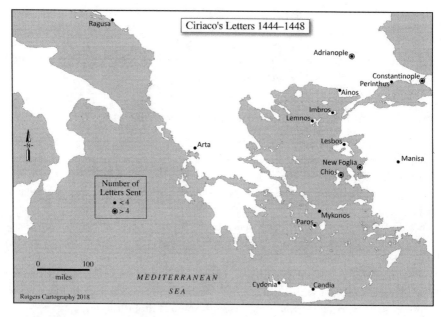

FIGURE 2.2   Ciriaco's correspondence 1444–1448.
Courtesy of Rutgers Cartography Lab

between Hungarian crusaders and the sultan Murad II.[57] In the first letter, probably but not certainly addressed to Andreolo Giustiniani-Banca, Ciriaco recounted the arrival of Hungarian and Serbian ambassadors to the Ottoman court and the subsequent peace negotiations.[58] He enclosed a copy of Ladislas of Hungary's letter to Sultan Murad and two copies of Murad's reply, one in an "enhanced" translation.[59] These documents mix the normal diplomatic function of gathering and circulating news updates with the concern for translation and language typical of humanist circles; because he combines the two, Ciriaco's letter does not fit easily in either genre.[60]

A mix of diplomatic strategy, travel writing, and political argument characterizes the document Ciriaco sent to Pope Eugenius IV in late 1441. Written in the immediate aftermath of the Council of Florence, the goal of the missive was to persuade Eugenius to appoint Ciriaco papal representative to Ethiopia.[61] In support of his argument, Ciriaco outlines his travels to date to impress the pope with the breadth of his contacts and depth of his experience of the Mediterranean world. Because of the emphasis on his travels, the document is often called the Itinerary (*Itinerarium*). While it covers roughly the same timeframe as Scalamonti's *Life*, some scholars have noted the differences in the order of locations visited; the persuasive nature of the piece means that Ciriaco was not emphasizing chronology but content.[62] Ciriaco wanted the assignment for a combination of antiquarian and diplomatic reasons—his success with John VIII Palaeologus meant that he was well positioned to gain the King of Ethiopia's signature agreeing to church union, and he was eager to explore the Upper Nile and North African coast. While the form is a long and persuasive letter, it also shares characteristics of a travel narrative. Furthermore, the autograph copy presented to Cosimo de Medici and a second version sent to Leonello D'Este suggests that the point of the document went beyond a specific request for patronage from Ciriaco to Eugenius, to whom it was directed; the goal was also to build Ciriaco's reputation as an experienced and knowledgeable traveler and passionate proponent of Crusade among other elite audiences.

During his 1444–1448 trip around the Eastern Mediterranean, Ciriaco's most frequent correspondent was his friend, business associate, and fellow humanist Andreolo Giustinian-Banca. The majority of surviving letters are preserved in a single manuscript, likely copied from Andreolo's originals on Chios in 1473 by the itinerant scribe Nicola Ugolino.[63] It is certainly possible that Ciriaco had other frequent correspondents whose letters have not survived, but it is clear from the contents of the letters that the two men shared a passion for the classical world. Ciriaco's letters to Andreolo fit within the framework of other Renaissance letters between friends; he used the correspondence to update Andreolo on his travels, describe the people he encountered and the cities he explored, and strive to entertain and comfort his distant friend.[64] In the spring of 1444, Ciriaco wrote twice to Andreolo in quick succession. In the first instance, describing his journey from Chios to Foglia Nuova, Ciriaco engaged in mythological fantasy, imagining the ships as Greek sea nymphs playing in the waves.[65] In the second, Ciriaco relayed the news of a Genoese–Neapolitan treaty, commenting, "Yesterday, dearest Andreolo, I wrote to you and, to cheer you up, described our joyful voyage in a rather expansive composition."[66] In another letter, Ciriaco debunked the myth of his own demise, writing that he was surprised Andreolo believed such a rumor since he joked that he was under the god Mercury's special protection.[67]

The overlap between Ciriaco's notebooks and letters is particularly apparent in communications with Andreolo about his visit to Athens and his observations of the monuments there. In January and February 1444 Ciriaco traveled across the Greek mainland, stopping at Patras, Corinth, and Athens. In March 1444 he sent a document to Andreolo in Chios describing three ancient monuments he saw in Athens. Bodnar observes: "This document, usually referred to as a letter, has all the earmarks of an excerpt made by Cyriac from his travel journals for presentation" to Andreolo.[68] In the document, Ciriaco describes the Parthenon as the Temple of Minerva designed by Phidias, quotes Pliny's praise of Phidias, and gives a detailed description of the building's overall structure and embellishments. He then says: "I took pains to include a drawing of this absolutely splendid building, as far as in me lay, in this notebook that I am keeping of my current travels through Greece."[69] No drawing accompanies the description in the manuscript containing copies of Ciriaco's correspondence, but Ciriaco's drawing of the Parthenon survives in autograph form in a presentation copy of his drawings and inscriptions made for Piero Donato, bishop of Padua[70] (see Figure 2.3). This episode demonstrates the blurred boundaries of Ciriaco's correspondence and its ability to shade into other forms of communication: his description plus drawing of the Parthenon were in his now lost notebooks but survive in two presentation copies, one to Donato, the other to Andreolo in a scribal copy, as part of a letter collection without the drawing. In light of the complexities of this material, one might ask what constitutes a "letter" distinct from other textual modes of knowledge circulation.

Ciriaco's correspondence intersects with three overlapping networks of communication in the fifteenth-century Mediterranean: commercial, diplomatic, and humanist or antiquarian travel. While each set of letters have distinct and idiosyncratic qualities, his letters to Bruni are part of a network of humanist correspondence in which individuals engaged with the classical past demonstrated their own learning and debated questions of interpretation and style. His diplomatic correspondence fits into a growing network of official and unofficial representatives charged with gathering and sharing news as well as persuading and negotiating rulers into trade and military agreements. His letters to Andreolo articulate and strengthen a friendship as well as describing and documenting his travels across the Eastern Mediterranean, making these letters both personal and part of a larger set of travel writings.[71] Ciriaco emerges from his letters as part of a Mediterranean network of overlapping and intersecting commercial, diplomatic, and scholarly exchanges.

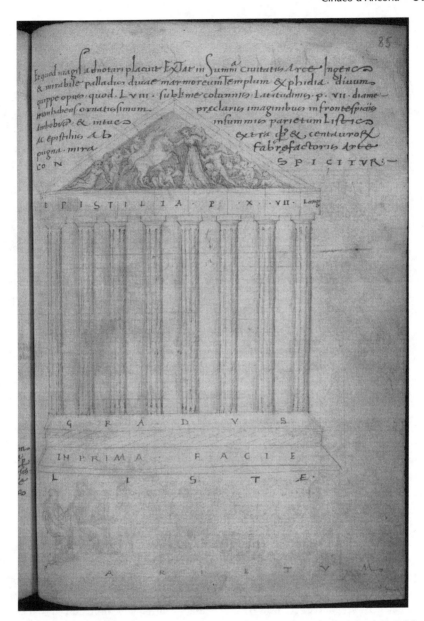

FIGURE 2.3 Ciriaco's drawing of the Parthenon, Athens, fifteenth century. bpk Bilda-gentur/Staatsbibliothek zu Berlin, Ms Ham. 254, Blatt 85r.
Courtesy of Art Resource

More generally, Ciriaco's lived experience fits into larger Mediterranean patterns, demonstrating some typical features for merchants, diplomats, and humanists. As a merchant, he learned the traditional skills of accountancy, vernacular literacy, and cross-cultural negotiation through an apprenticeship and partici-pated in the commercial networks that tied Europe to North Africa and the Middle East. During his travels, he faced typical dangers and setbacks: pirate raids, storms, and transportation delays. Cyriac layered diplomatic functions atop his merchant activities, offering a view of changing diplomatic practice in the mid-fifteenth century. As a scholar, Cyriac took inspiration from early writers such as Dante and Petrarch, but he took the humanist passion for the classical past out of the literary realm and instead applied it to the physical remains of the Greek and Roman past that littered the shores of the Mediterranean.

The limits of correspondence networks

As both his letters and his experience are part of Mediterranean networks of communication, Ciriaco's letters seem to be good candidates for network ana-lysis, a tool that has offered many useful insights in other cases of commercial, diplomatic, and intellectual correspondence. As I have suggested earlier, network analysis is not the best tool to apply to Ciriaco's letters. In order to understand why not, we need to consider two factors: the precise definition of a "network" and the place of the letters in Ciriaco's corpus.

The idea of the network—in the sense of connections between people—has been part of the scholarly landscape since the 1940s, but over the last decade has become an increasingly common way for scholars to conceptualize and analyze all sorts of interactions.[72] A classic example of a network focuses on the history of long-distance trade.[73] While there are multiple definitions of business net-works, they share several common elements: networks are non-hierarchical, layered on social affiliations, and necessitate a high degree of trust among mem-bers. Participants in a network replace reliance on legal institutions with informal cooperation that relies on reputation and status within the network.[74] Scholars have used network analysis to understand trade relationships in the Mediterra-nean, the Baltic, and the Atlantic; in their analyses, patterns emerge, demonstrat-ing the "thickness" or importance of different types of relationships within groups.[75] These aggregate patterns can challenge assumptions derived from legal or descriptive sources and offer evidence about how trade actually functioned in practice. Francisco Apellaniz, for instance, uses network analysis to overturn traditional interpretations of Venetian trade in the Eastern Mediterranean. Ven-etian legislative sources indicate that Venetian patricians dominated and shaped commerce, but Apellaniz shows that in fifteenth-century Alexandria, there were a number of lower-rank Venetians, Greeks, Jews, and Egyptians "negotiating, flaunting, and frequently breaking the rules."[76]

Moving from the precise concept of a business network to more general con-ceptions of social networks—a web of connections between people—network analysis has been used to answer political and cultural questions as well as eco-nomic ones. Historical sociologist John Padgett and his collaborators have applied the insights of network analysis to understand Medici family dominance in Florence, or more broadly how power worked within the Florentine elite. Padgett and Ansell's 1993 article "Robust Action and the Rise of the Medici" used a relational database to reconstruct multiple types of networks in Florentine society: marriage alliances, trade partnerships, real estate holdings, employment in the Medici bank, loan guarantors, and friendships.[77] Padgett and Ansell use this material to locate "holes" in the network and argue that Cosimo de Medici's power came from his ability to fill those holes and harness the power of multiple networks. Padgett and Paul McLean have used some of the same data to ask questions about the level of competition in the Florentine marketplace, and McLean's independent work has focused on the creation of the relational self through the composition and circulation of patronage letters.[78]

The ubiquity of the network in scholarly analysis is driven in part by our increased computing power and the ability to capture, analyze, and visually represent big sets of data. It is also driven by the pervasiveness of networks in contemporary society.[79] As we become habituated to thinking and talking explicitly about our own position in social networks, networks seem a persuasive way to explain the behavior of historical actors as well. There are, however, several critiques of networks as analytical tools. One critique comes from historical sociologists, who argue that network analysis offers an inadequate conceptualization of human agency on the one hand and of culture on the other.[80] Others have argued that network analysis does not explain change over time, or how networks transform or even fail, since most studies focus on examples of successful networks.[81] A final critique is the overuse of the term "network," or the idea that anything can be a network.[82] In the words of one scholar, network analysis has become "a terminological jungle in which any newcomer may plant a tree."[83] Once one sees networks everywhere, it becomes so broad and imprecise a term that it is impossibly vague and therefore not useful.

Returning to the question of Ciriaco of Ancona's correspondence, what might be the benefits and drawbacks of applying network analysis to his letters? The first difficulty arises with the letters themselves: as Ciriaco's description and drawing of the Parthenon demonstrate, it is not always easy to determine what is and is not a letter. The second problem is that of numbers; here a comparison with Francesco Datini's correspondence is useful. There are fewer than 100 surviving letters to or from Ciriaco. The Datini archive is huge, containing about 150,000 letters, including 125,000 commercial papers and 25,000 private and family letters.[84] This massive body of material has been subject to network analysis and has revealed many insights into the functioning of late medieval commerce.[85]

One of the main benefits using network analysis on the Datini material is that it allows scholars to perceive and visualize hidden patterns in large sets of data. The patterns of Ciriaco's correspondence, on the other hand, are perfectly obvious without needing to use network analysis. His main correspondent was Giustiniani-Banca, and he also exchanged letters with fellow humanists and with those useful to his strategic political goals. In fact, the element that emerges most strongly from Ciriaco's letters and notebook fragments is the one thing network analysis tries to remove from the equation: the sense of a single, unique, and idiosyncratic individual. Ciriaco's appeal comes from the fact that he is not predictable; his uniqueness opens many doors to the key people and moments of Renaissance culture. In contrast, network analysis takes the persuasive power away from the extraordinary individual, revealing through repetition and pattern the daily, often unreported or underreported, lived experience of a wide group of people. Network analysis can indeed be a powerful tool, depending on one's questions, but it is not universally applicable.[86] Ciriaco's case shows the limits of the network.

Notes

1 Lorenzo Mehus, ed. *Kyriaci Anconitani Itinerarium nunc primum ex ms. cod. in lucem erutum ex. bibl. illus. clarissimique Baronis Philippi Stosch* … Florence, 1742, 55, accessed at https://books.google.com/books?id=-NY_AAAAMAAJ&pg=PR3#v=onepa ge&q&f=false. The letter is discussed in Jean Colin, *Cyriaque d'Ancône: le voyageur, le marchand, l'humaniste* (Paris: Maloine Editeur, 1981), 285, and in Marina Belozerskaya, *To Wake the Dead: A Renaissance Merchant and the Birth of Archaeology* (New York: W. W. Norton & Co, 2009), 42. Racaneto was appointed by Eugenius IV in September 1440.
2 Lisa Kaborycha, "Introduction," in *A Corresponding Renaissance, Letters Written by Italian Women 1375–1650* (Oxford: Oxford University Press, 2016), 2–8; see also the Introduction to this volume.
3 John Najemy, *Between Friends: Discourses of Power and Desire in the Machiavelli-Vettori Letters of 1513–1515* (Princeton, NJ: Princeton University Press, 1993), 18–57; Deanna Shemek, "Letter Writing and Epistolary Culture," in *Oxford Bibliographies: Renaissance and Reformation,* ed. Margaret King. New York: Oxford University Press, 13 March 2013, DOI: 10.1093/OBO/9780195399301-0194.
4 Eve M. Duffy and Alida C. Metcalf, *The Return of Hans Staden* (Baltimore, MD: The Johns Hopkins University Press, 2013), 9–11.
5 Alfredo Trifogli, "Prefazione," in *Ciriaco d'Ancona e la cultura antiquaria dell'umanesimo: atti del convegno internazionale di studio: Ancona, 6–9 febbraio 1992,* ed. Gianfranco Paci and Sergio Sconocchia (Reggio Emilia: Diabasis, 1998), 10.
6 Edward W. Bodnar, *Cyriacus of Ancona and Athens* (Brussels: Latomus, 1960), 2–72.
7 Erin Maglaque, *Venice's Intimate Empire: Family Life and Scholarship in the Renaissance Mediterranean* (Ithaca, NY: Cornell University Press, 2018), 48–52.
8 Bodnar, *Cyriacus of Ancona and Athens,* 70–2; Bodnar has edited and translated five diary fragments in Bodnar and Clive Foss, eds., *Cyriac of Ancona, Later Travels.* The I Tatti Renaissance library, vol. 10 (Cambridge, MA: Harvard University Press, 2003), 61–82, 91–144; 151–78; 187–207; 299–355.
9 Scalamonti's *Life* is edited and translated in Charles Mitchell, Edward W. Bodnar, and Clive Foss, *Life and Early Travels.* The I Tatti Renaissance library, vol. 65 (Cambridge, MA: Harvard University Press, 2015), 3–171; Bodnar and Mitchell's edition of the Life with a fuller introduction was previously published as Francesco Scalamonti, Charles Mitchell, and Edward W. Bodnar, "Vita Viri Clarissimi et Famosissimi Kyriaci Anconitani," *Transactions of the American Philosophical Society* 86, no. 4 (1996): i–246.
10 On Datini, see Miner's contribution to this volume; on merchant letters more generally see Armando Petrucci, "L'Europa reimpara a scriversi," in *Scrivere lettere: Una storia plurimillenaria,* by Armando Petrucci (Bari, Italy: Laterza, 2008), 204–6; and

Francesca Trivellato, "Merchants' Letters across Geographical and Social Boundaries," in *Correspondence and Cultural Exchange in Europe, 1400–1700*, ed. Francisco Bethencourt and Florike Egmond (Cambridge: Cambridge University Press, 2007), 80–103. On the problem of distinguishing commerical letters from other genres of corespondence, see Jessica Goldberg, "The Use and Abuse of Commercial Letters from the Cairo Geniza." *Journal of Medieval History* 38, no. 2 (2012): 127–54.

11 Francesco Senatore, *Uno Mundo de carta: forme e strutture della diplomazia sforzesca* (Naples: Liguori, 1998), for an example of diplomatic correspondence, see Franca Leverotti, ed. *Carteggio degli oratori mantovani alla corte sforzesca (1450–1500)*. Vol. I. Rome: Ministero per i Beni e le Attività Culturali, Ufficio Centrale per i Beni Archivistici, 1999.

12 Cecil H. Clough, "The Cult of Antiquity: Letters and Letter Collections," in *Cultural Aspects of the Italian Renaissance: Essays in Honor of Paul Oskar Kristeller*, ed. Cecil H. Clough (Manchester, UK: Manchester University Press, 1976), 33–67; Clémence Revest, "Au miroir des choses familières. Les correspondences humanistes au début du XVe siècle," *Mélanges de l' École Française de Rome* 119, no. 2 (2007): 447–62; Francesco Petrarch, *Letters on Familiar Matters I–XXIV*. 3 vols. Translated by Aldo S. Bernardo (New York: Italica, 2005).

13 Bodnar et al., *Life*, 75, 93.

14 For examples of more traditional correspondence networks, see the case studies at http://republicofletters.stanford.edu/casestudies/index.html.

15 Bodnar et al., *Life*; Bodnar et al., *Later Travels*; Bodnar, *Cyriacus of Ancona and Athens*; Bodnar, *Cyriacus of Ancona's journeys in the Propontis and the northern Aegean, 1444–1445*. Memoirs of the American Philosophical Society, vol. 112. Philadelphia: American Philosophical Society, 1976; Bodnar, "Ciriaco d'Ancona and the crusade of Varna: a closer look," *Mediaevalia* 14 (1988): 253–80.

16 *Ciriaco d'Ancona e la cultura antiquaria dell'umanesimo: atti del convegno internazionale di studio: Ancona, 6–9 febbraio 1992*, edited by Gianfranco Paci, Sergio Sconocchia, and Accademia marchigiana di scienze, lettere ed arte-Ancona (Reggio Emilia: Diabasis, 1998), 269–89.

17 Colin, *Cyriaque d'Ancône*.

18 Belozerskaya, *To Wake The Dead*.

19 Bodnar, "Introduction," in *Later Travels*, ed. Bodnar and Foss, pp. ix–xxii; Colin, *Cyriaque d'Ancône*, 3–206; Belozerskaya, *To Wake The Dead*, 3–60.

20 Bodnar et al., *Life*, 15.

21 Bodnar et al., *Life*, 7, 15.

22 Bodnar et al., *Life*, 47.

23 Bodnar et al., *Life*, 49.

24 Belozerskaya, *To Wake The Dead*, 75–7; William Miller, *Essays on the Latin Orient* (Cambridge: Cambridge University Press, 1921), 311.

25 Bodnar et al., *Life*, 65.

26 Bodnar et al., *Life*, 91–7.

27 Elizabeth McCahill, "Finding a Job as a Humanist: The Epistolary Collection of Lapo Da Castiglionchio the Younger." *Renaissance Quarterly* 57, no. 4 (2004): 1308–45.

28 One of Ciriaco's early methods of communicating with other humanists was to exchange vernacular poetry; for examples of these verses, see Bodnar et al., *Life*, 18–27 and 39–43.

29 Colin, *Cyriaque d'Ancône*, 391–4; Filefo's letters from 1427–1434 are included in Bodnar et al., *Life*, 273–91.

30 Paolo Viti, "Filelfo, Francesco," in *Dizionario Biografico degli Italiani* 47 (1997), www.treccani.it/enciclopedia/francesco-filelfo_(Dizionario-Biografico).

31 Bodnar et al., *Life*, 275, 287.

32 Bodnar et al., *Life*, 291.

33 Bodnar et al., *Life*, 187.

34 Bodnar et al., *Life*, 187–97.

35 Davide Canfora, *La Controversia di Poggio Bracciolini e Guarino Veronese su Cesare e Scipione* (Florence: Olschki, 2001); John Oppel, "Peace vs. Liberty in the Quattrocento: Poggio, Guarino, and the Scipio-Caesar Controversy," *Journal of Medieval and Renaissance Studies* 4 (1974): 220–65.

36 Giuliana Crevatin, "La politica e la rhetorica: Poggio e la controversia su Cesare e Scipione," in *Poggio Bracciolini, 1380–1980, nel VI centenaria nella nascita*, ed. Riccardo Fubini, 281–342 (Florence: Istituto Nazionale di studi sul Rinascimento, 1982); Marianne Pade, "Guarino and Caesar at the Court of the Este," *La corte di Ferrara e il suo mecenatismo 1441–1598*, ed. Marianne Pade, Waage Peterson, and Daniela Quarta (Modena: Panini, 1990), 75–92.

37 Bodnar et al., *Life*, 197.

38 Belozerskaya, *To Wake*, 161.

39 Bodnar et al., *Life*, 199.

40 Hester Schadee, "Caesarea Laus: Ciriaco d'Ancona praising Caesar to Leonardo Bruni." *Renaissance Studies* 22, no. 4 (2008): 435–49.

41 Ennio I. Rao, *Curmudgeons in High Dudgeon: 101 Years of Invectives, 1352–1453* (Messina: Sfameni, 2007).

42 Bodnar et al., *Life*, 225–31.

43 Bodnar et al., *Life*, 225–7.

44 Foss points out that Poggio wrote a letter of recommendation for Ciriaco in 1438; "Introduction," in *Life*, ed. Bodnar et al., xvi; negative judgments of subsequent scholars are summarized in Piergiorgio Parroni, "Il latino di Ciriaco," in *Ciriaco d'Ancona e la cultura antiquaria dell'umanesimo: atti del convegno internazionale di studio: Ancona, 6–9 febbraio 1992*, edited by Gianfranco Paci, and Sergio Sconocchia (Reggio Emilia: Diabasis, 1998), 269–89.

45 Schadee, "Caesarea Laus," 439–40; Parroni, "Il latino," 282–3.

46 Schadee, "Caesarea Laus," 440.

47 Belozerskaya, *To Wake the Dead*, 107–26 calls him a spy as well as a diplomat; see also Bodnar, "Varna," 254.

48 Bodnar et al., *Life*, 77–87.

49 Bodnar, *Life*, 75–7.

50 Francesco Pall, "Ciriaco d'Ancona e le crociata contro i Turchi," *Bulletin de la section historique, Academie Roumaine* 20 (1938): 9–68.

51 Isabella Lazzarini, *Communication and Conflict: Italian Diplomacy in the Early Renaissance, 1350–1520* (Oxford: Oxford University Press, 2015), 15, 125.

52 Lazzarini, *Communication and Conflict*, 132.

53 Ludwig Bertalot and Augusto Campana, "Gli scritti di Iacopo Zeno e il suo elogio di Ciriaco d'Ancona," *La Bibliofilia* 41 (1939): 374; Kenneth M. Setton, *The Papacy and the Levant, 1204–1571* (Philadelphia, PA: American Philosophical Society, 1978), vol. 2, 64; Colin, *Cyriaque d'Ancône*, 311–16.

54 These letters are discussed in Colin, *Cyriaque d'Ancône*, 314–15 and appear in the *Commentariorum Cyriaci Anconitani nova fragmenta notis illustrata*, edited by Annibale Olivieri degli Abbati (Pesaro: Gavelliis, 1763), accessed at https://books.google.com/books?id=CJp12QUfQB4C&dq=Commentariorum%20Cyriaci%20Anconitani%20nova%20fragmenta%20notis%20illustrata&pg=PP1#v=onepage&q=Commentariorum%20Cyriaci%20Anconitani%20nova%20fragmenta%20notis%20illustrata&f=false.

55 Pall, "Ciriaco d'Ancona"; Bodnar, "Varna," 253–4.

56 Discussed Bodnar, "Varna," 259–67; letters edited and translated in Bodnar, *Later Travels*, 3–99.

57 For an overview of the Crusade of Varna, see Setton, *Papacy and the Levant*, II, 66–107.

58 Bodnar, *Later Travels*, 37–9; discussed in Setton, *Papacy and Levant*, II, 78.

59 Bodnar, *Later Travels*, 39–47.
60 Brian Maxson, *The Humanist World of Renaissance Florence* (Cambridge: Cambridge University Press, 2014), 85–106 investigates the mix of humanism and ambassadorial culture, identifying specific ritual occasions where humanist learning was necessary for diplomacy.
61 Bodnar, "Varna," 270; Colin, *Cyriaque d'Ancône*, 317–24 with partial French translation 320–3. The letter exists in three copies: the autograph copy presented to Cosimo de Medici is dated 13 November 1441; I have not seen it. Another copy, sent to Lionello D'Este, was copied by Felice Feliciano and edited by G. Colucci in *Delle antichità Picene* 15 (Fermo, 1792), 119–23, accessed at https://hdl.handle.net/2027/gri.ark:/13960/t7gq85j0k?urlappend=%3Bseq=131. A third copy, which Bodnar characterizes as a draft that was never sent, is edited by Mehus, *Itinerarium*, 1–52.
62 Colin, *Cyriaque d'Ancône*, 386, Mitchell and Bodnar, "Vita," 10–11.
63 Bodnar, *Later Travels*, 379.
64 There is an extensive literature on epistolary friendship in Renaissance Italy; see Najemy, *Between Friends*; Richard Trexler, *Public Life in Renaissance Florence* (New York: Academic Press, 1980), 131–58; Dale Kent, *Friendship, Love, and Trust in Renaissance Florence* (Cambridge, MA: Harvard University Press, 2009); Amyrose McCue Gill, "Fraught Relations in the Letters of Laura Cereta: Marriage, Friendship, and Humanist Epistolarity," *Renaissance Quarterly* 62, no. 4 (2009): 1098–129.
65 Bodnar, *Later Travels*, 21–5.
66 Bodnar, *Later Travels*, 25.
67 Bodnar, *Later Travels*, 87.
68 Bodnar, *Later Travels*, 411.
69 Bodnar, *Later Travels*, 19.
70 Bodnar, *Later Travels*, 411 and Plates I–II, includng the Roman architect Giuliano da Sangallo's copy of the Parthenon drawing.
71 Maglaque, *Venice's Intimate Empire*, 48–52.
72 Bonnie H. Erickson, "Social Networks and History: A Review Essay." *Historical Methods: A Journal of Quantitative and Interdisciplinary History* 30, no. 3 (1997): 149–57.
73 The letters of the Cairo Genizah have focused scholarly attention on the case of the Magribi traders, Jewish merchants who operated across the medieval Mediterranean. There is an active scholarly debate on the degree to which these traders relied on reputation or on legal institutions for contract enforcement. Avner Greif, *Institutions and the Path to the Modern Economy: Lessons from Medieval Trade* (Cambridge: Cambridge University Press, 2006) argues for the importance of reputation among the Magribi traders; his position has been challenged by Jessica Goldberg, *Trade and Institutions in the Medieval Mediterranean: The Geniza Merchants and Their Business World* (Cambridge: Cambridge University Press, 2012) and by Jeremy Edwards and Sheilagh Ogilvie, "Contract Enforcement, Institutions, and Social Capital: The Maghribi Traders Reappraised," *The Economic History Review* 65, no. 2 (2012): 421–44; for Greif's response, see "The Maghribi Traders: A Reappraisal?" *The Economic History Review* 65, no. 2 (2012): 445–69; for further discussion of this material see Miner's essay on Datini in this volume.
74 Stuart Jenks, "Conclusion," in *The Hanse in Medieval and Early Modern Europe*, edited by Justyna Wubs-Mrozewicz, 255–81 (256) (Leiden: Brill, 2014); for a definition that emphasizes social relationships, see Andrea Caracausi and Cristof Jeggle, "Introduction," *Commercial Networks and European Cities, 1400–1800*, eds. Andrea Caracausi and Christof Jeggle (London: Pickering & Chatto Publishers, 2014), 1–12 (2); for a definition that contains a geographical element, see Wim Blockmans, Mikhail Krom, and Justyna Wubs-Mrozewicz, "Maritime Trade around Europe 1300–1600: Commercial Networks and Urban Autonomy." In *The Routledge Handbook of Maritime Trade around Europe 1300–1600* (London: Routledge, 2017), 1–15 (4).

75 The collection *Commercial Networks and European Cities, 1400–1800,* eds. Andrea Caracausi and Christof Jeggle contains a range of case studies; see also Quentin van Doosselaere, *Commercial Agreements and Social Dynamics in Medieval Genoa* (Cambridge: Cambridge University Press, 2009); David Hancock, *Oceans of Wine* (New Haven, CT: Yale University Press, 2009).

76 Francisco Apellániz, "Venetian Trading Networks in the Medieval Mediterranean," *Journal of Interdisciplinary History* 44, no. 2 (2013): 157–79 (157); see also his "Florentine Networks in the Middle East in the Early Renaissance," *Mediterranean Historical Review* 30, no. 2 (2015): 125–45.

77 John F. Padgett and Christopher K. Ansell, "Robust Action and the Rise of the Medici, 1400–1434," *American Journal of Sociology* 98, no. 6 (1993): 1259–1319.

78 Paul D. McLean and John F. Padgett, "Was Florence a Perfectly Competitive Market? Transactional Evidence from the Renaissance," *Theory and Society* 26, no. 2/3 (1997): 209–44; McLean, *The Art of the Network: Strategic Interaction and Patronage in Renaissance Florence* (Durham, NC: Duke University Press, 2007).

79 Duncan J. Watts, *Six Degrees: The Science of a Connected Age* (New York: Norton, 2003); Albert-laszlo Barabasi and Jennifer Frangos, *Linked: The New Science of Networks* (New York: Basic Books, 2002).

80 Mustafa Emirbayer and Jeff Goodwin, "Network Analysis, Culture, and the Problem of Agency." *American Journal of Sociology* 99, no. 6 (1994): 1411–54.

81 David Hancock, "The Trouble with Networks: Managing the Scots' Early-Modern Madeira Trade." *The Business History Review* 79, no. 3 (2005): 467–91.

82 Blockmans, Krom, and Wubs-Mrozewicz, "Maritime Trade," 3; Jenks, "Conclusion," 255.

83 Hancock, "The Trouble," 468.

84 www.istitutodatini.it/schede/archivio/eng/arc-dat2.htm.

85 In addition to Miner's contribution, see Angela Orlandi, "Networks and Commercial Penetration Models in the Late Medieval Mediterranean: Revisiting the Datini," in *Commercial Networks and European Cities, 1400–1800,* edited by Andrea Caracausi and Christof Jeggle) (London: Pickering & Chatto Publishers, 2014), 81–106; Ingrid Houssaye Michienzi, *Datini, Majorque et le Maghreb (14e–15e siècles): Réseaux, espaces méditerranéens et stratégies marchandes.* The Medieval Mediterranean (Leiden: Brill, 2013), 96.

86 This conclusion echoes that of Mike Burkhardt, "Networks as Social Structures in Late Medieval and Early Modern Towns: A Theoretical Approach to Historical Network Analysis," in *Commercial Networks and European Cities, 1400–1800,* edited by Andrea Caracausi and Christof Jeggle (London: Pickering Chatto, 2014), 13–40.

PART II
Rulers and subjects

3

SAVING NAPLES

The king's malaria, the barons' revolt, and the letters of Ippolita Maria Sforza[*]

Diana Robin and Lynn Lara Westwater

On 12 November 1475, Ferrante, king of Naples, lay dying in Carinola, thirty miles north of his home at Castel Nuovo in the capital. His daughter-in-law Ippolita Maria Sforza posted a series of letters to her brother Galeazzo Maria Sforza, duke of Milan, describing the king's symptoms and warning him of the danger the king's illness posed (Figure 3.1).[1] While Duke Alfonso, Ippolita's husband and the king's son and heir, was suffering from the same sickness, the barons of the realm stood ready to seize the throne for themselves were the king to die. In bulletins sent hourly by couriers to Rome and from there to Milan, Ippolita updated her brother on the king's condition and begged him to send troops and arms south to defend her husband's succession to the throne should Ferrante die. If the barons staged another revolt as they had in 1458–1459, her own survival and that of her husband and their two children would depend on the duke of Milan.[2]

Seventeen years earlier, in June 1458, Ferrante himself had dispatched letters to Francesco Sforza, duke of Milan, warning that Ferrante's father Alfonso, who was then king of Naples, was dying. Ferrante's letters about his father's illness suggest that the aging king had fallen prey to malaria.[3] His dispatches to Sforza anticipate the anxious letters Ippolita Sforza would send to Galeazzo a generation later, describing her father-in-law's decline in November 1475. In these letters, Ippolita also used filial language to address her brother, just as Ferrante had called himself "figliolo" ("son") in addressing Francesco Sforza.[4] In 1455, the duke of Milan and the king of Naples had drawn up a marriage pact betrothing Ippolita (then ten years old) to the king's grandson Alfonso (then seven).[5] The king then strengthened his pact with Sforza that year by joining the alliance between the other great Italian powers concluded at Lodi.[6] Ferrante in his 1458 dispatches to Francesco and Ippolita in her 1475 letters to Galeazzo were playing similar cards: their kinship and their mutual enemies. In the earlier crisis around King Alfonso's illness, during the First Barons' Revolt, Francesco and Ferrante had stood united against

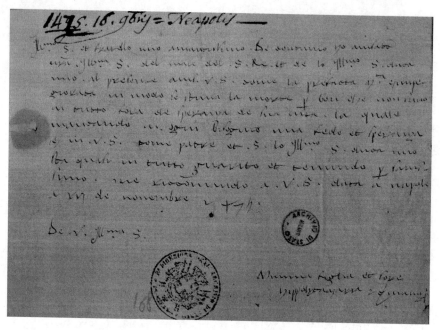

FIGURE 3.1 Ippolita Maria Sforza to Galeazzo Maria Sforza. Naples, 16 November 1475. Archivio di Stato di Milano, Potenze Sovrane, Sforzesco, 227, c. 168. Permission: Ministero per i Beni e le Attività Culturali, Archivio di Stato di Milano, protocol number 3207/28.13.11, 11 June 2018

the claims of Jean d'Anjou, first cousin of King Louis XI of France and pretender to the Neapolitan throne. Two years after King Alfonso's death, Jean had arrived in the Regno with the support of the most powerful barons of the realm and an army ready to claim the throne.[7] The First Barons' Revolt was crushed when Francesco Sforza, Cosimo de' Medici, and the pope supported Ferrante. Now, seventeen years later, faced with the prospect of the king's imminent death, Ippolita Sforza and her husband Alfonso feared a second revolt by the barons of Naples.

The crisis of 1475

When Ferrante came down with a virulent form of malaria in November 1475, Ippolita immediately wrote to Galeazzo. Her letters document the course of the disease that struck Ferrante and, to a lesser degree, Alfonso. With the barons again at the gates of the realm, Ippolita appealed by letter to her brother to come to the defense of her family and its reign and to strengthen the alliance between Naples and Milan. Her letters describe Ferrante's and Alfonso's struggle to survive the soaring fevers and paroxysms of the disease at its height and to come to terms with the political peril in which Naples found itself. Her letters also underscore the precariousness of her situation and her fear that Aragonese rule could end. Ippolita's detailed account of the illness's trajectory sheds light on a little-known chapter of fifteenth-century Italian political history and the epidemiology of a disease, identified as tertian, double tertian, quartan, and, less commonly, quotidian fever in early modern Europe.[8]

Ippolita Maria Sforza: writer of letters

Tall, strikingly blond, and classically educated, Ippolita Sforza and her convoy of nobles, professors and poets, royal cavalrymen, and bearers entered the kingdom of Naples on 14 September 1465.[9] Ippolita came to Naples at the age of twenty to marry Alfonso. Schooled by the humanist Baldo Martorelli in Latin rhetoric and poetry and by Constantine Lascaris, the Greek refugee scholar who dedicated his grammar, the *Erotemata*, to her, Ippolita was already famous in the northern Italian courts for delivering a Latin oration in honor of Pope Pius II at age fourteen.[10] Like many noblewomen of her generation, she began early to collect her letters, both those she wrote and those she received.

Ippolita arrived in Naples with her own library of classical texts. When shown her elegant rooms in the Castel Capuano, she ordered a study (*studiolo*) built for her own use to have a separate place to read, write, and receive her friends. She also asked her mother to send her family portraits so that she could display her impressive clan in the rooms where she entertained and worked.[11] Artists, poets, architects, and men of letters were soon drawn to her, as a woman of learning, taste, and talent with an income of her own. She received works dedicated to her from members of the king's literary academy, including Lorenzo Valla, Flavio Biondo, Antonio Cornazzaro, Francesco Galeota, Benedetto Gareth, Masuccio Saliterno, Antonio Becedelli (Panormita), and the academy head, Giovanni Pontano, who would later become her secretary.

Since both of her parents had died by 1468, soon after her arrival in Naples, Ippolita addressed almost all her letters, often two or three a week, to her pleasure-loving older brother Galeazzo. He was now prince of the realm, though he had shown little interest in the politics of the powerful Lombard state. Her previous letters to her parents and brother had typically been filled with stories of hunting trips she and her husband Alfonso had taken, games they enjoyed playing, books they read and discussed, and the interesting friends who hosted them. Now, dependent on the court news and gossip she picked up at Castel Nuovo, Ippolita soon became Galeazzo's reliable adviser in political as well as private matters. She learned the protocols of diplomacy from the principal Milanese ambassador to Naples, Antonio da Trezzo, who served both her grandfather and her father. Da Trezzo managed to ride the rapids of the Milan–Naples axis until Galeazzo fired him in 1470. Galeazzo's subsequent ambassadors at the court of Naples found working for the duke of Milan to be a revolving door. Within four years, he hired and fired three seasoned diplomats, despite their loyal representation of his interests.[12]

By 1475, Ippolita – the only ambassador her brother could not fire – found herself in a high-stakes game between the two most powerful states in Italy. As early as June 1472, Ippolita famously served as a member of her brother Galeazzo's diplomatic team. When rebels threatened to unseat Ferrante's kinsman John II of Aragon in Barcelona on 14 July 1472, Galeazzo at first supported Ferrante's longtime adversary Jean d'Anjou's plan to send warships from Genoa to aid the rebels. Ippolita – working together with Galeazzo's ambassador Francesco Maletta, her husband Alfonso, King Ferrante, and his longtime friend and adviser Count Diomede Carafa – drew up an agreement in which Galeazzo pledged not to support Jean and the rebels.[13] Milan and Naples were thus prevented from going to war. Even after Galeazzo's assassination in 1476, Ippolita's influence and counsel, letters, and orations continued to be sought after and cited not only in Milan and Naples but in Rome and Florence as well. In the wake of the Pazzi conspiracy in Florence in 1478, Ippolita, who used her dual position as a representative of the ducal family in Milan and the royal family in Naples, was instrumental in campaigning with Pope Sixtus IV and Ferrante to restore Lorenzo de' Medici to power.

When the deadly strain of malaria struck the house of Aragon in 1475, letters were Ippolita's arsenal. Via her longtime friends, the Milanese nobleman Carlo Stendardo who remained in Rome during the king's illness, and Galeazzo's ambassador to Sixtus IV, Sacramoro da Rimini, with whom the pope was said to be "innamorato" ("in love"),[14] Ippolita kept up a rapid tattoo of dispatches to her brother. She and her delegates relied on mounted postal riders traveling from Naples to Rome, and from Rome to Milan. Judging by the dating of her letters and those of her correspondents, her postal carriers could make the trip from Naples to Rome in two or three days, but Rome to Milan could take another week.[15] Thus, many days after the peril of the king's illness subsided, Galeazzo – still assuming the king's death was imminent, as Ippolita had indicated in her first malaria letters – was preparing troops to march into the Neapolitan kingdom to defend Aragonese rule in case of the king's death.

The malaria letters and the language of kinship

Ippolita's daily letters to family and friends had evinced a certain lighthearted style, varied, jaunty, and casually entertaining. Now, in November 1475, when Ferrante and Alfonso came down with malaria, her dispatches assumed a sober tone. They adhered to one topic and one only: the king's and her husband's symptoms, appearance, and chances of recovery. Ippolita also filled her letters with key diplomatic information and her strategic assessment of the kingdom's perilous political situation. They detailed her father-in-law's and husband's pain and suffering, day and night. Ippolita's own clinical eye-witness account of her husband Alfonso's sickness, observed first-hand at their home in the Castel Capuano on 12 November, contrasts markedly with the second-hand reports of her father-in-law's suffering which she received from the king's doctors in Carinola:

I can inform your most illustrious lordship that my above-mentioned lord consort has as of today been sick for eight days with painful and bloody diarrhea and a fever that is a double tertian, and he has not yet shaken the fever, which has been caused by choler, since with his diarrhea he expelled a great quantity of choleric matter that was quite unhealthy.

(Appendix 2, Letter 1)[16]

The duke's disease was violent at the onset but the symptoms quickly receded.

As pervasive as the subject of disease is throughout Ippolita's letters to Galeazzo in November 1475, kinship and its obligations among the members of an elite clan such as the Sforza are equally marked. Her "malaria letters" constantly invoke her fraternal relationship with Galeazzo and their shared love as siblings. Ippolita continually refers to the likeness that exists between a brother's and a father's love, reminding Galeazzo that he is not only "a good brother" but now "like a father to her." In turn, she hopes to be considered "a most obedient daughter" to Galeazzo. By the same token, Ippolita's and Galeazzo's letters interweave kinship created through blood ties with kinship by marriage. Ippolita's husband Alfonso is considered not simply Galeazzo's brother-in-law but his blood brother. Their children are seen as both hers and his. On 12 November she wrote to her brother:

The king ... is worse off than my most illustrious lord the duke. So just imagine, your lordship, how I feel, and were it not for the great faith and hope I have in you, my lord, who are like a father to me, I would be half mad with worry ... I pray that, if the worst befalls the lord king, may God prevent it, your lordship will be willing to demonstrate to my lord the duke, who will certainly be completely well because he is already recovering, that you are a good brother, that you love me and likewise my children, and that you will show him what your lordship has in mind since you consider me a most obedient daughter.[17]

Her use of paternal and filial language served a highly instrumental purpose by reminding her brother of the strength of his obligations and duties if the situation worsened.

In three subsequent letters, Ippolita reveals her worst fears to Galeazzo about the king's deteriorating condition in Carinola. In the first of these letters, she tells Galeazzo her plan to send a trusted Milanese courtier, Carlo Stendardo, to stay in Rome so that she "can more surreptitiously relay news hour by hour by means of the cavalry post of what is happening with the lord king and also with my lord duke, who can be considered healthy."[18] In two subsequent letters, she intimates that she and her brother Galeazzo need to lay the groundwork now for her husband Alfonso's succession to the throne, and prepare to fight were Ferrante to die. The physicians and others in charge of the king's treatment have reported that his condition has worsened and death is thought to be imminent. She informs her brother, however, that Alfonso is "improving so much that he can be judged healthy, and he has started to walk about his chamber." She suggests that her husband is ready to assume the rule: "regarding the kingdom, all the provisions that are considered necessary are being made by my lord duke, with of course mature deliberation and according to the requirements the situation seems to demand." Ippolita concludes this letter with the most powerful of her declarations to her brother, meant surely as a formal pledge: "Please deem that in any event this kingdom [of Naples] belongs to you and your most illustrious children." She asks that her brother regard her letter as having been penned in her own hand, though it bears the signature of her personal secretary, the eminent poet Pontano.[19]

The periodicity of the king's illness: 18–25 November

While Ippolita's earlier letters charted a downward curve in the king's health, the report she sent her brother on 18 November suggested an upturn. In the second week of the king's illness, her letters to Galeazzo chronicled a textbook case of malaria, in which the convulsions, spiking fevers, and severe pain on the first day were followed by remission of the symptoms on the second day; on the third day, a recurrence of the same symptoms was again followed by a fourth day free from pain. In classic malaria, the periodicity of the cycle might be sustained for several weeks, as occurred in Ferrante's case in 1475. As the king's illness worsened, the fate of the Regno hung in the balance.

Many of Ippolita's letters written between 18 and 25 November record the timing of King Ferrante's symptoms, often in lurid detail. Her hopefulness in this letter, written on 18 November, predicts a happy ending for both the king and his son – as long as the king's convulsions remain in remission:

> I wish to let you know that my duke is improving so much that I can declare him entirely healthy ... His majesty the lord king has made such great improvement between yesterday and today, according to letters from the doctors and others who are caring for his majesty, that they declare him to be free from illness and out of danger as long as the frequency of his paroxysms gradually diminishes.
>
> *(Appendix 2, Letter 3)*

This cautious optimism quickly evaporated the next day, when Ippolita wrote that the king had suffered an unexpected and alarming convulsion on the preceding night. This letter provides the most graphic accounts of the king's suffering and the frightening periodicity of the disease:

> Today I must tell you that his majesty last night had a new paroxysm that the doctors had not expected. It was very severe and painful, and frightening to everyone because it was sudden as well as severe and violent. And in the end he expelled a dead worm with abundant and impure feces.

These events have led to the conclusion that his illness is highly dangerous. However, it was feared that another paroxysm would follow, but up
until 20 hours it did not occur. Certainly, if it does not recur, it would
provide great hope. On the contrary, if it does recur, it would make the
situation extremely dangerous.

(Appendix 2, Letter 4)

As the illness's extremes continued to manifest themselves, Ippolita's precision in
relaying the doctors' reports conveyed not only the cyclical nature of the disease
but also the accompanying side effects such as intestinal parasites. Underlying all
her descriptions of the disease's symptoms is her anxiety about the future of the
Aragonese crown. On 23 November, she continues to relay the details of the
king's pathology and specific procedures the doctors undertook to cure him,
including bleeding:

In order to continue my updates regarding the course of his majesty's illness, I am sending your highness the news that his majesty (subsequent to
the paroxysm on Tuesday, that is, on the 21st of this month at 18 hours)
felt entirely reborn after they took two suction cups of blood and gave
him various medicinal remedies for the lower body. And from that time
up until the present hour he has achieved a remarkable improvement, as
witnessed by the fact that he passed the day yesterday very well, and was
able to attend to some business, which he would not have been able to do
if his mind had been clouded by bodily pain and suffering. Yesterday
evening he had a small attack, but it was very weak and caused him very
little pain.

(Appendix 2, Letter 7)

Belying her guarded optimism in her 23 November letter, Ippolita's next two bulletins, each dated 25 November 1475, to her courtier Carlo Stendardo in Rome
and her brother Galeazzo illustrated an escalation in the extreme peaks and valleys
of the king's fevers. After the news of the king's great improvement in the 23 and
24 November dispatches, Ippolita told Stendardo that the king suffered an unexpected and extremely painful paroxysm between four and five hours in the morning of the 24th. Writing on the afternoon of the 25th to Carlo Stendardo, she
was hopeful the same had not happened the previous night.

By means of our letters of the 23rd and 24th you were informed about
the improvements of the lord king, and his health is only progressing. It is
nevertheless true that the night before the 24th between four and five
hours, his majesty had an unexpected seizure. It was not without pain and
a good bit of torpor. Around morning time his condition had eased, such
that he had a much better day yesterday, and he was in good spirits.

(Appendix 2, Letter 8)

Before she could even finish these words, she added that a courier from Cari-nola arrived with the news that the king had suffered another attack overnight, though it had been less violent.

Later on 25 November, Ippolita again highlighted the periodic nature of the disease in a letter to her brother. The king suffered attacks, recovered, and relapsed again, all within a single day. Suddenly the extremes of fever and recovery alternated with even greater frequency than before.

> By means of the letters I wrote yesterday your highness was apprised by me of the great improvement of his majesty the lord king. By means of this letter I wish to let you know that the night before last at around five hours his majesty was overtaken by a paroxysm, which was quite unexpected and not without pain. He passed the day well yesterday: he was in good spirits ... This past night he was again overcome by a paroxysm, yet a light one. His strength is good, and we are quite encouraged, and his illness day by day is diminishing and good health returning.
>
> *(Appendix 2, Letter 9)*

While detailing the ups and downs in the king's health, Ippolita continues to underscore the contrast between her father-in-law and husband's prospects. The king's health remained fragile, but she told Galeazzo her husband was "totally recovered" and "devoting himself to getting stronger." In other words, Ippolita continued to reassure her brother that duke Alfonso was fit to rule.

On 27 November, Ippolita reported to her brother Galeazzo that the king was at last free from the sky-rocketing fevers and nightly convulsions that had plagued him. While Alfonso was now free from all symptoms, the king had begun to have copious nosebleeds, which were judged "a great natural benefit."

Intimations of a second Barons' revolt

On 27 November 1475, two weeks after the onset of the malaria that had endangered King Ferrante and Duke Alfonso's lives, Ippolita reported that a delegation of the most powerful barons in the Regno had arrived at Castel Capuano. In her letter to Galeazzo, she lists among the barons who presented themselves two of the largest landowners in the kingdom of Naples – Duke Giovanni Caracciolo of Melfi and Prince Girolamo Sanseverino of Bisignano.[20] A decade later, these two men would play leading roles in the Second Barons' Revolt (1485–1486). She wrote:

> The gentlemen of Naples who went [to Carinola] to visit his majesty, the lord king, have returned today [to Naples]. They report having seen his majesty in very good spirits, and that he was indeed strong, given the gravity of the illness he experienced. His majesty is now free of the tertian paroxysm which occurred in the day, and though he still has the nighttime one, it is

nevertheless diminishing ... Because of all these things it is believed that his majesty is now out of danger. I wanted to notify your highness of this. The lord my consort has been impeded by his infirmity, and therefore he is weak in the legs and sick to his stomach, and we are attending to this. For the last several days the barons of the realm have started to arrive here: that is, the count of Fundi and his sons; the duke of Melfi and the duke of Sora; and today the duke of Andri, the prince of Bisignano, the count of Sant' Angelo and the count of Capaccio arrived.

(Appendix 2, Letter 11)

As the barons waited in hopes of seeing Alfonso, Ippolita proudly unfurled, for their edification, the beautifully penned letters – with their ducal seals of gold – in which Galeazzo promised Ippolita and Duke Alfonso his unconditional backing were the king to die (Appendix 2, Letter 5; Figure 3.2).[21] To Alfonso, Galeazzo wrote:

21 November 1475. To [Alfonso] Lord Duke of Calabria, written in the prince's own hand: I have been so saddened and worried about your lordship's illness, but even more so by that of his majesty the king, your father, since it has reached a dangerous point. I pray that God will allow him to live and prosper. But if it were in the divine plan for Him to arrange otherwise, I tell you to take courage and maintain a strong and constant mind, since if such a need arose I will do anything for your lordship that you ask and I will wager all of my resources and even, if needed, my own person for the conservation and stabilization of your state. And I will put everything I have on the table without reservation, since your good is my own. I pray you to attend to recovering your full health. Galeazzo.[22]

Ippolita would even more proudly have displayed to the barons the letter Duke Galeazzo had sent to Antonello Petrucci, royal secretary to the king of Naples (also dated 21 November). In this hyperbolic letter, the duke of Milan passionately stated his determination to stand by the duke and duchess of Calabria and their children, no matter what his support might involve:

To lord Antonello Petrucci, the king's secretary. With sadness and much distress we have learned of the danger to his majesty the lord king and we find ourselves in as much anguish as can be imagined in this world, because when things on the one side and the other are properly accounted for and examined, our good or ill fortune [that is, of the two states] is entirely shared, and so do we want it to be, with no exception. This situation is upsetting and painful; and however much greater the warnings and the needs, so much more do we resolve to be prompt and prepared. If God arranged otherwise with his majesty, may God forbid this, we promise – for the preservation of the well-being and the state of the most illustrious duke, our brother and

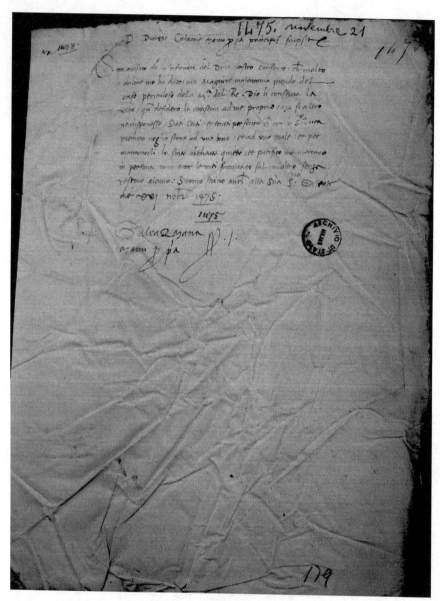

FIGURE 3.2 Galeazzo Maria Sforza to Ippolita Maria Sforza. Milan, 21 November 1475. Archivio di Stato di Milano, Potenze Sovrane, Sforzesco, 227, c. 179. Permission: Ministero per i Beni e le Attività Culturali, Archivio di Stato di Milano, protocol number 3207/28.13.11, 11 June 2018

brother-in-law, and of our sister, his wife – to subject everything we have in this world and even our own person, if it will be necessary, to whatsoever risk or need. In that circumstance we exhort you, even if such exhortation is not necessary, to use your customary faithfulness, sincerity, and diligence as regards the lord duke and lady duchess, since in addition to this being your duty, we, too, will remain in your debt for this. I pray you be pleased to keep me apprised of what is needed and what will transpire. Galeazzo Maria, in his own hand.[23]

As Ippolita herself underscored, Galeazzo's written word manifested the power of letters to forestall revolt.

In Ippolita's final letter in what we have presented as a case study of fifteenth-century malaria and epistolary practice, she again addresses her courtier Stendardo. She reports that her husband, the duke, has returned to the life he lived when he was healthy, while the king, despite occasional alarming symptoms, is also on the road to recovery. Her final "malaria dispatch" on 29 November 1475 ends with Ippolita's celebration of her brother Galeazzo's efforts to secure the Regno and his sister's life not with arms but with letters:

> This morning the most illustrious duke my lord got up and dressed and walked for more than an hour … His majesty the lord king yesterday had another natural benefit of blood that poured from his nose, around 3 ounces, and he had a very good day; and the attack of the previous night had not occurred again at the usual time, according to the report from three hours at night that we received. By the mounted messenger who left yesterday between 18 and 20 hours we wrote you at length according to what occurred to us. In this letter we will only tell you that the most illustrious duke our brother, because of the letters he wrote and the preparations he made, has earned more fame, respect and glory than he would have if he had overcome a great army.
>
> *(Appendix 2, Letter 13)*

Notes

* We are grateful to Sharon Strocchia for her help diagnosing as malaria the illness King Ferrante and Duke Alfonso faced and to the editors of this volume for their extensive suggestions.
1 See Appendix 2 for English translations of letters not already published.
2 On the barons' revolts see David Abulafia, "The Inception of the Reign of King Ferrante I of Naples: The Events of Summer 1458 in the Light of Documentation from Milan," in Abulafia, ed., *The French Descent into Renaissance Italy, 1494–1495: Antecedents and Effects* (Aldershot, UK: Ashgate, 1995), 71–89; Vincent Ilardi, "Towards the Tragedia d'Italia: Ferrante and Galeazzo Maria Sforza, Friendly Enemies and Hostile Allies," in Abulafia, 91–122; Eleni Sakellariou, "Institutional and Social Continuities in the Kingdom of Naples between 1443 and 1528," in Abulafia, ed., *Descent*, 327–353.
3 Alan Ryder, *The Kingdom of Naples under Alfonso the Magnanimous: The Making of a Modern State* (Oxford: Oxford University Press, 1990), 140–141, 424. Alfonso had

almost died of malaria in 1426; he contracted what appears to have again been malaria in May 1458 and died on 27 June that year.

4 Abulafia, "Inception," 82.

5 Carlo Canetta, "La sponsalie di casa Sforza con casa d'Aragona," *Archivio storico lombardo*, ser. 1, vol. 9, fasc. 1 (1882): 136–144 and 10 (1883), 769–782; Evelyn Welch, "Ippolita Maria Sforza, Duchess of Calabria," in Abulafia, ed., *Descent*, 123–136 (esp. 125).

6 Georges Peyronnet, "The Distant Origins of the Italian Wars: Political Relations Between France and Italy in the Fourteenth and Fifteenth Centuries, "in Abulafia, ed., *Descent*, 41; Abulafia, "Inception," 73, 89, 94, 96.

7 Ilardi, "Tragedia," 104–106.

8 Robert R. Sallares, *Malaria and Rome: A History of Malaria in Ancient Italy* (Oxford: Oxford University Press, 2002), 1–11; Charles M. Poser and George W. Bruyn, *An Illustrated History of Malaria* (New York and London: Parthenon, 1999), 5–7. See also our note on the history of malaria in Appendix 1.

9 For recent studies of this influential but understudied figure, see Ippolita Maria Sforza, *Duchess and Hostage in Renaissance Naples: Letters and Orations*, translated and edited by Diana Robin and Lynn Lara Westwater (Toronto: Iter Press, 2017), esp. 1–41; Welch, "Ippolita Maria Sforza," in Abulafia, ed., *Descent*, 123–136; M. Serena Castaldo, "Nota Biografica," in Ippolita Maria Sforza, *Lettere*, ed. M. Serena Castaldo (Alessandria: Edizioni dell'Orso, 2004), 68–98; Giovanni Pontano, *Correspondenza di Giovanni Pontano secretario dei dinasti aragonesi di Napoli (2 Novembre 1474–20 gennaio 1495)*, ed. Bruno Figliuolo (Battipaglia [Salerno]: Laveglia & Carlone, 2012), 3–68 and 402–404; Gregory Lubkin, *A Renaissance Court: Milan under Galeazzo Maria Sforza* (Berkeley, CA: University of California Press, 1994), 19, 23–25, 27, 42–46, 48, 51, 54, 64, 81, and 244; and Abulafia, ed., *Descent*, 6, 83, 94, 112–114, 118, and 120.

10 See Sforza, *Duchess*, 185–189, for the text and translation of her oration for Pope Pius II.

11 Sforza, *Duchess*, 20, 82; Welch, "Ippolita Maria Sforza," in Abulafia, ed., *Descent*, 127–128.

12 Sforza, *Duchess*, 25–28.

13 Ilardi, "Tragedia," in Abulafia, ed., *Descent*, 114–115.

14 Battioni, "Sacramoro da Rimini," in *Dizionario biografico degli italiani [DBI]* vol. 89 (2017), 555–558.

15 The time lag between sending and receiving letters traveling from Naples to Milan and vice versa is especially marked in the flurry of letters Ippolita and her brother exchange in the period 20–28 November 1475.

16 This and other previously unpublished letters are in Appendix 2.

17 Sforza, *Duchess*, 128.

18 Ibid, 129.

19 Ibid, 130.

20 Franca Petrucci, "Giovanni Caracciolo," *DBI*, vol. 19 (1976), 377–380; Alessio Russi, "Girolamo Sanseverino," *DBI*, vol. 90 (2017), 296–298.

21 In a later letter to Carlo Stendardo (Sforza, *Duchess*, 130–131), Ippolita recounts her pleasure at showing the barons her brother's letters. Galeazzo wrote three on the same day, one to Ippolita (Appendix 2, Letter 5) and one each to Alfonso and the king's secretary Antonello Petrucci (cited below in notes 22 and 23).

22 Archivio di Stato di Milano, Potenze Sovrane, Sforzesco (hereafter ASM/PS/S), 227, c. 175.

23 Ibid., c. 176.

24 Sforza, *Duchess*, 155 (23 January 1482).

25 Sforza, *Duchess*, 31–35; 145–156.

26 Sforza, *Duchess*, 35, 198, 201, 208.

27 Sallares, 1–11; Poser and Bruyn, 5–7.

28 Hippocrates, *Epidemics* 1.11.

29 Sallares, 14–19.
30 Sallares, 7–9.
31 Ryder, 348.
32 Herlihy, 49–53.
33 ASM/PS/S, 227, c. 165.
34 See Sforza, *Duchess*, 62n4.
35 Giovanni Pontano, *Correspondenza*, Letter 11, 13-14.
36 Pontano, *Correspondenza*, Letter 12, 14.
37 Pontano, *Correspondenza*, Letter 13, 15.
38 ASM/PS/S, 227, c. 179. Galeazzo wrote two other letters the same day promising his support, one to Duke Alfonso (c. 175) and one to Antonello Petrucci, the king's secretary (c. 176). See notes 22 and 23.
39 That is, to Alfonso.
40 Letter draft, ASM/PS/S, 227, c. 180–181.
41 Pontano, *Correspondenza*, Letter 14, 15-16.
42 Pontano, *Correspondenza*, Letter 15, 16-17.
43 Carlo Stendardo.
44 Sacromoro (Pontano, *Correspondenza*, 17n2).
45 Antonello Petrucci, count of Aversa and secretary to the king (Pontano, *Correspondenza*, 17n3).
46 Aniello Arcamone, count of Borrello, Aragonese ambassador in Rome (Pontano, *Correspondenza*, 17n4).
47 Pontano, *Correspondenza*, Letter 16, 17-18.
48 Draft of letter, ASM/PS/S, 227, c. 187.
49 Pontano, *Correspondenza*, Letter 17, 18-19.
50 They are, respectively: Onorato Caetani with his sons Baldassare and Pier Bernardino; Giovanni Caracciolo, Pietro Giovan Paolo Cantelmo, Francesco del Balzo, Girolamo Sanseverino, Giovanni Leonardo Caracciolo, and Guglielmo Sanseverino (Pontano, *Correspondenza*, 19n1).
51 Pontano, *Correspondenza*, Letter 18, 19.
52 Carlo Stendardo.
53 Pontano, *Correspondenza*, Letter 21, 22.
54 Carlo Stendardo.

EPILOGUES

-I-

Ippolita Maria Sforza's epistolary chronicle of an outbreak of malaria in the royal family in Naples in November 1475 suggests a happy ending. Her continuing sense of her place within and responsibility to her family – the Sforza in Milan and the Aragonese in Naples – was both her ballast and her source of power. Years later she would again convey her deep connection to both families and underscore their intertwined fates in a letter to the young duke of Milan, Giangaleazzo Sforza, who was her nephew, future son-in-law, and heir:

> Your most illustrious lordship will recognize in the letters of your magnificent ambassadors the extraordinary love and fatherly concern that his majesty the king has for your excellency's needs as well as for the preservation of your state, concerning which the king has no motive and purpose other than that which he has for his own state. And so we, who are in the middle between that state there and this state here, can and do bear witness in such a way that, to anyone with sound judgment and especially to your illustrious lordship, [our connection] should be unquestioned because of the many ties and common interests which so clearly bind us together ... Nonetheless, we are informing your illustrious lordship that from this side, as a daughter, a wife, and a mother, and from the other side, as a mother, aunt, sister, and descendant of the family, we are completely prepared to undergo any trouble, effort, and danger.[24]

-II-

Yet the story Ippolita Maria Sforza's later letters would tell is dark. These letters portray a world in which Galeazzo, her beloved but flawed older brother, would be assassinated in 1476, the great maritime Italian city of Otranto would be occupied by the Turkish army in 1480–1481,[25] and Naples and Milan would face off against Venice and Rome in the long wars of Ferrara in 1482–1484.[26] In 1485–1487, the long-dreaded Second Barons' Rebellion broke out and the largest landowners in the kingdom attempted unsuccessfully to remove King Ferrante from the Neapolitan throne. On the heels of that crisis, Ippolita's 1488 death deprived Milan and Naples, still the most powerful states on the peninsula, of their most important intermediary. In 1494, the failure of these states to maintain a lasting alliance would lay Italy open to the French invasion of the Regno and lead to the fall of the house of Aragon.

APPENDIX 1

A note on the history of malaria

Malaria has been known to physicians since classical antiquity, though it was not known by its modern name until the nineteenth century. From the fifth century BCE to the Renaissance, the disease was identified as tertian, quartan, and less commonly quotidian fever. Periodicity is its chief characteristic: Tertian fever – a day of fever alternating with a day without – was thought the most dangerous, because of its severe periodicity.[27]

Frequent citations of the disease in the Hippocratic corpus indicate that malaria was present in the Mediterranean by the fifth century BCE. The *Epidemics* of Hippocrates, for example, describes malaria and notes that "acute disease occurs in the fever called semi-tertian, which is more fatal than the others."[28] The ancient physicians of the first and second centuries CE – Pliny the Elder (24–79 CE), Galen (129–199 CE), and Celsus (fl. 14–37 CE) – all offer detailed descriptions of symptoms characteristic of malaria.[29]

In early modern Europe, malaria was believed to be a disease that came from the vapors that arose from swamps, marshes, and wetlands; hence its name from the Italian *mal'aria* (bad air).[30] Consequently, in enlightened Naples, a program to drain the swamp-lands was launched in 1447.[31] Thirteenth-century Pisa, writes David Herlihy, was so decimated by epidemics of tertian fever that it resembled cities subsequently devastated by the Black Death.[32]

In assessing the importance of Ippolita's account of her father-in-law's and her husband's battle with malaria as an index of daily life in early modern Naples, even for royalty, the dating of her letters is important. The fact that her letters chronicle the course of a virulent outbreak of malaria in November agrees with what we know about the seasonality of the disease.

APPENDIX 2
The malaria letters

Translation Diana Robin and Lynn Lara Westwater
1. Ippolita Maria Sforza to Galeazzo Maria Sforza. Naples, 12 November 1475[33]

Most illustrious prince and most excellent lord, most honorable brother.

If before receiving this letter your most illustrious lordship has heard word of my most illustrious consort's illness, please do not attribute it to any failing on my part, since I was hoping to notify you when things were certain, and depending on the inclinations of the writer, this illness could be depicted by others in quite different ways. At present I can inform your most illustrious lordship that my above-mentioned lord consort has as of today been sick for eight days with painful and bloody diarrhea and a fever that is a double tertian, and he has not yet shaken the fever, which has been caused by choler, since with his bloody diarrhea he expelled a great quantity of choleric matter that was very unhealthy. He was given a medicine that reduced his attacks, the restless paroxysms, and his expulsions, and improved his urine. Today he has had no paroxysm. And although at the beginning of the diarrhea, the doctors were very concerned that this illness was dangerous, given the other symptoms that accompanied it, they are now reassured that with divine help it will come to a quick and happy end, since they see sickness diminishing. Tonight they will give him another medicine that is hoped will improve his health. I will provide updates to your lordship, to whom I commend myself. From Castel Capuano, Naples, 12 November 1475.

Of your same most illustrious dominion[34]
your most affectionate sister, Ippolita Maria, duchess of Calabria
Simon P. secretary.

N.B. For other letters from Ippolita (dated 12–16 November) on the malaria crisis, see Duchess and Hostage, *pp. 127–130 (letters 68–71).*

2. Ippolita Maria Sforza to Galeazzo Maria Sforza. Naples, 16 November 1475[35]

Most illustrious prince and excellent lord, most loving brother,
In the two other letters I wrote in my own hand, I informed your most illustrious lordship of the illnesses of the lord king and of my most illustrious consort. In this letter I wish to let you know that my lord duke is improving so much that he can be judged healthy, and he has started to walk about his chamber. By the grace of our Lord God, he is out of any danger. But as concerns his majesty the lord king, he has worsened considerably and is in great danger, according to the news given by the doctors and others in charge of his care and treatment. And therefore, regarding the kingdom, all the provisions that are considered necessary are being made by my lord duke, with of course mature deliberation and according to the requirements the situation seems to demand. I wanted to give your most illustrious lordship news about everything, as my duty requires, and I will continue to do so daily as the situation unfolds. I do not write in my own hand, as I did in my previous two letters, since I am continually caring for my lord duke and am busy tending to necessary tasks. Kindly trust this letter as if it were in my own hand, and please reciprocate the trust and love the lord duke my consort and I have for you, as do your nephews and niece, whom you can and must consider your own offspring. Please deem that in any event this kingdom belongs to you and your most illustrious children. My lord, all my hope rests in your most illustrious lordship.
Written 16 November.
Ippolita Maria.
Giovanni Pontano, secretary.

3. Ippolita Maria Sforza to Galeazzo Maria Sforza. Naples, 18 November 1475[36]

Most illustrious and excellent prince and lord, my most loving brother,
In the other letters I sent your excellency the news that the lord king and my most illustrious consort were ill. By means of this letter I wish to let you know that my duke is improving so much that I can declare him entirely healthy. He has started to walk around his chamber and he is continually spending time with and being visited by friends and servants. His majesty the lord king has made such great improvement between yesterday and today, according to letters from the doctors and others who are caring for his majesty, that they declare him to be free from illness and out of danger, as long as the frequency of his apoplectic fits gradually diminishes and every treatment helps his health and brings significant improvement to his strength and vitality. Because of these events, I wanted to send news by means of this letter in order to fulfill my duty and to provide comfort to your most illustrious lordship. Commending myself as always to your lordship. From Castel Capuano, Naples, 18 November 1475.
Of your most excellent and illustrious dominion your most loving sister, Ippolita Maria Visconti, duchess of Calabria, etc. Giovanni Pontano, secretary.

4. Ippolita Maria Sforza to Galeazzo Maria Sforza. Naples, 19 November 1475[37]

Illustrious prince and most excellent lord, my most loving brother,

By means of my letter yesterday I notified your highness of the condition and state of his majesty the lord king's health and of his improvement. Today I must tell you that his majesty last night had a new paroxysm that the doctors had not expected. It was very severe and painful, and frightening to everybody because it was sudden as well as severe and violent. And in the end he expelled a dead worm, with abundant and impure feces. These events lead to the conclusion that his illness is highly dangerous. However, it was feared another paroxysm would follow, but up until 20 hours it did not occur. Certainly, if it does not recur, it would provide great hope. On the contrary, if it does recur, it would make the situation extremely dangerous. My lord duke, with God's grace, has recovered his health and well-being. It is nonetheless true that tonight, in order to eliminate completely the slight fever that has persisted, they are going to give him a light purge. I will keep your highness apprised of everything in order to fulfill my duty and so that your most illustrious lordship will know the course of the illness I mentioned above. Commending myself as always to your highness. Written in Castel Capuano, Naples, 18 November 1475.

Of your most excellent and illustrious dominion your most affectionate sister, Ippolita Maria, duchess of Calabria. Giovanni Pontano, secretary.

5. Galeazzo Maria Sforza to Ippolita Maria Sforza. Milan, 21 November 1475[38] [Figure 3.2]

To the lady duchess of Calabria, written in the prince's own hand,

I have been told of the illness of the duke your husband, which has greatly saddened me. But I feel even greater sorrow at the precarious situation of his majesty the king. I hope God preserves his life as much as I hope he preserves my own. But if He ordained otherwise, rest assured and count upon the fact that with the said lord duke I want to share good fortune and ill fortune. To keep his state obedient, calm, and peaceful I will risk my own person and will put everything I have on the table without reservation, as I have also written to his lordship.[39] Galeazzo, 21 November 1475

Galeazzo Maria
In his own hand

6. Galeazzo Maria Sforza to Ippolita Maria Sforza. Milan, 22 November 1475[40]

Galeazzo, 22 November 1475

To the most illustrious lady Ippolita Maria, duchess of Calabria,

This morning by the same means of a letter in our own hand we wrote to your ladyship about your husband what we felt was necessary to write regarding the illness of his majesty the king. This evening we received your letters from the 14th of this month, to which – although they have already been executed upon because of the abovementioned letters of ours, and it is not necessary to reply further –

(Continued)

(Cont).

I will nevertheless reply to you to express more thoroughly our thoughts on the matter, that is, if God ordained otherwise with the lord king, we desire in any circumstance to share good fortune or ill fortune with you and with your husband and my brother. In case of need, he can rely on us and our resources as much as he could rely on his own resources and his own person, since truly in such circumstance we will forget everything that has occurred between his majesty the king and us. We love him in the recesses of our heart as a father, as regards matters of state. Pray your said husband to take courage, since we will take action rather than just talk if such a need arose, may God forbid. And yet, if it did occur, although we do not suspect that even the smallest leafy frond will be disturbed, yet to ensure the security and greater stability of his holdings, and to command from the beginning greater trust and authority, we believe that his most illustrious lordship should give the gen d'armes one hundred or two hundred thousand ducats and commit that decisively, since it would act to extinguish every evil thought, if someone in his kingdom and state tried to create trouble, and for those who are outside the kingdom, it would foil every plot that might be attempted against his lordship. You will assure him, as stated, that he can avail himself of us as he would of himself, and if he has difficulties, we want to share them and we do not doubt that his excellency of Florence will be of the same mindset and determination.

P.S.

Show this letter that we have written to you to Carlo Stendardo; to Messer Zaneschi for intelligence purposes; and, if he agrees, you can also show it to Messer Anello.

7. Ippolita Maria Sforza to Galeazzo Maria Sforza. Naples, 23 November 1475[41]

Most illustrious prince and excellent lord, my most affectionate brother,

In order to continue my updates regarding the course of his majesty's illness, I am sending your highness the news that his majesty (subsequent to the paroxysm on Tuesday, that is, on the 21st of this month at 18 hours) felt entirely reborn after they took two suction cups of blood and gave him various medicinal remedies for the lower body. And from that time up until the present hour he has achieved a remarkable improvement, as witnessed by the fact that he passed the day yesterday very well, and was able to attend to some business, which he would not have been able to do if his mind had been clouded by bodily pain and suffering. Yesterday evening he had a small attack, but it was very weak and caused him very little pain. And up to the present hour, that is the 23rd of this month at twenty hours, the news I have received is that his majesty's condition is good and constantly improving. I am giving your most illustrious lordship news about everything so that you can follow the course of this illness. I commend myself always to your lordship. I write nothing of my lord duke because the little after-effects of his illness are so insignificant that they are hardly noticeable, and they are due to weakness more than anything else. From Castel Capuano, Naples, 23 November 20, 20 hours, 1475.

Of your most excellent and illustrious dominion your most affectionate sister, Ippolita Maria, duchess of Calabria. Giovanni Pontano, secretary.

8. Ippolita Maria Sforza to Carlo Stendardo. Naples, 25 November 1475[42]

Duchess of Calabria, etc.
  Carlo,[43]
  By means of our letters from the 23rd and 24th you were informed about the improvements of the lord king, and his health is only progressing. It is nevertheless true that the night before the 24th, between four and five hours, his majesty had an unexpected seizure, and it wasn't without pain and a good bit of torpor. Around morning time his condition had eased, such that he had a much better day yesterday and he was in good spirits. We have not heard by means of the letters we are receiving from there if the same thing happened again last night. We have hope that he is only progressing, since if it were otherwise, a mounted messenger would have come flying to tell us. And please inform our reverend monsignor of Piacenza[44] about all of this. As to other matters, we wrote to don Antonello[45] about the lost letter, and he wrote back to us that he never saw, in these days of the illness, a letter of ours addressed to the most illustrious lord duke of Milan, nor to the monsignor of Piacenza, but only some packages addressed to you; and that he wrote to don Anello[46] asking him to explain how such a thing occurred. Don Antonello says that letter that began domino meo singularissimo was his, that he wrote in his own name to the most illustrious lord duke of Milan when the lord king was in such grave danger, and that he sent that letter to said monsignor; and that he has already received a response, because it was sent on wings. Inform us how many letters of ours you have received, and when, and be prompt in writing. We have heard from Carinola that his majesty the king this past night had an attack, but it was quite mild. From Castel Capuano, Naples, 25 November, hour 16. Giovanni Pontano, secretary.

9. Ippolita Maria Sforza to Galeazzo Maria Sforza. Naples, 25 November 1475[47]

Most illustrious prince and most excellent lord, my most affectionate brother,
  By means of the letters I wrote yesterday your highness was apprised by me of the great improvement of his majesty the lord king. By means of this letter I wish to let you know that his majesty, the night before last, at around five hours, was overtaken by a paroxysm, which was quite unexpected and not without pain. He passed the day well yesterday: he was in good spirits and enjoying himself and had pleasant conversations. This past night he was again overcome by a paroxysm, yet a light one. His strength is good, and we are quite encouraged, and his illness day by day is diminishing and good health returning. Whatever occurs, your highness will be informed by means of a letter from me. Regarding my lord duke, since he is totally recovered, I will write no further details other than to say that he is devoting himself to getting stronger. Commending myself always to your sublime lordship. From Castel Capuano, Naples, the day 25 November, hour 12, 1475.
  Of your most excellent and illustrious dominion your most affectionate sister, Ippolita Maria, duchess of Calabria. Giovanni Pontano, secretary.

10. Galeazzo Maria Sforza to Ippolita Maria Sforza. Milan, 26 November 1475[48]

Galeazzo, 26 November

To lady Ippolita Maria, duchess of Calabria

We fully understood everything your ladyship says in your letters from November 16 and respond that we are extremely pleased and relieved to hear of the good recovery of the most illustrious lord duke of Calabria, your husband and our brother. But on the contrary, regarding the worsening of his majesty the lord king's illness, we are extremely distressed and anguished. It seems unnecessary to repeat to you again our determination that you will have understood quite thoroughly from the three letters written in our own hand and in others and how – in order to maintain that realm in peace and due reverence to the lord duke your husband and our brother and also to your ladyship, and for the realm's preservation and the honor of his lordship – we are ready and willing to put up everything that we have in the world and even to expose our own person to every danger. If such were necessary we would not fail and we will do whatever the lord duke your husband and our brother will order and desire for us to do. I wish to let your ladyship know that if his majesty the king were to pass from this mortal life, may God forbid, we have chosen to send to your lordship and ladyship the illustrious lord messer Ludovico our brother, with a most honorable corps. I wish also to let your ladyship know that we have notified all of our gens d'armes in Romagna to be ready to ride when and where his excellency the lord duke your husband and my brother and also your ladyship tell them to ride, and that they should obey your lordship and ladyship as they would me. But if you wish to make use of our gens d'armes in Lombardia, your highnesses should notify us immediately so that we will immediately pay them to ride out.

11. Ippolita Maria Sforza to Galeazzo Sforza. Naples, 27 November 1475[49]

Most illustrious prince and most excellent lord, my most affectionate brother,

The gentlemen of Naples who went to visit his majesty the lord king returned today. They report having seen his majesty in very good spirits, and that he was indeed strong, given the gravity of the illness he experienced. His majesty is now free of the tertian paroxysm, which occurred in the day, and though he still has the nighttime one, it is nevertheless diminishing. Last night his majesty had a great natural benefit because of its own accord his nose erupted with blood. Because of all of these things it is believed that his majesty is out of danger. I wanted to inform your highness of this. The lord duke my consort has been impeded by his infirmity, and therefore he is weak in the legs and sick to his stomach, and we are attending to this. For the last several days the barons of the realm have started to come: that is, the count of Fundi and his sons; the duke of Melfi and the duke of Sora; and today the duke of Andri, the prince of Bisignano, the count of Sant'Angelo and the count of Capaccio arrived.[50] I provide this information to your highness, to whom I commend myself. From Castel Capuano, Naples, 27 November – 1475, hour 23.

This evening, by means of a trusted person of mine who came from Carinola, I was told in person, on behalf of the doctor who is in my service (that is, messer Silvestro), that he is not yet certain about the lord king's illness and for three or

(*Continued*)

(Cont).

---

four more days he would not feel comfortable affirming that he is out of danger, and that he is also very wary and fearful about this. I will learn from him, once these days have passed, what his assessment of the situation is, and I will inform your sublime lordship accordingly.

Of your most excellent and illustrious dominion your most affectionate sister, Ippolita Maria, duchess of Calabria. Giovanni Pontano, secretary.

12. Ippolita Maria Sforza to Sacramoro da Rimini. Naples, 28 November, 1475[51]

Most reverend monsignor,

I think that your reverend lordship, as you left, must have given orders for our Carlo[52] to follow; and likewise he was informed in writing by us as to what he should do, and that he shouldn't leave there under any circumstances. Nevertheless we had to tell him that he should consult Bonifatio Cagnola. Your lordship will be able to write him again, if you are already traveling, if after your departure circumstances change for him. And if you have not left, give him full orders as to what he has to do and how during your absence. From Castel Capuano, Naples, 28 November 1475.

Duchess of Calabria, etc. Giovanni Pontano, secretary.

N.B. For other letters from Ippolita (dated 28–29 November) on the malaria crisis, see Duchess and Hostage, *pp. 130–132 (letters 72–73).*

13. Ippolita Maria Sforza to Carlo Stendardo. Naples, 29 November 1475[53]

Duchess of Calabria, etc.

Carlo,[54]

This morning the most illustrious duke my lord got up and dressed and walked for more than an hour, and then he ate at the table, as he was accustomed to doing when he was healthy. It is nevertheless true that last night and the night before, because of the moon's movement, he suffered some perturbations. His majesty the lord king yesterday had another natural benefit of blood that poured from his nose, around 3 ounces, and he had a very good day; and the attack of the previous night had not occurred again at the usual time, according to the report from three hours at night that we received. By the mounted messenger who left yesterday between 18 and 20 hours we wrote you at length according to what occurred to us. In this letter we will only tell you that the most illustrious duke our brother, because of the letters he wrote and the preparations he made, has earned more fame, respect and glory than he would have if he had overcome a great army. From Castel Capuano, Naples, 29 November 1475, at the second hour. Giovanni Pontano, secretary.

4

ISABELLA D'ESTE'S EMPLOYEE RELATIONS*

Deanna Shemek

The correspondence of Isabella d'Este (1474–1539), marchesa of Mantua, is known to be rich in information about the construction of the arts and antiquities collection she assembled in her famous display space, the *studiolo*, and, by extension, about the sixteenth-century European market for luxury goods ranging from paintings, sculptures, and musical instruments to clothing, textiles, jewels, perfumes, and specialty food items, all of which she acquired through correspondence with friends and trusted agents.[1] Less systematically studied is the fact that these letters, which survive in a massive archive, also reveal a good deal about how this Renaissance princess related to the people she employed. Letters Isabella exchanged with and regarding various court functionaries open a window onto some of the practical operations of early modern courts as contexts for labor of many kinds.

There are some oft-cited vignettes. A perennial favorite among art historians are peremptory posts Isabella sent from Ferrara about two years into her marriage (February 1490) to Francesco II Gonzaga, marchese of Mantua, to the painter Giovanni Luca Liombeni in Mantua: she orders him to finish, on schedule, the decorative motifs in her newly conceived *studiolo*, unless he prefers to be thrown into a dungeon.[2] Or there is the letter she wrote to her loyal Ferrarese correspondent, Bernardino Prosperi, in 1503 complaining about how ill served she had been by an agent whom she had instructed to buy gloves for her in Spain. Rejecting the gloves, she wrote to Prosperi:

> [I]n case he slanders us for returning them by saying that they were good, please do us the service of showing several pairs to the most reverend cardinal our brother [Ippolito d'Este], who has excellent judgment; ask him to turn them inside out and see if these are Ocañan gloves for the likes of us. Then, if he should hear talk of this matter, he can testify to their condition and the meager diligence of Sanz.[3]

And then there is the sensational story of Isabella's reported attack on one of her ladies-in-waiting, whose hair she snipped off, apparently, in a jealous rage about her husband's flirtations.[4] These sorts of stories circulate in the archive and in publications, exchanged with knowing nods and eyebrows raised to indicate that thanks to this paper trail, we can see who Isabella d'Este *really* was. Certainly, as an executive Isabella could be severe with people who crossed her or did their jobs poorly, and these letters reveal both the entitled temperament of a princess and some of the tensions that must have characterized life at the Gonzaga court. Yet, a comprehensive evaluation yields also some counterbalance to this picture: Isabella liked to reward good work.

Nowhere was this truer than among her diplomatic and communications network. The many letters she exchanged with Bernardino Prosperi about *his* services suggest how gratifying it could be to perform well for the marchesa of Mantua. Prosperi was Isabella's assiduous reporter of news from Ferrara and a key figure in the network of informants that kept her apprised of events throughout Italy. She wrote to him on 20 March 1498:

> If it were not for your letters, we would never have news of our birth-place again ... because we have no one else but you who tells us about it. For this reason, your letters are all the more dear to us, and you merit praise and thanks for them ... If you continue thus, we will reward your work all the more.[5]

Isabella did reward Prosperi and treated him as a valuable correspondent and a friend for many years. When his wife was pregnant in 1494, she sent him an eagle stone (or aetite) as a good luck charm for the child's healthy delivery.[6] And in 1505, she granted Prosperi's request that she take one of his daughters into her court as a lady-in-waiting: a placement that effectively committed her to covering a significant portion of the girl's dowry. Writing to Prosperi, she assured him:

> We have gladly accepted your daughter, Eleonora, whom we like both on her own account and because of whose daughter she is. We hope to be served well by her and that you and your wife will be consoled, for we will treat her well. Set your mind at ease about this and think no more about it. Turn instead to raising and placing your other daughters ... [Y]ou must promise us again to allow us to gratify you always in anything you need, both in memory of the service you gave to the dear departed madonna, our mother, and for your own virtues and goodness.[7]

Another figure who stands out is the Mantuan ambassador Giorgio Brognolo, who served as Isabella's buyer in Venice for precious gems, fabrics, glassware, marble, books, and the like.[8] The letters to Brognolo, like those to Prosperi and other high-level courtier diplomats like Baldassarre Castiglione, Jacopo d'Atri, and Isabella's tutor and personal secretary, the humanist Mario Equicola, convey consistent respect and appreciation for excellent services.[9] It was Brognolo who handled delicate matters like the 1509 Roman negotiations for the dowry of Eleonora Gonzaga when she married Pope Julius II's nephew, Francesco Maria della Rovere. And Brognolo negotiated the 1510 political crisis that saw the emperor, the king of France, and the pope himself bidding for Isabella's son, Federico, as a hostage in exchange for the liberation of her husband, Francesco Gonzaga, from Venetian imprisonment.

Letters to Brognolo are easy to trace in the Gonzaga diplomatic correspondence, but they have not been considered from the standpoint of Isabella's employee relations. What they suggest is a polished style of management that seems to take a page from modern manuals of best practices: the marchesa routinely recognized people's talents, rewarded their achievements, and made them feel valued. At the same time, she had little compunction in terminating people for bad service: we can trace the hard downfall, for example, of Leonello Marchese, who governed as Isabella's commissioner in the troubled court of Solarolo in Romagna, which she had acquired years earlier as her sole possession. When Marchese surprised and betrayed her in 1536 by turning out to be corrupt, she threw him out on his ear, dismissing him in a blistering letter.[10]

The ten-year-old Federico Gonzaga did, in fact, travel to Rome and lived a life of luxury as Pope Julius II's friendly hostage, into his early teens. A letter Isabella sent to Matteo Ippolito, his guardian in the papal court, instructing him about his management of Federico's staff scolds Ippolito for insubordination and makes explicit some of Isabella's thinking about employee management. She writes:

> We are amazed that you would take the liberty of firing any servant who has been assigned by the lord or by us to Federico. If they are behaving badly, discreet warning from you should suffice. And if it should not, then a word to the lord would be in order, but you should not simply have dismissed them. You should ask him about it and fire no one without His Excellency's sharing in the decision, unless Federico for some just cause wishes to dismiss them, though except for truly scandalous cases, he must defer to the lord his father.
>
> We also hear that you keep Federico in such servitude that he has lost his spirit, that he is not allowed to invite anyone to eat with him unless you give him permission, that you scold him in public, that sometimes you strike him or threaten with your hand that you will do so, that you make him eat according to your appetite and you subject him to many other forms of servitude that are inappropriate for the firstborn son of a lord and your patron.
>
> We are not at all pleased about this, nor will the lord be pleased when he hears of it, as he will. Too many people know about it, and this will require that for his honor we take measures you will not like. Hence, we order you to show more respect for Federico and his servants, and we

remind you that you are not his superior, you are employed in his service. And since he has been raised to exercise authority, you should accustom him and deftly correct him in private regarding things he does not know; and under no circumstances whatsoever are you to communicate to him through your actions or your effects that we do not want him to have this authority ... You must correct the servants as a father or a brother would, according to their age. To be useful and bring honor to your patron, you should communicate well among yourselves and not become the talk of the court.

You are in a position to bring yourself great honor and profit, if you will control your temper and use the prudence that is appropriate to the task you have undertaken. We know you love Federico and that you dislike it when things are done badly, and that this causes your outbursts, but it will not do to behave imperiously, to the embarrassment of your patron and his servants.[11]

A sifting of Isabella's correspondence for information about her dealings with employees and service providers reveals a highly effective executive who understood how to run the complex organization of the Gonzaga court. Like other courts of the time, Mantua's was staffed by a combination of multi-generation families long in service to the Gonzaga, and people hired through various processes of recommendation and interview. While the famous letters pertaining to Isabella's *studiolo*, her diplomacy, and her shopping have revealed her working relations with artists, ambassadors, and artisans, a notable part of her correspondence records her management of cooks, seamstresses, wet nurses, apothecaries, stable masters, and others who got things done at the Gonzaga court.[12]

Ferrante Gonzaga, too, went abroad as a young man. As she prepared the staff who would accompany this son, she wrote to one of her longtime servants, Giovanni di Casale, about why his son had not been selected for Ferrante's entourage:

Know that since our son Ferrante must go to the imperial court, and since it is necessary to send him with a minimal entourage, we recognize the necessity that those who go with him be people of a sort who have proven that he will be well served and satisfied in all his needs. This is something we are most certain would not be the case if we had chosen to send Scipione, your son, because to speak with you frankly, he is the most ignorant and negligent person possible, someone who busies himself with everything but serving his lord, and who keeps company and uses language completely alien to the place where he is. We assure you that our respect for you made us tolerate him up to now, in the belief that surely he would come to his senses, but he went from bad to worse, to the extent that since Ferrante has departed, we have dismissed him completely and forever. And we would do this again if we hadn't already done it. So you must excuse us, and believe that what we are telling you is merely the truth. Be advised that in our view, if you want to punish your son, you must put him in the service of a lord who will once in a while punish him appropriately for his insolence. If we can be of service to you in anything else, we will do so readily.[13]

Isabella's sensibility for occasion and the impact of Gonzaga events on even the lowliest members of her court emerges from a letter she sent to Girolamo Stanga on 19 July 1493. As she was preparing for the arrival of her first child, she realized that the delivery of birth announcements could generate welcome income for those who would be chosen to bear happy news to Gonzaga subjects far and wide. She wrote to Stanga (Figure 4.1):

> Since it is public knowledge that we are pregnant, even though we do not share this information willingly, we want you to request a favor from the most illustrious lord our consort, and do this in such a way that he cannot refuse. Ask His Excellency to be content to leave to us the selection of the people who will deliver the birth announcements. We have many poor servants, and if we don't give them this income now, we don't know when we will be in a position to reward them. It seems to us honorable that those who have long been in our service should reap the fruits of our first efforts before others do. Even if someone has already inquired with our aforesaid lord about these errands and if he has raised their hopes, we want you to insist that he revoke what he has told them.[14]

Isabella d'Este was served by hundreds of workers, some of whom emerge in her letters only once or twice. There are, for example, the cooks: Comatre Patrizia whom Isabella brings with her to Naples in 1496 to cook healthy food for Francesco while he is stationed there;[15] the vegetable gardener's wife whom she assigns to cook for her squire while he is quarantined for plague;[16] the cook who was sent to her from the marchese of Monferrato, her future in-law, but whom she sent back because he was saddled with a family who would also need support; the "old cook" for whom she sought an apprentice but whom, she declared, she would "under no circumstances remove from his position."[17] And there was Isabella's favorite cook, Massimo. Good cooks were apparently hard to find, and in her later years she especially valued them because she had ceased to be able to enjoy most food. In 1533, when Massimo signaled a preference not to return to her service after a stint in the employ of Isabella's sons, Ercole and Ferrante, she wrote to Ferrante:

> I stand in immense need of him, because truly I have found myself for some time now to be so lacking in appetite that after the departure of Massimo and the death of Piangilato, no cook has appeared who knows how to prepare anything that tastes good to me, though I have had

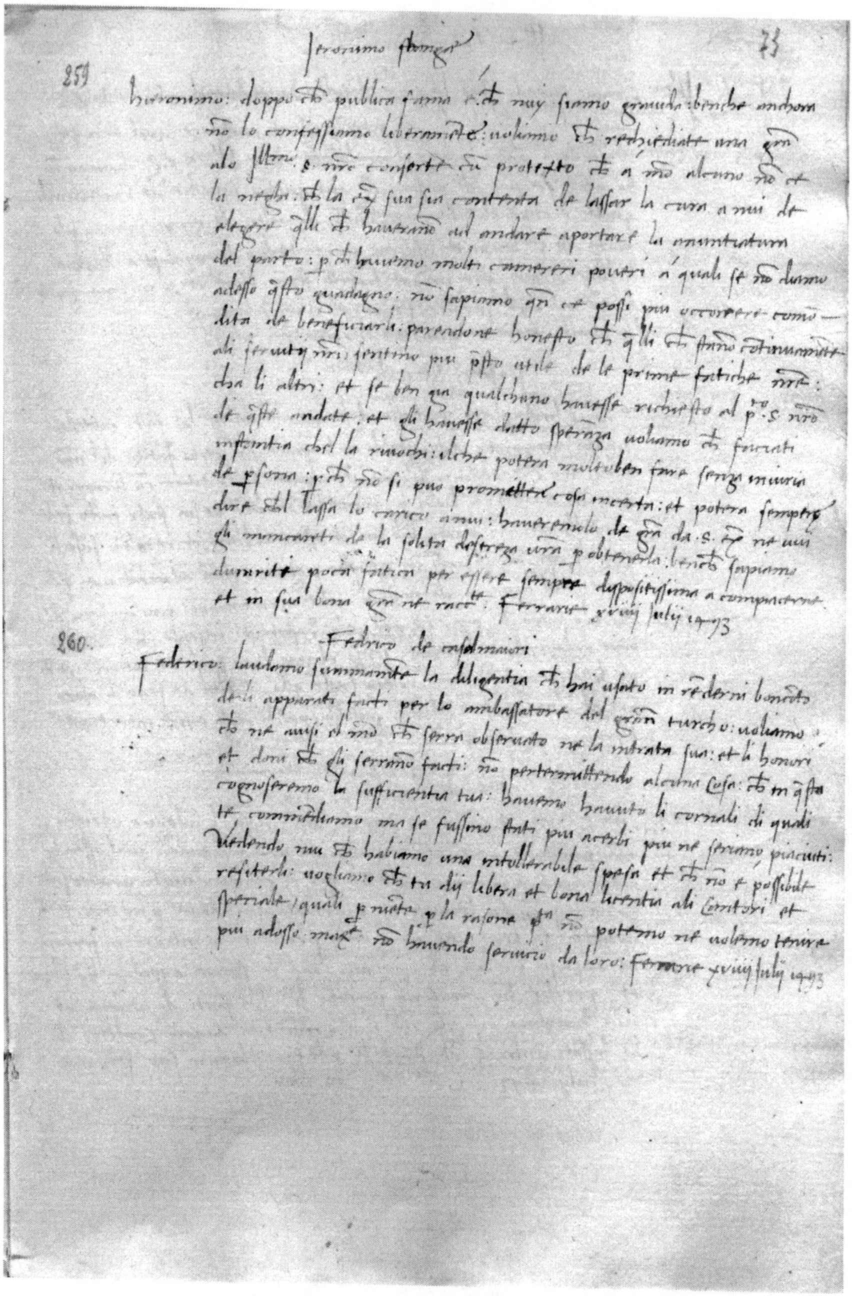

FIGURE 4.1 Isabella d'Este to Girolamo (Jeronimo) Stanga, 19 July 1493. Archivio di stato di Mantova, Archivio Gonzaga, libro 3, c. 73r. Printed with permission, Ministero per i Beni e le Attività Culturali

searches conducted in several places to try to find one. Your Lordship, who does not need such delicacies since you have the stomach of a young man and a soldier, will do me a great favor and accommodation if you will please me in this, if, that is, Massimo is content to come. For I have never wished for anyone to serve me against his will.[18]

We might take Isabella's claim about coerced service as a mere rhetorical formula, but this was not the case, at least for Massimo. She wrote again eight days later:

Even if I could expect from him the most delicate dishes anyone could desire, I would dismiss a cook who served me unwillingly. And so, Your Lordship may calm his spirits if Massimo declines to come into my service because he does not fancy returning to Mantua and wishes instead to roam, to see the world, and to try to set aside some earnings. Though on account of this news I suffer more than a little, this is no reason for you not to keep him in your service. On the contrary, I will be pleased if you are well served by him.[19]

Isabella liked good food and wine, as we can see from the many orders she posted for these things. She also cared a lot about her clothing and, as we have noted in the case of defective gloves, she was impatient with faulty wardrobe items. One person who suffered from Isabella's perfectionism was a Jewish woman named Sara (Sara Judea) who must have regretted being accorded the dubious privilege of making Isabella's caps. A letter from Milan to Giovanni Battista Cattaneo on 24 August 1514 records the marchesa's displeasure with one of these:

Contrary to what you wrote us, the cap that you sent us along with your letter of the 21st was not at all satisfactory. Its flaw is that the bands are too close to one another, which makes the gathers too tight. We are sending it back to you so that you can return it to Sara and she can immediately make another with wider gathers and also more gold, because this one has much less gold than the first one did, which is the opposite of what we wrote you we wanted.[20]

On 2 September, Isabella wrote again to say that the remade cap, too, was unsatisfactory, but Sara appears a number of times in the correspondence and seems to have remained in Isabella's employ despite her rather poor job performance.

We learn of Isabella's laundress, Marmirola, only on account of her death from plague. In July 1527, Isabella wrote to Matteo Casella to ensure provisions for Marmirola's son, who was left in the care of a third party:

I ordered that the boy's father be sent to fetch him and bring him here. And since I understand that that poor woman had some money and rings in her possession that could help feed her poor little son if they were recovered, in the most urgent of terms I pray you intervene with all your authority to see that diligence is used in getting back those rings and that money. I say nothing of her personal belongings, because since this woman died of plague I think they have been burned. For every loving action you take in this case, I will be obliged to you more than a little, aside from the fact that it will be pious and holy.[21]

A subsequent letter orders the boy's father to assume his paternal duties or suffer punishment.

This kind of individual attention for her servants' welfare was not unusual in Isabella's court, but the most spectacular case of it may be Isabella's work on behalf of her steward, Carlo Bozino. Bozino had the misfortune to be captured by Tunisian pirates when they took one of Isabella's barges as it headed home to Mantua after her escape from the Sack of Rome. Isabella worked tirelessly to get back her stolen belongings, but also her people. Two of the three servants who were captured were soon freed by the Venetian Giovanni Contarino, but poor Bozino was left behind for lack of sufficient ransom. His predicament led Isabella to write to the nobleman Enea Pio of Carpi and Sassuolo on 7 May 1528, asking Pio to mobilize the offices of her nephew, Ercole II d'Este, who was on his way to France to marry the king's daughter, Renée. Her idea was an elaborate mobilization of the royal gift economy:

> Since poor Bozino remains a prisoner of that king [of Tunisia], who bought him for four hundred and thirty ducats and who refuses to free him without making a big profit, we cannot help but yearn for the release of the poor young man, for whom we feel extreme compassion, having understood that he is kept in chains and is very badly treated. We would like, with Your Lordship's mediation, to be granted a great favor by Don Ercole. Since we understand through reliable channels that His Most Christian Majesty can claim great friendship and authority with the king of Tunisia, we would like Don Ercole to request a letter from His Majesty to that king, in favor of the poor captive. We would like the letter to result in that king's making a gift of the captive to His Majesty, or his releasing him for the price that he paid for him, because Bozino's brothers will make every effort to find the money to pay his ransom. We pray Your Lordship please work with the aforesaid lord, our nephew, to achieve our much-desired aim. You may assure His Lordship that at this time he could do nothing that would please us more.[22]

Not every servant of Isabella's was saved by such ruses, even when her troubles resulted from no fault of her own. Mentioned above is the great benefit accorded to young women who were admitted into service in Isabella's court. These figures deserve a full-length study, which is not my task here. Suffice it to say that Isabella sponsored dozens of these girls, who received something of an education at court, even if only through their experience of being trained to dance and to socialize as part of her entourage. The marchesa of Mantua was indeed famous for the beautiful women she surrounded herself with, all of them dressed in enviable wardrobes and charged with being charming in her company. Acceptance into this company brought with it Isabella's personal commitment both to find a marriage match suitable for each girl and to her liking, and to enhance the girls' prospects by augmenting their dowries. But sometimes life got in the way of these happy endings.

A case in point is the unfortunate Zoanna Boschetta. Zoanna's father, Albertino, was a co-conspirator in the treasonous attack of Giulio and Ferrante d'Este against their brother, Duke Alfonso d'Este, in 1506. Giulio and Ferrante were incarcerated, and Zoanna's father was executed. As a collateral result, Zoanna herself was told that she could no longer stay in Isabella's court because she was unmarriageable. Isabella wrote to her in Ferrara, where she had fled for her safety:

> Since what happened with your father has stained his family to the extent that we believe no one can be found who will wish to become his relative or yours, and because we raised you at court and would not like to see you end up in a situation that is not useful and honorable for you, we think the best thing would be for you to be willing to serve God and enter a convent; and we have written asking Madonna Cassandra to speak to you about this in our name. But then we decided also to write you this letter encouraging you to take this path as the safest and most honorable one. If you do so, we will provide you with the things you need and will never fail to favor and support you just as we do our other girls, so that the convent you enter will know that we hold you dear. Think hard and well about this, and listen to the advice of Madonna Cassandra, who is informed of our wishes. You will be happier with each passing day, given the many troubles of girls who marry and stay in this world.[23]

The historical record of early modernity bears precious few traces of figures such as the lady-in-waiting, the boy servant, and the steward as individuals. A suggestive exception to this documentary reticence, however, can be found in the routine court management correspondence of women such as Isabella d'Este. The marchesa of Mantua's epistolary interactions regarding court operatives at many different levels, from the ambassador to the laundress, reveal, to be sure, one powerful woman's distinctive administrative persona. They also offer glimpses of the inner, day-to-day workings of her court, and the otherwise undetectable men, women, and children who lived and labored there.

Notes

* A shorter version of this essay appeared in *Itinera chartarum. Nel 150° dell'Archivio di Stato di Mantova. Studi in onore di Daniela Ferrari* (Milan: Silvana, 2018), 195–200.
1 Among the many studies on Isabella's acquisitions and her relations with artists and literary figures who sometimes served her, see Alessandro Luzio and Rodolfo Renier, *La*

coltura e le relazioni letterarie di Isabella d'Este Gonzaga, edited by Simone Albonico (Milan: Sylvestre Bonnard, 2005), Clifford M. Brown and Anna Maria Lorenzoni, *Isabella d'Este and Lorenzo da Pavia: Documents for the History of Art and Culture in Renaissance Mantua* (Geneva: Librairie Droz S.A., 1982), and Evelyn Welch "Shopping with Isabella d'Este," in *Shopping in the Renaissance. Consumer Cultures in Italy, 1400–1600* (New Haven, CT and London: Yale University Press, 2005), 246–73; 352.

2 See the letters 48 and 49 (2 October and 12 November 1491) in Isabella d'Este, *Selected Letters*. Translated and edited by Deanna Shemek (Toronto and Tempe, AZ: Iter Academic Press and Arizona Center for Medieval and Renaissance Studies, 2017). Except where indicated, all letters cited below will refer to this edition, by letter number. For manuscript images of this and other correspondence of Isabella d'Este, see the online resource, *IDEA Letter/e*, in *IDEA: Isabella d'Este Archive* http://isabelladeste.web.unc.edu.

3 Isabella d'Este, *Selected Letters*, letters 376 and 377 (18 July 1506).

4 On this episode, see Sarah D. P. Cockram, *Isabella d'Este and Francesco Gonzaga: Power Sharing at the Italian Renaissance Court* (Surrey, UK and Burlington, VT: Ashgate, 2013), 121–25; as well as Alessandro Luzio, "Isabella d'Este nelle tragedie della sua casa (1505–1506)." *Atti e memorie dell'Accademia virgiliana di Mantova* Nuova serie, 5 (1912): 55–95; appendix 18.

5 Isabella d'Este, *Selected Letters*, letter 164.

6 Isabella d'Este, *Selected Letters*, letter 78 (2 February 1494). On these stones see Jacqueline Musacchio, *The Art and Ritual of Childbirth in Renaissance Italy* (New Haven, CT and London: Yale University Press, 1999), 140.

7 Isabella d'Este, *Selected Letters*, letter 356 (15 June 1505).

8 Brognolo's service to Isabella began soon after her arrival in Mantua as Francesco II Gonzaga's bride. Francesco had appointed him Gonzaga ambassador to Venice in 1489. Roberto Zapperi, "Brognolo, Giorgio," *Dizionario biografico degli italiani* 14 (1972): www.treccani.it/enciclopedia/giorgio-brognolo_(Dizionario-Biografico).

9 On Equicola's relations with Isabella see Chapter III, "In the Service of Isabella d'Este," in Stephen Kolsky, *Mario Equicola: The Real Courtier* (Geneva: Librairie Droz, 1991), 103–69.

10 Archivio Gonzaga, busta 2936, cc. 127v–128r (31 March 1536).

11 Isabella d'Este, *Selected Letters*, letter 468 (22 July 1511).

12 Among the recent research drawing from Isabella's correspondence, see Cockram, *Isabella d'Este and Francesco Gonzaga*; Carolyn James, "Marriage by Correspondence: Politics and Domesticity in the Letters of Isabella d'Este and Francesco Gonzaga, 1490–1519," *Renaissance Quarterly* 65/2 (2012) 321–52; James, "An Insatiable Appetite for News: Isabella d'Este and a Bolognese Correspondent," in *Rituals, Images, and Words: Varieties of Cultural Expression in Late Medieval and Early Modern Europe*, edited by F. W. Kent, and Charles Zika (Turnhout, Belgium: Brepols, 2005) 375–88; Matteo Basora, "'La prima donna del mondo': Isabella d'Este epistolografa tra lettere e arti. Edizione e analisi linguistica di missive autografe e dei copialettere" (Pavia: Università degli Studi di Pavia Facoltà di Lettere e Filosofia, 2011); Monica Ferrari, "Un'educazione sentimentale per lettera: Il caso di Isabella d'Este (1490–1493)," www.retimedievali.it (2009); Paul H. D. Kaplan, "Isabella d'Este and Black African Women," in *Black Africans in Renaissance Europe*, edited by T. F. Earle and Kate J. P. Lowe (Cambridge: Cambridge University Press, 2005) 125–54; Kate Lowe, "Isabella d'Este and the Acquisition of Black Africans at the Mantuan Court," in *Mantova e il Rinascimento italiano. Studi in onore di David S. Chambers*, edited by Philippa Jackson and Guido Rebecchini (Mantua: Sometti, 2011), 65–76; Roberta Iotti, "Phenice unica, virtuosa e pia. La corrispondenza culturale di Isabella," in *Isabella d'Este. La primadonna del Rinascimento*, edited by Daniele Bini [*Quaderni di civiltà mantovana*] (Mantua: Bulino, 2006) 167–83.

13 Isabella d'Este, *Selected Letters*, letter 648 (19 August 1522).

14 Isabella d'Este, *Selected Letters*, letter 75 (19 July 1493).

15 Isabella d'Este, *Selected Letters*, letter 132 (29 September 1496).
16 Isabella d'Este, *Selected Letters*, letter 365 (9 May 1506).
17 Isabella d'Este, *Selected Letters*, letter 584 (22 February 1518).
18 Isabella d'Este, *Selected Letters*, letter 798 (3 February 1533).
19 Isabella d'Este, *Selected Letters*, letter 799 (11 February 1533).
20 Isabella d'Este, *Selected Letters*, letter 517 (25 August 1514).
21 Isabella d'Este, *Selected Letters*, letter 719 (29 July 1527).
22 Isabella d'Este, *Selected Letters*, letter 728 (7 May 1528).
23 Isabella d'Este, *Selected Letters*, letter 384 (30 August 1506).

5

LETTERS AS SOURCES FOR STUDYING JEWISH CONVERSION

The case of Salomone da Sesso/Ercole de' Fedeli[*]

Tamar Herzig

The efforts to convert the Jews in the Italian peninsula became increasingly institu-
tionalized in the sixteenth century, following the establishment of Houses of Catechumens, first in Rome (in 1543) and then in other cities. Because of the wealth
of material originating in the archives of the Houses of Catechumens and in those
of the tribunals of the Roman Inquisition, which prosecuted converts suspected of
reverting to Judaism, these institutions' records have served as the primary lens
through which Jewish conversion in Italy has been explored in the late twentieth
and twenty-first centuries.[1] At the same time, detailed examinations of the letters
penned by inquisitors, bishops, and cardinals have helped to elucidate the ways in
which the Tridentine Church strove to discipline and control catechumens and
neophytes, as well as the limits of its endeavors.[2]

The achievements of the campaign to convert the Jews from the mid–sixteenth
through the eighteenth century were doubtlessly remarkable.[3] Nonetheless, focusing primarily on this era has elided the historical significance of the growing
importance that Italian elites had already begun to ascribe to Jewish conversion in
the pre-Reformation era.[4] Local studies suggest that a surge in the number of
converts was apparent in the early fifteenth century, and that its second half saw
a rise in Jews' baptisms.[5] In the absence of ample institutional documentation, letters assume an even greater significance for the study of Jewish conversion in the
Quattrocento than they do for subsequent centuries. Still, they have remained
largely neglected in scholarship on converts and the debates sparked by their baptism in Renaissance Italy.[6]

This essay focuses on a case study that demonstrates how the epistolary genre
might be used to expound the phenomenon of Jewish conversion to Christianity
in the fifteenth century. It draws on the correspondence preserved at the Archivio Gonzaga, in the State Archives in Mantua, and at the historical archive of
the Este rulers, now in the State Archives in Modena. The Archivio Gonzaga,

one of the most complete European archives for a ruling dynasty of the late medieval and early modern eras, contains numerous missives documenting daily life in the court cities of Renaissance Italy.[7] Although the Estensi's archive suffered considerable losses following its transfer from Ferrara to Modena in 1598, it too preserves illuminating letters from the fifteenth and sixteenth centuries.[8]

The letters explored in this study pertain to the baptism of two Jewish men, one in Mantua and the other in Ferrara, in 1491. Their close reading, I propose, therefore enables us to refocus scholarly attention on the pre-Tridentine roots of Italian elites' investment in converting the Jews. No less importantly, it sheds light on certain aspects of Jewish conversion that are rarely revealed in the sources generated by ecclesiastical institutions. As a specific type of ego-documents, letters tell us a lot about the self-perception of converts and about the motivations and concerns of agents of conversion, including laymen and laywomen.[9] In the absence of autobiographies or diaries authored by Italian apostates from Judaism or by their convertors in the fifteenth century, letters also provide an invaluable window for their thoughts and feelings regarding religious conversion, albeit not always in a straightforward manner.[10]

Convert identity and self-fashioning in letters

Most of the letters discussed below pertain to the best-known convert in fifteenth-century Ferrara, Salomone da Sesso (or Sasso, d. after 1521), who according to scholars of Jewish history was one of the two greatest Jewish artists of Renaissance Italy.[11] Praised in a dispatch of the extraordinarily discerning connoisseur Isabella d'Este (1474–1539) as a goldsmith who was "very able (*molto virtuoso*) and refined in his craft," Salomone created exquisite pieces of jewelry and engraved swords and is remembered primarily for the "Queen of Swords" that he made for Cesare Borgia (1475–1507) (Figure 5.1).[12] At the height of his success, he converted and assumed the new name of Ercole dei Fedeli.[13] Although art historians have long been aware of his artistic accomplishments,[14] the precise circumstances leading to his baptism in 1491 have hitherto remained obscure.[15] Previously unexplored letters pertaining to the conversion of Salomone and his relative Angelo have now made it possible to reconstruct the vicissitudes that led to their baptisms, as well as the controversy regarding conversionary practices that these kindled.[16]

The son of a Jewish moneylender, Salomone was born in Florence in the mid-1450s and grew up in Bologna. By 1487, he was already employed as court goldsmith of Eleonora of Aragon (1450–1493), the duchess of Ferrara. Following the marriage of Eleonora's daughter to Marquis Francesco Gonzaga (1466–1519) in 1490, Salomone accompanied Isabella d'Este to Mantua.[17] Shortly after arriving in Mantua, the young *marchesa* began generating both official and personal correspondence,[18] and it is through the letters that she and her consort wrote and received that much of the information about the conversion of Salomone and his less-famous relative may be gleaned.[19]

FIGURE 5.1 Cesare Borgia's engraved *cinquedea*, attributed to Salomone da Sesso/ Ercole de' Fedeli, c. 1498/9. Casa Caetani, Rome. Photo: Dr. Elizabeth Bemis. Reproduced with permission of the Fondazione Camillo Caetani

Thus, we learn from a letter that Isabella sent Francesco Gonzaga on March 22, 1491 that when issuing the "usual proclamation regarding the Jews for the Holy Week," which forbade Mantua's Jews to leave their homes, she exempted solely Salomone da Sesso and his three Jewish apprentices, who were granted complete freedom of movement.[20] As this missive indicates, Salomone's talent brought him privileges that set him apart from his fellow Jews. Nonetheless, other letters reveal that he remained closely attached to Jewish society. In the course of 1491, he interceded with Mantua's rulers in favor of three other Jews: his brother-in-law Davide Finzi,[21] a certain Deodato,[22] and his relative Angelo di Vitale, who was working at his service. Angelo was arrested in Mantua, even though the marquis had previously issued a safe-conduct, at Salomone's request, allowing him to pass through Gonzaga lands. On August 16, Salomone therefore sent a letter to Pietro Gentile da Camerino, who accompanied Francesco Gonzaga in his travels, asking him to remind the marquis of his promise and protesting the failure to respect Angelo's safe-conduct (Figure 5.2).[23]

That Salomone da Sesso engaged in letter-writing should come as no surprise, because goldsmiths were usually literate. Practicing a craft that involved close contact with upper-class clients, Renaissance goldsmiths were at the very top of the artisanal hierarchy in terms of their social status. Thus, as Pamela H. Smith observes, they were more self-conscious than other artisans and were certainly aware of the role of writing in enhancing their reputation. While only a few of them—famously, the goldsmith-sculptor Benvenuto Cellini (1500–1571)—authored autobiographies, many goldsmiths did leave behind other kinds of written records.[24]

Of course, Salomone was not just a goldsmith; he was also a Jew. Robert Bonfil has characterized the flourishing of letter-writing as one of the chief forms

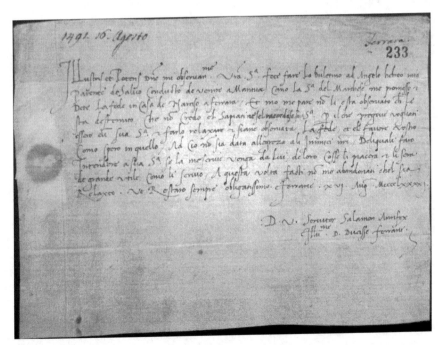

FIGURE 5.2 Salomone da Sesso's letter of August 16, 1491 to Pietro Gentile da Camerino. Archivio di Stato di Mantova, Archivio Gonzaga, busta 1232, c. 233. Reproduced with permission of the Archivio di Stato di Mantova

of cultural expression of the Jews in Renaissance Italy, although the letters that he had in mind were those written in Hebrew by Jewish men and addressed to their learned counterparts in other communities.[25] As far as the correspondence of early modern Jews with Christians was concerned, Bonfil argues that the only significant dialogues of this kind took place on a purely intellectual plane.[26] These found an expression in the later epistles that Jewish poet Sarra Copia Sulam (1600?–1641) exchanged with Venetian men of letters,[27] or in the correspondence of the Jew Benedetto Blanis (c.1580–1647), who shared his occult knowledge with members of the Medici court in Florence.[28] Letter-writing in the vernacular also formed a key aspect of Jews' participation in the "republic of merchants" in the making.[29]

Salomone da Sesso's letter of 1491, written in the vernacular by a Jew who was neither a leader of his community nor a *letterato* or a merchant and addressed to a Christian recipient, does not belong to any of these genres of Jewish letter-writing. Rather, it fits into a category of missives regularly dispatched by fifteenth-century goldsmiths as well as by other artists, that of the *supplica* (sppulication).[30] A specific genre of epistolary writing, Renaissance *suppliche* requested favors, privileges, or other forms of grace from state authorities. They differed significantly from the typologies of missives that learned Jews and Jewish merchants authored, since both of these categories were meant to be exchanged among equals whereas supplications inevitably reflected unequal power relations. Nonetheless, *suppliche* can still tell us much about friendship, family, and patronage ties. Indeed, in central and northern Italy they were often addressed to the supplicants' patrons and were regularly sent by the relatives or friends of imprisoned culprits, who petitioned for their release or for the mitigation of their penalties.[31]

The supplication requesting Angelo di Vitale's release was signed "Salomone, goldsmith of the most illustrious lady, the Duchess of Ferrara,"[32] attesting to Salomone's confidence in his privileged position as Eleonora of Aragon's protégé, and in the high esteem with which his artistic skills were held at the Ferrarese court.[33] Significantly, Salomone did not designate himself as a Jew, in sharp contrast with his identification in the missives of Isabella d'Este, Francesco Gonzaga, and Eleonora of Aragon prior to his baptism, in which he was always identified as Jewish.[34] The difference between the goldsmith's self-fashioning in his dispatch and the way the aristocratic rulers who commissioned luxury items from him identified him assumes an even greater significance when we take into consideration the letters that he authored after his baptism.

Four such letters have been discovered to date. They were all addressed to Isabella d'Este, and dealt with specific works that he was making for her. The first was sent on October 14, 1504, while the neophyte was working chiefly for Isabella's father Duke Ercole d'Este (1431–1505), who hired him as his own court goldsmith after Eleonora's demise. It was signed: "Ercole, goldsmith of the most illustrious lord, the Duke of Ferrara" (Figure 5.3).[35] The second was drafted on August 17, 1505, a few months after Duke Ercole's death and before Salomone/Ercole began his employment as court goldsmith to Ferrara's new

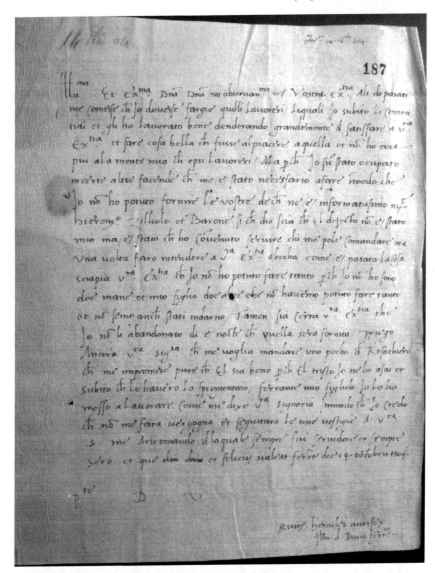

FIGURE 5.3 Salomone da Sesso/Ercole de' Fedeli's letter of October 14, 1504 to Isabella d'Este, signed "Hercules aurifex Illustrissimi Domini Ducis Ferrarie." Archivio di Stato di Mantova, Archivio Gonzaga, busta 1890, c. 187. Reproduced with permission of the Archivio di Stato di Mantova

duchess Lucrezia Borgia (1480–1519), so he identified himself merely as "Ercole the goldsmith."[36] The convert's two later dispatches, from May 14 and July 15, 1506, were penned after he had taken a position as Lucrezia's court goldsmith. The former was signed: "Ercole, goldsmith of the most illustrious duchess of Ferrara," and the latter: "Ercole, goldsmith of the duchess."[37]

Just as he did in the letter to Pietro Gentile prior to his baptism, Salomone/
Ercole continued to identify himself in the letters sent after his conversion solely
by his profession, omitting any mention of his religious affiliation. Whereas his
name was changed upon baptism, the goldsmith's profession was the one element
of his identity that remained constant throughout his adult life. Yet even if in his
own missives he refrained from alluding to his Jewish origins, when others
referred to him in writing they sometimes noted his past identity as a Jew.[38] This
was true for both Jews and Christians who mentioned the goldsmith in their missives. Thus, while a Jew named Abram identified him in a letter to Francesco
Gonzaga as "Salomone da Sesso, who is now called Ercole"—implying that the
goldsmith was still the same person notwithstanding his name change—Isabella
d'Este sent a missive to her agent in Ferrara, asking him to procure a gilded book
cover from "Master Ercole, who used to be a Jew."[39]

Such persistent reminders of the past from which they had sought to detach
themselves were a common feature in lives of baptized Jews throughout the
early modern era,[40] but the letters drafted by Salomone/Ercole demonstrate how
converts were able to resist them. By emphasizing his unchanged professional
identity in the way he signed his missives, Salomone/Ercole fashioned himself as
a man who was, first and foremost, a goldsmith admired for his artistic virtuosity. As his case demonstrates, the comparison of letters that Jews wrote before
and after their conversion with those that others wrote about them enables us to
better understand how neophytes strove to forge a new sense of self, drawing on
those aspects of their identity that were unaltered by baptism.

Letters as a medium for debating conversionary policy

Let us now return to the goldsmith's first extant letter of August 16, 1491. Although
Francesco Gonzaga received it, in a missive sent four days later he instructed the
podestà (chief magistrate) of Mantua Ermolao Bardolini to disregard Salomone's
plea to honor Angelo di Vitale's safe-conduct.[41] Salomone then enlisted the support
of Eleonora of Aragon, who on August 20 sent a missive to the marquis of Mantua,
asking him to grant this wish so that "Salomone the Jew, our goldsmith," who
expressed his intention to go to Mantua to try and assist his relative, would not tarry
away from Ferrara where his services to the duchess were very much in need.[42]
Refusing his mother-in-law's request, Francesco Gonzaga went on to order Angelo's repeated interrogation under torture, until the defendant finally confessed to
having stolen from the Mantuan Jew Jacob with the aid of an unnamed Christian
woman, with whom he also admitted having had sexual relations.[43] Jacob as well as
the leaders of the Jewish populace in Mantua were keen on seeing Angelo pay with
his life for his purported crimes.[44]

Not only were Salomone's attempts to save his relative unsuccessful, but the
goldsmith himself was arrested in Ferrara just a few days later. The dossier of his
trial, like most of Ferrara's criminal records from the fifteenth and sixteenth centuries, has not survived.[45] Its loss renders the missives generated by members of

the Este and Gonzaga courts all the more valuable for reconstructing the turn of events that culminated in the goldsmith's conversion to Christianity.

In a letter that Francesco Gonzaga sent Eleonora of Aragon on September 7, he noted that Salomone had committed "very enormous errors" in the city of Mantua, and that "he had upset all the Jews there," in addition to having defrauded the marquis of "eighteen to twenty" ducats while forging a gold chain for him.[46] A Jew named Bonaventura played a key role in incriminating Salomone, and in a dispatch of September 8 Francesco ordered his podestà to interrogate Angelo under torture again about Salomone's alleged crimes, at Bonaventura's presence.[47] As was common in the fifteenth century, the marquis refrained from communicating sensitive information in writing, and merely instructed his podestà to ask Bonaventura for more information about Salomone's transgressions once he met him.[48]

A letter that Eleonora of Aragon sent Isabella d'Este on September 10 explicitly mentions one of the charges that had been brought against her favorite goldsmith:

> Salomone the Jew, our goldsmith, is in prison here [in Ferrara] for sodomy and other bad things; and it seems that there [in Mantua] a servant of his likewise finds himself in prison. Recognizing his error, the aforementioned Salomone has repented and decided to become a Christian, and his Excellency the most illustrious lord Duke our consort thought to pardon him, in order to gain his soul. I therefore greatly beg you that you should wish to intercede with the aforementioned marquis [of Mantua] so that he pardons the aforementioned servant, since he has also converted and wants to become a Christian, so that this will be a double gain.[49]

In her analysis of Eleonora's epistolary communication with her daughter, Monica Ferrari has stressed the mother's care to instill in Isabella the behavior of a dutiful wife submissive to her husband's desires.[50] Yet Eleonora's letter of September 10, 1491, written after the failure of her own efforts to convince the marquis of Mantua to liberate Angelo, discloses her willingness to rely on Isabella's conjugal ties for obtaining a favor for her court goldsmith against Francesco's will. The marquis had already ordered on September 10 that Angelo be sent to the gallows,[51] but because of the latter's secret baptism in prison his execution was deferred.[52] On September 15, Isabella did as her mother requested and sent a letter to her consort, who was in Venice at that time, entreating him to pardon Angelo.

Isabella argued that absolving the delinquent Jew would be a merciful deed, in compliance with a tradition instituted by Christ. To support her claim she quoted, in Latin, the verse from Ezekiel 33:11: "I will not the death of the sinner, but that he be converted and live" ("*nolo mortem peccatoris, sed ut convertatur, et vivat*").[53] Used by St. Benedict to introduce his monastic rule, this verse was frequently cited in subsequent centuries to emphasize the importance of the conversion of sinners.[54] Like the letters penned by other fifteenth-century patrician women, then, this missive disclosed Isabella's familiarity both with sacred texts in Latin and with religious ideals that were popularized in vernacular devotional texts and sermons.[55] At the same time, it is a rare testimony of an educated laywoman's confidence in resorting to theological arguments for justifying controversial conversionary means, such as the pardoning of convicted criminals.[56]

On that very day, however, Francesco Gonzaga sent a letter to his podestà expressing his anger upon learning that a certain procurator had appeared on Angelo's behalf insisting that the culprit should not be put to death because after his baptism he became a new person, and in fact was no longer called Angelo. This argument was based on the theological understanding of baptism as a rite of passage that signified an individual's symbolic death and spiritual rebirth. The indelible spiritual mark of the sacrament of baptism was supposed to turn the neophyte into a new person, a change of identity that was reaffirmed by the imposition of a new name.[57] Francesco Gonzaga dismissed such theological arguments as "frivolous reasoning."

Although the view that a non-Christian's baptism amounted to the death of his or her old self was a longstanding theological notion, in the fifteenth century there was no judicial consensus regarding its implications concerning the fate of baptized Jewish criminals.[58] Indeed, magistrates in important Italian cities such as Rome and Bologna refused to absolve Jewish culprits who consented to baptism.[59] In the same vein, the marquis of Mantua stated that whatever Angelo's new Christian name was, he wanted him hanged by the following Monday.[60]

Francesco's letters reveal a much more skeptical attitude to the transformative power of baptism than the view put forward in the missives of his mother-in-law or his wife. Clearly, the marquis did not regard the conversion to Catholicism of convicted Jewish offenders who were sentenced to death as categorically different from the conversion of condemned Christian criminals who repented their earlier sins.[61] In a missive of September 17 to Isabella, the marquis asked her to forgive him for not complying with her request, explaining that he was convinced that having been such a bad Jew, Angelo would prove to be an even worse Christian.[62] Like Isabella, Francesco also resorted to theological argumentation, but while his consort had done so to justify the convert's pardoning, the marquis used it in support of Angelo's capital punishment. Francesco added that, if the criminal's conversion really was motivated by a genuine concern for the state of his soul, death should actually please him, since it would be better for him to die while in such a good condition—that is, right after his baptism and before he had the chance to sin again.[63]

At this stage, the duke of Ferrara intervened in person. Although his wife was the one who masterminded the conversion of her Jewish protégé Salomone and his relative, Ercole d'Este wholeheartedly backed her efforts.[64] On September 19, he sent a letter to his daughter, explaining that he did not wish Angelo to perish, "because he has converted to Christianity." Ercole beseeched Isabella to do all within her power to postpone the execution until her husband's return from Venice. On his way back, Francesco was supposed to pass through Ferrara, and

Ercole hoped to convince him to spare Angelo's life.[65] Isabella succeeded in putting off the execution, and when the marquis met his father-in-law he finally agreed to pardon the baptized Jew. On September 22 Francesco sent Isabella a letter affirming that although the convert really did merit a capital punishment—on which the marquis had previously insisted—he now agreed to pardon him as a favor to her father.[66]

The correspondence among members of the Este and Gonzaga courts in 1491 bears witness to the potentially conflicting judicial and theological understanding of the meaning and implications of baptism in the pre-Tridentine era, and to the distrust of some lay rulers in regard to the sacrament's effectiveness in bringing about a criminal's genuine transformation.[67] In Francesco's letters, we find the same attitude toward the persistence of a convert's old identity that was expressed in a missive that the Jews of Mantua sent him in September 1491, and which he then forwarded to Bardolini, protesting the endeavors to have Angelo di Vitale pardoned and insisting that he should be executed for the crimes he had committed as a Jew prior to his baptism.[68] Thus, letters by members of two rival communities of faith surprisingly reveal a shared view of the limited effect of religious conversion.

Letters on the spectacle of conversion

Letters are also our main sources for detailed descriptions of the baptismal ceremony of Salomone da Sesso, which was celebrated on October 9, 1491, shortly after Angelo di Vitale's release from Mantua's prison and his return to Ferrara.[69] The event was recounted in three missives that Isabella d'Este's informants Bernardino de' Prosperi, Francesco da Bagnacavallo, and Girolamo Magnanino sent her from Ferrara on October 10. On the following day, Eleonora of Aragon reported it in a letter to Ercole d'Este, who was out of town at that time.

According to the letters addressed to Isabella, the festivities began with a grand procession headed by Duchess Eleonora that accompanied Salomone and his nine-year-old son from Ferrara's castle—a symbol of the ducal family's political power—to the cathedral, which functioned as the city's liturgical heart. There, the bishop of Ferrara baptized the two Jews.[70] Eleonora of Aragon presented Salomone at the baptismal font and the goldsmith was christened Ercole, in honor of her husband. Alfonso d'Este, Eleonora's eldest son and the ducal heir, acted as godfather to Salomone's son, who was christened Alfonso.[71] In her missive, Eleonora related how her court goldsmith then delivered an oration in which he affirmed that his decision to convert resulted from the realization that Christianity was the true faith, "and he put forward many texts in Hebrew to prove [the veracity of] the Trinity, the advent of Christ and His virgin birth, His passion, and the baptism."[72]

The duchess, who praised the convert's eloquence, evidently strove to present his speech as the successful outcome of her efforts to secure the baptism and pardoning of Salomone and his relative Angelo. She therefore refrained from mentioning the last part of Salomone's public address, which hinted at the dubious circumstances that culminated in his crossing of the religious boundary. According to Bagnacavallo's letter, though, "afterward he recounted in his defense what had been the cause of his having been imprisoned because of the Jews, saying that he was hated by the Jews of Mantua."[73] Prosperi's dispatch similarly mentioned the convert's allusion to alleged misdeeds in Mantua that had set in motion the turn of events leading to his baptism.[74] Hence, two of the missives addressed to Isabella disclosed the coerced aspect of Salomone's conversion, thereby casting a shadow on the overall triumphal tone of his oration in praise of Christianity's superiority over Judaism—an aspect that Duchess Eleonora sought to underscore in her own letter to her consort.

***

Because of the loss of criminal court records, only the letters preserved at the Gonzaga and Este archives have made it possible to uncover the complex turn of events that ultimately brought the acclaimed Jewish goldsmith Salomone da Sesso to the baptismal font. Previously assumed to have embraced Christianity willingly, "inspired either by God or by [hope for] material gain,"[75] these letters have revealed not only that Salomone actually converted under duress, but also that Jews played an instrumental role in implicating him and his relative in grave crimes, thereby pushing them to consent to baptism in order to save their lives. A systematic examination of those letters, moreover, has elucidated the attitudes of both Jews and Christians toward neophytes, demonstrating how these differed from the ways in which the converts in question presented themselves in writing.

The correspondence among the Este and Gonzaga rulers has also disclosed the importance that letter-writing assumed in a debate concerning a controversial conversionary strategy. Whereas other religious controversies in the late Quattrocento found their expression in public disputations, letters served as the primary medium through which those favoring the practice of absolving baptized Jewish criminals in 1491 advocated their views, and their opponents justified its rejection. Furthermore, since letters were perceived as an unthreatening form of communication in the service of family interests, and were often the only genre in which laywomen wrote,[76] their analysis is essential for unearthing the pivotal roles that patrician women such as Eleonora of Aragon and her daughter Isabella could play in facilitating Jewish conversion to Christianity. Bearing witness to the importance that such upper-class Renaissance women ascribed to converting the Jews, letters attest to their engagement in the religious controversies of their age, as well as to the influence that they could exert, often behind the scenes, in promoting specific ideologies.

The close reading of unpublished letters is particularly well suited for expounding the dramatic dynamics that often came into play in the individual cases of conversion that were typical of central and northern Italy, in contrast with the mass conversions of Jews in Iberia and in the Spanish-ruled regions of southern Italy.[77] No less importantly, letters document the theoretical and practical meanings of religious conversion in the pre-Reformation era, a period for which other kinds of sources, of a more institutional nature, are relatively scarce. Thus, it is chiefly through letters that we may uncover the intricacies, contested significance, and implications of Jewish conversion to Catholicism half a century before the establishment of the Roman Inquisition, and many decades prior to the foundation of Houses of Catechumens in Ferrara (in 1576–1584) or in Mantua (in 1588).[78]

Abbreviations

ASMo = Archivio di Stato di Modena.
ASMt, AG = Archivio di Stato di Mantova, Archivio Gonzaga.

Notes

* Support from the Israel Science Foundation (grant no. 389/15) is gratefully acknowledged. I thank Yonatan Glazer-Eytan, Moshe Sluhovsky, Kenneth Stow, and the participants of the *Renaissance of Letters* workshop for their helpful comments and suggestions.
1 See especially Adriano Prosperi, "L'Inquisizione Romana e gli ebrei," in *L'Inquisizione e gli ebrei in Italia*, ed. Michele Luzzati (Rome: Laterza, 1994), 67–120; Brian Pullan, *The Jews of Europe and the Inquisition of Venice: 1550–1620* (Totowa, NJ: Barnes and Noble, 1983); Marina Caffiero, *Battesimi forzati: Storia di ebrei, cristiani e convertiti nella Roma dei papi* (Rome: Viella, 2004); Pietro Ioly Zorattini, *I nomi degli altri: Conversioni a Venezia e nel Friuli Veneto in età moderna* (Florence, 2008); Natalie E. Rothman, *Brokering Empire: Trans-Imperial Subjects between Venice and Istanbul* (Ithaca, NY, 2011), 87–162; Matteo Al Kalak and Ilaria Pavan, *Un'altra fede: Le Case dei catecumeni nei territori estensi (1583–1938)* (Florence: Olschki, 2013); Samuela Marconcini, *Per amor del cielo: Farsi cristiani a Firenze tra Seicento e Settecento* (Florence: Firenze University Press, 2016). See also the articles collected in the special issue of *Ricerche per la storia religiosa di Roma* 10 (1998): "*Dall'infamia dell'errore al grembo di Santa Chiesa": Conversioni e strategie della conversione a Roma nell'età moderna.*
2 Studies of the correspondence of cardinals Guglielmo Sirleto (1514–1585) and Carlo Borromeo (1538–1584), for instance, document these prelates' occasional disagreements with official ecclesiastical policy regarding the Jews and their hoped-for conversion, as well as their independent-mindedness in the pursuit of solutions to specific problems involving converts. See especially Renata Segre, "Il mondo ebraico nei cardinali della controriforma," in *Italia judaica: Gli ebrei in Italia tra Rinascimento ed Età barocca. Atti del II convegno internazionale, Genova 10–15 giugno 1984* (Rome: Ufficio centrale per i beni archivistici, 1986), 119–138; Segre, "Il mondo ebraico nel carteggio di Carlo Borromeo," *Michael: On the History of the Jews in the Diaspora* 1 (1972), 163–260.
3 Renata Segre, "Neophytes during the Italian Counter-Reformation: Identities and Biographies," *Proceedings of the Sixth World Congress of Jewish Studies* 2 (1973), 131–142: 132. See also Adriano Prosperi, "La Chiesa e gli ebrei nell'Italia del '500," in *Ebraismo e antiebraismo: Immagine e pregiudizio*, with a preface by Cesare Luporini (Florence: Giuntina, 1989), 171–183.
4 Peter A. Mazur, *Conversion to Catholicism in Early Modern Italy* (New York and London: Routledge, 2016), 18–42, 66–82, provides an overview of Jewish conversion to Christianity in Italy from the mid-1540s onward. No such overview exists for the fifteenth century. On current trends in studying the history of Jewish conversion to Christianity in the Italian peninsula see the special issue of *Materia giudaica* 19: 1–2 (2014): *Strategie e normative per la conversione degli ebrei dal Medioevo all'età contemporanea.*

Atti del Convegno Internazionale, Ravenna 30 settembre–2 ottobre 2013, ed. Mauro Perani.

5   Anna Esposito, *Un'altra Roma: Minoranze nazionali e comunità ebraiche tra Medioevo e Rinascimento* (Rome: Il Calamo, 1995), 154–157; Elisabetta Traniello, *Gli ebrei e le piccole città: Economia e società nel Polesine del Quattrocento* (Rovigo: Minelliana, 2004), 160–176. See also Ariel Toaff, *Il Vino e la carne: Una comunità ebraica nel Medioevo* (Bologna: Il Mulino, 1989), 181–195. For additional studies that mention individual cases of Jewish conversion in Quattrocento Italy see the bibliographic references in Tamar Herzig, "Rethinking Jewish Conversion to Christianity in Renaissance Italy," in *Renaissance Religions*, ed. Nicholas Terpstra and Peter Howard (Turnhout: Brepols, forthcoming), nn. 5, 19.

6   Scholars have been concerned mainly with the representations of Jewish conversion in the various literary, musical, and theatrical genres in which they began to feature in the last decades of the fifteenth century, notably in humanist orations, *sacre rappresentazioni*, and popular songs. See Stephen Bowd, "The Conversion of Margarita: A Wedding Oration in Fifteenth-Century Brescia," *Archivio italiano per la storia della pietà* 25 (2012): 140–166; Pietro Delcorno, "Corruzione e conversione in una sacra rappresentazione fiorentina: *La rappresentazione di dua hebrei che si convertirono* (c. 1495)," *Cheiron* 57–58 (2012): 273–310; Don Harrán, "'Adonai con voi' (1569), a Simple Popular Song with a Complicated Semantic About (What Seems to Be) Circumcision," in *The Jewish Body: Corporeality, Society, and Identity in the Renaissance and Early Modern Period*, ed. Maria Diemling and Giuseppe Veltri (Leiden and Boston, MA: Brill, 2009), 427–463: 428–429 and n. 6.

7   Daniela Ferrari, "The Gonzaga Archives of Mantua and Their Rearrangements over the Centuries, along with an Overview of Archival Materials on Mantuan Jewry," in *Rabbi Judah Moscato and the Jewish Intellectual World of Mantua in the 16th–17th Century*, ed. Giuseppe Veltri and Gianfranco Miletto (Leiden: Brill, 2012), 145–160: 145–155.

8   Umberto Dallari, *Inventario sommario dei documenti della Cancelleria ducale estense (sezione generale) nel R. Archivio di Stato di Modena* (Modena: Società Tipografica Modenese, 1927), 3–5; Guido D'Angiolini and Claudio Pavone (ed.), *Guida Generale degli Archivi di Stato Italiani* (Rome: Ministero per i Beni Culturali, 1981–1994), vol. 4, 1001–1003.

9   On Renaissance letters as ego-documents see Peter Burke, "Representations of the Self from Petrarch to Descartes," in Roy Porter, *Rewriting the Self: Histories from the Renaissance to the Present* (London and New York: Routledge, 1997), 17–28: 21–24.

10 Diaries and autobiographies written by converts or potential converts from Judaism only became common toward the end of the early modern era. For these sources and the methodological problems involved in treating them as ego-documents see Adelisa Malena, "I demoni di Alvisa: Il racconto autobiografico di Alvisa Zambelli *alias* Lea Gaon," in *La fede degli italiani: Per Adriano Prosperi, vol. 1*, ed. Guido Dall'Olio, Adelisa Malena, and Pierroberto Scaramella (Pisa: Edizioni della Normale, 2011), 383–402; Malena, "Fra conversione, penitenza e possessione: La vita di Alvisa Zambelli, ebrea convertita (1734–1735)," in *Spazi, poteri, diritti delle donne a Venezia in età moderna*, ed. Anna Bellavitis, Nadia Maria Filippini, and Tiziana Plebani (Verona: QuiEdit, 2012), 281–289 (for an autobiography), and Joseph B. Sermoneta, "Tredici giorni nella casa dei conversi: Dal diario di una giovane ebrea del 18° secolo," *Michael: On the History of the Jews in the Diaspora* 1 (1972): 261–315; Kenneth Stow, *Anna and Tranquillo: Catholic Anxiety and Jewish Protest in the Age of Revolution* (New Haven, CT: Yale University Press, 2016), 1–18 (for a contested diary).

11 Moses A. Shulvass, *The Jews in the World of the Renaissance* (Leiden: Brill, 1973), 240. See also Franz Landsberger, "The Jewish Artist before the Time of Emancipation," *Hebrew Union College Annual* 16 (1941), 321–413: 377–378; Cecil Roth, *The History of the Jews of Italy* (Philadelphia, PA: Jewish Publication Society of America, 1946), 199.

12 Isabella d'Este praised Salomone's virtuosity in a letter to Ludovico Sforza of May 15, 1491 (ASMt, AG, 2904, lib. 136, c. 94ʳ). Isabella was reputed for her "refined and

experienced eye" when scrutinizing artworks and luxury items, and her commissions from goldsmiths had a notable impact on the Renaissance market for jewelry: Francis Ames-Lewis, *Isabella and Leonardo: The Artistic Relationship between Isabella d'Este and Leonardo da Vinci, 1500–1506* (New Haven, CT: Yale University Press, 2012), 19–39; Evelyn Welch, *Shopping in the Renaissance: Consumer Cultures in Italy, 1400–1600* (New Haven, CT: Yale University Press, 2005), 252–253.

13 Tamar Herzig, "Nuns, Artists, and Baptized Jews: The Vestition Ceremony of Suor Theodora, *Quondam Hebrea*," *Memorie domenicane* n.s. 46 (2015), 241–262.

14 Like other goldsmiths who specialized in jewelry, most of his works were melted down at some point. He is remembered primarily for his lavishly engraved swords, on which see Sergio Masini and Gianrodolfo Rotasso, "Le armi nella storia," in *Le armi degli Estensi: La collezione di Konopiště* (Bologna: L. Cappelli, 1986), xxi–xxviiii: xxviii; Mina Gregori, *In the Light of Apollo: The Italian Renaissance and Greece, December 22, 2003–March 31, 2004* (Athens: The Hellenic Culture Organization, 2003), 401–402; Daniele Diotallevi, "Arte e armi per Cesare," in *Cesare Borgia di Francia: Gonfaloniere di Santa Romana Chiesa, 1498–1503. Conquiste effimere e progettualità statale. Atti del Convegno di Studi (Urbino, 2003)*, ed. Marinella Bonvini and Monica Miretti (Ostra Vetere: Tecnostampa, 2005), 427–445; Marià Carbonelli Buades, "Cèsar Borja i l'art. Tres episodis," *Revista Borja* 2 (2009), 325–357: 331.

15 The most recent biographical account of the goldsmith's life in Roberta Bianco, "Ercole dei Fedeli," in *Dizionario Biografico deli Italiani* (Rome: Istituto della Enciclopedia Italiana, 1960–), vol. 43 (1993): 131–132 reiterates earlier mistakes regarding some major events in his life in Angelo Angelucci, *Catalogo della armeria reale* (Turin: Candeletti, 1890), 307, and Constantino G. Bulgari, *Argentieri gemmari e orafi d'Italia*, part 4: *Emilia* (Rome: Palombi, 1958–1974), 350.

16 Only one letter pertaining to Salomone's conversion was ever published, partially, in Luciano Chiappini, "Eleonora d'Aragona, prima duchessa di Ferrara," *Atti e Memorie della Deputazione Ferrarese di Storia Patria* 6 (1956): 1–156: 75–76. Excerpts of Isabella d'Este's letter regarding Angelo's conversion are cited in Alessandro Luzio and Rodolfo Renier, *Il lusso di Isabella d'Este, marchesa di Mantova* (Rome: Forzani, 1896), 45–46. For the turn of events leading to Salomone's baptism see Tamar Herzig, "The Prosecution of Jews and the Repression of Sodomy in Fifteenth-Century Italy," in *L'Inquisizione romana, i giudici e gli eretici: Studi in onore di John Tedeschi*, ed. Anne Jacobson Schutte and Andrea Del Col (Rome: Viella, 2017), 59–74. See also the reconstruction of Salomone's life in Herzig, *A Convert's Tale: Art, Crime, and Jewish Apostasy in Renaissance Italy* (Cambridge, MA: Harvard University Press, in press).

17 He later returned to Eleonora's court, as noted in Isabella's letter to her mother of March 24, 1490 (ASMt, AG, 2904, lib. 136, c. 14^v), now available in English in Isabella d'Este, *Selected Letters*, ed. and trans. Deanna Shemek (Tempe, AZ: Arizona Center for Medieval and Renaissance Studies, 2017), 30. However, he was back in Mantua in early 1491 (Herzig, *A Convert's Tale*).

18 On Isabella's correspondence see Shemek, "In Continuous Expectation: Isabella d'Este's Epistolary Desire," in Dennis Looney and Deanna Shemek (eds.), *Phaethon's Children: The Este Court and Its Culture in Early Modern Ferrara* (Tempe, AZ: Arizona Center for Medieval and Renaissance Studies, 2005), 269–300: 277; Shemek, "Isabella d'Este and the Properties of Persuasion," in *Women's Letters across Europe, 1400–1700: Form and Persuasion*, ed. Jane Couchman and Ann Crabb (Aldershot: Ashgate, 2005), 123–140: 125–127; Shemek, "'Ci ci' and 'pa pa': Script, Mimicry, and Mediation in Isabella d'Este's Letters," *Rinascimento*, seconda serie 43 (2005), 75–91: 77; Shemek, "Introduction," in Isabella d'Este, *Selected Letters*, ed. and trans. Shemek, 1–19.

19 For Isabella's patronage relations with other artists, as revealed in her correspondence, see Ames-Lewis, *Isabella and Leonardo*.

20 Isabella d'Este's letter to her husband, of March 22, 1491 (ASMt, AG, 2904, lib. 136, c. 82ᵛ). The text in the original letter preserved in ASMt, AG, 2107, fasc. II, c. 103ʳ is identical to the one in Isabella's copybook, although it bears the date of March 26 which, in light of Francesco's response to the missive—which was sent on March 26—appears to be an error. In his reply, Francesco approved Isabella's renewal of the *grida* (ASMt, AG, 2107, fasc. I.1, c. 5ʳ, also copied into ASMt, AG, 2904, lib. 137, c. 12ʳ).

21 Isabella d'Este's letter to Ludovico Sforza of May 15, 1491 (ASMt, AG, 2904, lib. 136, c. 94ʳ).

22 Salomone's intervention is noted in the instructions that Francesco Gonzaga sent his secretary, Antimaco, from Ferrara on May 4, 1491 (ASMt, AG, 2904, lib. 137, c. 38ᵛ).

23 Salomone da Sesso's letter of August 16, 1491 to Pietro Gentile da Camerino (ASMt, AG, 1232, c. 233). That Pietro Gentile accompanied Francesco Gonzaga in his travels is noted in Isabella d'Este's letter to Antimaco of September 14, 1491 (ASMt, AG, 2991, lib. 1, c. 41ᵛ).

24 See Pamela H. Smith, "In a Sixteenth-Century Goldsmith's Workshop," in *The Mindful Hand: Inquiry and Invention from the Late Renaissance to Early Industrialisation*, ed. Lissa Roberts, Simon Schaffer, and Peter Dear (Amsterdam: Royal Netherlands Academy of Arts and Sciences, 2007), 33–57: 44–45. On fifteenth-century artisanal literacy in general see Smith, "Why Write a Book? From Lived Experience to the Written Word in Early Modern Europe," *Bulletin of the German Historical Institute* 47 (Fall 2010), 25–50.

25 Robert Bonfil, *Jewish Life in Renaissance Italy*, trans. Anthony Oldcorn (Berkeley, CA: University of California Press, 1994), 233–239. Letter-writing was one of the pillars of the primary education of Italian Jewish boys, who were trained in drafting epistles to their relatives on a daily basis. Some of these letter collections are available in critical editions: *Letters of Jewish Teachers in Renaissance Italy*, ed. Yacov Boksenboim (Tel Aviv: Tel Aviv University Press, 1985) [in Hebrew]. See also *Letters of the Carmi Family: Cremona, 1570–1577*, ed. Yacov Boksenboim (Tel Aviv: Tel Aviv University Press, 1983) [in Hebrew]; *Letters of Rabbi Leon Modena*, ed. Yacov Boksenboim (Tel Aviv: Tel Aviv University Press, 1984) [in Hebrew]; *The Letters of the Rieti Family: Siena, 1537–1564*, ed. Yacov Boksenboim (Tel Aviv: Tel Aviv University Press, 1987) [in Hebrew]; *Letters of Jews in Italy: Selected Letters from the Sixteenth Century*, ed. Yacov Boksenboim (Jerusalem: Yad Yitzhak Ben Zvi and the Hebrew University of Jerusalem, 1994) [in Hebrew]; Cédric Cohen Skalli and Michele Luzzati, *Lucca 1493: Un sequestro di lettere ebraiche. Edizione e commento storico* (Naples: Università degli Studi di Napoli "L'Orientale," 2014).

26 Bonfil, *Jewish Life in Renaissance Italy*, 238.

27 See Benjamin Ravid, "How 'Other' Really Was the Jewish Other? The Evidence from Venice," in *Acculturation and Its Discontents: The Italian Jewish Experience between Exclusion and Inclusion*, ed. David N. Myers *et al.* (Toronto: University of Toronto Press, 2008), 19–55: 28–30, and the letters in Sarra Copia Sulam, *Jewish Poet and Intellectual in Seventeenth-Century Venice: The Works of Sarra Copia Sulam in Verse and Prose, Along with Writings of Her Contemporaries in Her Praise, Condemnation, or Defense*, ed. and trans. Don Harrán (Chicago, IL: University of Chicago Press, 2009), esp. 115–249.

28 Edward Goldberg, *Jews and Magic in Medici Florence: The Secret World of Benedetto Blanis* (Toronto: University of Toronto Press, 2011), and see the correspondence in *A Jew at the Medici Court: The Letters of Benedetto Blanis Hebreo (1615–1621)* (Toronto: University of Toronto Press, 2011).

29 Francesca Trivellato, "A Republic of Merchants?" in *Finding Europe: Discourses on Margins, Communities, Images ca. 13th–ca. 18th Centuries*, ed. Anthony Molho, Diogo Ramada Curto, and Niki Koniordos (Oxford: Berghahn Books, 2007), 133–158. On Jewish merchants' epistolary practices in the seventeenth and (especially) eighteenth

century see Trivellato, *The Familiarity of Strangers: The Sephardic Diaspora, Livorno, and Cross-Cultural Trade in the Early Modern Period* (New Haven, CT: Yale University Press, 2009), esp. 177–193.

30 See Evelyn Welch, *Art and Society in Italy 1350–1500* (Oxford: Oxford University Press, 1997), 121–123. As Welch points out, the letters written by artists employed by the princely rulers of Italian states rarely dealt with abstract artistic or intellectual matters. For the best-known artistic correspondence that did concern such issues see Deborah Parker, *Michelangelo and the Art of Letter Writing* (Cambridge: Cambridge University Press, 2010).

31 Cecilia Nubola, "Supplications between Politics and Justice: The Northern and Central Italian States in the Early Modern Age," in *Petitions in Social History*, ed. Lex Heerma van Voss (Cambridge: Cambridge University Press, 2002), 35–56. See also Paolo L. Rossi, "The Writer and the Man: Real Crimes and Mitigating Circumstances: *Il caso Cellini*," in *Crime, Society and the Law in Renaissance Italy*, ed. Trevor Dean and K. J. P. Lowe (Cambridge: Cambridge University Press, 1994), 157–183: 173–180.

32 Salomone da Sesso's letter of August 16, 1491 to Pietro Gentile da Camerino (ASMt, AG, 1232, c. 233): "Servitor Salamon Aurifex Illu[strissi]me D[omine] Ducisse Ferrarie." On Renaissance artists' choice of names when signing their works, their letters, and other documents that were written on their behalf see Welch, *Art and Society in Italy*, 87.

33 In Renaissance Italy, skilled goldsmiths were considered artists rather than craftsmen: Susan Mosher Stuard, *Gilding the Market: Luxury Fashion in Fourteenth-Century Italy* (Philadelphia, PA: University of Pennsylvania Press, 2006), 150, 176–178.

34 For instance, in Isabella d'Este's letter to Ludovico Sforza of May 15, 1491 (ASMt, AG, 2904, lib. 136, c. 94^r): "Salomone da Sesso hebreo et aurifice dilectissimo de la Ill[ustrissi]ma n[ost]ra m[ad]re"; in Francesco Gonzaga's letter to Eleonora of Aragon of September 7, 1491 (ASMt, AG, 2904, lib. 139, c. 52^v): "Salomone da Sesso hebreo"; and in Eleonora of Aragon's letter to Isabella d'Este of September 10, 1491 (ASMt, AG, 1185, c. 194): "Salamon hebreo n[ost]ro orevese."

35 Salomone da Sesso/Ercole [de' Fedeli]'s letter to Isabella d'Este of October 14, 1504 (ASMt, AG, 1890, c. 187), signed: "Hercules aurifex Illu[strissimi] D[omini] Ducis Ferr[ari]e."

36 Salomone da Sesso/Ercole [de' Fedeli]'s letter to Isabella d'Este of August 17, 1505 (ASMt, AG, 1240, c. 334), signed: "Hercules orevexe." It appears as if the author initially considered adding an indication of his former status as Duke Ercole d'Este's court goldsmith by adding the word "formerly" (*olim*) after the designation "Ercole the goldsmith," but then desisted from noting his previous employment by the late duke.

37 Salomone da Sesso/Ercole [de' Fedeli]'s letter to Isabella d'Este of May 14, 1506 (ASMt, AG, 1241, c. 300), signed: "Hercules Aurifex Ill[ustrissi]me Ducisse Ferra-[rie]," and his missive to Isabella of July 15, 1506 (ASMt, AG, 1241, c. 301), signed: "Hercules auriffice della duchessa."

38 Although in the records of the Ferrarese court—whose duchess and duke had secured the goldsmith's baptism—he was usually designated simply "Master Ercole the goldsmith," even ducal officials sometimes alluded to his Jewish origins, as when recording a payment made in 1503 to "Ercole the goldsmith, the former Jew" (ASMo, Camera Ducale, Amministrazione della casa, *Munizione e Fabbriche*, no. 42, c. 4^r: "M[aestr]o Hercule oreveso già hebreio [sic]").

39 See Abram's letter to Francesco Gonzaga of December 13, 1493 (ASMt, AG, 1232, c. 820): "Salamo[n]e da Sexo chiamato mo Hercules" (on this letter and its author's identification see Herzig, *A Convert's Tale*), and Isabella d'Este's letter to Girolamo Ziliolo of January 21, 1494 (ASMt, AG, 2991, lib. 4, c. 20): "M[aest]ro Hercule qual era Judeo" (noted in Luzio and Renier, *Il lusso di Isabella d'Este*, 46).

40 Segre, "Neophytes during the Italian Counter-Reformation," 132. On convert identities in the early modern era see Elisheva Carlebach, *Divided Souls: Converts from*

Judaism in Germany, 1500–1750 (New Haven, CT: Yale University Press, 2001) and, for the more complex problem of Iberian *conversos*, Renée Levine Melammed, *A Question of Identity: Iberian Conversos in Historical Perspective* (Oxford: Oxford University Press, 2004).

41 Francesco Gonzaga's letter to Ermolao Bardolini of August 20, 1491 (ASMt, AG, 2904, lib. 139, c. 27ʳ).

42 Eleonora of Aragon's letter to Francesco Gonzaga of August 20, 1491 (ASMt, AG, 1185, c. 177): "Salamo[ne] hebreo n[ost]ro Aurifice."

43 Ermolao Bardolini's letter to Francesco Gonzaga of August 30, 1491 (in ASMt, AG, 2440). This letter is noted in David S. Chambers and Trevor Dean, *Clean Hands and Rough Justice: An Investigating Magistrate in Renaissance Italy* (Ann Arbor, MI: University of Michigan Press, 1997), 243.

44 The possible reasons for this are delineated in Herzig, *A Convert's Tale*. In his letter to Ermolao Bardolini of September 15, 1491 Francesco Gonzaga reported the Mantuan Jews' complaints about the endeavors to secure Angelo's exoneration following his conversion to Christianity while detained in Mantua's prison (ASMt, AG, 2904, lib. 139, c. 60ᵛ).

45 These records were either lost in a fire or destroyed in subsequent centuries: Diane Yvonne Ghirardo, "The Topography of Prostitution in Renaissance Ferrara," *Journal of the Society of Architectural Historians* 60:4 (December 2001): 402–431: 408, 425.

46 Francesco Gonzaga's letter to Eleonora of Aragon of September 7, 1491 (ASMt, AG, 2904, lib. 139, c. 52ᵛ): "Intendo ch[e] è stato sostenuto lì a Ferrara Salomone da Sesso hebreo, quale in certa collana che me fece li messi passati me robbati diceotto o vinti ducati ultra ch[e] la è comisso alcuni errori molto enormi ne la cita n[ost]ra, et in specie i[n] mettere sottosopra tuti li zudei ch[e] lì sono."

47 Francesco Gonzaga's letter to Ermolao Bardolini of September 8, 1491 (ASMt, AG, 2904, lib. 139, c. 53ᵛ).

48 On Francesco's preference for communicating sensitive information through reliable intermediaries rather than conveying it in writing see Sarah D. P. Cockram, *Isabella d'Este and Francesco Gonzaga: Power Sharing at the Italian Renaissance Court* (Burlington, VT: Ashgate, 2013), 32–33.

49 Eleonora of Aragon's letter to Isabella d'Este of September 10, 1491 (ASMt, AG, 1185, c. 194)

50 Monica Ferrari, "Un'educazione sentimentale per lettera: Il caso di Isabella d'Este (1490–1493)," *Reti medievali* 10 (2009): 351–371.

51 Francesco Gonzaga's letter to Ermolao Bardolini of September 10, 1491 (ASMt, AG, 2904, lib. 139, c. 56ʳ).

52 Angelo's baptism was noted in Isabella d'Este's letter to Francesco Gonzaga of September 15, 1491 (ASMt, AG, 2991, lib. 1, c. 44ʳ) and in Francesco Gonzaga's letter to Ermolao Bardolini of September 15, 1491 (ASMt, AG, 2904, lib. 139, c. 60ᵛ).

53 Isabella d'Este's letter to Francesco Gonzaga of September 15, 1491 (ASMt, AG, 2991, lib. 1, c. 44ʳ), noted in Luzio and Renier, *Il lusso di Isabella d'Este*, 45–46.

54 Cf. Ezek 33: 11. St. Jerome translated this verse in the Vulgate version as "nolo mortem impii sed ut revertatur impius a via sua et vivat" but St. Benedict, in the introduction to his monastic rule, cited it as "nolo mortem peccatoris sed convertatur et vivat." See *The Rule of Saint Benedict*, ed. and trans. Bruce L. Venarde (Cambridge, MA: Harvard University Press, 2011), 6. Medieval authors often cited St. Benedict's Latin version; cf. Sharon Roubach, "The Hidden Apocalypse: Richard of Saint-Vanne and the Otherworld," *Journal of Medieval History* 32 (2006): 302–314: 311–312, n. 45; James W. Marchand, "An Unidentified Latin Quote in Piers Plowman," *Modern Philology* 88:4 (May 1991): 398–400: 399.

55 This also characterizes the letters penned by patrician women such as Alessandra Macinghi Strozzi (1407–1471) earlier in the Quattrocento: Maria Luisa Doglio, "Letter

Writing, 1350–1650," in *A History of Women's Writing in Italy*, ed. Letizia Panizza and Sharon Wood (Cambridge: Cambridge University Press, 2000), 13–30: 16–17.

56 On Isabella's education, which exposed her to Latin and to ancient authors, see Shemek, "Isabella d'Este and the Properties of Persuasion," 125. According to Molly Bourne, *Francesco II Gonzaga: The Soldier-Prince as Patron* (Rome: Bulzoni, 2008), 31, her consort had only "a serviceable if rudimentary knowledge of Latin."

57 Adriano Prosperi, "Battesimo e identità cristiana nella prima età moderna," in *Salvezza delle anime, disciplina dei corpi: Un seminario sulla storia del battesimo*, ed. Adriano Prosperi (Pisa: Edizioni della Normale, 2004), 1–65: 53–55. See also Caffiero, *Battesimi forzati*, 272–273; Cristina Galasso, *Alle origini di una comunità: Ebree ed ebrei a Livorno nel Seicento* (Florence: Olschki, 2001), 114–115.

58 In his 1558 legal tract, Marquardus de Susannis (d. 1578) noted the lack of consensus in the matter, although he presented the opinion that baptism should not lead to the exoneration of a convicted Jewish criminal as the majority opinion, citing earlier jurist Filippo Decio (1454–1535) to support this claim. Marquardus de Susannis, *Tractatus de Iudaeis et aliis infidelibus circa concernentia originem contractuum, bella, foedera, ultimas voluntates, iudicia, & delicta Iudaeorum & aliorum infidelium, & eorum conversiones ad fidem* (Venice: Cominus de Tridino, 1558), 139–140.

59 Unlike Francesco Gonzaga, though, they were willing to grant baptized Jewish convicts a less painful death: Rossella Rinaldi, "Topografia documentaria per la storia della comunità ebraica bolognese," in *Banchi ebraici a Bologna nel XV secolo*, ed. Maria Giuseppina Muzzarelli (Bologna: Il Mulino, 1994), 29–87: 64–65; Esposito, *Un'altra Roma*, 154, n. 95.

60 Francesco Gonzaga's letter to Ermolao Bardolini of September 15, 1491 (ASMt, AG, 2904, lib. 139, c. 60^v).

61 On the conversion of condemned criminals and the symbolic value of their public execution see Adriano Prosperi, *Delitto e perdono: La pena di morte nell'orizzonte mentale dell'Europa cristiana, XIV-XVIII secolo* (Turin: Einaudi, 2016), esp. 40–68, 353–380.

62 The proceedings of the Inquisition's tribunal in Venice record a similar utterance by a Jewish man, who assured a Christian noblewoman in 1555 that if one had not been a good Jew, he could never become a virtuous Christian (Pullan, *The Jews of Europe and the Inquisition of Venice*, 244).

63 Francesco Gonzaga's letter to Isabella d'Este of September 17, 1491 (ASMt, AG, 2904, lib. 139, c. 61^v): "[N]o[n] dubitiamo, si come lo è stato cativo zudeo, serria pegior[e] Christiano. Et meglio è p[er] lui tanto ch['e]l è in bono esser[e] e ben disposto ch['e]l se ne morà." A similar attitude toward repentant criminals, whose public execution was regarded as an edifying moment in which "the killing of a human being simultaneously created a soul in paradise," was adopted by other Italian magistrates in the fifteenth century: Adriano Prosperi, "Conversion on the Scaffold: Italian Practices in European Context," in *Space and Conversion in Global Perspective*, ed. Giuseppe Marcocci, Aliocha Maldavsky, Wietse de Boer, and Ilaria Pavan (Leiden: Brill, 2014), 44–60: 51.

64 Eleonora's role in securing these baptisms and another conversion from Judaism in 1491 is analyzed in Herzig, *A Convert's Tale*.

65 Ercole d'Este letter to Isabella d'Este of September 19, 1491 (ASMt, AG, 1185, c. 201): "[N]ui desideramo ch[e] dicto Angelo no[n] p[er]isca maxime essendossi facto Christiano."

66 Francesco Gonzaga's letter to Isabella d'Este of September 22, 1491 (ASMt, AG, 2904, lib. 139, cc. 63^v–64^r).

67 For the baptism of Jews who consequently received pardons for their transgressions in post-Tridentine Italy see Pullan, *The Jews of Europe and the Inquisition of Venice*, 271–272; Segre, "Neophytes during the Italian Counter-Reformation," 132;

Katherine Aron-Beller, *Jews on Trial: The Papal Inquisition in Modena, 1598–1638* (Manchester: Manchester University Press, 2011), 165.

68 The marquis of Mantua forwarded this letter to his podestà, but like most letters of this kind its copy was not kept along with the copies of his own letters (cf. Cockram, *Isabella d'Este and Francesco Gonzaga*, 33). Nonetheless, the Mantuan Jews' complaints in the letter were summarized in Francesco Gonzaga's missive to Ermolao Bardolini of September 15, 1491 (ASMt, AG, 2904, lib. 139, c. 60ᵛ). A similar notion concerning the immutability of a converted Jew's self was later implied in the Jew Abram's dispatch to Francesco Gonzaga of December 13, 1493 (ASMt, AG, 1232, c. 820).

69 The baptismal ceremony is also recorded in one Ferrarese chronicle, but its description is the least informative of the five accounts recounting the festivities. See Bernardino Zambotti, *Diario Ferrarese dall'anno 1476 sino al 1504*, ed. Giuseppe Pardi, *Rerum italicarum scriptores*, ed. L. A. Muratori, vol. 24/7:2 (Bologna: Nicola Zanichelli, 1934), 223.

70 The bishop of Ferrara (in 1474–1494) was Bartolomeo della Rovere, nephew of Pope Sixtus IV: Luciano Chiappini, Werther Angelini, and Amerigo Baruffaldi, *La chiesa di Ferrara nella storia della città e del suo territorio, secoli XV–XX* (Ferrara: Gabriele Corbo Editore: 1997), 13–14.

71 Letters sent to Isabella d'Este by Bernardino de' Prosperi, Francesco da Bagnacavallo, and Girolamo Magnanino, on October 10, 1491 (ASMt, AG, 1232, cc. 40, 93, 167). Salomone's wife and three other children were baptized on another occasion (Herzig, *A Convert's Tale*).

72 Eleonora of Aragon's letter to Ercole d'Este of October 11, 1491 (ASMo, Archivio Segreto Estense, Casa e Stato, 132), cited in Chiappini, "Eleonora d'Aragona," 75–76.

73 Francesco da Bagnacavallo's letter to Isabella d'Este of October 10, 1491 (ASMt, AG, 1232, c. 93).

74 Bernardino de' Prosperi's letter to Isabella d'Este of October 10, 1491 (ASMt, AG, 1232, c. 40); see Herzig, "The Prosecution of Jews," 67–69.

75 As suggested in Angelucci, *Catalogo della armeria reale*, p. 308.

76 As noted in Deanna Shemek, "Letter Writing and Epistolary Culture," *Oxford Bibliographies Online: Renaissance and Reformation*, ed. Margaret L. King (Oxford: Oxford University Press, 2013).

77 The history of the Jews in the southern parts of the Italian peninsula that were subject to the Spanish crown diverged from that of their coreligionists in central and northern Italy (except for the Spanish-ruled duchy of Milan, from which the Jews were expelled in 1597). The Sicilian version of the Spanish Edict of Expulsion was promulgated as early as 1492, and in 1541 Jews were also expelled from the Kingdom of Naples. On the "New Chrisitian" who formed their own community in Naples see Peter A. Mazur, *The New Christians of Spanish Naples, 1528–1671: A Fragile Elite* (Houndmills: Palgrave Macmillan, 2013). For Sicily see Nadia Zeldes, *The Former Jews of this Kingdom: Sicilian Converts after the Expulsion, 1492–1516* (Leiden: Brill, 2003). In the central and northern parts of the peninsula Jews either converted alone or, in the case of male converts such as Salomone da Sesso, instigated the conversion of their entire families (see n. 5 above).

78 On the foundation of the House of Catechumens in Mantua see Mazur, *Conversion to Catholicism in Early Modern Italy*, 25–26. Preparations for the establishment of a House of Catechumens in Ferrara were already underway in 1576, though it officially began its activity in 1584: Andrea Faoro, "Prime ricerche sulla Casa dei catecumeni di Ferrara," in *Ebrei a Ferrara, ebrei di Ferrara: Aspetti culturali, economici e sociali della presenza ebraica a Ferrara (secc. XIII–XX)*, ed. Laura Graziani Secchieri (Florence: Giuntina, 2014), 219–231.

PART III

Humanism, diplomacy, and empire

6

WRITING A LETTER IN 1507

The fortunes of Francesco Vettori's correspondence and the Florentine Republic

Christopher Bacich

Stanford Libraries' Special Collections houses a short letter dated June 25, 1507. The executive council responsible for Florence's foreign policy, the *Dieci di libertà e balìa* (the Ten of Liberty, Authority, and Power), drafted the missive and dispatched it to one "Francesco Vettori" (1474–1539). It ordered him to seek out an audience with the Holy Roman Emperor, Maximilian I (1459–1519). At the time, Vettori was a young member of the Florentine elite with experience holding various posts in the government. The Ten dispatched the letter to Vettori only because Florence's leader, Piero Soderini (1452–1522), had failed to convince the council to entrust this diplomatic mission to his secretary, Niccolò Machiavelli (1469–1527). The appointment of Vettori to the German embassy brought him into a close working relationship with Soderini and Machiavelli that eventually proved pivotal in the lives of all three men.

The letter's tone betrays anxiety and perhaps even a slight sense of dread. Maximilian I had announced his intent to travel to Rome and be crowned Holy Roman Emperor by the pope, a gesture designed to challenge France's involvement on the peninsula by forcefully reaffirming Italy's belonging to the empire. The Florentines knew they would be obligated to expose themselves as the enemy of one or the other of two great European powers, France (Florence's historic ally) or the empire. The Ten had reason to be anxious.

The appointment of Vettori to his embassy resulted from trying circumstances for Florence both at home and abroad. For more than a decade, Florence had experienced internal convulsions and the external menace of foreign powers. The expulsion of the Medici in 1494, the establishment of a Republic under the leadership of Girolamo Savonarola (b. 1452) and his subsequent execution in 1498, followed by the installation of Piero Soderini in 1502 as the first and only *Gonfaloniere di giustizia a vita* ("Standardbearer of Justice for Life") left deep fissures in Florentine society. In addition, these were the first years of the Italian

Wars (1494–1559), a time of nearly continuous warfare. The involvement of France and the Holy Roman Empire in Italian affairs, coupled with the ambitions of powerful neighbors and the rebellion of cities under Florentine dominion, made the years immediately preceding Vettori's mission to Maximilian some of the most challenging of Florence's history.

Vettori's mission to Maximilian's court was delicate and led to continual debate in Florence. Internally, pro- and anti-German forces battled one another over the best policy to follow vis-à-vis the emperor's planned sojourn. Externally, Florence's reputation as the staunch ally of Maximilian I's primary rival, Louis XII of France (1462–1515), hampered Vettori's efforts to establish a relationship of trust with the emperor. These difficulties contributed to a constant reshuffling of priorities for Vettori during his embassy and induced the Republic to expand his authority as it sought to reach an acceptable agreement with Maximilian I.

Vettori's mission additionally inspired him to craft a somewhat obscure but noteworthy work of Renaissance literature, the *Viaggio in Alemagna* (Journey to Germany). Ostensibly a collection of prurient tales, the *Viaggio* espouses a rather pessimistic vision of human nature and existence. Although Vettori's grim perspective on human life likely originated with his 1507 embassy, evidence shows he cannot have authored the *Viaggio* before the beginning the intense, two-year period of correspondence with Machiavelli. In that exchange, Vettori and Machiavelli continuously returned to the question of how best to navigate events and wrestle with fortune. Again and again, Machiavelli proposed to Vettori the power of reason, discourse, and planning, while Vettori repeatedly responded by arguing for the futility of reason and attempts at calculation and discourse. Examining episodes in Vettori's career and his correspondence with Machiavelli enriches our understanding of the worldview on display in the *Viaggio*.

Finally, the microhistory of Vettori's letter reveals that this Renaissance artifact endured its own tumultuous journey as it passed in and out of various archives and libraries. Markings and inscriptions testify to a variety of locations where the letter was placed for safekeeping. All the same, those very markings hint at the possibility of an insecure location, one from which the letter could be pilfered and then put to sale on the market.

Fortune smiles on Francesco: Vettori's *mandato*

Vettori's *mandato*, which specified the scope and limits of his mandate abroad, charged him with two tasks. First, he must

> Go right away, as soon as you can toward Germany to find his Majesty, the King of the Romans, wherever you learn he is to be found. Having arrived, seek out an audience with him. Once you have gone through the proper ceremonies and presented him with letters of credence from our most excellent *Signori*, quickly make him understand that we sent you to his Majesty because news of his journey to Italy reached this city. And as [his] devoted

children we took delight in it and are hoping the best for it, as befits such a great Prince. Moreover, let him know that through you we want him to understand that we dispatched you as swiftly as possible in order to request with all our soul that other ambassadors of ours might soon meet and honor him in a favorable location, as is proper for us to do. Moreover, we would like to offer him all that will be beneficial to him for his journey, as the afore-mentioned ambassadors will make clearer, as soon as his Majesty persists in this purpose. In explaining all these things, use those words and terms that seem most appropriate to you without altering the effect.[1]

In presenting Vettori's second task, the tone of the *mandato* becomes more anxious:

In your lodgings near his Majesty, diligently observe everything—whether or not he really means to come, and by what means, and with what people, and by means of what route, and what customs they follow, and with what provisions they actually travel—in order to give us the most accurate information possible. Indeed, this must be your greatest concern, because this is what matters now.

The letter finishes with the Ten setting firm limits to Vettori's scope of action:

And above all, we remind you that as regards any plan [you may discover] or request that should be made of you [regarding Florence], keep things vague, referring to the need to inform us of everything and to the arrival of new ambassadors.[2]

These limits were typical of the type of office to which Vettori had been appointed, that of a *mandatorio*, which stood far below ambassador. A *mandatorio* had less latitude for negotiation and ordinarily could not commit to agreements or sign treaties.[3] Undoubtedly the delicacy of the mission had convinced the Ten that the diplomat should have as little license as possible in order to insure total control of the outcome (Figure 6.1).

Vettori was only thirty-three at the time of his appointment, but already had some important experience in government. He came from a wealthy family that was part of the Florentine magnate class, the *ottimati*. The Vettori family's wealth derived from nearly a century of involvement in the wool trade. Francesco's father was a soldier and was entrusted with important assignments and offices under both the Medici and the Republic.[4] When his father died in office in 1495, the Ten appointed Francesco to complete his term as Captain of Pistoia. In 1504 Soderini appointed him to the *Dodici Buoniuomini* ("The Twelve Good Men") and then to the *Otto di Guardia* ("The Eight of the Guard"), the council in charge of Florence's police force. In 1505 he held the office of *Podestà* in Castiglione Aretino, not far from Arezzo.[5] All in all, in 1507 Francesco could be considered a trustworthy mag-nate with some valuable political experience.

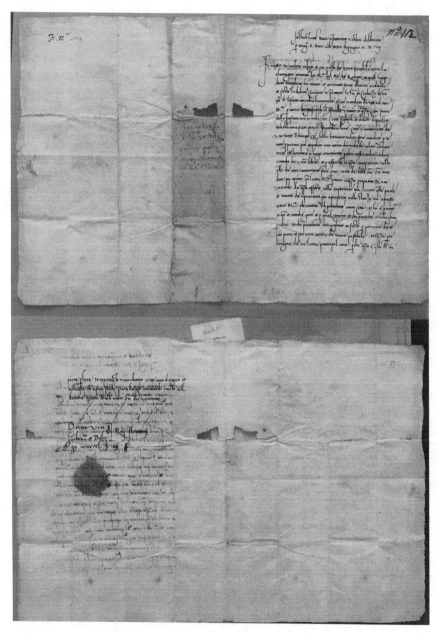

FIGURE 6.1 The *mandato* dispatched to Francesco Vettori on June 25, 1507. "Letter, June 25, 1507, Florence," MS, Misc 0076. Courtesy of Department of Special Collections, Stanford University Libraries

Vettori's mission amounted to an insurance policy on the part of Florence, in the event their longstanding alliance with France should fail them. Five years earlier, in 1502, two ambassadors from the court of the Holy Roman Emperor, Maximilian I, arrived and informed the Florentines that the emperor was planning to depart on crusade after traveling to Rome for his coronation.[6] They then presented the Florentine government with Maximilian's "request" for financial support for his project. Such a plan implied that he would be traversing Italy with a vast army, a fact that would force the Florentines to decide between Maximilian I and his main rival in Italy, Louis XII of France. Indeed, Maximilian I had already once descended into Italy in 1496, precisely to break Florence's pact with France. The emperor failed at that time, but the presence of his ambassadors in Florence in 1502 sent a clear message that he had not given up hopes of fracturing the alliance between Florence and France.[7]

Vettori's *mandato* came five years later in 1507 because Maximilian I found himself delayed by several circumstances, including a war for control of Bavaria that ended late in 1505. Maximilian's decision in October of 1506 to call the Diet of Constance (April 30–July 26, 1507) only intensified fears in the Republic.[8] When further rumors reached Florence in the summer of 1507 that the emperor had expanded his plans from merely being crowned in Rome to also restoring lands to the Church and integrating Italy into the empire once again, debate began in the Republic as to whom should be sent to treat with the emperor.[9] Vettori's *mandato* records the outcome of that debate.

The debate pitted Soderini and his candidate, Machiavelli, against magnates who wanted one of their own to consult with the emperor. The appointment to offices such as those of *mandatorio*, ambassador, and others had become a flashpoint between Soderini and the magnates and may help explain part of the intensity of the debate. Diplomatic embassies had slowly evolved from onerous burdens to coveted awards.[10] Before the eruption of the debate, accusations that he appointed men ill-suited for office had already surfaced against Soderini. The accusations were most likely driven by frustration over the increased difficulty for *ottomati* to complete their *cursus honorum*. Moreover, these diplomatic offices paid salaries.[11] Hence in the debate over whom to send to Maximilian I, more than qualifications and honor were at stake—money was as well.

These issues likely contributed to Machiavelli's rejection. Even if Machiavelli served as secretary of the Ten, he did not belong to the magnate class. Further, he had become a favorite of Piero Soderini, who had fallen out of favor with many magnates by 1507. These two factors, combined with his well-known devotion to the alliance with France, made Machiavelli a particularly unsavory candidate for the *ottomati*, especially for the newly formed pro-German bloc. Soderini had briefly won Machiavelli's appointment on June 19, but debate erupted again and Soderini surrendered to the will of the magnates. Vettori's *mandato* is dated June 25. The five-day debate must have been exceptionally intense, with Vettori emerging as the compromise candidate.[12]

Soderini's struggle with the magnates over whether to send Machiavelli has its roots in the history of the office he held, unique in Florentine history: Soderini served as the one and only "Standardbearer of Justice for Life." Florentines intentionally established the office in imitation of the Venetian Doge. The restructuring of Florence's government happened as a result of the upheavals that followed the execution of Girolamo Savonarola in 1498, though that restructuring belonged to a longer process that began with the invasion of Charles VIII of France and the ouster of Piero de' Medici in 1494.

Piero's expulsion initiated a period marked by radical governmental reforms that would culminate in Soderini's appointment as Standardbearer of Justice for Life. The invasion of Charles and the expulsion of Piero de' Medici seemed to confirm Savonarola's prophecies that God would establish a new age through his servant, King Charles VIII of France. Largely by means of his followers' initiatives, Florentine government underwent a number of modifications inspired by Savonarola's prescriptions, the most radical of which was the creation of a new Great Council.[13] Contemporary chroniclers generally agree that the Great Council came about because of popular pressure upon Florentine elites to open up the government to greater representation among the non-elite classes.[14] After its establishment in late December 1494, the Great Council alone possessed the power to pass legislation. The magnates saw the Great Council as being in the hands of non-elites—the *popolo*—and resented it.[15]

After Savonarola's execution, the tensions between the *popolo* and magnates only intensified, with the *popolo* taking aim at the precursor to the council that drafted Vettori's *mandato*, the *Dieci di balìa* (Ten of Authority and Power). For at least two centuries, Florence had granted *balìa* (extraordinary authority and power) to councils like the Ten.[16] Generally, such councils were temporary, established under specific circumstances, and assigned definitive goals.[17] Nevertheless, by the turn of the sixteenth century, the Ten had become an almost permanent fixture of Florentine government, wielding the power to declare war, make peace, hire soldiers, appoint military commissioners and enter into alliances. Members of the *popolo* believed that the Ten had conspired to prolong war, in order to burden the *popolo* with heavy taxes and shake faith in the abilities of the Great Council to govern Florence.[18] For more than a year, the Great Council refused to approve candidates to sit on the Ten. Finally in September 1500, the magnates and *popolo* came to an agreement, but one that stripped the Ten of all real power, a fact driven home by the change in title from the *Dieci di balìa* (Ten of Authority and Power), to the *Dieci di libertà* (Ten of Liberty).[19] Not two years later, Piero Soderini would reverse that change as Standardbearer of Justice for Life.

Soderini's appointment to that office took place in 1502 because of an apocryphal story related about Savonarola. 1502 was an arduous year for Florence as it grappled with the ongoing rebellion of Pisa and the revolt of Arezzo. Moreover, in 1501 Cesare Borgia (1475–1507) had demanded that Florence reestablish Medici rule or face his wrath and in 1502 he was again on Florentine borders.

These crises paralyzed the Great Council and rendered it incapable of raising funds for continued military action.[20] At the heart of the matter lay the refusal of many magnates to continue to lend money to the Republic or even participate in government because of the Great Council's adoption of a policy that eliminated payments of interest to the regime' creditors for the war on Pisa.[21] The gridlock that ensued in the Great Council forced a discussion about a rather ambiguous suggestion that Savonarola had made years before: that Florence reform its government in the image of Venice.[22] Although Savonarola had never advocated a specific institutional form, in 1502 champions for the establishment of a Doge of Florence succeeded in convincing Savonarola's followers—the *Piagnoni* or *Frateschi*—that their late leader had indeed intended just such a reform.[23] This move inaugurated one of the most radical innovations of Florentine government in its history. In September 1502, the Great Council established a new figure, the Standardbearer of Justice for Life.[24]

Soderini's magnate origins, governmental experience and careful political positioning all influenced his election as Standardbearer of Justice for Life. He held several eminent and powerful positions in Florentine government, including—among numerous others—sitting on the Ten and the *Signoria*, the supreme executive council of Florence. He had also served as the Florentine ambassador to the Duke of Savoy, the Holy Roman Emperor, and the King of France. Additionally, Soderini had carefully kept his distance from the Mediceans and the *Piagnoni* and was without children—a crucial element in order to assure that the Standardbearer of Justice for Life would not mutate into a dynastic prince. All these factors converged to make Soderini appear to be the perfect candidate for the new position.[25]

Thus, in 1507 when Soderini presented Machiavelli as his candidate to parley with Maximilian I, the debate morphed into one as much about Soderini's leadership as about the embassy, and offers a glimpse of how contested the Standardbearer's position had become after five years. Soderini needed to reaffirm his authority because of the novelty of his office and continued resistance from a growing bloc of magnates. Ever since the execution of Savonarola, a number of magnates had aspired to wrest control of Florentine government from the Great Council through the establishment of a smaller, aristocratic senate that would control finances and foreign policy.[26] Upon accession to his new office, Soderini knew many magnates expected control of Florentine government to be entrusted to them.[27] With this in mind, he not only restored to the Ten all the powers the Great Council had stripped away in 1500—including *balìa*—but he also entrusted to it the day-to-day operation of the government, effectively replacing the *Signoria*.[28] The signature on Vettori's *mandato* reads the *Dieci di libertà e balìa* (The Ten of Liberty, Authority and Power) because of changes introduced into Florentine government by Soderini, designed to placate the magnates.

Nevertheless, Soderini retained a non-magnate as secretary of the Ten, Machiavelli. During the fifteenth century, in every type of government—republic, oligarchy, monarchy—there was a marked growth in the authority of the chancery, combined with its ever-greater submission to the ruling power. Hence, though the Ten was composed of magnates, Soderini's effective control over Florence passed through its chancery and, therefore, through Machiavelli. Rejection of Machiavelli for the embassy to Maximilian I was tantamount to a repudiation of Soderini's rule.

In 1509, Vettori returned from his embassy to Maximilian I commanding the respect and admiration of his peers but support for Soderini had only continued to erode. In 1512, four young Florentine magnates confronted Soderini and forcibly removed him from office. They brought him to the house of Francesco Vettori, who proceeded to intercede with the *Signoria*, insisting they legally depose Soderini and allow him to go into exile. Vettori likely saved Soderini's life and, in Vettori's estimation, fell afoul of both the Medici and Republican factions. Soderini's failure to secure Machiavelli's nomination as *mandatorio* to Maximilian I's court finished well for the Standardbearer of Justice, once it became clear the only way his tenure would be *for life* is if it ended with his premature death. Vettori stepped in to prevent that outcome.[29]

Mission impossible: Francesco Vettori's fortunes in Germany

The mission entrusted to Francesco Vettori was anything but simple and straightforward and the shifting priorities of that mission, coupled with the continuous amplification of his authority in the German court, serve as a good example of the essentially fluid nature of Renaissance diplomacy.[30] The decision to appoint Vettori a *mandatorio* undoubtedly sprang from the necessity of preserving the goodwill of Louis XII of France. Had the Republic sent an ambassador to Maximilian, it could very well have been interpreted as a sign of the intention to break with the French and forge a new alliance with the empire. Indeed, precisely to prevent this misunderstanding, the Florentines instructed their ambassador to Louis XII to reassure the king that Vettori's embassy to Maximilian I did not mean they were abandoning their venerable alliance with France.[31] Moreover, the Ten specified that Vettori's *mandato* would be identical to that of the previous *mandatorio* to Maximilian, Bernardo Ricci.[32] The Republic was acting with supreme caution, as it sought to navigate the tricky waters between its ancient allegiance to France and the real possibility of war with the Holy Roman Empire.

Given the enduring nature of the alliance with France and the primacy given it by Soderini (ex-ambassador to France), Vettori found himself in an exceptionally challenging position at Maximilian I's court and one that greatly hindered him in fulfilling his mission. That mission implied the basic duties expected of any Renaissance diplomat—representation, negotiation and information gathering—but the Florentine alliance with France hobbled Vettori from the outset in his attempt to adequately fulfill those duties.[33] Indeed, Vettori's letters to the Ten complain of the constant distrust he met at Maximilian I's court.[34] In turn, these circumstances forced the Florentine government to continuously discuss and debate how much authority Vettori should be given to engage the emperor.

The details of Vettori's particular embassy reveal how the importance assigned to the diverse responsibilities associated with a diplomatic mission could wax or wane, depending upon specific circumstances. His *mandato* specifically commanded Vettori to avoid negotiation by "keeping things vague." While Vettori carried letters of credence from the Republic, as a *mandatorio* he could not fully represent it. Further, the Ten's instruction to the French ambassador to reassure Louis XII about Vettori's presence at Maximilian I's court demonstrates that, in this case, the lowest level of representation served Florence best. Finally, the Ten specified to Vettori that his "principal concern" must be to gather information.

Though the relevant importance of diplomatic responsibilities might shift over the course of an embassy, Vettori's mission also illustrates that those responsibilities were always intimately related. By appointing Vettori as a *mandatorio* and, further, sending him alone, information gathering became a difficult task to accomplish. Unlike an ambassador, a *mandatorio* could not seek a regular audience with the emperor without a compelling reason. Vettori spoke no German. Although Latin served as the *lingua franca* at court, establishing relationships with any local informants became nearly impossible. Additionally, the Republic's decades-long pro-French stance had alienated it from most other Italian powers, so that Vettori found he could not easily trust the little information that might be gleaned from other Italian ambassadors.[35]

After a month, the Ten began to appreciate the virtual impossibility of acquiring any valuable information without expanding Vettori's mandate. Though Vettori never held any other title than *mandatorio*, over the course of his German mission the Ten gradually invested him with authority that seemed ambassadorial in all but name. In a letter dated July 31, 1507, the Ten instructed Vettori to raise the issues brought to their attention by the emperor's ambassadors in 1502, when the Florentines were first made aware of his plans to travel to Italy. The emperor immediately responded positively, instructing his ambassador in Rome to begin discussing the issue with Florentine ambassadors there. Maximilian I increased the demand of 40,000 ducats he had made in 1502 to 50,000. That decision suddenly transformed Vettori's mission into one where representation and negotiation took center stage.

Indeed, on November 30, Vettori composed a letter which was read aloud to the Ten and that brought about a fateful decision on their part. Vettori wrote of his encounter with Maximilian's personal secretary and ambassador, Mathias Lang (1468–1540). He wrote, "After having examined your letters, I told him that in his request in the name of His Majesty you saw three difficulties." The first of these, Vettori explained to Lang, was the threat of war. Loaning such a vast amount of money to Maximilian would mean effectively declaring Florence the enemy of the King of France, who would undoubtedly despoil the many Florentine merchants in France of their property and instruct his allies—Venice, Lucca and Pisa—to declare war on Florence, a war that would only hinder Maximilian I's plan to make his descent into Italy.[36] Next, Vettori noted to Lang that after four years of continuous war, Florence could not even amass 40,000 ducats, let alone 50,000. Finally, he had communicated to Lang that

> the third difficulty (a great embarrassment to you) is that the city has little
> income, almost nothing, and that if it were to pay this money, it would
> have to extract it from all the citizens, each of whom should pay his share
> according to his wealth. But to do so is impossible, especially since the
> Emperor wants this money as a mere beginning of his activity, without
> wanting to promise anything.

Indeed, highlighting the contrast between his mandate and actual duties, Vettori
explained that although he thought it may have been opportune to have placed
on the table the question of Pisa (which in 1507 still proclaimed its independence from Florence), he decided against it, since "you wrote to me to stick to
generalities."[37]

The end of Vettori's letter provoked strong reactions and an important response:

> But to respectfully tell you my thoughts, the motives for your delay in
> coming to a resolution are good. Delaying sometimes helps. Yet some-
> times it may also provoke the opposite effect, if you run out of time
> before concluding something. Our city can well remember it, for she has
> done it before to her great disadvantage.[38]

After his letter had been read, debate broke out. Some officials wanted to send
ambassadors to substitute Vettori; others still feared offending Louis XII; still others
favored granting Vettori a new mandate, officially granting him the authority to
negotiate with the emperor. In the end the Ten decided to send a new, more specific *mandato*, while continuing to withhold from Vettori the power to conclude
any agreement.[39] And in a nod to Soderini, the Republic decided to send the secretary of the Ten, Machiavelli, to deliver these new instructions.

Machiavelli arrived in December 1507 and he and Vettori eventually became
fast friends.[40] Upon delivery of the instructions, Machiavelli wrote to the Ten
about his plans to return, but Vettori insisted he remain. Desperate to gather
more information, Vettori welcomed the opportunity of having a sharp, experienced diplomat by his side to act as an informant, secretary and analyst.[41]

Between the two, Vettori proved the more skeptical about Maximilian's chances
of becoming a real threat to Florence. In the beginning, Vettori had written with
alarm about the potential threat of imminent invasion. In early February both men
were sure that Maximilian's decision to launch a first assault on Venice would be
devastating to Italy. But after the emperor's humiliation at the hands of the Venetians in February 1508, while Machiavelli continued to tout the threat of invasion,
Vettori began to pepper his correspondence with the Ten with cynical remarks
expressing his misgivings about Maximilian's ability to do any real harm.[42]

Indeed, Maximilian I's support at the Diet of Constance waxed and waned over
the months of its duration. The emperor convened the Diet in October 1506, after
receiving word of the death of his son, Philip I (1478–1506). Philip had inherited
Burgundy and the Low Countries from his mother and Maximilian I feared losing

control of Philip's territories that bordered upon France. He judged Italy to be the best place in which to challenge Louis XII and called the Diet in order to garner support for the long-planned Italian campaign.[43] Initially, the majority of princes, realms and cities promised generous assistance for the Italian campaign, with even the Swiss cantons committing troops for the force that was to gather in October 1507.[44] Nevertheless, troops arrived late and in numbers vastly lower than expected, as did the money pledged for the venture.[45] The emperor's army was not only defeated by the Venetian and French forces in February 1508, but the Venetians captured a considerable piece of imperial territory in Friuli and the Tyrol. This humiliating campaign effectively ended Maximilian I's grand designs in Italy, proving Vettori's assessment of the situation more accurate than that of his comrade Machiavelli.

The variegations of Vettori's mission to Germany demonstrate the essentially malleable nature of Renaissance diplomacy and how little titles and offices mattered on the ground. Though the Ten appointed Vettori a *mandatorio*, they simultaneously assigned him a complicated and arduous task: to convince the Emperor Maximilian I that Florence was joyful at the news of his planned trip to Italy and ready to support him, but without committing the Republic to anything concrete, while gathering as much information as possible about how the planned campaign was proceeding. Notwithstanding the difficulties and limitations associated with the embassy, Vettori served as Florence's most important representative to Maximilian I, negotiating with him and gathering critical information for the Republic in a moment of crisis. When Vettori finally returned to Florence in March 1509, he re-entered his city recognized as a faithful, clever and successful Florentine official. His career was only beginning. For the rest of his life Vettori would serve the Republic and then the Medici, most often as an ambassador. He had exceeded expectations in fulfilling the terms of this initial mission.

Confronting fortune: Vettori, Machiavelli and the *Viaggio in Alemagna*

Vettori's embassy inspired him to pen a short piece of literature, the *Viaggio in Alemagna (Journey to Germany)*. Salacious, comical and often very dark, Vettori's *Viaggio* is a highly provocative work. It follows the thirty-three-year-old Vettori on his journey through Italy to Constance. For the most part eschewing the details of his diplomatic mission, the *Viaggio* occupies itself with the stories narrated by Vettori's hosts or his fellow travelers in various hostels and inns. Indeed, part diary and part novella, the *Viaggio* resists classification.[46] As a travel diary of Vettori's 1507 journey from Florence to Germany, it has proven to be quite accurate.[47] Additionally, it provides a type of "narrative frame" that creates a space in which the primary action takes place.[48] Vettori's hosts or his fellow travelers convey that action over the course of twenty-one novellas. The tales recounted by Vettori's storytellers are reminiscent of those found in Boccaccio's *Decameron*, though Vettori replaced a stable companionship with a fluid and seemingly random set of narrators.[49] The *Viaggio in*

Alemagna established Vettori as a gifted and ingenious author of a distinctive kind of travel writing that emerged from the journey he was instructed to take on behalf of the Florentine government in their 1507 letter.

Vettori claimed that the reason he composed the *Viaggio* was for both the pleasure he took in writing it and the pleasure he hoped to grant his audience in reading it. At a certain point in the *Viaggio*, he claims his brother, "according to whose own judgement is a learned man," found his work and told him he was astounded that "I should waste time writing such frivolous things—novellas and fables—and that after having read it, he regretted having wasted his time doing so. He did not criticize the type of writing but its material." Vettori responds that "I had written it in order to satisfy myself and not him."[50] And later he comments, "I chose such material because it pleased me."[51] Pleasure in reading and writing sufficed as a *raison d'être* for the Viaggio in Vettori's view.

Indeed, pleasure served an important place in Vettori's vision of human nature, a vision that some critics have seen as darkly pessimistic. Indeed, the *Viaggio* finishes with a disquisition on pleasure as the motor force behind all human action. On the last evening of the *Viaggio*, Vettori, two traveling companions and their retinue cannot sleep. Some of the party begin to play cards and one of his companions laments the practice of gambling. Vettori's other companion responds to his denunciation and finishes the *Viaggio*, remarking,

> I take it for granted that everything men do in this world, they do for pleasure. And this is demonstrated every day by experience, starting with those who live in fear of God and who precisely observe our religion. Clearly they have no other reason than pleasure because they persuade themselves—as is the truth—that having left the body, the soul will enjoy its triumph in the heavenly realm and taste all of the blessedness and happiness that one can imagine and that it will be reunited with the body in order to always be at ease and in gladness. [And it is the same for] those who live according to the world—those who place their pleasure in ambition, in eating, in sex, in amassing money, in adorning their family with good habits.

For Vettori, the pursuit of pleasure encourages human beings to engage what he considered to be their primary activity, the attempt to deceive one another:

> I thought to myself in how many ways, with what cleverness, with how many different arts, with how much industry will a man devise to deceive another. And because of this variety the world is more beautiful: the brain of this one sharpens itself to find new skill in defrauding and the brain of the other sharpens itself to guard against being defrauded. And indeed the entire world is swindling, starting with religious people, then going to jurists, then to doctors, astrologers, secular princes, and in all those who surround them, in all arts and exercises, and day by day things get finer and sharper.[52]

Vettori's views here echo those he expressed to his brother, Paolo, in a letter dated May 15, 1512, where he wrote, "the entire world is swindling."[53] The *Viaggio* and this letter indicate that Vettori espoused a rather negative view of human motivation and action, and sought to explore these issues in different kinds of writing, including his correspondence. Vettori's experience during the embassy to Maximilian's court had shaped his worldview. At the same time, the *Viaggio*, written sometime after 1513, was also informed by his experience of the final years of Soderini's tenure (1509–12), the victorious return of the Medici (1512) and his subsequent assignment as ambassador to Rome (1513–15).[54]

The 1507 *mandato* vaulted Vettori into social circles in which European powers interacted with one another, seeking to protect and advance their interests. By the time Vettori began the *Viaggio*, he had the opportunity to observe and attempt to navigate the machinations of Maximilian I, Louis XII, Pope Julius II, the rebellious French clergy at the Council of Pisa and the Medici pope, Leo X. He likely based his particularly damning description of Cardinal William Biçonnet in Book IV of the *Viaggio* upon Cardinal Saint-Malo, whom Vettori presumably met at the Council of Pisa (1511–12).[55] Encounters with figures such as Saint-Malo or Mattias Lang in the court of Maximilian I took place regularly in the circles in which Vettori moved evermore, beginning in 1507. Indeed, by the time he composed the *Viaggio*, living within the world of Renaissance diplomacy must have made swindling and the possibility of being swindled Vettori's quotidian concern for years.

Vettori's famous correspondence with his friend and companion on the embassy to Germany, Machiavelli, provides another source for understanding the evolution of his perspective. Machiavelli initiated their correspondence immediately after being released from prison in the hopes that Vettori might help him engineer a reconciliation with the Medici through Pope Leo X (Giovanni di Lorenzo de' Medici, 1475–1521, r. 1513–21). John Najemy has closely analyzed the two-year correspondence between Machiavelli and Vettori and argued that Vettori played a crucial role in the development of Machiavelli's in dialogue with his friend Vettori.[56] It seems plausible to posit the same for Vettori: the ideas he expressed in the *Viaggio* may have equally been influenced by the dialogue with Machiavelli.

Much of the correspondence between Machiavelli and Vettori dealt with how to face the vicissitudes of fortune, especially vis-à-vis political events. In fact, in a now renowned letter, dated December 10, 1513, Machiavelli shared the news of having composed *The Prince*. For the most part, Machiavelli touted the power of reason and discourse as weapons against Fortune. But Vettori's expressed a deep reserve about the efficacy of such weapons. Indeed, in one of his last letters Vettori explains to Machiavelli that, in the end, the Fates control all human action.[57]

Vettori's skepticism regarding the powers of human reason, expressed in his correspondence with Machiavelli, may have developed by means of his personal experience as a diplomat. In his correspondence with Florence during the first months of his mission, Vettori expressed his certainty about Maximilian's imminent invasion.[58] As his mission went on, he lost that certainty and became more doubtful about the emperor's plans. Vettori reported a similar experience to Machiavelli, regarding the election of Giovanni di Lorenzo de' Medici as Pope Leo X. Though he had personally visited with and spoken to each voting cardinal, still he was utterly blindsided by the Medici's election to the papal throne.[59] The realization of how misguided was his initial certainty about Maximilian I and Cardinal de' Medici, coupled with his experience in dealing with figures such as Matthias Lang and a host of other officials and diplomats in secular and papal courts, undoubtedly influenced the vision of human nature he expressed in the *Viaggio*.

Between the years of his embassy to Maximilian I through those in which he served as ambassador to Leo X's papal court, Vettori appears to have become increasingly suspicious of reason's capabilities to adequately anticipate and plan for events. Reason principally served to advance one's interests at any cost and protect oneself from the duplicity of others who sought the same for themselves. His years as a diplomat had led Vettori to adopt a fairly cynical view of human nature. He proclaimed that view in correspondence, especially with Machiavelli, and expressed it as literary art in his *Viaggio in Alemagna*. The career upon which the *mandato* of 1507 launched Francesco Vettori became a catalyst for action, experience and thoughtful reflection. And it produced more correspondence; indeed some of the most famous letters of the Italian Renaissance.

Epilogue: the afterlife of a renaissance letter

Stanford University's Special Collections now houses the letter, across a continent and an ocean from where it was composed. Its own itinerary brings us into the world of antiquarians and collectors, estates and auctions, archives and *fondi*. That itinerary cannot be fully reconstructed and certain questions still remain unanswered—including those stemming from the possibility a theft along the way—but tracing the letter's journey nonetheless reveals how its own history continued, long after Francesco Vettori's had ended.

The materiality of the letter offers clues as to its journey. Creases and perforations, notes and markings, numerals and letters: all hint at travel and resting places along the way. In the upper left-hand corner of 2v the inscription "F. IIa," taken together with a matching inscription in the right-hand corner of 1r, "n÷112," attests to the fact that the letter was placed in an archive, its place being recorded as the 112th document in *filza* IIa (Figure 6.2). A note at the center of the right-hand side of 2v proclaims to the reader the nature of the epistle, "Instrutione a Fr.co Vettori quando andò nella Alemagna al Re de Romani"

FIGURE 6.2 Detail of archival inscriptions on Vettori's *mandato*, indicating *filze* IIa, n. 112. "Letter, June 25, 1507, Florence," MS, Misc 0076. Courtesy of Department of Special Collections, Stanford University Libraries

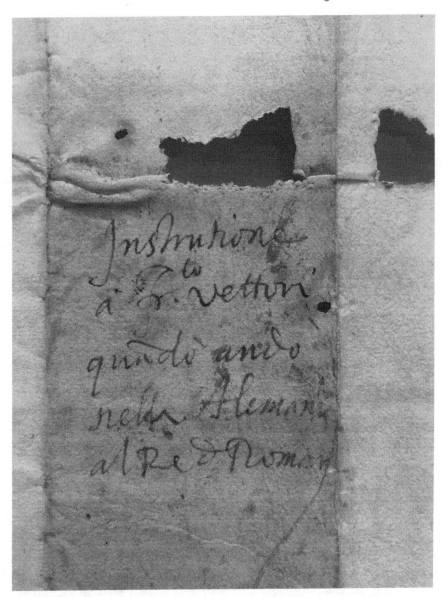

FIGURE 6.3 Detail of archival inscription on Vettori's *mandato*: "Instrutione a F.co Vettori quando andò nella Alemagna al Re de Romani" ("Instruction given to Francesco Vettori when he went to the King of the Romans in Germany"). "Letter, June 25, 1507, Florence," MS, Misc 0076. Courtesy of Department of Special Collections, Stanford University Libraries

("Instructions to Francesco Vettori when he went to Germany to the King of the Romans") (Figure 6.3). Hence, someone noted what Vettori's letter was and then deposited it in a place for safekeeping, most probably an archive in Italy.

The letter's journey from Italy to Stanford can be partially reconstructed starting from a document belonging to the Manuscript Division of the Stanford Libraries. It records that the university acquired Vettori's 1507 letter from Alan G. Thomas in July of 1978. According to an obituary published in the newspaper *The Independent*, Thomas (1911–92) "bought most notably at the Phillipps manuscript sales of 1965–77."[60] Those sales put up for auction documents collected by Sir Thomas Phillipps (1780–1862), who had amassed a collection of books and documents that included more than 60,000 manuscripts by the end of his life.[61] The Sotheby's sales of 1965–77 offered at auction the considerable final remnant of Phillipps' collection.[62] Phillipps came into possession of Vettori's documents in 1836, when he purchased them at auction from the estate of Richard Herber (1774–1833). Herber, in turn, had acquired them from Elector Palatine Karl Theodor (1724–99), who had purchased the entirety of the Vettori family archive in 1758.[63]

Hence, a plausible itinerary of the 1507 letter to Francesco begins to take shape. Sometime after his death in 1539, Vettori's letter passed into the hands of his descendants, who gathered it together with other books, manuscripts and documents, as they slowly amassed a private archive over the next two centuries. In 1758, the letter traveled to Munich, where it found its home in the library of Elector Palatine Karl Theodor until the early nineteenth century. At some point in the early 1800s, the missive was brought to England by Richard Herber and then purchased by Thomas Phillipps in 1836. The letter made up part of the Phillipps Collection until it was acquired by Alan Thomas either in 1968 or 1972. In 1978, the missive made its final journey to its home in Stanford University's Special Collections.

Yet certain pieces of evidence seem to challenge this reconstruction. First, the Sotheby's catalogues of the Phillipps collection auctions make no reference to the 1507 letter to Vettori.[64] Next, the inscriptions in the corners of folios 1r and 2v (see Figure 6.2) also present difficulties to the hypothesis that the 1507 missive came to Stanford via the Phillipps collection. Those inscriptions served to catalogue the letter, noting its place in *filza* IIa as document n. 112. An examination of a few hundred letters to Francesco Vettori from the Phillipps collection that were claimed by the Italian state confirm that none of them have similar inscriptions to those found on the 1507 missive.[65]

Thus, an alternative hypothesis presents itself. The 1507 missive to Francesco Vettori made its way into another archive, possibly a state archive.[66] In 1569 and 1570, Cosimo I (1519–74) ordered all documents relative to the *stato vecchio* (old state) be turned over for the creation of a new archive.[67] Then, in 1778, new legislation under Grand Duke Peter Leopold established the Diplomatic Archive of Florence, by which documents were collected from suppressed religious organizations, certain magistrates and some family archives.[68] In either of these moments, the 1507 letter to Francesco Vettori might have made it to a state archive, where it lay as document no. 112 in *filza* IIa, until it was pilfered and made its way to the market. Until an

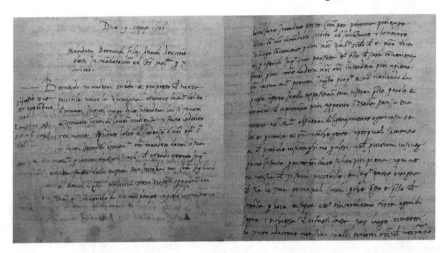

FIGURE 6.4 *Mandato* dispatched to Bernardo de Ricci on September 9, 1506, of which Francesco's *mandato* is an exact copy. Archivio di Stato di Firenze, *Signori, Missive, Legazioni e Communicazioni*, 26, f. 157r and 157v. Courtesy of the Ministero per i Beni e le Attività Culturali, Archivio di Stato di Firenze

examination of the Vettori manuscripts held in the British Library can be carried out, the possibility Vettori's letter was stolen from an Italian archive cannot be ruled out.

One final note: research completed in the Florentine archives yielded an interesting fact regarding the 1507 missive's origin. As noted by Rosemary Jones, Francesco received the same mandate as Bernardo de Ricci a year earlier.[69] In seeking out Bernardo's *mandato* in the Florentine archives, the origins of Francesco's letter were revealed: the 1507 letter to Francesco Vettori is an exact copy of the letter sent to Bernardo in September 1506 (Figure 6.4). The text of the letter appears just after the sentence quoted by Jones. It would seem that, since Vettori had received the same *mandato*, the Florentine chancery decided to copy, word for word, Bernardo's *instructione*. It is a reminder of how Renaissance bureaucracies produced letters, including formulaic requests to different people to perform certain tasks necessary to the operations of state.

***

Though it comes to fewer than three hundred words, the *mandato* drafted by the *Dieci di libertà e balìa* to Francesco Vettori in 1507 carries within its few lines, its folds and creases—its very materiality—a tremendously rich history. The letter acts as a locus where the Italian Wars intersect with extraordinary governmental reforms in Florence, where the friendship between two Renaissance humanists and a number of their writings have their origins, and where inscriptions and markings attest to the places where in succeeding centuries the letter found its home.

Appendix

Instructione data a Francesco Vectori deliberata per e' magnifici signori Dieci ad xxv di giugno m. d. vii

Francesco tu andrai subito et piu presto ché ti sara possibile verso la Alamagna a trovare la Maestà del Re de Romani, in quel luogo, dove intenderai lui si trovi, et arrivato farai d'havere audienza et facte le debite cerimonie et presentate le lettere di credenza de' nostri excelsi Signori li farai intendere brevemente essere mandato da noi ad sua Maestà per causa di significarli che essendo venuto in questa città fama della passata sua in Italia, noi come figliuoli et devoti di quella ne habbiamo preso piacere, sperandone bene, come e, conveniente da uno tanto Principe et lielho haviamo voluto fare intendere per te, come per persona piú expedita cum animo dimandarlo subito ad incontrare et honorare in luogo conveniente per altri nostri ambasciadori secondo che è nostro debito, et per offerirli in questa sua passata tucto quello che sarà conveniente farsi per noi, come da decti nostri ambasciadori intenderà più apieno, quando la sua Maestà perseveri in questo proposito et non variando da questo effecto, nella expositione tua userai quelle parole et termini che ti parranno più a proposito. Nella stanza tua apresso a sua Maestà observerai diligentemente omni cosa: se lei è per venire et quando et cum che gente et per qual camino, et che pratiche vi si tenghino per altri; et che provisioni vi si veghino in facto per poterzene dare più piena et più vera notitia che ti sarà possibile: et in questa parte bisogna che sia la tua principal cura, perche questo e, quello che im/porta per hora et soprattutto ti ricordiamo circa omni disegno et richiesta che ti fussi facta stare largo rimettendo il tucto al darcene notitia et alli nuovi oratori che verranno.

Decem viri Libertatis et baliẹ Reipublicẹ Florentinae. Ego Marcellus Virgilius scripsi.

***

Instructions given to Francesco Vettori, deliberated by the magnificent lords of the Ten on June 25, 1507.

Go right away, as soon as you can toward Germany to find his Majesty, the King of the Romans, wherever you learn he is to be found. Having arrived, seek out an audience with him. Once you have gone through the proper ceremonies and presented him with letters of credence from our most excellent *Signori*, quickly make him understand that we sent you to his Majesty because news of his journey to Italy reached this city. And as [his] devoted children we took delight in it and are hoping the best for it, as befits such a great Prince. Moreover, let him know that through you we want him to understand that we dispatched you as swiftly as possible in order to request with all our soul that other ambassadors of ours might soon meet and honor him in a favorable location, as is proper for us to do. Moreover, we would like to offer him all that will be beneficial to him for his journey, as the aforementioned ambassadors will make clearer, when his Majesty persists in this purpose. In explaining all these things, use those words and terms that seem most appropriate to you without altering the effect. In your lodgings near his Majesty, diligently observe everything—whether or not he really means to come, and by what means, and with what people, and by means of what route, and what customs they follow, and with what provisions they actually travel—in order to give us the most accurate information possible. Indeed, this must be your greatest concern, because this is what matters now. Above all we remind you that as regards any plan or request that should be made of you, keep things vague, referring to the need to inform us of everything and to the arrival of new ambassadors.

The Ten Men of Liberty, Authority, and Power of the Republic of Florence. I, Marcello Virgilio, have written this.

Notes

1 I would like to express my deep gratitude to William Connell, Marcello Simonetta, Paolo Nanni, Francesca Klein and the editors for their help and suggestions. MS Misc 0076, Special Collections, Stanford University Libraries.
2 MS Misc 0076.
3 Rosemary Devonshire Jones, *Francesco Vettori, Florentine Citizen and Medici Servant* (London: Athlone Press, 1972), 11–12, 17.
4 R.J.F. Hughes, *Francesco Vettori: His Place in Florentine Diplomacy and Politics* (London University PhD. Thesis, 1958), i–v; Devonshire Jones, *Francesco Vettori*, 1–9.
5 Devonshire Jones, *Francesco Vettori*, 15–17.
6 On Maximilian, see Hermann Wiesflecker, *Kaiser Maximilian I. Das Reich, Österreich Und Europa an Der Wende Zur Neuzeit* (Vienna: Verl. f. Geschichte u. Politik, 1971) and Heinrich Ulmann, *Kaiser Maximilian I. Auf Urkundlicher Grundlage Dargestellt* (Stuttgart: J. G. Cotta, 1884).
7 Nicolai Rubinstein, "Firenze e il problema della politica imperiale in Italia al tempo di Massimiliano I," *Archivio Storico Italiano* 116, no. 1 (417) (1958): 5–13.
8 Rubinstein, "Firenze e il problema," 18–22.
9 Rosemary Devonshire Jones, *Francesco Vettori*, 14.
10 Riccardo Fubini, "Diplomacy and government in the Italian city-states of the fifteenth century (Florence and Venice)," in *Politics and Diplomacy in Early Modern Italy: The Structure of Diplomatic Practice, 1450–1800*, ed. Daniella Frigo, trans. Adrian Belton (Cambridge, UK: Cambridge University Press, 2000). See also Paolo Margaroli, *Diplomazia e Stati Rinascimentali: Le Ambascerie Sforzesche Fino Alla Conclusione Della Lega Italica (1450–1455)* (Florence: La Nuova Italia Editrice, 1992).
11 Alison Brown, *Medicean and Savonarolan Florence: The Interplay of Politics, Humanism, and Religion* (Turnhout: Brepols, 2011), 151.
12 Roslyn Pesman, "Machiavelli, Piero Soderini, and the Republic of 1494–1512," in *The Cambridge Companion to Machiavelli*, ed. John M. Najemy (Cambridge; New York: Cambridge University Press, 2010), 55.
13 On the timeliness of Savonarola's appeal, see Rudolf von Albertini, *Firenze dalla repubblica al principato storia e coscienza politica* (Turin: Einaudi, 1970), 10–19. On just how many those followers may have been and their political strength in Florence in the first years after the Medici expulsion, see Polizzotto, *The Elect Nation*, 9–17; on the Great Council, see John M. Najemy, *A History of Florence 1200–1575* (Malden, MA: Blackwell Pub, 2006), 381–90.
14 Najemy, *A History of Florence*, 381–2.
15 See, for example, Sergio Bertelli, "PETRUS SODERINUS PATRIAE PARENS," *Bibliothèque d'Humanisme et Renaissance* 31, no. 1 (1969), 95.
16 Guidi, *Lotte, pensiero*, 100–1.

144 Appendix

17 Najemy, *A History of Florence*, 128.
18 Roslyn Pesman Cooper, "L'elezione di Pier Soderini a Gonfaloniere a Vita: NOTE STORICHE," *Archivio Storico Italiano* 125, no. 2 (454) (1967): 148.
19 Sergio Bertelli, "Pier Soderini 'Vexillifer Perpeutuus Reipublicae Florentinae' 1502–1512," in *Renaissance: Studies in Honor of Hans Baron*, eds. Hans Baron, Anthony Molho, and John A. Tedeschi (Dekalb, IL: Northern Illinois University Press, 1971), 348; Najemy, *A History of Florence*, 402–3.
20 On this crisis see Bertelli, "PETRUS SODERINUS" 93–8, "Pier Soderini 'Vexillifer Perpeutuus,'" 335–47, and "Machiavelli and Soderini," *Renaissance Quarterly* 28, no. 1 (1975): 1–10; and Pesman Cooper, "L'elezione di Pier Soderini," 145–85.
21 Pesman Cooper, "L'elezione di Pier Soderini," 149–50.
22 Najemy, *A History of Florence*, 385.
23 Riccardo Fubini, "L'uscita dal sistema politico della Firenze quattrocentesca dall'istituzione del Consiglio Maggiore alla nomina del Gonfaloniere Perpetuo," in *I Ceti Dirigenti in Firenze Dal Gonfalonierato Di Giustizia a Vita All'avvento Del Ducato: Comitato Di Studi Sulla Storia Dei Ceti Dirigenti in Toscana: Atti Del 7. Convegno, Firenze, 19–20 Settembre 1997*, ed. Elisabetta Insabato (Lecce: Conte, 1999) 42.
24 Pesman Cooper, "L'elezione di Pier Soderini," 163.
25 Pesman Cooper, "L'elezione id Pier Soderini," 170–80.
26 Albertini, *Firenze*, 19; Butters, *Governors and Government*, 44–5; Fubini, "L'uscita dal sistema politico," 40; Najemy, *A History of Florence*, 408.
27 It should be noted that there is debate as to Soderini's true intentions as *Gonfaloniere a vita*. Bertelli in "PETRUS SODERINUS," "Pier Soderini 'Vexillifer Perpeutuus'" and "Machiavelli and Soderini" as well as Fubini, in "L'uscita dal sistema politico" argue that Soderini was laying the groundwork to become a Renaissance Prince. In my opinion, Pesman Cooper is more convincing in her evaluation of Soderini as dedicated to the structure of government established by the 1502 reform. See, in particular, Pesman Cooper, "Pier Soderini: Aspiring Prince or Civic Leader?" *Studies in Medieval and Renaissance History* 1 (1978): 69–126; see also Najemy, *A History of Florence*, 409.
28 Bertelli, "Pier Soderini 'Vexillifer Perpeutuus,'" 348–9 and "Machiavelli and Soderini." 14.
29 Devonshire Jones, *Francesco Vettori*, 55–66.
30 Daniella Frigo, "Introduction," in *Politics and Diplomacy*, 8.
31 Butters, *Governors and Government*, 117.
32 Devonshire Jones, *Francesco Vettori*, 17.
33 See Isabella Lazzarini, *Communication and Conflict: Italian Diplomacy in the Early Renaissance, 1350–1520* (Oxford, 2015), "Renaissance Diplomacy," in *The Italian Renaissance State*, eds. Andrea Gamberini and Isabella Lazzarini (Cambridge; New York: Cambridge University Press, 2012), and "L'informazione politico-diplomatica nell'età della Pace di Lodi: raccolta, selezione, trasmissione. Spunti di ricerca dal carteggio Milano-Mantova nella prima età Sforzesca (1450–1466)," *Nuova Rivista Storica*, LXXXIII, n. II (Maggio-Agosto, 1999): 247–80.
34 Devonshire Jones, *Francesco Vettori*, 23.
35 Devonshire Jones, *Francesco Vettori*, 21–5.
36 Louis Paulin Passy, *Un Ami de Machiavel: François Vettori: Sa Vie et Ses Oeuvres*, v. 2 (Paris: Plon-Nourrit, 1914), 302.
37 Passy, *Un Ami de Machiavel*, 303, 304.
38 Passy, *Un Ami de Machiavel*, 306.
39 Devonshire Jones, *Francesco Vettori*, 24.
40 See John Najemy, *Between Friends: Discourses of Power and Desire in the Machiavelli-Vettori Letters of 1513–1515* (Princeton, NJ: Princeton University Press, 1993).
41 These are Devonshire Jones' findings "Some Observations," 93–113.

42 Devonshire Jones, "Some Observations," 107; *Francesco Vettori*, 26.

43 Wiesflecker, *Kaiser Maximilian I*, v. 3, 354.

44 Rubinstein, "Firenze e il problema," 116, n. 1 (417) (1958), 20.

45 Rubinstein, "Firenze e Il Problema" 116, n. 2 (418) (1958), 150.

46 Ezio Raimondi, *Politica e Commedia: Dal Beroaldo Al Machiavelli* (Bologna: Il mulino, 1972), 187.

47 Vettori, *Scritti Storici*, 384.

48 Giuseppe Giacalone, Il Viaggio in Alamagna di F. Vettori e i miti del Rinascimento (Arezzo: Università di Siena, Facoltà di magistero in Arezzo, Istituto di letteratura e filologia moderna, 1982), 11.

49 Filippo Grazzini, "Per la strade di Alamagna con e senza Machiavelli: viaggio, scrittura e motivazione in Francesco Vettori," in *Compagni di viaggio*, ed. Vincenzo De Caprio (Viterbo: Settecittà, 2008), 7.

50 Vettori, *Scritti Storici*, 40.

51 Vettori, *Scritti Storici*, 60.

52 Vettori, *Scritti Storici*, 32.

53 Vettori, *Scritti Storici*, 371.

54 See Georges Ulysse, "Le Viaggio in Alamagna de Francesco Vettori." *Italies*, 1998, 44 and Jean-Marc Rivière, "Le regard du voyageur dans la formation politique du citoyen: L'exemple de Francesco Vettori," *Italies*, 2014, 74.

55 Vettori, *Scritti storici e politici*, 371.

56 In *Between Friends*, Najemy writes, "A close reading of the letters reveals that Vettori was an important *punto di riferimento* for Machiavelli, personally, politically, and intellectually. He was a source of judgment and approval that mattered a great deal, a compelling adversary in their exchanges on politics and diplomacy, and, most of all, a discerning, sympathetic, but critical reader of Machiavelli's letters," 9.

57 Najemy, 113–14, 307–9.

58 See, for example, letters dated, July 26–August 5, 2011, September and October 9 in M. Louis Passy, *Un ami de Machiavel; François Vettori, Sa vie et ses oeuvres*, v. 2 (Paris: Librairie Plon, 1914), 226–9; 239–46; 260–5.

59 Najemy, *Between Friends*, 102.

60 Hamlyn, "Obituary."

61 Alan Bell, "Phillipps, Sir Thomas, baronet (1792–1872)," in *Oxford Dictionary of National Biography*, eds. H.C.G. Matthew and Brian Harrison (Oxford: Oxford University Press, 2004), 91–3.

62 Bell, "Phillipps," 94.

63 Sotheby & Co. (London, England) and Thomas Phillipps, *Catalogue of the celebrated collection of manuscripts formed by Sir Thomas Phillipps, Bt*; New Series: Fourth Part (London: Sotheby: June 1968), 79.

64 See Sotheby & Co. (London, England) and Thomas Phillipps, *Catalogue*, New Series: Fourth Part (June 1968) and Eighth Part (July 1972).

65 These are now housed in the state archives in Florence and listed as *Acquisti e doni*, 353–5.

66 The markings appear to be from the seventeenth or possibly eighteenth century.

67 *Fonti per La Storia Degli Archivi Degli Antichi Stati Italiani*, eds Fabio Antonini, Andrea Guidi, Giacomo Giudici, Alessandro Silvestri, Filippo de Vivo (Roma: Ministero dei beni e delle attività culturali e del turismo, 2016), 26–8.

68 *Fonti per La Storia*, 43–5.

69 Signori, Missive, Legaz. e Comm., 26, fo 157r, September 9, 1506: 'Mandata Bernardi Filiii Bernardi de Ricciis electi in mandatarium ad Caesarem Maestem per x viros," ASF, quoted by Jones, *Francesco Vettori*, 17.

7

MINDING GAPS

Connecting the worlds of Erasmus and Machiavelli

William J. Connell

The charting of epistolary networks in time and space has become a practice common in early modern studies.[1] The advantages are obvious. Letter mapping makes possible the rapid visualization of intellectual communities. Major letter writers are highlighted, but also lesser-known figures who served as transit hubs in the circulation of information and ideas. Knowledge concerning the rhythms and limits of a correspondence—knowledge that historians and biographers would sometimes acquire through years of patient reading—becomes evident at a glance, available to inform sophisticated readings of the letters in a correspondence. One of the risky temptations in this sort of work, however, lies in a tendency to read an epistolary network as a substitute for a person's social and intellectual network. Letters appear to tell so much about their writers and their addressees that they often crowd out other evidence. And the mapping of letters—according to person addressed, places to and from, and date written—albeit extremely useful, through a somewhat artificial process of abstraction and reification, may have the effect of limiting our understanding of a person's social and intellectual world.

Particularly useful then, both because they remind us that epistolary evidence has boundaries and because they spur us to look at other sources, are the chronological gaps in a surviving correspondence. A person who at other times wrote letters with a certain frequency may have slacked off during a certain period for personal reasons. Letters that were actually written may simply be lost to us owing to any number of causes, some of them immediate to a letter's sender and recipient, some instead related to the circumstances of collection and archiving. Where such gaps exist, the historian or biographer not unreasonably attempts to fill them by extrapolating from the letters that do survive, by gleaning information from literary texts (especially their prefaces), and by diving into the notarial, judicial, fiscal, and commercial archives that are so extensive from the early modern period, many, perhaps most of them, still inadequately explored. And the information from these other sources may well describe a network noticeably different from the one that results from epistolary mapping.

Gaps in two well-known correspondences figure quite prominently in my ongoing study of the intellectual world of Niccolò Machiavelli (1469–1527) and Desiderius Erasmus (1466–1536).[2] The Florentine and the Dutchman almost certainly did not exchange letters. Erasmus is not named in Machiavelli's correspondence, and while Machiavelli is named once in Erasmus' correspondence, the mention (in a letter an Italian sent to Erasmus) dates from 1535, seven years after Machiavelli's death, and the writer does not assume that Erasmus has read him but rather tries to introduce Erasmus to what Machiavelli wrote in the *Discourses*.[3] The silence has understandably contributed to a general impression, with serious consequences for scholarship, that the two men were hardly aware of each other's existence. But there are significant lacunae in the surviving correspondences of the two men, and my attempts to supplement them with other kinds of documents have turned up evidence that suggests there were real contacts between the circles of Machiavelli and Erasmus in the first decades of the sixteenth century.

The idea that Machiavelli and Erasmus stood at opposite poles—both geographic and intellectual—owes much to Augustin Renaudet's rich survey of 1954, *Érasme et l'Italie* (1954). Renaudet stressed Erasmus' lack of interest in the accomplishments and personalities of the Italian Renaissance and he emphasized differences in outlook between Machiavelli and Erasmus, frequently using the Florentine Secretary as a foil to the pious northern humanist.[4] Over the next half-century scholarship on the Renaissance and Reformation stressed these differences even further, arguing that Erasmus' brand of Christian humanism was far removed from the skeptical, secularizing approach of Machiavelli. In her carefully researched history of the reception of Erasmus in Italy, Silvana Seidel Menchi stated that hypotheses concerning the reading of Erasmus by Machiavelli were "insufficiently proven."[5] Allying herself with Renaudet against attempts by earlier scholars to show connections between Machiavelli and Erasmus, she argued that it was only during the hardening of the Reformation and Counter-Reformation, when Erasmus was falsely stigmatized as a "heretic," that for artificial and political reasons Machiavelli and Erasmus were paired in contemporary sources.

To be sure, scholars in earlier phase of Renaissance studies could point to similarities in the writings of Machiavelli and Erasmus as evidence of a general Renaissance "culture" or "spirit." Erasmus' criticisms of the Roman Catholic Church find many parallels in Machiavelli's writings. When the two authors discuss topics like princes, courtiers, tyranny, Fortune, and warfare, moreover, a dialogue of sorts seems to emerge. But in the absence of hard connections, similarities of this sort were usually attributed to indirect influence or to the *Zeitgeist*. J. H. Hexter once referred to the "loom of language and the fabric of imperative" that resulted in similarities he found in the writings of Machiavelli, Thomas More, and Claude de Seyssel—although he tried unfairly to dismiss Erasmus from the group.[6] In recent decades, however, scholarly specialization and the different religious outcomes in Protestant and Catholic Europe served inexorably to differentiate

Erasmus' "Northern" or "Christian" humanism from the more secularizing and republican thought exemplified by Machiavelli in Italy.[7] The distance was moreover enhanced in Erasmus scholarship by a generation of Catholic historians (especially after Vatican II) that wished to underline his orthodoxy,[8] and, in Machiavelli scholarship, by the followers of the biographer Roberto Ridolfi, who mistakenly portrayed Machiavelli as a writer largely self-taught, distant from the intellectual currents of contemporary Europe, rooted in Tuscan soil.[9]

Instead, during the first two decades of the sixteenth century—that protean period before Luther's break with the Church when so many ideas and institutions were in flux—there were real connections between the circles of Erasmus and Machiavelli. This was the period when Erasmus was at his most daring in his criticism of the Church and of princes; meanwhile Machiavelli was more thoroughly engaged with European intellectual discourse than scholars have imagined.

Erasmus at San Marco

The first of the two lacunae discussed here appears in the correspondence of Erasmus. The edition of Erasmus' letters by Percy Stafford Allen is one of the crown jewels of early modern scholarship.[10] The most recent count of the surviving letters totals 3,098, of which 1,958 letters were written by Erasmus and 1,140 were sent to him by others.[11] As Léon-Ernest Halkin and, later, Lisa Jardine demonstrated, letters were the preeminent way in which Erasmus promoted himself to sixteenth-century readers.[12] The majority of these letters were kept in copy by Erasmus and published by himself, often with editorial changes. In 1501 he wrote to Jacob Batt asking for copies of any letters in his possession.[13] By the end of 1505 he was planning on publishing a volume of his letters.[14] Erasmus clearly saw his correspondence as an instrument for constructing a continent-wide network of "friends" or "followers" in accordance with meanings contemporary both to Erasmus and to us.

However, as can be seen from the chronological chart compiled by Christoph Kudella (see Figure 7.1), a dramatic quantitative leap in the number of letters surviving from Erasmus' correspondence took place only in 1515–1516, with the publication of the most influential edition of the *Adages* (1515) and the Greek New Testament: the *Novum instrumentum omne* (1516).

Most interestingly, there is a falling-off in the correspondence that began with Erasmus' stay in Italy in the second half of 1506. Although there were prior years for which twenty or more letters written by Erasmus survive, for the near five years between his departure from Paris in August 1506 and his departure from England for Paris on April 10, 1511, only nineteen letters survive in all. Twelve were written by Erasmus, and seven were addressed to him.[15] Between December 1508 and April 1511, moreover, no letters written by Erasmus have come down to us at all. What happened? In fact, as he later confessed to Beatus Rhenanus in a letter of 1521, when he was in Siena in 1509, a friend delivered

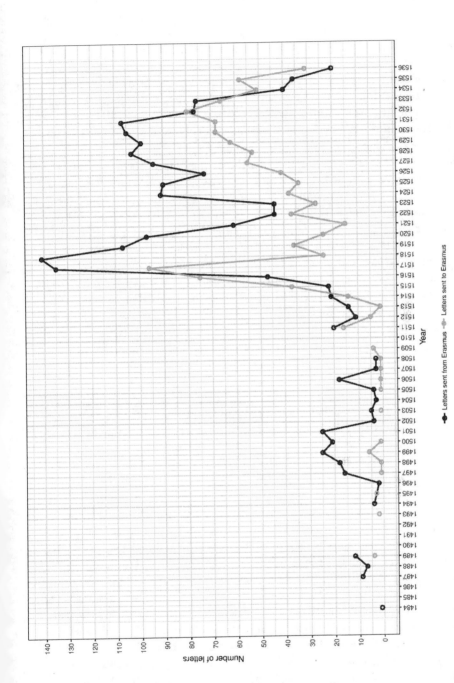

FIGURE 7.1 Letters from and to Desiderius Erasmus, 1484–1536. Christoph Kudella, *The Correspondence Network of Erasmus of Rotterdam: A Data-Driven Exploration*. PhD thesis, University College Cork, 2018. Line chart courtesy of Christoph Kudella

to him a volume of his own manuscript letters purchased from a bookseller in Rome. Startled, Erasmus burned the lot of them, and he continued for some time to burn his own letters when copies or originals came his way.[16] The motive is unclear, but in all likelihood Erasmus had written things he regretted. In the quest for patronage he perhaps revealed too much of himself. He may well have criticized powerful persons, including perhaps Julius II—at a time when Erasmus was dependent on Julius for the dispensation that freed him from the obligation of residence at his monastery in Steyn.[17]

The large gap in Erasmus' correspondence occurs unfortunately in one of the most interesting periods of his career. It begins with his arrival in Italy and continues through his return to England and the composition of *The Praise of Folly* down to his departure for France, where *Folly* would be published. The epistolary lacuna, and above all a desire to learn more about the impact on the Dutchman of Italy, has prompted curiosity but little new knowledge ever since Pierre de Nolhac's *Érasme en Italie*, published at the end of the nineteenth century.[18] The story has thus been told and retold how, in 1506, Erasmus accepted an appointment as traveling tutor to the two sons of Henry VII's Genoese royal physician; how he traveled to Turin, where in a matter of days he was awarded a doctorate in theology on September 4;[19] how he traveled to Bologna, but since Julius II was going to attack the city he passed on to Florence; how he returned to Bologna with his young charges in time to witness the entry of Julius on November 11; how upon completing his term as tutor he went to Venice to work with Aldus Manutius; and how he visited Rome, from whence, upon the accession of Henry VIII, he returned to England in 1509.

Our ignorance concerning the brief visit to Florence in 1506 has often been noticed, given Florence's libraries, monuments, humanists, and artists. We are not even sure how long Erasmus stayed in Florence. De Nolhac thought he was there "no more than six weeks."[20] One quite recent study surprisingly abbreviates the time to "ten days or so."[21] The only activity in Florence we are certain of is that Erasmus was translating Lucian. On his journey to Italy, Erasmus had passed through Paris and left two books to be published with the printer Badius. One of them comprised his translations of Euripides' *Hecuba* and *Iphigenia at Aulis*; the second was a volume of Lucian translations that he and More had prepared together. The Euripides was published in Paris in September 1506; the Lucian, however, would not appear until November; and in the meantime, as we know from its dedication, Erasmus sent from Italy, a set of additional Lucian translations, which he said he had done while in Florence, that Badius then inserted between folios that had already been printed.[22] Given that the new work was substantial, comprising Lucian's *Hercules, Eunuchus, De sacrificiis*, and *Convivium*, plus a further eighteen brief dialogues, for a total of twenty-two, the work of translating is likely to have required a sojourn greater than ten days.[23] Julius was already marching with his army toward Bologna while Erasmus was in Turin in early September. Erasmus will have reached Bologna by the end of September and it is likely he spent much of October in Florence.

A letter that Erasmus wrote twenty years later from Basel offers further information on the time in Florence. The funny epistle describes for Erasmus' correspondent how a thunderclap in Basel set off an explosion in a gunpowder magazine. Since in Basel the gunpowder was stored next to a brothel, Erasmus tells how the blast sent prostitutes and their clients scurrying half-naked through the streets.[24] Erasmus then writes that the loud noise recalled a thunderclap he witnessed in Florence years earlier, when he was waiting for news that it was safe to return to Bologna.[25] As he tells it, he was sitting in the privy attending to nature (*in secessu sedens ad exonerare alvulum*) when he heard a tremendous thunderclap.[26] He rushed back to his companions and told them that soon they would hear some unpleasant news. Sure enough, soon a physician hurried by who told them that three nuns had been struck by lightning, one had died immediately, one was near death, and for the third there was little hope.

These chance details suggest a little more concerning Erasmus' situation in Florence. An entry in the diary kept by a Florentine shopkeeper, Luca Landucci, dates the lightning strike to November 4, 1506. Landucci writes that the nunnery—the Dominican establishment of Santa Caterina[27]—was struck while the nuns were praying, and he says that one of those who died was the daughter of the humanist, Niccolò Michelozzi.[28] November 4 happens also to have been the day on which Erasmus posted a letter from Florence (in which two other letters were enclosed) to Servatius Rogerus, the prior of his monastery in Steyn, explaining that he would soon be returning to Bologna now that it was safe.[29]

The nunnery's location, which was adjacent to the Dominican convent of San Marco (see Figure 7.2), almost certainly means that Erasmus was working in the Library of San Marco, which was in effect Florence's public library, on the day of the thunderstorm.

It has always been assumed that the Greek text of Lucian that Erasmus and More used for their translations that were published in 1506 was the Aldine edition published in 1503.[30] Interestingly, the catalog of the San Marco Library that was compiled circa 1500—thus shortly before Erasmus' visit—lists a printed Lucian volume that is almost certainly the *editio princeps* published by Lorenzo da Alopa in Florence in 1496, as well as a manuscript containing thirty-seven of Lucian's dialogues.[31] A scholar who compared the Aldine with the *editio princeps* considered the Aldine inferior, calling it "corrupt in accents and spellings."[32] Although the earlier set of Lucian translations done in England by Erasmus and More was in all probability based on the Aldine, it would be interesting to determine whether the twenty-two additional dialogues that Erasmus translated while in Florence were again based on the Aldine, or possibly on the better 1496 edition or the San Marco manuscript.

The Basel letter of 1526 indicates that Erasmus made some acquaintances at the library. Who these persons may have been—they are referred to simply as "*caeteri*"—is a matter for speculation. Michelozzi, for instance, whom the doctor may have been seeking with news regarding his daughter, was a locally important figure who had been secretary to Lorenzo the Magnificent. Later he

FIGURE 7.2 Piazza San Marco, Florence. Gray circle: Convent and Library of San Marco. Black circle: Nunnery of Santa Caterina. In a detail from the map of Florence, *Nova pulcherrimae civitatis Florentiae topographia accuratissime delineata*, drawn by Stefano Buonsignori and published in 1584. Courtesy of the Fotothek des Kunsthistorischen Instituts in Florenz-Max Planck Institut, Inst.Neg. 11.047

would succeed Machiavelli in the Chancery.[33] But there is no firm indication that Erasmus met him, and nowhere does he name him. Any correspondence that Erasmus might have had with Florentines while in Italy, or friendships with them that he might have made with them, have left not a trace. The massive correspondence from later years evinces little interest in Florence. During the remainder of his Italian sojourn Erasmus returned to Florence only once or twice, and then just in passing.[34] Evidently Florence held few attractions for him. One clue as to the source of this disregard may be found in a story Erasmus later told from his time in Venice. There, in 1508, Erasmus happened met the learned Bernardo Rucellai, a Florentine who was then in voluntary exile. In the story Erasmus renders his Latin name "Oricellarius" as "*Ocricularius*," or "craggy-assed," and he marvels that a man who could write Latin at the level of Sallust, when asked to speak it, remained dumbfounded and refused.[35] Indeed, by the early 1500s in Florence most learned conversation was conducted in the vernacular. Erasmus instead, throughout his career, spoke in Latin while shunning the vernacular languages, including both Italian and his native Dutch.[36] The abandonment of spoken Latin in Florence perhaps explains why, throughout his remaining the years, Erasmus shied away from Florence and Florentines. Still, some persons in Florence seem to have remembered Erasmus' visit of 1506.

Machiavelli's "Erasmus"

There were subsequent editions, including Aldine editions, of the two books Erasmus was working on in 1506—the Euripides he had left in Paris before coming to Italy and the Lucian whose final portion he completed in Florence and sent to Paris. The most curious of the editions of these two books were published in Florence, where someone seems to have remembered Erasmus' visit. The two books appeared as the first and third volumes of a set of five Erasmian volumes issued by the Giunta press between 1518 and 1520. As Seidel Menchi noted long ago, the Florentine selection is somewhat odd.[37] There seems to be a program at work, but not one determined by Erasmus, who had few if any contacts in Florence. The result was a choice representing Erasmus as a writer more secular and more political than he really was. Absent were important works belonging to Erasmus' religious program, for instance the very popular *Enchiridion militis christiani*. Nor was Erasmus the stylist and grammarian represented, save in a minor way, in an addendum to a republished schoolbook. Meanwhile, the pieces of a political character were enhanced.

Once the publication dates are corrected for the Florentine *ab incarnatione* style (with the year beginning March 25),[38] the order and content of the five books appears as follows:

1. The translations by Erasmus of Euripides' *Hecuba* and *Iphigenia at Aulis*, published in December 1518. Based on an Aldine edition of 1507, with a preface added by the Florentine editor and typesetter Antonio Francini.[39]

2. *The Praise of Folly*, published in 1518 *ab incarnatione* and after the first volume, so, in modern style, in early 1519, but before March 25, 1519. Based on an Aldine edition of 1515.[40]

3. Erasmus' and More's translations of Lucian, based on an Aldine edition of 1516, but the surprising addition of More's *Utopia*. Published in July 1519.[41]

4. A schoolbook consisting of a preface by Aldus, the first four books of Priscian's Grammar, and the *De octo partium orationis constructione … Erasmo Roterodamo autore*—although that work was probably written by William Lily or John Colet and only revised by Erasmus. Published in January 1520.[42]

5. Political works: Erasmus' *A Complaint of Peace*, his translation of Isocrates' *Ad Nicoclem*, his *Education of a Christian Prince* and *Panegyric to Philip of Burgundy*, and his translations of four works of Plutarch: *De discrimine adulatoris et amici*, *De utilitate capienda ex inimicis*, *An principe requiri doctrinam*, and *Cum principibus debere disputare* all based on an Aldine edition of September 1518. The Florence volume adds Erasmus' *Sileni Alcibiadis* and *Oratio de virtute*—works that notably treat princes and tyrants.[43] Published in February 1520.[44]

Many of the Giunti books, as in these instances, comprised texts borrowed from Aldine editions that were repackaged for the local Florentine market.[45] Oddly, therefore, none of these volumes contained a dedication (usually to a Florentine patrician), and only the first included a somewhat generic preface by the press's humanist editor, Antonio Francini. In the case of the Lucian volume (no. 3), there doesn't seem to have been an effort made to sell the book, since a press inventory of 1604 reveals copies still on the shelf.[46] The failure to promote it seems all the more remarkable given the miscellany's addition of *Utopia*, which in 1519 was a bestseller. Giunti volumes usually included prefaces and dedications that indicated prominent Florentines, yet here only the first volume included such a preface—a generic statement written by the humanist scholar and press employee Antonio Francini that gives no clue as the purpose of the printing.[47]

The mystery behind the Florentine Erasmus set begins to unravel with the examination of a dedicatory letter that Francini wrote for another book that was published soon after. In 1520 the Giunti press published a Latin translation of the *Onomasticon* of Julius Pollux, a vocabulary and phrase-book written by a second-century Greek rhetorician.[48] And there was a dedicatory letter from Francini unusually addressed not to a Florentine but to Thomas Linacre, who had himself visited Florence during the last years of Lorenzo de' Medici and in 1520 was serving as royal physician to Henry VIII.[49] Francini's letter discusses the progress of letters at Florence from the time of Lorenzo the Magnificent down to the papacy of Leo X. He praises the writings of the English humanists, and he writes that only recently he had seen through the press More's *Utopia*, together with a number of Lucian's dialogues.[50] Francini regrets that he was too young at the time to have met Linacre in Italy, but he gives the name of the person who convinced him to dedicate the book to Linacre: their mutual friend, a teacher of Francini's, one Giampiero Machiavelli.[51]

The mention of a "Machiavelli" in connection with Linacre, More, and (by extension) Erasmus is intriguing. Roberto Weiss and Carlo Dionisotti noticed it long ago, and each searched unsuccessfully for a connection to the famous Niccolò. Giampiero in fact does not appear in Florence's ordinary fiscal and baptismal records, or in the genealogies of the Machiavelli family.[52] There is a gap, moreover, in the surviving Machiavelli correspondence, precisely in the relevant years.

Machiavelli's surviving personal correspondence, as organized in the edition by Franco Gaeta, comprises 335 letters, eighty-seven of them written by Machiavelli and 254 addressed to him by other persons[53] (see Figure 7.3). One or two others have been discovered since Gaeta's publication, but they are not from the period discussed here, and a definitive count awaits the edition directed by Francesco Bausi for the Edizione Nazionale delle Opere di Niccolò Machiavelli.[54] Although 335 is a large number, the surviving Machiavelli correspondence is only a tenth of the size of Erasmus' correspondence. Unlike Erasmus, Machiavelli did not seek out copies of his letters after sending them, nor did he keep copies himself. Most notably, he did not keep copies of his letters and in only a few instances were preliminary drafts (*minute*) preserved among his papers. The letters to Francesco Vettori and Francesco Guicciardini, which comprise the richest part of his correspondence, survive only because the Vettori and Guicciardini families later shared the originals with Machiavelli's grandson, Giuliano de' Ricci, who copied them

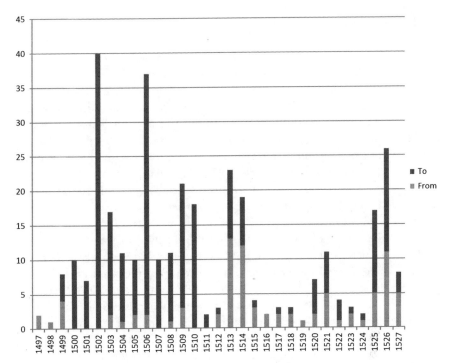

FIGURE 7.3 Letters from and to Niccolò Machiavelli, 1497–1527. Niccolò Machiavelli, *Lettere*, ed. Franco Gaeta = vol. 3 [1984] in Machiavelli, *Opere*, 4 vols. in 5
(Turin: UTET, 1984–1999). Graphic: William J. Connell

and then possibly destroyed them.[55] Machiavelli was keenly aware that certain of
his letters would be shown around by his correspondents, and he seems to have
written to a restricted circle of friends. He did not communicate directly with the
powerful via letters, as Erasmus sometimes did, but rather via friends who spoke on
his behalf rather than write. Thus while the Machiavelli correspondence is quite
revealing—often more so psychologically than the Erasmus correspondence—it is
not nearly so detailed. And then between January 31, 1515 and April 15, 1520,
there is a great falling-off.

We have only ten letters written by Machiavelli (including the two on those
dates) and only two that were addressed to him. Most of Machiavelli's own letters from this five-year period were brief notes to a nephew, Giovanni Vernacci,
who was working in a trade venture in Pera, the European section of Constantinople. With the exception of a missive to Ludovico Alamanni of 1517, the
correspondence tells us little. Yet these were the very years in which *The Prince*
was completed and dedicated,[56] and in which Machiavelli wrote the *Discourses
on Livy*, *Mandragola*, and the *Art of War*.

Unfortunately, since Machiavelli tended to describe himself in the few letters
to his distant nephew as lonely and out of favor, there has been a tendency on

the part of biographers to fill the void by exaggerating Machiavelli's isolation.[57] Although he worried about finances, his access to social and intellectual life was unrestricted. In 1515 he suffered a serious reversal when he failed to win the favor of the Medici, but his near complete despair was soon relieved in part when he was welcomed to the circle of patricians, writers, and artists that met in the Rucellai Gardens. There is even a report that Machiavelli attended the meeting of Leo X and Francis I in Bologna in December 1515 that resulted in the Concordat of Bologna, and that he was treated with distinction by the French chancellor, Antoine Duprat.[58] In short, Niccolò Machiavelli was hardly isolated and, even though not employed by the Medici, he was circulating in the upper echelons of Florentine intellectual life and he would have had opportunity—and motives, given their content—for reading and discussing the works of Erasmus, whose reputation, in 1515–1520, was at its acme.

Meanwhile, Giampiero Machiavelli, who was involved in Florentine Erasmus publications, turns out to have been close to Niccolò. He held, in fact, the benefice at the Church of Santa Andrea in Percussina, the hamlet where Niccolò kept the ancestral farm at which he famously wrote *The Prince*.[59] Giampiero proved so difficult for previous scholars to pin down because he was a priest who was moreover the illegitimate son of the priest in a rural parish.[60] And it is through understanding of Giampiero's career and whereabouts that a concrete connection between the circle around Machiavelli and the humanists of Northern Europe, including Erasmus, may now be established.

Giampiero and Thomas Linacre got to know each other during the latter's stay in Italy from 1487 to 1499. From a surviving letter we know that Linacre was still corresponding with Giampiero in Florence in 1513.[61] Meanwhile, Giampiero was studying law in Florence's university and he took holy orders and was tonsured in 1498. In 1504 he was involved in the publication in Bologna of a *Paraphrasis* of the first three books of Lucretius' *De rerum natura*, for which he possibly wrote an appendix defending the immortality of the soul.[62] By 1507 Giampiero was serving as *scolasticus*, or grammar master, in the Cathedral school, known as the Collegium Eugenianum. Further advancement stalled, however, when in 1510 the Savonarolan faction blocked his appointment to a chaplaincy in the Cathedral. Soon after, Giampiero resigned his post as *scolasticus* and accepted a position as the traveling preceptor during the university studies of a promising and extremely wealthy young cleric, Lorenzo Bartolini, to whom Niccolò was related by marriage.[63]

An account book preserved in the private archive of the Bartolini–Salimbeni family happens to record the expenses of young Lorenzo Bartolini during the travels with his preceptor Giampiero.[64] By matching accounting entries that offer firm dates with notarial contracts and snippets of information from other sources, it has been possible to compile a list of the impressive individuals with whom the two Florentines came into contact. These included the jurist Filippo Decio and the members of a humanist circle in Paris that included Christophe de Longueil, Guillaume Budé, the anti-Arabist physician Pierre Brissot, Jacques Lefèvre d'Étaples, Josse Clichtove, and Gérard Roussel. Linacre himself may have met the two Florentines in France in 1514, when he accompanied Mary Tudor to her wedding with Louis XII. Longueil was subsidized by Bartolini while in Rome learning Greek from 1516 to 1519.

As Bartolini was completing his studies, a trip together with Longueil was planned to visit the humanist circle in England and Erasmus in Flanders prior to Bartolini receiving his baccalaureate. Budé sent introductions to More and Erasmus.[65] Surviving letters from Longueil confirm meetings with Linacre and Richard Pace while in England, although the death of John Colet (September 10, 1519) possibly cast a shadow on the group's visit.[66] After crossing the channel the three visited Erasmus himself, on October 15 in Louvain, after which Bartolini received his degree in Paris and the two Florentines traveled back to Florence. Unfortunately, the meeting of Longueil with Erasmus became unpleasant, leading to a strained and polemical relationship between the two humanists. To the Florentine Bartolini, Erasmus reached out separately, but only a year and a half later (!), thanking him for the earlier visit, apologizing for having failed to welcome him more warmly, and regretting that since then they had exchanged no letters.[67]

The call on Erasmus must have been disappointing for the young Bartolini. The visit seems to have been envisaged as a culminating point for his studies in Northern Europe. In these years travelers from around Europe were visiting Erasmus on journeys that resembled pilgrimages.[68] With the knowledge of this back-story, a more detailed account of Giunti Erasmian series may now be offered. For, although they had been away in France since 1513, both Giampiero Machiavelli and Lorenzo Bartolini were thick with the Giunti Press. Giampiero, as already seen, had been a teacher of Antonio Francini, the humanist who supervised the Giunti publication of Greek and Latin texts. And it was Giampiero who in 1520 made the connection with Linacre for the publication of Julius Pollux. Lorenzo Bartolini was instead the actual dedicatee of the Giunti *Iliad*, which was published with a fine dedicatory letter from Francini on October 1, 1519—in time for copies to have reached Paris in advance of the conferral of Bartolini's baccalaureate.

As for the Erasmus series, it was published without the customary attention to the domestic Florentine market. It was probably no coincidence that the first three of the volumes—the Euripides, *Praise of the Folly*, and the Lucian-*Utopia*— were published by July 1519, in advance, therefore, of the visits of the two Florentines to England and Louvain. Bartolini would have had these books on hand to present to Erasmus and More as examples of the Florentine interest in classical learning and, in the case of the first and third volumes, as a way of saying to Erasmus that his visit of 1506, when he was working on Euripides and Lucian, was still remembered.

The fourth and fifth books of the Erasmian series were instead published almost immediately after the return of the preceptor and his pupil to Florence in 1520. The fourth simply updated an existing grammatical textbook by including a new (and soon to become influential) grammar, *On the Eight Parts of Speech*, that they must have picked up in England or Flanders. But the fifth and last volume, which has to do with princes, is best explained by returning to Giampiero's cousin, Niccolò.

Niccolò Machiavelli had been unemployed since 1512, when he was fired from the Florentine chancery. Even worse, in 1513, he was arrested, tortured, and briefly imprisoned on a false charge of conspiracy. There had been attempts to bring him into the Medicean patronage fold, but after 1515 he came in for savage criticism on account of the harsh lessons and alleged impiety of *The Prince*. Still, he had important friends who hoped eventually to secure him employment with the Medici. A number of these friends, in addition to Giampiero and Lorenzo Bartolini, were involved with the Giunti. If one were to choose the most "Machiavellian" of Erasmus's writings, they seem all to be gathered in the fifth Giunti volume. Indeed there is reason to believe they were selected with a view to easing Machiavelli's situation. If Machiavelli's *Prince* could be seen simply as one voice, along with those of Erasmus, Isocrates, and Plutarch, addressing problems inherent in princeship and statecraft, the sharper messages of *The Prince* would be contextualized and therefore blunted.

The Erasmus volume on princes appeared in February 1520 in Florence. We know from correspondence that Filippo and Lorenzo Strozzi, themselves patrons and dedicatees of the Giunti, were arranging to introduce Machiavelli to Cardinal Giulio de' Medici with a view to restoring him to favor. Niccolò's meeting with the Cardinal took place took place in March 1520, only a few weeks after the publication of the fifth Giunti volume.[69] Given the context, it seems reasonable to suggest that the Erasmian book on princes was published by Niccolò's friends in an effort to mollify criticisms of *The Prince*. And it worked. The Cardinal smiled on Machiavelli. Soon after he was appointed official historiographer of Florence; and, in 1521, he published his *Art of War*—with the Giunti Press.

Conclusion

Charting letters in time and space is a useful and, by now, a necessary exercise in scholarship. But the greatest surprises for historians may lie not in the data positively affirmed in the graphs and charts, but in the lacunae those graphs and charts reveal. Erasmus' decision to burn his letters written during the period 1506–1511 means we remain largely in the dark about his relations with Italians and about events prior to the publication of *The Praise of Folly*. The falling-off of Machiavelli's correspondence in the period 1515–1520 has meant we could only speculate about what was happening in his life while he was writing the *Discourses* and *Art of War*. Our understanding of the two writers, and of the relation between the Renaissance and Reformation, has been unduly affected by these two lacunae. Imagine how differently the scholarship concerning this period would have developed if there had survived a thick file of Erasmus' correspondence with Italians from his time in Italy, or if we had a folder of Machiavelli's letters in which he discussed with his friends how eagerly he was reading Erasmus. Erasmus and Machiavelli belonged to intellectual worlds that were connected more intensively than their letters have permitted us to see.

Notes

1 A version of this chapter was presented at a conference of the Fondazione Luigi Firpo in Turin organized by Enzo Baldini and Massimo Firpo. Hans Blom, Kathy Eden, Nelson Minnich, Randolph Starn, and Hans Trapman kindly commented on an early draft. Stanford University's "Republic of Letters" project, the "Cultures of Knowledge" project at Oxford University, and the "Circulation of Knowledge and Learned Practices in the 17th-century Dutch Republic" group at the Huygens ING are at the forefront of current research. Examples of earlier quantitative approaches to correspondence include Federigo Melis, *Aspetti della vita economica medievale* (Siena: Monte dei Paschi, 1962), on the commercial correspondence of Francesco Datini; my own study, William J. Connell, "Appunti sui rapporti dei primi Medici con i comuni del territorio fiorentino," in Connell, *Machiavelli nel Rinascimento italiano* (Milan: FrancoAngeli, 2016), 194–210; and Barbara Stephenson, *The Power and Patronage of Marguerite de Navarre* (London: Routledge, 2004).

2 See William J. Connell, "Machiavelli's Utopia," *Times Literary Supplement*, no. 5931 (December 2, 2016), 15–17.

3 Giovanni Angelo Odoni to Erasmus, [March?] 1535, in Desiderius Erasmus, *Opus epistolarum*, ed. P. S. Allen, 12 vols. (Oxford: Clarendon Press, 1906–1958) [cited hereafter as "Allen"] no. 3002. On this letter, see Leandro Perini, "Gli eretici italiani e Machiavelli," *Studi storici*, 10 (1969), 877–918: 880–883; Silvana Seidel Menchi, "Sulla fortuna di Erasmo in Italia. Ortensio Landi e altri eterodossi della prima metà del Cinquecento," *Schweizerische Zeitschrift für Geschichte*, 24 (1974), 537–634: 549–560; and Giuliano Procacci, *Machiavelli nella cultura europea dell'età moderna* (Bari: Laterza, 1995), 125.

4 Augustin Renaudet, *Érasme et l'Italie* [1954], pref. Silvana Seidel Menchi (Geneva: Droz, 1998), 95–102, 309–320.

5 Silvana Seidel Menchi, *Erasmo in Italia, 1520–1580* [1987], 2d ed. (Torino: Bollati Boringhieri, 2007), 357 n. 4. Her conclusion was at odds with suggestions by Delio Cantimori, Eugenio Garin and Luigi Firpo, among others.

6 J. H. Hexter, *The Vision of Politics on the Eve of the Reformation: More, Machiavelli, and Seyssel* (New York: Basic Books, 1973), 179–202.

7 See William J. Bouwsma, *A Usable Past: Essays in European Cultural History* (Berkeley, CA: University of California Press, 1990), 225–246. Bouwsma followed Renaudet in seeing Valla as the only important point of contact between Italian humanism and the North.

8 For an amusing counter-attack on the positive reception of Erasmus by the contemporary Catholic Church, see Father Stanley L. Jaki's "Introduction," to Christopher Hollis, *Erasmus* (Fraser, MI: Real View Books, 1997), vii–xxxii.

9 Roberto Ridolfi, *Vita di Niccolò Machiavelli*, 7th rev. ed. (Florence: Sansoni, 1978). On Machiavelli's supposed "exile," see Connell, *Machiavelli nel Rinascimento*, 68–74.

10 The Allen edition is cited above in note 3. The French translation, *La Correspondance d'Érasme*, ed. Marie Delcourt et al., 12 vols. (Brussels: Presses Académiques Européenes, 1967–1984), is complete. The English translation, *The Correspondence of Erasmus* [cited hereafter as "*Letters*"], in the *Collected Works of Erasmus* (Toronto: University of Toronto Press, 1974–) [cited hereafter as *CWE*], is still in progress. The Dutch translation, *De correspondentie van Desiderius Erasmus* (Rotterdam: Donker, 2004-), now comprises sixteen of a projected twenty-two volumes.

11 See the superb work of Christoph Kudella, "The Correspondence Network of Erasmus of Rotterdam: A Data-Driven Exploration," PhD thesis, University College Cork, 2018, some of which he kindly shared with me.

12 Léon-E. Halkin, *Erasmus ex Erasmo: Érasme éditeur de sa correspondance* (Aubel: Gason, 1983); Lisa Jardine, *Erasmus, Man of Letters: The Construction of Charisma in Print* (Princeton, NJ: Princeton University Press, 2015; 1993).

13 Erasmus to Jacob Batt, April 5, 1501, Allen, no. 151, 1:55, and in *Letters*, 2:29.

14 Erasmus to Franciscus Theodericus, end of 1505, Allen, no. 186, 1:415, and in *Letters*, 2:100.
15 See Allen, nos. 200–202, 1:431–433, and in *Letters*, 2:123–155.
16 Erasmus to Beatus Rhenanus, May 27, 1521, in Allen, no. 1206, 4:499, and in *Letters*, 8:218. Erasmus mentioned the burning of his correspondence again in the January 30, 1523 letter to Johann von Botzheim: Allen, 1:37, and in *Letters*, 9:350. Erasmus' explicit account of the destruction of his letters inexplicably escaped Renaudet, *Érasme et l'Italie*; J. K. Sowards, "Two Lost Years of Erasmus: Summary, Review, and Speculation," *Studies in the Renaissance*, 9 (1962), 161–186; and Jardine, Erasmus, *Man of Letters*. Compare Halkin, *Erasmus ex Erasmo*, 24–25, who noticed it and accepted it as an unwelcome fact.
17 For the dispensation, dated January 4, 1506, see Allen 3: xxix–xxx, and in *Letters*, 2:103–106.
18 Pierre de Nolhac, *Érasme en Italie*, 2d ed. (Paris: Klincksieck, 1898).
19 Luigi Firpo, "Erasmo da Rotterdam a Torino," in Firpo, *Gente di Piemonte* (Milan: Mursia, 1983), 41–65; Paul F. Grendler, "How to Get a Degree in Fifteen Days: Erasmus' Doctorate in Theology from the University of Turin," *Erasmus of Rotterdam Society Yearbook*, 18 (1998), 40–69; Irma Naso, "La laurea in teologia di Erasmo da Rotterdam a Torino," in *Erasmo da Rotterdam e la cultura europea*, ed. Enrico Pasini and Pietro B. Rossi (Florence: SISMEL—Edizioni del Galluzzo, 2008), 291–311; Patrizia Cancian, "4 settembre 1506, Torino: il diploma di laurea di Erasmo," ibid., 313–315.
20 De Nolhac, *Érasme en Italie*, 16.
21 Alexandre Vanautgaerden, *Érasme typographe. Humanisme et imprimerie au début du XVIe siècle* (Geneva: Droz, 2012), 78.
22 Vanautgaerden, *Érasme typographe*, 83–84, describes the process of insertion.
23 The twenty-two dialogues added comprise forty-five large pages in the modern edition of Erasmus' works. See *Luciani dialogi*, ed. Christopher Robinson, in Desiderius Erasmus, *Opera Omnia*, ordo primus, tomus primus (Amsterdam: North-Holland, 1969), 572–617. Robinson lists the added dialogues on 370.
24 Erasmus to Nicolas Wary, September 26, 1526, Allen, no. 1756, 6:418, and in *Letters*, 12:369–370.
25 De Nolhac, *Érasme en Italie*, 14–16, misreads the letter and situates the Basel explosion and brothel in Florence. The explosion, which occurred on September 19, 1526, is described in Fridolin Ryff's chronicle, published in *Basler Chroniken*, vol. 1, ed. Wilhelm Vischer and Alfred Stern (Leipzig: Hirzel, 1872), 54.
26 On excretion and thunder, compare Strepsiades in Aristophanes, *Clouds*, 391: "When I shit, it's like thunder." Erasmus' *alvulus* ("small womb") is a *recherché* term for the anus.
27 Santa Caterina was a recent foundation of Savonarolan inspiration.
28 Luca Landucci, *Diario fiorentino dal 1450 al 1516*, ed. Iodoco del Badia (Florence: Sansoni, 1883), 279. Michelozzi's daughter may have been one who survived. Records from Santa Caterina in the Archivio di Stato di Firenze, *Corporazioni religiose soppresse dal governo francese*, 106, vol. 12, fol. 1v, list two daughters of Ser Niccolò Michelozzi, Cecilia and Domitilla, who both entered S. Caterina on November 30, 1505, although, according to Biblioteca Nazionale Centrale di Firenze, Ms. Landau Finlay, 72, fols. 68r–69v, neither appears to have died in 1506, since their deaths were recorded in 1571 and 1565 respectively. Sharon Strocchia kindly supplied these references.
29 Erasmus to Servatius Rogerus, November 4, 1506, Allen no. 200, 1:431–433, and in *Letters*, 2:123–125.
30 Martin H. H. Engels discovered Erasmus's personal copy of the Aldine Lucian in 1973 and argued that it was the basis of the 1506 translations. See Egbertus van Gulik, *Erasmus and his Books*, trans. J. C. Grayson, ed. James K. McConica and Johannes Trapman (Toronto: University of Toronto Press, 2018), 291.
31 In the San Marco inventory of 1500, published in Berthold L. Ullman and Philip.A. Stadter, *The Public Library of Renaissance Florence: Niccolò Niccoli, Cosimo de' Medici and*

the Library of San Marco (Padua: Antenore, 1972), 240, no. 982, "Dialogi aliquot Luciani, in volumine impresso, corio rubro" probably refers to the 1496 Lucian printed in Florence. Ibid., 259, no. 1158, "Luciani XXXVII dialogi, in membranis" refers to a manuscript that was part of Giorgio Antonio Vespucci's 1499 donation to the convent's library, now in the Biblioteca Laurenziana and described in detail in Francesca Gallori and Simone Nencini, "I libri greci e latini dello scrittoio e della biblioteca di Giorgio Antonio Vespucci. Introduzione e catalogo," *Memorie domenicane*, 28 (1997), 203–207.

32 C. R. Thompson, *The Translations of Lucian by Erasmus and St. Thomas More* (Ithaca, NY: privately printed, 1940), 19–20. The 1496 and 1503 Lucian editions are listed in the *Short-Title Catalogue of Books Printed in Italy* 2d ed. (London: British Library, 1986), 396. On the ways in which Lucian was read, see David Marsh, *Lucian and the Latins: Humor and Humanism in the Early Renaissance* (Ann Arbor, MI: University of Michigan Press, 1998).

33 Paolo Viti, "Michelozzi, Niccolò," in *Dizionario biografico degli italiani* (Rome: Istituto dell'Enciclopedia italiana, 1960–) [hereafter "*DBI*"], 74:264–267; Connell, "La lettera," 71, 77–78.

34 Erasmus passed through Florence in 1508, on the way from Ferrara to Siena; Nolhac, *Érasme en Italie*, 6. In 1509, when he returned to England from Rome, the first leg of his journey took him to Bologna and he is likely to have gone through Florence.

35 Desiderius Erasmus, *Apophthegmata*, Lib. VIII, Thrasea II, in *Desiderii Erasmi Roterodami opera omnia*, ed. Jean Le Clerc (Leyden, 1703–1706), IV, 363E. In October–November 1506, when Erasmus came to Florence, Bernardo had already left in voluntary exile and the discussions in the "first phase" of the Rucellai Gardens had concluded: Felix Gilbert, *History: Choice and Commitment* (Cambridge, MA: Harvard University Press, 1977), 215–246: 226–227.

36 On Erasmus and vernaculars, see Arthur Richter, *Erasmus-Studien* (Dresden: Johannes Päsler, 1891), Anhang A ("Erasmus' Sprachkentnisse"), XIX–XXIV. On his lack of Italian, see Léon-E. Halkin, *Erasmus: A Critical Biography*, trans. John Tonkin (Oxford: Blackwell, 1993), 67. For earlier developments in Italy, see Sarah Stever Gravelle, "The Latin-Vernacular Question and Humanist Theory of Language and Culture," *Journal of the History of Ideas*, 49 (1988), 367–386. Studies of "oral culture" in Italy have emphasized performance and preaching as opposed to learned discussion. See, for example, the number of *The Italianist*, 34, no. 3 (2014), dedicated to "Oral Culture in Early Modern Italy: Performance, Language, Religion."

37 The Florentine Erasmus series was first noticed by Silvana Seidel Menchi, "Alcuni atteggiamenti della cultura italiana di fronte a Erasmo, 1520–1536)," in *Eresia e riforma nell'Italia del Cinquecento. Miscellanea I* (Florence: Sansoni, 1974), 71–133: 79–86. See also Carlo Dionisotti, "La testimonianza del Brucioli" [1979], in Dionisotti, *Machiavellerie. Storia e fortuna di Machiavelli* (Torino: Einaudi, 1980), 193–226: 210–215.

38 William A. Pettas, *The Giunti of Florence: A Renaissance Printing and Publishing Family* (New Castle, DE: Oak Knoll Press, 2012), offers thorough descriptions of the individual volumes. Unfortunately in his massive catalogue he fails to adjust Florentine *ab incarnatione* dating to modern style. See also Decio Decia, Renato Delfiol, and Luigi Silvestro Camerini, *I Giunti, tipografi editori di Firenze, 1497–1570. Annali* (Florence: Giunti Barbèra, 1978) [cited hereafter as "Decia"].

39 Pettas, *Giunti of Florence*, 300, no. 122; Decia, 103, no. 111; Seidel Menchi, "Alcuni atteggiamenti," 84 n. 52; Dionisotti, "La testimonianza," 211.

40 Pettas, *Giunti of Florence*, 300, no. 121; Decia, 103, no. 112; Seidel Menchi, "Alcuni atteggiamenti," 84 n. 53; Dionisotti, "La testimonianza," 212. Pettas placed it first in order, but both Seidel Menchi and Dionisotti put it second in order of publication. Dionisotti specifically adjusted for the *ab incarnatione* date, situating it between January 1 and March 25, 1519.

41 Pettas, *Giunti of Florence*, 309, no. 136; Dionisotti, "La testimonianza," 212; Decia, 105, no. 118; Seidel Menchi, "Alcuni atteggiamenti," 84 n. 54.

42 Pettas, *Giunti of Florence*, 314–315, no. 144. See also Decia, 109, no. 129; Seidel Menchi, "Alcuni atteggiamenti," 84 n. 55. Dated January 1519 Florentine style. This was the second Giunti edition of a work already published in January 1517 that was based on an Aldine edition of 1514. The schoolbook's first edition is described in Pettas, *Giunti of Florence*, 288–289, no. 104. Only the "Erasmian" *De octo partium* was added in this second edition.

43 Pettas, *Giunti of Florence*, 314, no. 143.

44 Dionisotti, "La testimonianza," 213, corrected the 1519 *ab incarnatione* date to February 1520 in modern style.

45 Dionisotti, "Stampe giuntine," in Dionisotti, *Machiavellerie*, 176–192.

46 Decia, 105, no. 118.

47 According to Pettas, *Giunti of Florence*, 34–38, Francini was "[t]he most productive of the Giunti editors in the first half of the sixteenth century." See also Franco Bacchelli, "Francini, Antonio," *DBI*, 50:142–144.

48 Pettas, *Giunti of Florence*, 320–321, no. 153. Julius Pollux, *Vocabularium* (Florence: Giunta, 152), consulted in the Folger Library, Washington DC, shelf mark: 222-395f.

49 Charles B. Schmitt, "Thomas Linacre and Italy," in Francis Maddison, Margaret Pelling, and Charles Webster, eds. *Essays on the Life and Work of Thomas Linacre, c. 1460–1524* (Oxford: Oxford University Press, 1977), 36–75.

50 Antonio Francini to Thomas Linacre, in Julius Pollux, *Vocabularium* (Florence: Giunta, 1520), fol. 2A2v: "Omitto Thomam Morum cuius de Utopiensium Republica ingeniosissimum opusculum, Lucianique dialogos nonnullos in latinum sermonem tralatos et legimus et probamus." A loose English translation of the dedicatory letter is in John Noble Johnson, *The Life of Thomas Linacre, Doctor in Medicine: Physician to King Henry VIII, the Tutor and Friend of Sir Thomas More*, ed. Robert Graves (London: Lumley, 1835), 242–245, where the technical meaning of Francini's "legimus et probamus" (244) is lost.

51 Pollux, *Vocabularium*, fol. 2A2v: "Iohannis Petri Machiavelli tibi deditissimi nobisque amicissimi suasu."

52 Robert[o] Weiss, "Notes on Thomas Linacre," in *Miscellanea Giovanni Mercati*, 6 vols. (Vatican City: Biblioteca Vaticana, 1946), 4:373–380; Dionisotti, "La testimonianza," 214.

53 Niccolò Machiavelli, *Lettere*, ed. Franco Gaeta = vol. 3 in Machiavelli, *Opere*, 4 vols. in 5 (Turin: UTET, 1984–1989). See also the fine English translation: *Machiavelli and His Friends: Their Personal Correspondence*, trans. James B. Atkinson and David Sices (DeKalb, IL: Northern Illinois University Press, 1996) [hereafter "Atkinson-Sices"].

54 The only new discovery of a letter was published by Michele Luzzatti and Milletta Sbrilli, "Massimiliano d'Asburgo e la politica di Firenze in una lettera inedita di Niccolò Machiavelli ad Alamanno Salviati (28 Settembre 1509)," *Annali della Scuola Normale Superiore di Pisa*, Classe di Lettere e Filosofia, series 3, vol. XVI, no. 3 (1986), 825–854.

55 Connell, "La lettera," 55–61.

56 Connell, *Machiavelli nel Rinascimento*, 94–117, dates the dedication and presentation to May–June 1515.

57 Ridolfi's judgment (*Vita*, 254–255) regarding the second half of 1515 bleeds into the way.

58 Antoine Théodore Du Prat, *Essai sur la vie d'Antoine Du Prat* (Versailles: Dagneau, 1854), 112–114, cites certain "Mémoires domestiques." Marcello Simonetta kindly brought this to my attention.

59 Connell, "Datazione," 96–100.

60 My full archival study of Giampiero's career is forthcoming. The Machiavelli correspondence mentions him only once: Francesco Del Nero to Machiavelli, September 12, 1510, in Machiavelli, *Lettere*, 342–343: "messer Giovam Piero." Also in Atkinson-Sices, 207: "Messer Giovan Pietro."

61 Thomas Linacre to [Giam]Piero Machiavelli, December 14, [1513], in Robert[o] Weiss, "Notes on Thomas Linacre," in *Miscellanea Giovanni Mercati*, 6 vols. (Vatican City: Biblioteca Vaticana, 1946), IV, 373–380. See thefacsimile in T. J. Brown, "English Scientific Autographs I: Thomas Linacre, 1460-1524," *The Book Collector*, 13 (1964), 340–341. The letter is addressed to "Piero" Machiavelli, omitting an expected "Iohanni," but Weiss is surely correct in considering the identification secure. Linacre further addressed Giampiero as if he were a doctor in arts and medicine (Linacre's own degree), whereas Giampiero's doctorate (conferred years after Linacre's departure from Italy) was in canon and civil law. Linacre's reference to Giampiero's "prestantissimum iuvenem discipulum tuum" clearly indicates the latter's illustrious pupil, Lorenzo Bartolini, thus confirming Giampiero as the intended recipient.

62 Sergio Bertelli, "Noterelle machiavelliane. Ancora su Lucrezio e Machiavelli," *Rivista storica italiano*, 76 (1964), 774–792 (782–784), discussed the *Paraphrasis*. That the appendix may have been written by Giampiero is my suggestion.

63 Niccolò Machiavelli's great-uncle Guido was married to Lorenzo Bartolini's great-aunt, Giannetta, in his second marriage. The name "Giannetta" recurred thereafter for several generations in the Machiavelli family, suggesting a tie that continued during and beyond Niccolò's lifetime. See Pompeo Litta, *Famiglie celebri di Italia* (1781–1851), "Macchiavelli [sic] di Firenze," Tavola I; and *Istoria genealogica delle famiglie de' Salimbene di Siena e de' marchesi Bartolini Salimbeni di Firenze*, in Ildefonso da San Luigi, *Delizie degli eruditi toscani*, 23 vols. in 24 (Florence: Cambiagi, 1770–1789), XXIII (Appendice), 270, 275.

64 Archivio Bartolini-Salimbeni, Vicchio, 369. The account book was first identified by Götz-Rüdiger Tewes, "Die Medici un Frankreich im Pontifikat Leos X.," in Tewes and Michael Rohlmann, eds., *Der Medici-Papst Leo X. und Frankreich* (Tübingen: Mohr Siebeck, 2002), 11–116 (34 n. 48); see also Tewes, *Kampf um Florenz—Die Medici im Exil 1494–1512* (Cologne: Böhlau, 2011), 1051. Although he once intended to publish the account book, Tewes kindly informs me he no longer expects to do so. My study selected significant entries that will appear in a forthcoming book.

65 Guillaume Budé to Thomas More, August 12, 1519, in Louis Delaruelle, *Répertoire analytique et chronologique de la Correspondance de Guillaume* Budé (New York: Burt Franklin, n.d.), 73, no. 40; and Budé's letter in Greek to Erasmus, September 15, 1519, in Delaruelle, *Répertoire*, 78–79, no. 44; and Marie-Madeleine de la Garanderie, ed., *La correspondance d'Érasme e de Guillaume Budé* (Paris: J.Vrin, 1967), 206.

66 Christophe de Longueil to Thomas Linacre, May 7, 1521, in Longueil, *Orationes* (Florence: Giunta, 1524), 109v–110r: "Quod si tuae erga me voluntatis pignus aliquod apud me esse volebas, qui tam multa in ipsa Britannia anno superiore dedisses"; and Philipp August Becker, *Christophle [sic] de Longueil. Sein Leben und sein Briefwechsel* (Bonn and Leipzig: Schroeder, 1924), 142, for the date. For the meeting with Pace, see Longueil to Reginald Pole, August 22, 1522, in Longueil, *Orationes*, pp. 152v–153r: "ab eo [=Pace] humaniter in Britannia fuissem accaeptus"; with Becker, *Christophle de Longueil*, 193, for the date.

67 Erasmus to Lorenzo Bartolini, March 1, 1521, Allen, no. 1187, 4:445–446; *Letters*, 8:157–159.

68 For one semi-fictional Florentine example, see Bartolomeo Cerretani, *Dialogo della mutatione di Firenze*, ed. Raul Mordenti (Rome: Edizioni di storia e letteratura, 1990), 16.

69 On Machiavelli's meeting with Cardinal Giulio de' Machiavelli and its date in March 1520, see Ridolfi, *Vita*, 542 n. 2.

8

THE CARDINAL'S DEAREST SON AND THE PIRATE

Venetian empire and the letters of Giovan Matteo Bembo

Demetrius C. Loufas

In October 1519, life was not going very well for Pietro Bembo. "And because you care so deeply about how I am doing," he wrote to his dear friend Bernardo Bibbiena, "I can tell you that at no time in my life have I found myself so tormented as I now find myself." The celebrated man of letters, then a secretary to Pope Leo X, found himself navigating a quite difficult period of his extraordinary life. As dramatic as it sounds, Bembo was hardly exaggerating: his beloved father had died a few months earlier, his agent in Bologna had robbed him of more than 600 florins, and he had spent another 3,000 to marry off his niece. To top it all off, his back was still hurting, though this at least was beginning to improve.

In all of the disasters of 1519 for Pietro Bembo, there was at least one bit of good news to share.

> But to leave the melancholy things aside: I gave the hand of my oldest niece, Marcella, to a very good and virtuous gentleman, not only from my country but even from my own family, Messer Giovan Matteo Bembo, not rich but well-off enough, esteemed in this city and quite honored for his age, which is twenty-eight: I am very pleased with this. He took her hand yesterday: he will take her home in two or three days. On my end, I have nothing else pleasing to tell you.[1]

Pietro was satisfied enough with the match; a few happy sentences in an otherwise melancholy letter. Though he was optimistic about his new nephew-in-law, Pietro Bembo had no idea how important Giovan Matteo Bembo would prove, both in Pietro's own life and to the Venetian Republic. From the moment of the wedding until Pietro's death almost three decades later, Pietro and Giovan Matteo continuously maintained a warm—and largely written—bond. And in multiple ways, their relationship was defined by the vast distances that separated them.

Two decades later, Giovan Matteo Bembo himself would engage in a very different sort of correspondence with a very different sort of partner. In his role as an administrator at the edges of Venetian empire, Giovan Matteo would come face to face—or pen to pen—with the most terrifying pirate of his day, Hızır, the "Barbarossa." Unlike his warm communications with his uncle, the letters exchanged with Barbarossa were the remains of a 1539 summer standoff between the two men. Barbarossa, as the Ottoman Grand Admiral, and Giovan Matteo Bembo as a regional overseer, did literal and literary battle on the Dalmatian coast in the context of the Third Ottoman–Venetian War. Bembo prevailed in these tense exchanges and ultimately returned to the capital a hero, bringing the Republic of Venice a desperate victory in what was a disastrous war for the Venetians. The most enduring testament to his triumph, however, came more than two decades later when his letters with Barbarossa appeared in an edited volume, the *Lettere di principi, le quali si scrivono da principi, o a principi, o ragionan di principi*, published in 1562 by the printing house of Giordano Ziletti and an energetic Viterbese editor named Girolamo Ruscelli. Unlike in the published correspondence between Giovan Matteo Bembo and his uncle Pietro, Giovan Matteo was the star of the exchange included in this anthology. When considered together, however, the two sets of letters paint a picture of the chaotic world in which a cardinal and a pirate could share a pen-pal, and why the whole world would want to read what they wrote.

Bembus Pater and the Dearest Son

The promise that Pietro saw in Giovan Matteo quickly changed into profound admiration. Each letter exchanged between Pietro and Giovan Matteo contains the same language and sentiments that sustained their bond over the decades, and over great distances. From very early on in their correspondence, Giovan Matteo became Pietro's *Figliuolo Carissimo*, his "Dearest Son," a name that he would continue to use for his nephew throughout their entire correspondence. At the end of 1520, almost exactly one year after Giovan Matteo and Marcella's wedding, Pietro wrote to his nephew:

> As far as my feelings towards you, if you doubt them in any way, you commit an error because I love you not only as Uncle but also as Father, and I hope that my actions show you this more than my words.[2]

In the same spirit, Pietro signed each letter as *Bembus Pater*, the same name by which he referred to his own father in his famous work *De Aetna*, first published almost three decades earlier. Pietro's tender letters and consistent use of "Dearest Son" for Giovan Matteo contrast almost tragically with the tone Pietro adopted in his letters to his only biological son, Torquato. Torquato, a reliable source of frustration and disappointment for Pietro, suffered forms of address that were as volatile as the content of his father's letters; Pietro was as ready to address him warmly as "mio figliuolo" as he was to sternly call him out by name alone, "Torquato," or to plainly call him an idiot. Pietro rode Torquato especially hard about the poor attention he paid to his studies, taking his weakness in his studies as signs of much greater failings:

> For so long you have given me constant cause for pain by your weak spirit towards your studies, even if Messer Felice writes me in consonance with your letters, I hardly dare to believe either you or him. I know that every little occasion to avoid your studies is taken immediately by you as a great reason, and that you are not so constant in anything as in your weakness towards learning virtue and doctrine; this is not the work of a generous heart, which is what I wish yours were. And I also know that if you cheat me, you cheat yourself much more.[3]

Pietro's contentious relationship with his own son, painful as it was, accentuates the serene and productive bond that he shared with his nephew.[4]

The closeness of this bond seems to have benefitted from the drastically different paths that uncle and nephew took in life. As distant members of the same Bembo clan, Pietro and Giovan Matteo were inheritors of a long and celebrated history of service to the Republic of Venice. Their family was among the oldest in the Venetian Lagoon and had provided the city with a multitude of praiseworthy citizens; the Bembo family could claim no fewer than three saints, according to legend, not to mention scores of civic leaders upon which the Venetian Republic depended.[5] Both Giovan Matteo and Pietro were as well positioned as any Venetian patricians to serve Venice as their ancestors had done, bringing honor—and hopefully fortune—to the Bembo name. And yet, Pietro Bembo famously shirked his opportunities and responsibilities as a Venetian noble.[6] He managed to dodge his fate as a Venetian bureaucrat and took up residence at the great humanist courts of northern Italy before ultimately settling into a long Church career—all the while producing some of sixteenth-century Italy's most important works of poetry and prose.

Giovan Matteo, on the other hand, walked a much more conventional path for a Venetian patrician of the sixteenth century. Unlike Pietro—who turned away from this patrician heritage to pursue patronage and eventual fame in Ferrara, Urbino, and ultimately at Rome—Giovan Matteo Bembo embodied the ideal of a Venetian nobleman of the sixteenth century. Giovan Matteo served the republic for over half a century, doing his part not only to protect and administer Venice's overseas holdings but also to beautify them, growing his own wealth and prestige in the process.[7]

Giovan Matteo Bembo's legacy, to his family as much as to his city, has received some share of scholarly attention. By the time of his death sometime after 1570, he had assembled a healthy patrimony for his 10 legitimate children and one natural son. The pride of his collection of properties was his own personal residence, a relatively modest palace in the parish of Santa Maria Nova. Giovan Matteo left his mark on the property in at least one highly personal way, a monument to his long career in Venice's furthest imperial reaches. Set into the exterior wall of his palace rests a small figure of Saturn or Chronos in the guise of a wild-man, holding a disk. A plaque with a Latin inscription hangs below the figure stating "As long as this [the sun] rotates, the cities of Zara, Cataro, Capodistria, Verona, Cyprus and Candia will give testimony to his actions."[8] Giovan Matteo Bembo held important administrative offices in each of these locations during his long tenure as a Venetian officer and they clearly left their mark on him much as he left his mark on them in the form of fountains and public decorations.[9] Beyond the house at Santa Maria Nova and his liquid assets, Giovan Matteo Bembo's children inherited an extensive real estate portfolio; excluding the main residence of his palace, Giovan Matteo left his heirs nine houses, six *casette* or small houses, and five apartments, plus a villa and land at Ponte di Brenta outside of Padua.[10]

Giovan Matteo's ascendant career provided Pietro many good reasons to keep in frequent contact with him, even beyond the close and genuine bond that his letters illustrate. For Pietro, Giovan Matteo was not only a beloved member of his family, but was also one of his most important connections to the world of Venetian government and business. Pietro nurtured his nephew as Giovan Matteo faced the challenges of his increasingly important positions in Venetian administration and offered him guidance on even the most mundane problems. Giovan Matteo's career took him all over the empire and his numerous offices afforded him considerable influence and honor—though not always a lot of money. In one letter from late in 1541, Pietro told Giovan Matteo:

> Do not be sorry if the office that you have now [Regent of Capodistria] does not earn you money, because in doing beautiful works and making beautiful impressions as you tend to and certainly always will, wherever you land you will earn much greater and more enduring riches—honor and a good reputation: these things clear the path and open the doors to the highest levels.[11]

But Pietro's guidance was not without self-interest. His frequent requests for favors—typically recommendations—accompanied his alternating praise and advice regarding Giovan Matteo's rising fortunes. Pietro's letters are filled with moments in which he recommended people and cases to Giovan Matteo's attention. One otherwise typical letter from June 1525 included a brief reflection on how frequently Pietro made use of his nephew's position, before asking him to once again lend a much-needed hand; Pietro explained how "I know how many letters I have written you in recommendation of many people during your time in office; but they are all light in comparison to this one."[12]

Giovan Matteo's prestigious offices and useful connections made him the natural choice for Pietro's "procurator" for his business around the republic. Despite his high offices, Giovan Matteo was still Pietro's nephew and thus no request was too ordinary for Pietro to make of him. In his letters, Pietro often asked Giovan

Matteo to procure even small articles, like glass cups or all types of foods. On other occasions, Pietro sought more obscure items from Giovan Matteo, like his 1537 inquiry about the delivery of ancient silver coins from Zara where his nephew was then *conte*.[13] Pietro's orders to Giovan Matteo could also extend to important business matters, and with surprising frequency regarded rents and other issues from Pietro's properties on the Italian mainland.

Though he was Pietro's "Dearest Son" and occasional errand-boy, Giovan Matteo had much more in common with Pietro's father, Bernardo Bembo, than with Pietro himself. Until his retirement from civil service at the age of 82, Bernardo held varied and important offices of Venetian rule. At the time of Pietro's birth in 1470, Bernardo was serving one of his many terms as diplomat—this time, in the Kingdom of Castile—but Bernardo's resume also included terms as Head of the Council of Ten and Podestà of Ravenna.[14] Like Giovan Matteo, Bernardo typified the ideal Venetian noble of his era. He synthesized civic duty, republican pride, and a balanced engagement with humanistic pursuits. As Venetian *terra firma* holdings expanded in the fifteenth century, the administrators of this growing empire—like Bernardo—had rapidly increasing contact with the burgeoning humanist communities in northern Italy.[15] Bernardo was in an advantageous position for indulging his interests in philology, poetry, and classical texts, even as he fulfilled his political obligations.[16] Besides his energy and his connections, Bernardo was also equipped with a degree from Padua that only added to his ability to participate in humanist circles.[17] Bernardo was not among the first Venetian patricians to encounter or nurture humanism from northern Italy, but he was a perfect example of his generation of supporters of humanism and consumers of its products.[18] Both his personal and public expressions of this interest were widely admired by his contemporaries; whether he was adding to his immense manuscript collection or restoring Dante's tomb at Ravenna, Bernardo's refinement was praised by his peers.[19]

As close as he was to his father, and as perfectly as their interests outside of governance aligned, Pietro dragged his feet over every office that his father tried to secure for him. Pietro's upbringing was a model of Venetian patrician child-rearing but his overwhelming discomfort with patrician obligations emerged early in his adulthood. Throughout his 20s and 30s, Pietro's father put him in the running for government offices which, to Pietro's relief, he never won. In the second half of 1505 alone, Pietro was passed over for at least four different appointments in government.[20] Examples from his correspondence from the period highlight his contentment at dodging his preordained fate as a Venetian bureaucrat. In one letter to his younger brother Carlo, Pietro wrote that:

> I thank you and my other Magnificent Relatives, for the many efforts made on my behalf [to secure office]. And I also must thank the Most Illustrious Senate, both those that wanted me and those that did not want me; the first group for seeking to help me and the second group for actually helping me.[21]

While the letter itself is undated, it was written in the aftermath of more failed attempts to obtain election to a post for Pietro between July 1499 and March 1501. Pietro's desperation reached its peak toward the end of the letter when he pleaded, "I pray of you, if you love me, if you hold me dear," before asking his family to abandon their hopes for his career in the civic service. The miters and crowns of rule, Pietro continued, are for others and not him.

For all the similarities between Bernardo and Giovan Matteo, they differed in at least one essential fact that had less to do with their comportment or their priorities than with geopolitical circumstances. Bernardo was active during a period in which Venice encountered both great opportunities and major challenges, gains and losses in both territory and prestige. Giovan Matteo Bembo came of age during a much gloomier period in Venetian history. He received his first governmental appointment, as an official of the Wine Customs Office, in 1511; only two years after the Battle of Agnadello, in which Venice lost the Italian territories it had taken centuries to collect. For Venetians, the battle was the central moment in the War of the League of Cambrai, a war that threatened to destroy the entire republic. The Venetian reconquest of the lost territories in northern Italy, mostly completed by 1517, formed the context in which Giovan Matteo first participated in Venetian rule and certainly framed the series of governmental offices he would hold throughout the rest of his life. From his first appointment in 1511 to his final election in 1564, Giovan Matteo held at least a dozen different positions up and down the ranks of Venetian administration. Although several of his offices pertained to the city of Venice itself—his time as a wine customs official, his three appointments to the Quarantia Criminale, his seat on the Council of Ten—Giovan Matteo's career reflected a specialization in the governance of Venice's empire, both the eastern (*Stato da Mar*) and western wings (*terra firma*).[22] Despite the challenges of holding up a republic that had received a near-fatal blow, Venice's threatened position provided fertile ground for a young and talented patrician to showcase his abilities.

While the War of the League of Cambrai initiated an existential but relatively brief threat to Venetian rule over northeastern Italy, Venice's position in the east was arguably even less secure than its position in the west during the late fifteenth and early sixteenth centuries. Through careful diplomatic negotiation and a series of military triumphs, the Republic of Venice had been able to recover its *terra firma* possessions in the years after the devastating losses of 1509, essentially reconstituting its hold on the region within a decade. Meanwhile, Venetian losses to the Ottomans in the east were a regular and largely irreversible occurrence throughout the entire early modern period. By the end of the fifteenth century, the Ottomans had captured Venice's major possessions in the Peloponnese—Negroponte, Coron, and Modon—and were poised to inflict even more damage. Venice's territorial gains in the Eastern Mediterranean—a collection of islands and port cities that had been slowly gathered in the three centuries since the Fourth Crusade—was nearly extinguished by the Ottomans within a period of roughly 50 years.[23] In the first decades of the sixteenth century, Ottoman incursions into the Adriatic Sea only increased. This trend accelerated in the 1530s as the famous pirate, Barbarossa, arrived in the area as admiral of the Ottoman Navy. Barbarossa's campaign of 1539 would bring him a rare and unconventional defeat, delivered by Giovan Matteo Bembo, the Rector of Cataro.

The converging paths of Giovan Matteo Bembo and the Redbeard

Like Giovan Matteo Bembo, the pirate Barbarossa (Figure 8.1) had sought and made his fortunes largely in the Eastern Mediterranean. His origins are hazy, but it seems that he was born and given the name of Hızır on the island of Lesbos shortly after its 1462 Ottoman conquest.[24] Hızır's father, Ya'kub, was an Ottoman *sipahi* who settled on the island or was possibly born there himself as well.[25] Other sources state that Hızır's grandfather was a soldier from Yenice-i Vardar in Macedonia who received a plot of land on Lesbos as payment for his role in conquering the island, either as a janissary or a *sipahi*.[26] In either case, Hızır's father's family were recent arrivals to Lesbos, deeply connected to and reliant on its new Ottoman authorities. Hızır's mother, on the other hand, appears by all accounts to have been not only a local Greek woman, but the widow of a Greek Orthodox priest. The most important person in his family, however, was his elder brother, Oruç. From Oruç, the original pirate Barbarossa, Hızır inherited both his profession and, following Oruç's death in battle against the Spanish in 1518, his name.

By the 1530s, Hızır—by then Barbarossa, the "Redbeard"—had leveraged a career of piracy into more than could possibly have been imagined. As a result of his spectacular successes as a corsair, he had become the independent ruler of Algiers. In 1519, shortly after consolidating his power in Algiers in the wake of his brother's death, he willingly traded in sovereignty for a subservient but infinitely more powerful and prestigious position—Ottoman Governor of Algiers.[27] His most important Ottoman appointment came 14 years later when he was selected by Sultan Suleiman as Beylerbey, effectively Grand Admiral, of the Ottoman Navy.[28] Barbarossa's selection as Beylerbey of the fleet came as a direct result of the failings of the Ottoman Navy earlier in the decade. Andrea Doria, the Genoese admiral then employed by Emperor Charles V, had inflicted a series of defeats on the Ottomans around the Eastern Mediterranean. Doria's successes revealed the urgent need for reorganization of the Ottoman fleet at all levels, from the arsenal onwards; this was to become the task of Barbarossa.

By the time Sultan Suleiman proclaimed Barbarossa admiral of the fleet in 1533, Giovan Matteo Bembo had already spent the better part of a decade working in the eastern half of the Venetian empire. His first commission in the east came in 1522 when he was assigned command of a galley posted to the Adriatic, but the importance of his assignments quickly grew. By 1533, he had been selected to serve as the Rector, or overseer, of the critically important city of Zara, modern-day Zadar in Croatia. Within two decades of this appointment, he performed numerous similar roles throughout the Eastern Mediterranean: in Cataro (~1539), Capodistria (1541), Famagusta (1546), and Candia (1552)—not

HARIADENVS PIRATA
Turcicus.

Quòd se exerceret pugnis naualibus ille,
Amissa in bello dextera, causa fuit.
Et quia promeruit mulios cum laude triumphos,
Rettulit & forti parta tróphaa manu,
Præfectum Solymannus eum maris inde creauit,
Et Bassae emerito nomen habere dedit.

FIGURE 8.1 Portrait of Hariadenus, or Hayreddin, the Barbarossa. Paolo Giovio and Theobald Müller, Mvsaei Ioviani imagines artifice manu ad viuum expressae. Nec minore industria (Basel, 1577), "Hariadenus Pirata." Courtesy Department of Special Collections, Stanford University Libraries

to mention offices he tried and failed to secure, like that of Bailo of Corfù, a position he lost out on by only two votes.[29] For all of the heights that Giovan Matteo reached before his death in 1570, there was perhaps nothing that brought him greater fame than his 1539 victory over the pirate Barbarossa, when the Third Ottoman–Venetian War brought the pirate to Venetian shores once again.

Girolamo Ruscelli's letters: printing Giovan Matteo Bembo and Barbarossa

At each stage of Giovan Matteo's career, letters to and from Pietro Bembo continued to flow, but Pietro was not the only person with whom Giovan Matteo participated in a surviving published correspondence. His 1539 showdown with Barbarossa resulted in scriptural skirmishing as well as actual battle and their letters back and forth found their way into print more than two decades after their conflict. In 1562, Girolamo Ruscelli's anthology of letters, *Lettere di principi, le quali si scrivono da principi, o a principi, o ragionan di principi*, was published in Venice by the printing house of Giordano Ziletti. That the letters resurfaced in print more than 20 years after the events that they described has more to do with the changing tastes of early modern Italian readers than solely the lingering celebrity of Giovan Matteo Bembo himself.

Like other sixteenth-century anthologies of correspondence, Ruscelli's work was a lightly annotated collection of letters written to and by some of the major political and cultural figures of the fifteenth and sixteenth centuries. Andrea Doria, Baldassare Castiglione, Cosimo I de' Medici, Emperor Charles V, Cardinal Bessarion, King Francis I of France, the Ottoman Sultan Suleiman, and no fewer than five popes all find a place Ruscelli's anthology. Giovan Matteo Bembo joined this prestigious cohort for his correspondence with "Aradin Bassà, called Barbarossa." And, unlike his correspondence with his uncle, which largely survives only as Pietro's half of the exchange, Giovan Matteo's back and forth with Barbarossa preserves the voices of both men though with the mediation of Ruscelli as editor.[30]

Girolamo Ruscelli, the man largely responsible for this anthology, was an important and extremely active figure in the story of sixteenth-century Italian print. Originally from Viterbo, Ruscelli bounced around Italy before establishing himself in Venice in 1548. Throughout his travels, Ruscelli was an energetic participant in the developments of print and vernacular language in Italy. Although he is well known for his work even before his arrival in Venice, Ruscelli's final decades, spent in Venice, were a period of extreme activity.[31] From the first moments of his arrival in Venice, Ruscelli immediately began to insert himself into networks of literati within the city and the Veneto. He spent time in the circles of noted grammarians, authors, printers, and editors like Francesco Alunno, Giuseppe Orologi, Lodovico Dolce, and Paolo Manuzio. His network of correspondence reached even wider and, beyond Pietro Bembo himself, included Aretino, Cardinal Iacopo Sadoleto, and many others.[32]

Ruscelli had many reasons to contact, print, or otherwise attach himself to Pietro Bembo and his family.[33] Among the most important was Bembo's stature in a movement that Ruscelli sought to find his place in—the refining and elevation of vernacular literature. Pietro Bembo is well known as one of the heroes of the movement to legitimize vernacular Italian language as a serious medium for literature. Ruscelli, though a far cry from Bembo in fame, was an important advocate of this project in his own right.[34] In an editorial career of only 15 years in Venice, Ruscelli labored to nurture an Italian challenger to the dominance of Latin in the sphere of reputable writing. Ruscelli and his peers envisioned themselves as "champions of the vernacular" in its struggle for recognition, especially against accusations that it lacked regularity or that its corpus was too small.[35] In order to combat this, Ruscelli and others published works explicitly devoted to the standardization of the ascendant Tuscan; however, their mission sat just below the surface even in works not explicitly devoted to this subject. *Lettere di principi* must be counted among the works whose more subtle purpose was the advancement of vernacular language. For this grand project, an editor would have been hard-pressed to find a case more suitable for inclusion than the struggle between Giovan Matteo Bembo and Barbarossa.

The publication of *Lettere di principi* of course rested on much more than Ruscelli's admiration of the Bembi or any advantages gained by putting their letters to print. *Lettere di principi* also reflected broader tastes in sixteenth-century readership and anthologies of letters were an increasingly popular genre of sixteenth-century Venetian printing. A trend that began with Aretino in 1538—the publication of vulgar-language epistolaries—only grew in popularity over the course of the century. Four years after the publication of Aretino's personal correspondence, the first printed anthology of letters by multiple authors appeared, a project credited largely to Paolo Manuzio but that was quickly imitated by other printers and editors.[36] The growth of the genre has been attributed to several developments and is firmly tied to the excitement, embodied by men like Ruscelli, being poured into refining and standardizing an Italian vernacular modeled on the Tuscan of Dante and Boccaccio but championed by Pietro Bembo. Letter anthologies, like Ruscelli's, were intended at least in part as style-guides for would-be writers of all levels, as well as showcases of the beauty and power of the vernacular language. By the middle of the century, business was booming for the genre of epistolary anthologies and their didactic potential. Though it was not the first anthology of letters, or even Ruscelli's first, the *Lettere di principi* serves as a fine example of demand for books in this vein; it underwent two editions in as many years and received second and third volumes a decade later—Ruscelli's death in 1566 acting as no impediment.[37]

Letters to a pirate

Giovan Matteo Bembo's inclusion in Ruscelli's anthology centers on his 1539 standoff with Barbarossa. Barbarossa, already widely known as the terrifying corsair turned leader of the Ottoman Navy, needed little introduction from Ruscelli. Readers are informed only that "This Aradin is the famous Barbarossa the Second, the one from the time of the Rule of Charles V, there having been another before him who died in the time of Leone [Pope Leo X]."[38] In

August 1539, almost one year exactly since he had given an embarrassing defeat to the fleet of the Holy League at Preveza, this Barbarossa and his fleet returned to the Ionian and Adriatic Seas. During their campaign against the remaining Christian possessions in the region, they arrived at the Bay of Kotor—now in Montenegro—then, the Venetian territory of Cataro. On 9 August from Castel Novo di Cataro, near the mouth of the bay, Barbarossa sent Giovan Matteo, the Rector of Cataro, the first of what would be a long series of messages:

> To you, Rector of Cataro. For your information, from here a certain two of our boys fled as did certain Turks, all of which you have captured. Do, having seen this notice, return them without any delay, as I believe you will do. In addition, you must deliver into our hands a certain land called Risano. And having seen this present notice, correctly respond to it in its entirety.[39]

With his first message, Barbarossa set both the tone and the strategy for the many letters that followed. Barbarossa's attitude as it came through the letters suited a man as accustomed to victory as he was. Risano, the subject of his demand, was simply the next in a long list of Dalmatian towns the admiral had set his sights on. And his demands, fearsome as they were coming from the notorious Barbarossa, were given added weight by his latest conquest. Barbarossa's letter was written not just from his ship, but from Castel Novo di Cataro—a location much more important than Risano—recently taken by Barbarossa from the Spanish.[40] As direct as he was with his demands, his strategy operated on a subtler level as well. Barbarossa's "boys" and "certain Turks," of questionable existence, provided him with an alternative path to Risano. Should Giovan Matteo refuse to return the missing men, Barbarossa had reasonable cause to move deeper into the Bay of Cataro to "find" them.

In fact, the correspondence regarding this situation had begun before Barbarossa's scribes ever sat down to write his threats. Before Barbarossa's letters or his brief introduction, Ruscelli placed a letter from Giovan Matteo Bembo dated three days earlier than Barbarossa's first written salvo. In this letter—conveniently addressed to Signor General Capello, presumably the famed Venetian admiral Vincenzo Capello whom Barbarossa crushed the year before at Preveza —Giovan Matteo lamented the arrival of Barbarossa outside of Cataro even as he took comfort in the fortitude of his soldiers and the inhabitants of the city. All had been active in preparing for a siege, especially Giovan Matteo who "to tell the truth, have not slept in two months &, if I ever happened to fall asleep, it was fully clothed and by misfortune."[41] Only one man was arguably more devoted to saving Cataro than Giovan Matteo Bembo; days earlier, a friar had thrown himself into the water and found his way to the galley of Barbarossa himself. On board, he claimed to have discovered Barbarossa's plans to take Cataro and also to have seen some ambassadors of the King of France wandering the decks.[42]

For reasons left unstated but presumably thanks to the bold friar, Giovan Matteo knew that Barbarossa was lying about the captured boys and Turks in order to justify an excursion deeper into the Bay of Cataro.[43] And in the face of Barbarossa's threats and tricks, Giovan Matteo kept his responses extremely courteous, deflecting Barbarossa's aggressive message with deferential ignorance and innocence. He informed the "Most Excellent Sir" Barbarossa that he certainly did not have any Turk fugitives, as there was a truce between Venice and the Ottoman sultan.[44] Giovan Matteo also explained that, in regards to Risano, he lacked the authority to give it to anyone at all. He gave Barbarossa a further lesson in Venetian bureaucratic complexity by informing him that these requests would be best handled by our "Magnificent Orator, who currently finds himself meeting with the most fortunate Ottoman Emperor." Other than these two requests, Giovan Matteo informed Barbarossa that he was completely at his service—to do whatever he had the authority to do, of course.[45]

Barbarossa, incensed at what must have been unexpected noncompliance, took an even harsher tone in his next letter to Giovan Matteo:

> The truce that you spoke of, or really the peace, is in my hand to make and to unmake—even if the most high, most powerful, most exalted Signore, may God forever keep him victorious, along with all his Pashas, were content with truce, I would break it at my own will.[46]

Barbarossa's second message spoke to the high degree of autonomy he retained, or at least claimed to retain, even after he submitted himself to the Ottoman Sultan. Though he was then acting on behalf of the Ottoman ruler, Barbarossa at the very least wished to give the impression that he maintained sovereignty over the fleet he commanded and considered his own personal property.[47] Although enraged, a hint of alarm also appeared in Barbarossa's second letter; he demanded that Giovan Matteo "send one of your important men, & if you have any paper from the Great Sultan, let him bring it, & I will look at this truce you say the Great Sultan has with you."[48] Barbarossa, far away from Constantinople, clearly began to wonder if he had missed something since he last set sail from the capital.

As before, the rigid divisions of Venetian authority provided Giovan Matteo a convenient shield. He replied to Barbarossa that the Venetian Ambassador to the Ottomans, the magnificent Lorenzo Gritti, had made the truce with the Sultan and sent it to Venice; Giovan Matteo could not share it with Barbarossa, as such.[49] Before once again offering his services—none of them useful—to Barbarossa, Giovan Matteo thanked him for not putting his armada to use against the Venetians in the Bay of Cataro. Along with the letter but without the truce, Giovan Matteo agreed to send "to Your Excellency, according to your request, one of my men."[50] Giovan Matteo appeared not to have even followed through with this promise until days later; in Barbarossa's next two letters, he repeated his demand to speak with one of Giovan Matteo's men.[51]

As his attempts to trick or scare his way into Cataro and Risano faltered, Barbarossa moved his ships closer to the city and disembarked men and cannons in order to make a probing assault. For all his expertise as a captain, Barbarossa's brief expedition on land was easily driven off by the pathetically small army of Bembo and his captains.[52] In a moment of generous recollection, Giovan Matteo later placed words of praise—for himself—in the mouth of Barbarossa. Bembo, according to Barbarossa, did "not appear to be a man who would let him win, either by words or by action."[53] Hesitant about the possible truce, and having failed to compel Giovan Matteo Bembo either through persuasion or by this small show of force, Barbarossa ultimately left the Bay of Cataro—presumably, in the mind of Giovan Matteo, to try his trick on the nearby Venetian towns of Dulcigno, Budua, and Antivari. Giovan Matteo, the unceasingly prudent and dutiful administrator, wrote to warn them as such.[54]

Alongside the letters between Giovan Matteo and Barbarossa, Ruscelli included a letter by Giovan Matteo addressed to the Doge and Senate. This letter contains the main description of the skirmishes with Barbarossa's men, only mentioned briefly in the Bembo–Barbarossa correspondence. In this report, Bembo praised the work of his captains, his Slav auxiliaries, the women, children, and old men of the city, and even himself (through the mouth of Barbarossa). Yet he left out a critical part of the story in this message to the Senate—a piece of the story that, according to Ruscelli's anthology, he did share with his uncle three weeks later.[55] Giovan Matteo's argument that Venice and the Ottomans had a truce, supported by the King of France, was a bluff presumably based on the report given by the reckless but ultimately heroic friar that Giovan Matteo had written about in his letter to General Capello. That the bluff had worked seemed miraculous, but only later would he discover that small portions of his lie turned out to be somewhat true.

> I cannot help but believe that Our Lord God inspired me to write as I did and to guess that which I had no indication of [...] because up until that point I did not know that traveling with Barbarossa's armada were the French Ambassadors, nor did I know the Sultan's mind on this subject. And one can see that, even if he is a Turk and a Barbarian, he desired to keep his word.[56]

Although he conveniently forgot the role of the friar as he described his "seemingly prophetic" powers to his uncle, Giovan Matteo's commitment to his bluff of Barbarossa remains impressive. Giovan Matteo's claim that the "King of France, as everyone knows, is the author of our peace" remained false and the French representatives were not at all pressing for peace between Venice and the Ottomans, but their presence did ultimately help bring about the salvation of Giovan Matteo and Venetian Cataro.[57] The French, tired of Barbarossa lingering in the Bay of Cataro, implored the stubborn pirate to "stop wasting time battling these mountains [of the Dalmatian coast]" and attack southern, Spanish Italy instead.[58] When Barbarossa failed to heed their demands, they reached out to Constantinople and implored the Ottoman Sultan to make the pirate move; Barbarossa was ordered to depart for Puglia, a softer and much more worthwhile target. The stiff resistance he faced from Giovan Matteo, combined with the orders from Constantinople, led Barbarossa to finally, begrudgingly give in to the French demands and depart the Bay of Cataro. The war between Venice and the Ottoman Empire would not end until the following year; however, Giovan Matteo's letter suggests that Venice's efforts to make peace were beginning to find traction or to at least convince the Ottomans that there were more pressing threats. Even with the fortunate complaints of the French, Giovan Matteo believed that by responding with such conviction in his letters, he had given Barbarossa "the firm opinion that I knew all of these secrets, & because of this he decided to depart" (Figure 8.2).[59]

Giovan Matteo Bembo's successful resistance to Barbarossa was an ideal example of the power of a well-crafted letter, but their conversation also speaks to the second reason for the rise in readership of these volumes of celebrity correspondence—they were entertaining. By gathering, and probably tinkering with, the correspondence of celebrities of years recently passed, editors like Ruscelli appealed to a wider audience than their mainstays of literati, grammaticians, and aspiring writers. Scholars have long observed the impact of sixteenth-century disasters on the literature, strategies, and general mood of European—especially Italian—states. Between the disaster of Agnadello and the massive growth of Ottoman power, Venice's position suffered as much as any state's in the period.

The authors included in anthologies like Ruscelli's *Lettere di principi* reflected the tension of the times. Both the ruination of Italy and the conquests of the Turks were popular subjects for the letters included in this and similar anthologies. The theme of barbarism versus civilization more broadly appeared prominently in the letters chosen for these anthologies, which meant that correspondence by and regarding the Turks was a popular choice for inclusion.[60] In *Lettere di principi*, the inclusion of not only Giovan Matteo Bembo and Barbarossa but also Andrea Doria and Ottoman Sultan Suleiman the Magnificent speaks to the power of this literary trend.

Venice, struggling to hold onto its far-flung territories, took an increasingly evasive or even timid role during the tragedies and uncertainties of the period. Temperance, always an esteemed virtue in Venice, became even more dominant as a characteristic of Venetian diplomacy and strategy. The defeats of the sixteenth century, especially when contrasted with the tremendous spurts of growth Venice experienced in the preceding centuries, forced the republic to reevaluate its position in the region. Though Venice had been beaten in war many times, the defeat at Agnadello is accorded a much higher importance. Two factors rendered the loss of the Battle of Agnadello a much more difficult moment to forget. Firstly, the aggression of the League of Cambrai was a direct consequence of Venice's extended period of expansion. Its rapidly spreading mainland empire put it into direct conflict with the papacy over territory in Romagna, and its successes had

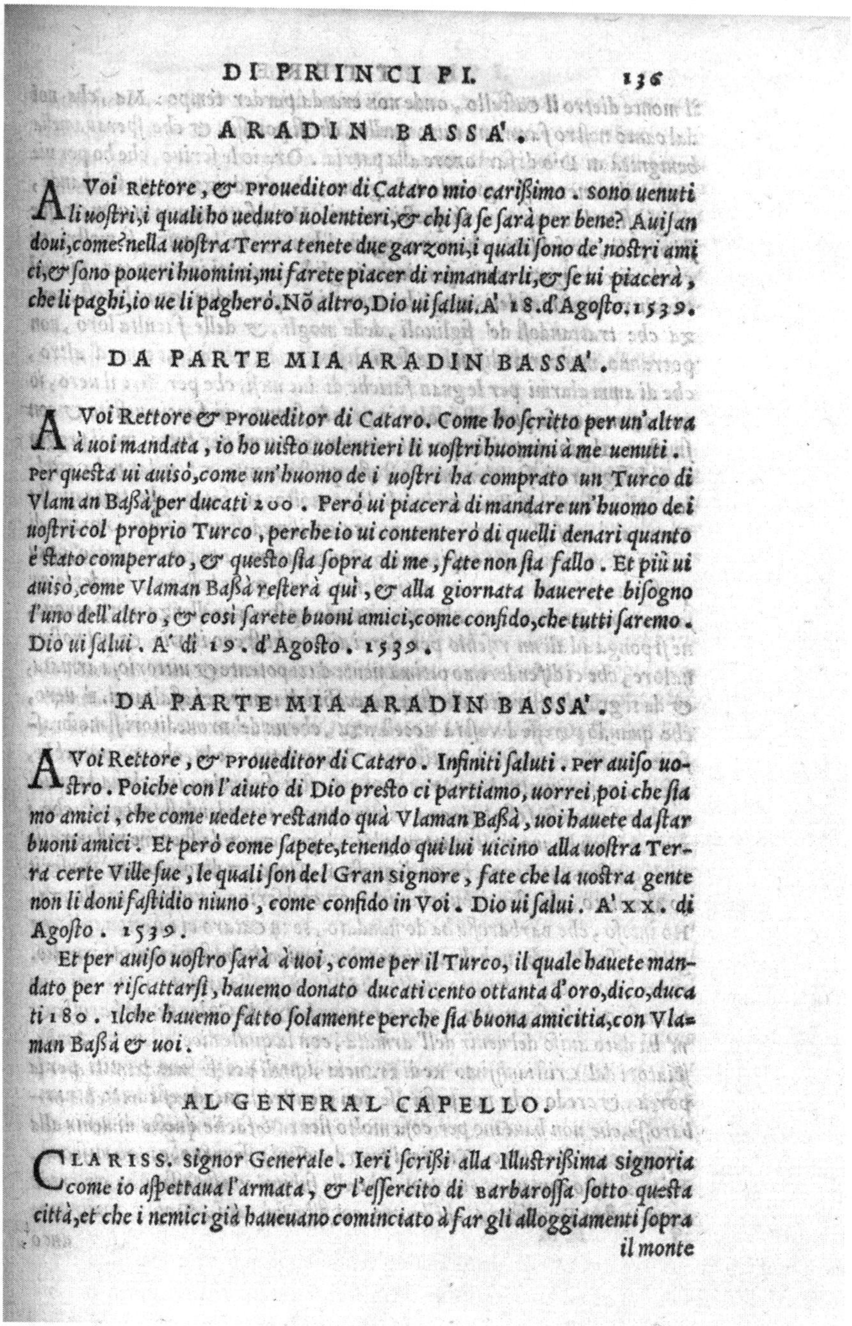

ARADIN BASSA'.

A Voi Rettore, & Proueditor di Cataro mio carißimo . sono uenuti
li uoſtri, i quali ho ueduto uolentieri, & chi ſa ſe ſarà per bene? Aui ſan
doui, come? nella uoſtra Terra tenete due garzoni, i quali ſono de' noſtri ami
ci, & ſono poueri huomini, mi farete piacer di rimandarli, & ſe ui piacerà,
che li paghi, io ue li pagherò. Nò altro, Dio ui ſalui. A' 18. d'Agoſto. 1539.

DA PARTE MIA ARADIN BASSA'.

A Voi Rettore & Proueditor di Cataro . Come ho ſcritto per un'altra
à uoi mandata, io ho uiſto uolentieri li uoſtri huomini à me uenuti .
Per queſta ui auisò, come un'huomo de i uoſtri ha comprato un Turco di
Vlaman Baßà per ducati 200 . Però ui piacerà di mandare un'huomo de i
uoſtri col proprio Turco, perche io ui contenterò di quelli denari quanto
è ſtato comperato, & queſto ſia ſopra di me, fate non ſia fallo . Et più ui
auisò, come Vlaman Baßà reſterà qui, & alla giornata hauerete biſogno
l'uno dell'altro, & coſi farete buoni amici, come confido, che tutti ſaremo .
Dio ui ſalui . A' dì 19. d'Agoſto. 1539.

DA PARTE MIA ARADIN BASSA'.

A Voi Rettore, & Proueditor di Cataro . Infiniti ſaluti . Per auiſo uoſtro . Poiche con l'aiuto di Dio preſto ci partiamo, uorrei, poi che ſia
mo amici, che come uedete reſtando quà Vlaman Baßà, uoi hauete da ſtar
buoni amici . Et però come ſapete, tenendo qui lui uicino alla uoſtra Terra certe Ville ſue, le quali ſon del Gran ſignore, fate che la uoſtra gente
non li doni faſtidio niuno, come confido in Voi . Dio ui ſalui . A' xx. di
Agoſto . 1539.

Et per auiſo uoſtro ſarà à uoi, come per il Turco, il quale hauete mandato per riſcattarſi, hauemo donato ducati cento ottanta d'oro, dico, duca
ti 180 . ilche hauemo fatto ſolamente perche ſia buona amicitia, con Vlaman Baßà & uoi .

AL GENERAL CAPELLO.

C LARISS. ſignor Generale . Ieri ſcrißi alla Illuſtrißima ſignoria
come io aſpettaua l'armata, & l'eſſercito di Barbaroſſa ſotto queſta
città, et che i nemici già haueuano cominciato à far gli alloggiamenti ſopra
                                                              il monte

FIGURE 8.2 Barbarossa's final, meeker letters to Giovan Matteo Bembo. Girolamo
Ruscelli and Francesco and Giordano Ziletti, *Lettere di principi: le quali o si scriuono da
principi, ò à principi, ò ragionan di principi* (Venice, 1562), f. 136r. Courtesy Department
of Special Collections, Stanford University Libraries

stoked its confidence enough to challenge Rome. This decision ultimately brought the League together against the Republic of Venice.[61] Secondly, the great magnitude of the loss put Venice itself at risk of conquest and the trauma of this fact triggered a lasting change both in Venice's political reality as well as its strategy for facing the world going forward. It left Venice hesitant to deploy its soldiers for decades to come, preferring to avoid any conflict that would threaten its empire, or its virtues of "prosperity and serenity."[62] Nor was Venice's crisis of confidence confined to its mainland Italian territories. Shame, confusion, and defiance dominated the minds of Venice's men of the sea in the wake of Ottoman naval victories, just as the defeat at Agnadello had stoked anxieties over the *terra firma* holdings.[63] Giovan Matteo Bembo's resistance to Barbarossa typified the new, more subtle approach of the republic in dealing with threats.

Giovan Matteo's double defeat of Barbarossa earned him fame back in Venice and beyond—a fact exemplified by his inclusion in Ruscelli's *Lettere di principi*. Another letter to Pietro Bembo included in the anthology, this time from Girolamo Fracastoro and sent five years after the standoff with Barbarossa, testified to Giovan Matteo's lingering legacy as a beloved overseer of the republic's Dalmatian cities:

> and when he left Zara, the people cried as if they had all lost their father and there was no woman nor man, great or small, who did not accompany him [to the port]. And after he embarked, those who did not have boats with which to follow him sat themselves on the pier and put their feet into the water to show that, if they were able, they would follow him beyond; and in Capo d'Istria and in Cataro they felt the same affection.[64]

But the publication of Giovan Matteo's verbal sparring with Barbarossa is important for much more than its role in shaping his celebrity. At the most basic level, the letters are important as one of the few published sources in which the words of Giovan Matteo Bembo survive. We can read a great deal about the life of Giovan Matteo Bembo through the letters of Pietro Bembo, but having this half of the conversation alone can only go so far. Recreating a dialogue by examining even fragments of Giovan Matteo's voice allows for a richer reading of both men. The means by which Giovan Matteo Bembo defeated Barbarossa also present an intriguing assessment of the role of Venetian administrators in connecting and in defending the republic in the aftermath of disasters like the naval battles of Zonchio and Preveza, or the Battle of Agnadello. More than ever, a Venetian Rector's ability to speak (and write) was envisioned as the republic's most important line of defense.[65] What few battles occur in the episode of Bembo and Barbarossa receive little comment in the letters of Ruscelli's anthology. Giovan Matteo's verbal victory matters much more than the skirmishes he directs, or even the near-divine intervention of the complaining French ambassadors. Giovan Matteo was prepared to defend Cataro using what meager resources the republic had been able to grant him, but through his writing he was able to disarm even the terrifying Barbarossa.

Conclusion

Almost 500 years later, Pietro Bembo and Barbarossa are still recognized as great figures—among the greatest of their time—in their very different fields. Giovan Matteo Bembo, for his part, has largely faded into the background of our story of the sixteenth century. Even Giovan Matteo's image no longer remains, lost to fire in the Great Council Hall of the Ducal Palace in 1577.[66] A house, a will, plaques, some contracts, and the printed praise of many illustrious men, he nonetheless left behind many artifacts that bear witness to his success and the republic that was both awed by it and grateful for it.[67] However, Giovan Matteo may ultimately be less notable for the virtue of his character or the skill of his command than as a nexus of some of the most important developments in sixteenth-century Italy. Exceptional as he was—in ability and in fortunate family connections—Giovan Matteo provides an opportune example of the deep bonds that connected seemingly disparate worlds. Together, the two sets of letters fill out the image of a man whose life as a civil servant not only brought him into contact with a cardinal and a corsair, but also made his relations with both part of the experience of reading printed letters in late Renaissance Italy. Giovan Matteo Bembo's letters—both those he wrote and those he received—traversed Venetian empire, geographically and thematically. In his Rector's chair, Giovan Matteo sat at the intersection of the major political, economic, and cultural developments of his time. His surviving correspondence showcases the ways in which Venetians, Ottomans, editors, administrators, and even the greatest men of letters of this era came together in the world of Venetian empire in the Adriatic.

Notes

1 Pietro Bembo, *Pietro Bembo: Lettere*, ed. Ernesto Travi, vol. II (Bologna: Commissione per i Testi di Lingua, 1987), 135.
2 Bembo, I:154–155.
3 Bembo, *Pietro Bembo: Lettere,* IV: 585.
4 The serious tone was not unwarranted. The futures of Bembo's children, born to a priest and a lowborn woman, would reasonably depend on their virtue more than upon their parentage. Sarah Gwyneth Ross, *The Birth of Feminism: Woman as Intellect in Renaissance Italy and England* (Cambridge, MA and London: Harvard University Press, 2009), 61.
5 Nella Giannetto, *Bernardo Bembo: Umanista e politico veneziano*, Civiltà Veneziana. Saggi. (Firenze: L. S. Olschki, 1985), 89–90.
6 Pietro Bembo ultimately served the Republic of Venice in a different capacity, but one much more suited to him. He was chosen as the official historian of Venice in 1529, though he did not live to see the publication of his work.
7 For his role in reorganizing the civic spaces of Famagusta, Cyprus in the 1540s, see Lorenzo Calvelli, "Archaeology in the Service of the Dominante: Giovanni Matteo Bembo and the Antiquities of Cyprus" in *Cyprus and the Renaissance, 1450–1650*, eds. Benjamin Arbel, Evelien Chayes, and Harald Hendrix (Turnhout, Belgium: Brepols, 2012).
8 For this and other important details on Giovan Matteo Bembo's palazzo, see Patricia Fortini Brown, *Private Lives in Renaissance Venice: Art, Architecture, and the Family* (New Haven, CT: Yale University Press, 2004), 191.

9   Lorenzo Calvelli, "Archaeology in the Service of the Dominante: Giovanni Matteo Bembo and the Antiquities of Cyprus," in *Cyprus and the Renaissance, 1450–1650*, ed. Benjamin Arbel, Evelien Chayes, and Harald Hendrix (Turnhout, Belgium: Brepols, 2012), 19–66.

10   Brown, *Private Lives in Renaissance Venice: Art, Architecture, and the Family*, 191–200.

11   Bembo, *Pietro Bembo: Lettere*, IV:392–393.

12   Bembo, *Lettere*, II:260.

13   Stanko Kokole, "The Silver Shrine of St. Simeon in Zadar: Collecting Ancient Coins in Fifteenth-Century Dalmatia," *Studies in the History of Art* 70, no. Symposium Papers XLVII: Collecting Sculpture in Early Modern Europe (2008): 110–127.

14   Carol Kidwell, *Pietro Bembo: Lover, Linguist, Cardinal* (Montreal: McGill-Queen's University Press, 2004), 3–8.

15   Margaret L. King, *Venetian Humanism in an Age of Patrician Dominance* (Princeton, NJ: Princeton University Press, 1986), 219.

16   Giannetto, *Bernardo Bembo: umanista e politico veneziano*, 85.

17   As educated as many patricians may have been, Bernardo's degree was still something of note. When mentioning Bernardo Bembo as one of the state attorneys in 1509, Sanudo refers to him as "Ser Bernardo Bembo, university laureate and knight" while his peers are only described with the generic "ser." Marin Sanudo, *Venice, Città Excelentissima: Selections from the Renaissance Diaries of Marin Sanudo*, ed. Patricia H. Labalme and Laura Sanguineti White, trans. Linda L. Carroll (Baltimore, MD: The Johns Hopkins University Press, 2008), 382.

18   King, *Venetian Humanism in an Age of Patrician Dominance*, 239.

19   Giannetto, *Bernardo Bembo: umanista e politico veneziano*, 133.

20   In this case, Pietro was up for diplomatic posts in France, the Holy Roman Empire, Spain, and Naples. Giannetto, *Bernardo Bembo: umanista e politico veneziano*, 248.

21   Bembo, *Pietro Bembo: Lettere*, I:121.

22   Sandra Secchi, "Bembo, Giovanni Matteo," *Dizionario Biografico degli Italiani* (Treccani, 1966), www.treccani.it/enciclopedia/giovanni-matteo-bembo_(Dizionario-Biografico).

23   Monique O'Connell, *Men of Empire: Power and Negotiation in Venice's Maritime State* (Baltimore, MD: The Johns Hopkins University Press, 2009), 23–28.

24   Heath W. Lowry, "Lingering Questions Regarding the Lineage, Life and Death of Barbaros Hayreddin Pasa," in *Frontiers of the Ottoman Imagination: Studies in Honour of Rhoads Murphey*, ed. Marios Hadjianastasis (Leiden and Boston, MA: Brill, 2015), 186.

25   An Ottoman fiefholding cavalryman, roughly analogous to a western knight.

26   Lowry, "Lingering Questions Regarding the Lineage, Life and Death of Barbaros Hayreddin Pasa," 186.

27   Ernle Bradford, *The Sultan's Admiral: The Life of Barbarossa* (New York: Harcourt, Brace & World, 1968), 80.

28   Bradford, 122–123.

29   He was later elected to his most prestigious position, Doge of Candia, though he declined the office, stating that he was too old to properly fill the role. Secchi, "Bembo, Giovanni Matteo."

30   Pietro's half of this exchange has survived in many printed versions. Letters to Giovan Matteo appear already in Francesco Sansovino's 1560 edition of *Delle lettere da diversi re, et principi, et Cardinali Et altri huomini dotti a Mons. Pietro Bembo scritte*. Most recently, letters to Giovan Matteo appear in Ernesto Travi's 1987 published edition of Pietro's correspondence.

31   He had met with great success in the city and eventually became too productive in his craft, oversaturating the market in 1554 and causing disastrous results for his business. Paolo Trovato, *Con ogni diligenza corretto: la stampa e le revisioni editoriali dei testi letterari italiani, 1470–1570* (Ferrara: UnifePress, 2009), 257.

32 Though his work included both great successes and horrible failures, Ruscelli remained a central figure in the Venetian print industry throughout the middle of the sixteenth century. Trovato, 244–245, 257.

33 *Lettere di principi* offers just one example of the many times that Ruscelli touched on the Bembo name over the course of his decades as an editor and publisher. In his personal correspondence, Ruscelli appears to have had at least some contact with Pietro Bembo and, in his editorial career, he had even printed works that included some of Bembo's writing. Giovan Matteo too had appeared already in Ruscelli's editions, not least of which as the recipient of the dedication to Ruscelli's 1556 edition of Paolo Giovio's *Dialogo dell'imprese militari e amorose*. Bembo is praised as the "most bright and honored gentleman, sir Gio. Matteo Bembo, most dignified Venetian Senator." Paolo Giovio, *Dialogo dell'imprese militari e amorose*, ed. Maria Luisa Doglio (Roma: Bulzoni, 1978), 23.

34 Trovato, 244, 257.

35 Brian Richardson, *Print Culture in Renaissance Italy: The Editor and the Vernacular Text, 1470–1600* (Cambridge: Cambridge University Press, 1994).

36 Richardson, 126.

37 Lodovica Braida, *Libri di lettere: le raccolte epistolari del Cinquecento tra inquietudini religiose e buon volgare* (Roma, Bari: GLF editori Laterza, 2014), 196–197.

38 Girolamo Ruscelli, *Lettere di principi: le quali o' si scrivono da principi, ò à principi o' ragionan di principi* (In Venetia: Appresso Giordano Ziletti, 1564), 138r.

39 Ruscelli, 138r.

40 In his third letter to Giovan Matteo, Barbarossa references this conquest, warning Bembo and explaining the scope of his desires. Ruscelli, 136r.

41 Ruscelli, 137v.

42 Ruscelli, 137v–138r.

43 Ruscelli, 140rv.

44 Ruscelli, 138r–145v.

45 Ruscelli, 138v.

46 Ruscelli, 135v.

47 Ruscelli, 138v.

48 Ruscelli, 138v.

49 Ruscelli, 136v.

50 Ruscelli, 136v.

51 Ruscelli, 140r.

52 Ruscelli, 140v–114r [sic.].

53 Ruscelli, 140v.

54 Ruscelli, 141v.

55 Giovan Matteo, in this letter at least, signed off in a way befitting a letter to the *Bembus Pater.* "Come Figliuolo, Gio. Matteo Bembo." Ruscelli, 144r.

56 Ruscelli, 143v–144r.

57 Ruscelli, 137v.

58 Ruscelli, 143v.

59 Ruscelli, 144r.

60 Braida, *Libri di lettere: le raccolte epistolari del Cinquecento tra inquietudini religiose e buon volgare*, 194–195.

61 Robert Finlay, "The Immortal Republic: The Myth of Venice during the Italian Wars, 1494–1530," *The Sixteenth Century Journal* 30, no. 4 (Winter 1999): 931–944.

62 Robert Finlay, "Fabius Maximus in Venice: Doge Andrea Gritti, the War of Cambrai, and the Rise of Habsburg Hegemony, 1509–1530," *Renaissance Quarterly* 53, no. 4 (Winter, 2000): 990.

63 For one contemporary Venetian perspective on the naval crisis and potential resolutions, see Cristoforo Canale, *Della milizia marittima: libri quattro di Cristoforo Canale trascritti e annotati da Mario Nani Mocenigo*, ed. Mario Nani Mocenigo (Venezia: Filippi editore, 2010).

64 Ruscelli, *Lettere di principi: le quali o' si scrivono da principi, ò à principi o' ragionan di principi*, 152r.

65 Along the lines of Margaret King's well-known image of Venetian patricians as the "walls" of the city. King, *Venetian Humanism in an Age of Patrician Dominance*, xxi.

66 Giovan Matteo appeared in a narrative painting by Jacopo Tintoretto, yet another sign of the tremendous esteem in which he was held in his city. Brown, *Private Lives in Renaissance Venice: Art, Architecture, and the Family*, 191.

67 In particular, petitions by Giovan Matteo pertaining to the license to print and profit from several works of his uncle. Marin Sanudo, *I diarii*, ed. Rinaldo Fulin et al. (Venice: F. Visentini, 1879–1903), 53:65 (22 March 1530) cit. in Brown, *Private Lives in Renaissance Venice: Art, Architecture, and the Family*. For an additional privilege case filed by Giovan Matteo, Cola Bruno, and Aldo Minuzio on Pietro Bembo's behalf, see Brian Richardson, *Printing, Writers, and Readers in Renaissance Italy* (Cambridge and New York: Cambridge University Press, 1999), 71.

PART IV
Science and travel

9

THE LITERARY LIVES OF HEALTH WORKERS IN LATE RENAISSANCE VENICE[1]

Sarah Gwyneth Ross

"How can I believe that you are a philosopher," Petrarch asked a physician-antagonist in one famous invective letter, *Contra medicum*, "when I know you are a mercenary mechanic? I gladly repeat this term, since I know that no other reproach stings you more."[2] Good to his word, he inflicted ten more puncture wounds of the same type in the ensuing paragraphs. He repeated he process in three other letters on the theme. Petrarch skewered physicians to exalt his preferred "pure" life of the mind. Capitalizing on the letter as a genre conveying the immediacy of conversation, he targeted with real punch the opportunities for social advancement that the medical profession afforded.

Medical doctors commanded more respect by the sixteenth century, as Nancy Siraisi and George McClure rightly stress.[3] In the first place, Petrarch's bold distinction between learning and healing was a straw man, since philosophy constituted a significant part of the physician's training. By the fifteenth century, moreover, the famous Platonist Marsilio Ficino, also a practicing physician, performed considerable cosmetic surgery on the medical profession's reputation. Ficino's own example went a long way toward crafting the figure of the physician-philosopher in Italy's cultural imaginary; his voluminous writings on the topic underscored the point repeatedly.[4] In the later sixteenth century, praise for physicians is not hard to find—even in some unlikely places. The Venetian feminist Moderata Fonte's *Worth of Women* (1600) categorically pays men few compliments, but her dialogue nonetheless credits several of her city's learned and generous physicians.[5]

Yet for all these advances, medical practitioners still had a tricky relationship to "letters" in their multiple meanings. In Cinquecento literature, physicians found themselves positioned between artisanal work and an unimpeachably "civil profession." In addition to the modern scholarly term "medical practitioners," I use the term "health *workers*," which conjures something more of the *labor* that some

Renaissance intellectuals still emphasized over the *learning* in this profession, as well as the distinctive way that the medical world's assorted professionals embodied the integration of book learning and experiential knowledge.[6]

The increased integration of learning and experience was an important cultural development of the Renaissance era, but not everyone was pleased about it. In his immensely popular *Piazza universale di tutte le professioni del mondo* (*Marketplace of All the World's Professions*, 1585), Tommaso Garzoni archly situated medical doctors between butchers and theologians.[7] Such attitudes of latter-day Petrarchs like Garzoni probably inspired the Venetian physician Fablio Glissenti, turning from medical to literary writing in the 1590s, to create a fictional character who lamented that the modern field of medicine included "surgeons, barber-surgeons, midwives, charlatans [and even] woodworkers, gondoliers, servants, and similar types, who ought to take an oar in hand, not a scalpel."[8]

Part of the ongoing humanist hostility to, suspicion of, or at least anxiety about medicine lay in contemporary diagnostic practices, including smelling and tasting patients' urine. Physicians also had social liabilities: their fathers sometimes came from the ranks of higher artisans, for instance pharmacists.[9] Even when parentage did not raise concerns, practicing medicine still meant association with the world of trade, including close collaborations with pharmacists that sometimes included conducting patient examinations or autopsies in apothecary shops.[10] As Siraisi notes, medicine in early Renaissance Italy developed a reputation as one of the professions that offered "opportunity for improving one's social status and that of one's descendants" even if "the social status conferred by even the most successful medical career was less than that conferred by the equivalent position in the law."[11]

Richard Palmer has offered the closest thing we have as yet to a prosopography of Venice's physicians. Without analyzing their social backgrounds in the aggregate, he stresses that the Venetian College of Physicians kept reducing its fees. The expressed aim was to lure good students away from the more expensive medical college at Padua, but the effect put doctorates in "arts and medicine" in less exalted hands.[12] The College perpetuated, then, something of the model embedded in tales told of the fourteenth-century celebrity physician Taddeo Alderotti, who was said to have been so poor as a boy that he had to peddle church candles in Florence.[13]

In short, if some illustrious medical humanists such as Girolamo Mercuriale sat comfortably in the center of the Republic of Letters by the sixteenth century, the ongoing association of doctors with artisans, as well as the notion that the profession of medicine welcomed social climbers, meant that practitioners had to exert themselves to earn citizenship in that community. University-educated doctors could only rest so much on their laurels.[14] Barber-surgeons and apothecaries had to do even more cultural work to earn humanist approval. In the Renaissance, doctor jokes were more the rage than lawyer jokes. Doctors' printed letters, which often took the form of medical advice (*consilia*) framed by as much rhetorical ornamentation as their writers' skill allowed, show them striving against prejudices for inclusion in the "Renaissance of Letters." Physicians tended to assert their humanistic credibility with an anxious insistence that seemed the very opposite of *sprezzatura*, the smoothness and nonchalance famously counseled by Castiglione.

This essay explores that reality, first, by inviting (re)consideration of Nicolò Massa (1485–1569), a doctor positively sweating to prove himself a man of letters and thus worthy of respect. Massa tried too hard; and that, as Pierre Bourdieu taught us long ago, is a sure sign of exclusion.[15] Massa's *Epistolarum medicinalium* (1558) leads us into one of the borderlands within the humanistic *respublica litterarum*. Massa's epistles show a medical professional's relative lack of literary dexterity, at least compared to card-carrying humanists. My aim is to present Massa as representative of a predicament faced by humanistic aspirants. These men and women were just as (or even more) committed to literary ideals and pursuits as their more illustrious contemporaries, but disciplinary or occupational constraints kept them in distinct regions of the "Renaissance of Letters," if not always on the outskirts. Massa's case ultimately leads us to contemplate others like him in the Venetian Republic. We will turn to Venetian health workers' encounters with literature in the aggregate, following their material and archival trails beyond correspondence, and concluding with some reflections on what letters and learning did for a range of historical actors. In so doing, we gain new purchase on the diversity of renaissances taking place during "The Renaissance."

Nicolò Massa: a lesson in trying too hard

Nicolò Massa (1485–1569) was among the few physicians mentioned in Francesco Sansovino's popular synopticon of Venetian excellence, *Delle cose notabili della città di Venetia* (1561). In a section devoted to Venice's leading philosophers and theologians, Sansovino praises Massa as "a celebrated physician and philosopher of exceedingly broad wisdom" whose works were "so widely in circulation that nearly everyone has a copy."[16] This tribute is singular: Massa is the only medical doctor upon whom Sansovino lavishes so much as a sentence. A few other physicians appear in a perfunctory list of urban professionals.[17]

What might have led Sansovino to favor Massa, a minor figure in the medical community compared to a pan-European celebrity such as Mercuriale? Part of the answer lies in the energy Massa expended courting cultural arbiters like Sansovino. For the first twenty-five years of his long career, Massa published Latin treatises aimed at medical audiences. As he sought greater prestige and wider fame later in his last decade, he turned to Italian humanism's defining genre: the letter. If scholastic treatises made you look smart but a bit medieval and lonely, letters made you look like a brilliantly innovative and well-connected Renaissance man. If you wanted to end up in a guidebook, the epistolary was the better medium for your message.

An aspiring physician's cursus honorum

In 1515, Massa took his first degree in surgery from the Venetian College of Physicians.[18] Such a degree licensed him to teach anatomy and dissection and conduct services as a blood-letter. These roles came with a certain degree of respect, and certainly more than that enjoyed by another category of health worker, apothecaries, whom the Venetian College registered and attempted to police. Still, the surgeon's credentials did not bring this ambitious young man the kind of broad cultural latitude that a degree in "arts and medicine" conferred. Accordingly, Massa took that second and more prestigious degree in 1521, also from the Venetian College. Such achievements enabled his medical and teaching career, but we should bear in mind that the Venetian College was not a full university. To gain the professional and cultural renown he aimed at, Massa had quite a bit left to prove—and he would do so.

By 1524, Massa was already serving as a physician at a prominent confraternity, the Scuola di San Giorgio, as well as at the convent of San Sepolcro. His reputation as a gifted society doctor serving wealthy urbanites and nobility from Italy to Poland grew with this success. Among Massa's claimed patients, we find the Venetian patrician Marco Goro, victim of a head wound, and Giovanni Broila, suffering a seemingly hopeless case of syphilis.

In 1527 Massa broadened his reputation among medical writers with his first publication, a treatise on syphilis. Over the next three decades, he authored five additional works—mostly in Latin and treating subjects from anatomy to fevers and the art of cutting vein, but one in Italian and treating the subject of logic (1550)—as well as three volumes of "epistles" touching on topics well beyond medicine in the larger field of philosophy. He also attended to numerous revisions and reprints of all these books. Small wonder, given that his publications would be the key to broadening his professional reputation—expanding his roster of patients—and to his credibility in broader cultural terms.

By the 1540s, Massa's growing medical reputation also brought him the honor (and burden) of serving on an unusually high number of degree examination committees for the Venetian College of Physicians. If the pan-European celebrity Vittore Trincavella served on the most committees, sponsoring students in 102 out of 105 graduations between 1545 and 1554, Massa came close behind, serving in the same capacity for thirty-three young men both Italian and foreign.[19] Massa's specialty was anatomy. He served his field as a forensic pathologist (especially in post-mortem dissections of syphilitic patients), as well as his city by conducting public dissections for pedagogical and for forensic medical and epidemiological purposes.[20] In the course of his research, teaching, public service, and publishing, he made a few refinements to Galenic medicine. Yet Massa's anatomical discoveries fell quickly under the shadow of Vesalius's monumental *De humanis corpora fabrica* (*On the Fabric of the Human Body*, 1543). Accordingly, it is not entirely surprising that this physician has long been just a footnote to Vesalius in histories of medicine, when he appeared at all.

Richard Palmer began to change that pattern of inattention, capitalizing upon the rich extant collection of Massa family papers to elucidate the energy and skill with which this physician, both through his medical work and by means of his shrewd investments, overcame poverty and a series of family tragedies to build a household and even considerable estate.[21] Nancy Siraisi has shown how Massa, together with other middle-rank physicians such as Orazio Augenio (c.1527–1603), accumulated professional capital through strategic epistolary networking.[22]

We can complicate the picture even further, since Massa's successes had as much to do specifically with engaging the *literary* as they did with property and politicking. Massa labored to strengthen the links between practical medicine and the "Renaissance of Letters." In his overwrought dedicatory epistles, and using other rhetorical techniques we will explore here, he positioned his technical and practical manuals not merely as *ars* but also as *scientia*.

From his first publication onward, Massa used the humanistic dedication to stake his claims to cultural legitimacy. Dedicating his *Liber introductorius anatomiae* (1536) to Pope Paul III, he construes the work as a literary offering—even if rather incongruously, given that this particular book outlined procedures for dissecting bodies. Yet Massa soldiered on rhetorically. Just as diligent farmers must rotate their crops to yield the best and most abundant produce, he informs the pontiff in a metaphor stretched to its tensile strength, so writers of all types should cultivate a variety of literature to produce the most perfect compositions. Highlighting his own intellectual versatility, he explains, "after I had already been zealously laboring in medicine for quite a while, I began to till literary fields, and I preserved the sweet fruits I found there."[23] Massa notes his practical experience in conducting dissections, but presents even this type of work as humanistic. His time in the anatomical theater, he insists, involved collaboration with "other cultivators of the liberal arts" including his friend, the nobleman Girolamo Marcello, whom he termed his "faithful Achates" and who, according to Massa's account, demanded that Massa write this little book.[24] In construing dissections as literary artifacts, Massa dipped his pen with anxious force into the inkwell of classical topoi. Consider, by contrast, how a writer comfortably possessed of financial, social, and cultural capital expresses the decision to publish, attributing it to peer pressure rather than personal ambition. The patrician, cardinal, and acknowledged prince of Venetian humanism Pietro Bembo also dedicated some of his work to Pope Paul III. Yet the dedicatory epistle to this same pontiff that Bembo included in his edition of Pope Leo X's correspondence seems far fresher and livelier, its tone almost casual. Noting that Latino Giovenale, the papal nuncio to Venice, had recently stayed with Bembo in Padua, he relates that Giovenale, after taking a bath to freshen up after the journey, wandered into Bembo's library and began looking through the books:

> [Giovenale] found a volume of letters written for Leo [...] which I had thrown into a little chest when I left Rome. He enjoyed reading them, since he had been close to Leo at the time, and he said to me, "Bembo, why don't you publish them? [...] they are part of the historical record; and you would be just the person to do this, since you're at work right now on writing the history of Venice."[25]

We hear in Bembo's dedicatory letter the rather complacent voice of the insider—*sprezzatura* indeed—rather than the urgent tone of the aspirant clear in Massa's prose.

Massa did not mind emphasizing his effort and labor as a scholar, professional, and family man. In fact, he was exceedingly proud of his exertions. As he narrates at length in his draft final testament, Massa rebuilt his family, which had fallen on hard times after his parents' deaths, and made his way up the professional ladder entirely through his own merit and labor, "without help from anyone else."[26] Massa's publications situated him as a medical humanist, which helped him professionally and thus fattened the family's bottom line. Yet Massa's ambitions extended into illustrious cultural territory in which competence and independence were not the best currency. To earn scholarly respect, Massa needed to display a slightly different kind of intellectual capital. His publications, above all his epistles, served this aim.

Letters make the man

Massa's strongest bid for literary legitimacy came toward the end of his career and took the form of his two-volume *Epistolarum medicinálium* (1558). This monument to his erudition redacted and expanded a 1550 collection that already enjoyed several editions in Latin and Italian in the intervening years. This revised version dispensed over 800 pages of diagnostic advice on common maladies, through Latin letters directed to patients, colleagues, and patrons. If treatises signaled credibility in a specific subject, letters showed the writer's reach of influence and, in their style and literary references, often a greater breadth of humanistic learning. As Nancy Siraisi urges, the letter collection as a genre deserves much more attention from historians of medicine than it has traditionally received. Physicians' epistles present their medical knowledge; many of their letters were *consilia*, case studies or short treatises, masquerading as correspondence. Letters also reveal professional networks and even contain a measure of their authors' social history.

Candice Delisle's work on scientific correspondence, and especially the letters of Conrad Gessner, shows how medical epistles, a new genre in the 1520s, bridged the republics of medicine and humanism.[27] At one level, correspondence served the scholarly and specifically disciplinary purposes of transmitting information, sometimes accompanied by objects—objectives later fulfilled, in large part, by specialized journals. At the same time, the medium of the letter sent a message about the writer's humanistic credentials and earned them a larger audience than other types of scientific writing typically had—though medical texts generally sold well.[28] In truth, the letter format could be a bit of a charade, since the content was often little different from a dissertation. "The epistolary form," Delisle summarizes, "seems a cover for other forms of medical discourse: disputations and controversies as well as short treatises."[29] The epistle marked the author as versed specifically in humanists' preferred vehicle for disseminating knowledge, in contrast to the scholastic treatise.

Massa's decision to invest in the epistolary mode at the culmination of his career, then, underscores his desire for humanistic clout. That desire, in turn, suggests his concern with forging a literary afterlife. With Cicero's model of discursive and epistolary posterity in mind, Petrarch had famously used the letter to ensure that a carefully curated image of himself as a scholar, philosopher, and citizen of the world outlived him.[30] Among physicians, letters proved the making of one doctor, Orazio Augenio, whose middling-rank social background did not afford him ready access to the courtly circles that contemporary figures such as Johann Lange enjoyed.[31] Early in his career, Massa resorted to the treatises typical of his profession; as death neared, he aimed for broader recognition as a man of wide learning. Letters were the most expedient way to enhance his reputation.

Still, far from appearing in his letters a comfortable physician–humanist confident in his role, Massa used his letters to defend, almost compulsively, his profession against literary detractors. Consider in particular Massa's 1556 epistle, "To All Scholars of the Good Arts and All True Lovers of Wisdom," an apologia for medicine's recognition as a humanistic discipline. Massa takes aim at the calumnies physicians suffer from grammarians or literary men—attacks based upon the lack of literary flair in medical texts. Physicians are unfairly maligned, Massa complains, for their clear, straightforward prose. He also turns critics' criticisms against themselves, accusing literary authors of weakening their own writing by making it too flowery. Truly great and "sublime" subjects such as theology and poetry "are quite ornate and sophisticated enough in and of themselves," he insists, and applying the "rouge" of rhetoric thus constitutes trivializing excess. "The same thing often happens to pretty women when they exert themselves in applying cosmetics to their faces," Massa continues; "instead of enhancing their beauty, they spoil it."[32] Accusing rhetoricians of irrelevance and even effeminacy, Massa construes medicine (like theology and poetry) as a field so inherently potent it must be discussed in a lean, muscular style. To do otherwise would be tantamount to coquettishness. Of course, there is plenty of rhetoric here. Given the cachet attached to eloquence in contemporary culture, Massa needed to fight rhetoricians with their own weapons, even as he claimed to resist intentionally the "siren-song" of ornament so as to write in the mode best befitting his subject matter.[33]

The tensions in this letter, which thread through *Epistolarum* as a whole, reveal that even an accomplished physician like Massa confronted a dilemma. On the one hand, he and his brethren hoped to dignify themselves and their profession by proving their capabilities not just as competent philosophers and doctors but also as broadly learned and eloquent writers worthy of membership in the humanist *respublica*. On the other hand, literary superfluity displayed by men supposed to be healing human bodies courted ridicule. In the popular literature of the day, physicians appear either as grasping, duplicitous mercenaries or supercilious windbags. Master Mercurio in Pietro Aretino's *Il Cortegiano* modeled the first type.[34] The character Callimaco's impersonation of a physician in Niccolò Machiavelli's *Mandragola* embodies elements of both negative stereotypes.[35] Tropes of the physician peddling useless herbal remedies eliciting Death's laughter abound in textual and visual

FIGURE 9.1 *An Old-Fashioned Renaissance Doctor*, etching by G.M. Mitelli, c. 1700.
Image credit: Wellcome Collection

imagery well into the eighteenth century (Figure 9.1). Massa felt he needed to
address the charge of insufficient learning more than that of ineffective remedies.

Massa's *Epistolarum medicinalium* is also a textbook case of trying too hard. In
this case, we see a physician trying too hard to play with the humanist elite.
Massa may have left us, in fact, a literary version of a phenomenon visible in the

material culture surrounding physicians as well. Consider, for instance, a medallion depicting the arch-humanist Pietro Bembo, attributed to Benvenuto Cellini. The obverse offers a clean image of Bembo with his title "cardinal." On the reverse, as we see here, a Pegasus elegant in its simplicity (Figure 9.2). By contrast, we have a medal commissioned by the physician Tommaso Rangone, also called Tommaso of Ravenna or Tommaso Filologo ("lover of words") (Figure 9.3). Bembo apparently needed just his name; Rangone let his multiply. On Rangone's medallion, moreover, we find a rather over-thought *impresa*: Zeus as eagle placing the infant Hercules to nurse at the breast of a reclining Hera, probably an oblique reference to Rangone's status as an adopted son. Below we confront a tangle of other motifs. The most public expression of his intellectual ambition is a self-funded funerary monument now wedged over a western door of the Basilica dei Santi Giovanni e Paolo in Venice, with a portrait containing every last symbol of learning to which he could lay any reasonable claim: books, astrolabes, *naturalia*, and all (Figure 9.4).

In his monuments of words, Massa aimed at a similar image of himself as a man of humanistic breadth and grace. The effects achieved did not always convey that message. Massa's epistles seem strained. The anxious physician's dedicatory letters are obviously formulaic. Still, the letter allowed him to show that he knew the language and form of humanistic exchange. At the same time, letters also allowed him to affiliate, however tenuously, with some intriguing realms of the *respublica litterarum* that might have seemed at first glance worlds away from Massa's Venice. Those connections substantiated in yet another way his value and cosmopolitanism.

Dr. Massa and the Queen of Poland

If letters inherently displayed the writer's networks, the first letter of an epistolary, usually a dedication, held special significance. Whether or not the dedicatee ever received a copy of the work or had any knowledge they had been honored, this choice set the writer in a specific cultural milieu. Nicolò Massa would therefore have chosen with the utmost care the two luminaries to whom he would offer his most ambitious publication: the two-volume *Epistolarum medicinalium*. The reigning doge Lorenzo Priuli was a relative no-brainer for a Venetian physician. Yet Massa made Priuli's letter the hinge between Volume 1 and Volume 2. For the more important spot, the dedication of Volume 1, Massa chose Bona Sforza, Queen of Poland. At first, Sforza might seem a peculiar choice. A closer look at Sforza and the interdisciplinary and heterodox circles around her, however, reveals that he made a brilliant selection in this broadminded and scientifically inclined patron.

Massa was the uncle of a rising star of medical humanism, Apollonio, suspected by some of being a Lutheran. Most of Catholic Europe's aspiring physicians traveled some distance to study at the premier universities of Bologna and Padua, and increasingly to take their degrees from the Venetian College of Physicians. Apollonio Massa, whose house lay a pleasant day's ride from Padua and

FIGURE 9.2 Benvenuto Cellini (attributed) medallion of Pietro Bembo, c. 1538.
Image credit: Courtesy of the National Gallery of Art, Washington, D.C. Image ID:
Samuel H. Kress Collection 1957.14.1015.b

FIGURE 9.3 Medallion of Tomaso Rangoni by Matteo Pagano della Fede, c. 1562.
Image credit: © Victoria and Albert Museum, London. Image ID: 2009CD9019

FIGURE 9.4 Statue of Tomaso Rangoni by Jacopo Sansovino (Venice).
Image credit: Didier Descouens (CC-BY-SA-4.0)

a twenty-minute walk from the examination halls of the Venetian *Studio*, instead took his degree at Wittenberg. This university had no great reputation for its medical faculty, but its Lutheran theologians were very well known. It did not look good, doctrinally speaking—as his uncle was well aware, to judge by ink he devoted to justifications for his nephew's decision (on purely academic grounds) elsewhere in his epistles.[36]

Since Massa aimed his *Epistolarum* not only at preserving his own medical reputation and showcasing his connections and clients but also boosting the career of a nephew with some pretty serious cultural liabilities, we can imagine Massa casting about for just the right potential "protectors" for the first volume. Italian potentates outside Venice might be impressive, but would look unpatriotic. Right as the Italian Wars ground to their dismal conclusion, this would have been a risky move for anyone, and Nicolò Massa did not have endless treasuries of cultural capital to burn. What about outside Italy? Dedicatees from France, the Holy Roman Empire, and Spain would have been even riskier choices on the same grounds. England was too remote and, even with Mary I on the throne, doctrinally suspect. The Dutch Republic furnished many excellent colleagues, but as yet few political figureheads of sufficient fame and duration to fawn at as potential patrons. In any case, Massa was in a slightly suspect line of work and had a potentially heterodox nephew to tout.

One cosmopolitan state presented Massa a perfect solution: Poland. As Joanna Kostylo has shown, sixteenth-century Poland-Lithuania proved a haven for heterodox thinking and a sanctuary for Italian religious refugees. A longstanding admiration of Polish elites for Italian humanist culture and the tradition of Polish aristocrats and culturally ambitious families sending their sons to study in Italian universities had helped to foster that receptive climate. By the early seventeenth century, Polish students constituted a "foreign nation" of over 1,300 students at the University of Padua, and the considerable population of Protestant students of medicine flocked to the more theologically lax *Studio* of Venice.[37]

Bona Sforza, patron of multiple circuits of exchange and a celebrated fomenter of Renaissance culture, as even the sharpest-tongued critic of court culture, Pietro Aretino, acknowledged, had little concern about doctrinal niceties.[38] She cared very much about promoting monarchical centralization on behalf of her husband, Sigismund I "the Old"—an unpopular policy among Polish nobles that led to her assassination in 1557. Upholding post-Tridentine Catholicism was definitely not on her agenda; her interests embraced science, especially botanical medicine. As Meredith Ray, Diana Robin, and Lynn Westwater have taught us, the women of the Sforza family engaged energetically in complex literary, political, and scientific projects.[39] Indeed, Bona of Savoy, wife of Duke Galeazzo Maria Sforza, kept a personal apothecary named Cristoforo de Brugora, noted for his botanical knowledge and garden.[40] Her grand-daughter and namesake, Massa's dedicatee Bona Sforza, brought an extensive retinue of Italian men to her Polish marriage. It included poets such as Celio Calcagnini, the astronomer Luca Guarico, and her personal physician Samuel ben Meshullam, one in a long tradition of Jewish recipients of medical degrees from the University of Padua.[41] Bona Sforza's other personal physician was one of the most famous Italian refugees then sheltering in Poland, the radical Antitrinitarian and *politique* Giorgio Biandrata.[42]

Since Sforza trusted her most intimate physical care to a Jew and an Antitrinitarian, it stood to reason that Sforza might be more than willing to sponsor a Venetian doctor with a (possibly) Lutheran nephew. Massa does not seem to have joined the ranks of Sforza's medical advisers, or her wider circles of protégées. Bad timing likely played a role. Sforza may or may not have had occasion to read the 1550 first edition of the *Epistolarum*, in which she is also the dedicatee of Volume 1, and she lay cold in her grave months before the 1558 reissue emerged. But Massa's dedication also had weak appeal. Even if Sforza read the 1550 edition, she might not have been sufficiently moved by the honor done her there to lavish patronage on this particular medical humanist.

The old surgeon's hand, dexterous in wielding a scalpel, proved shaky in penning a patronage letter. He missed many opportunities to signal Sforza's distinctive merits, and in so doing his own breadth of learning and cosmopolitanism. He praises Sforza only in the most standard ways—as pious, learned, and connected by ties of blood and marriage to powerful military men.[43] He relies on rhetorical questions that so often indicate ignorance of particulars. "What more can I say of your most holy manner of life? Or indeed what of your unparalleled discretion, and your vigilance in difficult times?" Massa asks.[44] Very little, apparently; he did not seem to know Sforza well enough to furnish details. In much the same way, Massa's dedicatory letter for the second volume, addressed to the humanist and reigning doge Lorenzo Priuli, rolls out a string of clichés about Venice's civic excellences and political stability.[45] In fact, when he tried to tailor his dedications, he sometimes wrong-footed the approach. The one distinctive theme Massa offers in his letter to Sforza is a winking reference to the fact that he and she were both getting on in years, and the hope that she would yet live to enjoy a "Nestorian old age." Such an expression would perhaps have offended his dedicatee more than comforting her if she ever saw it.[46]

Even if it would be hard to make a case for this letter's instrumental value, it still did useful humanistic work for its author. Massa's *Epistolarum* as a whole follows this dedication to Sforza in displaying for potential clients and for Latin readers more broadly the geographical reach of his connections, a common aim for letter writers of all specializations. In addition to a few other members of the Polish nobility, Massa addressed consilia to German patients and colleagues, especially Heinrich Stromer of Auerbach, whom he cultivated as a mentor for his nephew, the rising physician Apollonio Massa.[47]

Compared to masters of the learned letter such as Erasmus or Galileo, Massa appears limited.[48] He cleaved most to medical topics and kept his epistolary circle relatively tight. Of the sixty-four total letters in the 1558 edition, forty-five (70%) had Italian dedicatees, with only nine letters securely attributable to foreign recipients—professionals and nobility in Croatia, the Holy Roman Empire, and Poland. Of Massa's forty-five Italian named recipients, thirty-five were Venetians, meaning that Massa devoted about half the epistolary space in these volumes to showcasing connections just in his own city. And ten of these thirty-five letters he even directed to kin, with five featuring his nephew Apollonio, the physician, and another five Lorenzo, a secretary for the Venetian Senate. If we consider the types of recipients, too, Massa's immediate colleagues loom large: He addressed nineteen letters to men whom he either termed "physicians" or who are safely identifiable as such. Massa only wrote once to a member of the literary elite. His final epistle was addressed to Bernardino Feliciano, son of a noted Venetian orator and professor of rhetoric, placing this letter last to ensure that readers gave it special attention.[49]

The *Opera omnia* of Massa's contemporary, the celebrated medical humanist Vettore Trincavella (1496–1588), suggest greater reach, even if this collection also privileges Italian correspondence. While centered on the genre of medical advice letters to patients and colleagues in the Veneto, Trincavella's networks stretched to places absent in Massa's *Epistolarum*, including Milan and, above all, Bologna, the medieval capital of medical knowledge.[50] In stark contrast to both these physicians, moreover, consider the published correspondence of Erasmus, undisputed champion of the self-promotional humanistic epistle. Over 1,500 letters connected the Dutch intellectual to recipients scattered across the whole of Western Europe and covered almost every conceivable topic.[51]

Even if Massa's *Epistolarum* seems restricted by comparison, however, in his letters Massa showcased his medical knowledge, defended his profession, displayed his connections, and proved his ability to write a decent essay on a moral philosophical theme—for instance, "On the generation of man and his nobility," in the final letter dedicated to the humanist Bernardino Feliciano. Even the use of the letter form itself, moreover, signaled Massa's affiliation with a preferred humanist way of transmitting knowledge.

In the end, Massa got something like the credibility he sought by means of his letters. Not only did he appear in Sansovino's guidebook, he also became the central protagonist for his fellow physician Alvise Luisin's charming dialogue on learning and Stoical fortitude.[52] There were surely more skilled and inventive Latinists, smoother rhetoricians, and writers with greater breadth; yet, even if he sometimes visibly strained in working his letters, they still worked for him.

I emphasize the limitations evident in Massa's writing not to give him demerits but instead because they suggest a zone of intriguing interaction between the medical and literary *respublicae litterarum*. From within the borderland of these partly overlapping communities, Massa embodied the reality that writers had degrees of belonging. A university-educated man who wrote in Latin and published extensively, Massa unquestionably shared something with more famous men of science like Mercuriale or Galileo. His life circumstances and specialization limited him somewhat, even within the field of natural philosophy. A surgeon and anatomist by training, his straitened circumstances in youth had made him fast-track his studies toward earning power. If this gave him a somewhat bounded space even in the republic of medicine, it further restricted his range of motion in the Republic of

Letters. Unlike a Bembo or an Erasmus, Massa's life circumstances had prevented him from grazing for long years on Parnassus. That limitation showed in the number and content of his letters, the range of his dedicatees, and the slight awkwardness in his handling dedicatory epistles, a genre of writing that a seasoned literary humanist could make seem far less formulaic, imbuing the tropes with cleverer classical compliments designed to earn the admiration of patrons.

Massa then gives us a salutary nudge to beware of thinking of letters, the sinews of exchange, as too unitary a field or concept. The renaissances we find in letters have perhaps as many shadings as experiences of the Renaissance at large. Much depended on birth and circumstances; how much education you received or fought your way to achieve; and what you ended up doing to make ends meet. Continuing the thought, we turn now to the literary lives of Venetian medical practitioners who, inhabiting a yet shadier border territory of cultural aspiration than the well-educated and relatively well-known Massa, did not leave us volumes of printed *epistolae*—or any letters at all.

Venetian learning without letters

Venetians of many types had Renaissances. Artisans, merchants, professionals, and sometimes their relatives left in wills, inventories, and account books signs of their intellectual priorities. In my adventures in the Venetian archives, I have found that men and women connected with health work often proved the most ardent book-hoarders and the people most likely to burst through the testamentary boilerplate to ensure literary legacies or to make ethical bequests to kin and friends. Much like Nicolò Massa, so eager for recognition as a man of learning with wide connections, these humanists from the archives affiliated themselves vigorously with humanistic priorities.

Admittedly, the most elaborate contemporary libraries and collections, paradigmatically Pietro Bembo's, contained thousands of volumes and objects. Even if the scale of Venetians' collecting was comparatively diminutive, everyday people overall showed their cultural commitments more strongly than those more fortunate. Much as Albert Labarre and Marino Zorzi have found in examining other sets of book inventories, Venetian patricians' libraries appear puny; their median collection of books clocked in at an unimpressive thirty-two volumes.[53] The median book collection for Venetian physicians, by contrast, was 140 volumes—a figure that, intriguingly, outpaced that of lawyers (120 volumes), priests (ninety-two volumes), and secretaries (100 volumes). Only one barber-surgeon appeared in the records I examined; but he was a bibliophile, too. Zorzi de Agaziis owned 239 books. Even further down the professional ladder, six pharmacists popped up with literary collections that ranged widely (from five to 147 volumes) but whose median hovered at thirty-four volumes—two more than the median figure for patrician libraries, which is remarkable given that patricians had so much more wealth and so many more routes of cultural access than pharmacists.

To put apothecaries' libraries in sharper perspective, these artisans of the medical world had median collections three times larger than their nearest relatives on the socio-professional family tree. The retail merchants I located had median collections of twelve volumes, and other artisans' eleven volumes. Venetian medical practitioners also found ways to signal their literary passions beyond book hoarding, including in their naming practices. The pharmacist Adrian Vidal left an inventory of forty books, as well as a documentary trail leading to his children, whose distinctive classical names showcased their father's membership in the humanistic world. Some names drawn from the classical cannon were common enough, but Vidal got very creative. No garden-variety "Alessandros" or "Elenas"; Vidal's progeny included a Diodoro, Plinio, and Laelio.[54] Vidal's spirited choices mesh well with the recent work of Filippo de Vivo, who has recovered the lively interdisciplinary world of the Venetian apothecary's shop as a space (not unlike coffee-shops) for the exchange of political news and other matters of local and international interest.[55] In light of Vidal's book collecting and naming, we might wonder if they also served as venues for literary discussions.

Book historians warn us, with good reason, to consider inventories as false friends; they cannot tell us the same things about readers as more discursive evidence—for instance, letters, or the scholar's other great desideratum, the diary.[56] Yet Venetian physicians give us precious few letters. And, as James Grubb once cautioned, Venetians at large almost never give us diaries; *ricordanze* were things, he argued, that happened to other Italians.[57] That may be true on the whole, but I can offer one exception to the rule: the *giornali* of Nicolò Massa's colleague, Alberto Rini. Rini's journals, two account books with flashes of chronicling and self-writing squeezed into their narrow margins, recount a rich intellectual life and tight literary networks.[58] Rini had little disposable wealth, no wife, no surviving children, and no publication record. He did not even own his own home. But he was a record-keeping maniac.

In Rini's two books of memoranda spanning the years 1557 to his death in 1599, we watch him recording major family events and scribbling recipes and secrets with all the fervor that William Eamon and many others have taught us to expect early modern Europeans feeling.[59] But we also witness him, especially in the last decade of his life, buying books like a humanist. He inherited from his father and older brother a library of over 400 volumes, to which he contributed with increasing vigor. The Rini book inventory lists 500 titles. At the most generous estimate (counting Aristotle as a medical author), only 4% of that library pertained to medicine. Rini also circulated chronicles and other literary texts with card-carrying humanists, especially the historian Paolo Ramusio, from whom Rini borrowed manuscript redactions of the Latin chronicles of Doge Andrea Dandolo.[60] By borrowing the Dandolo manuscript from Paolo Ramusio, Rini acted, in the helpful terms Brian Maxson has given us, as a "social humanist"—someone who may not have published, but who corresponded with humanists who did.[61] Rini cultivated this connection to Ramusio for decades. He no doubt wrote letters back and forth in the process; but those have apparently been lost. All the same, Rini's scribbles show us a Renaissance in compelling miniature.

Beyond his and his family's activities, Rini kept close track of events in the wider civic world of Venice. In his brief but carefully crafted remarks, we witness his transformation from a reader of chronicles to a writer in that genre. The most elaborate of his entries concerns the December 1577 fire that struck the ducal palace. Rini recounts the progress of the conflagration as it made its way from a side street into the palace interior. He praises the coordinated efforts of fire-brigades from the Arsenale, regular citizens, and divine mercy, which saved most of the newer wing of the palace and nearby San Marco. The "exemplary virtue and industry" of Venetian workmen, he emphasizes, ultimately stamped out the fire.[62] Stressing the leadership of noblemen and the industry of commoners, Rini echoes tropes dating back to antiquity that segregated the polity's virtues according to social station.

Alberto Rini read his histories and chronicles well, and that should not necessarily surprise us. Nancy Siraisi attuned us long ago to the fact that medical men also read, collected, and, in the case of Girolamo Mercuriale and others of his high caliber, wrote histories.[63] And we are learning now from Hannah Marcus how much energy Italian physicians expended and risk they courted in getting access to, writing, and in some cases also censoring varied reading material, including prohibited books in and outside the field of medicine.[64] Rini, however, urges us to consider less the expansive nature of doctors' interests or the possible disciplinary homologies obtaining between the historical and the medical "case study," and more the personal desire of middling-sort physicians to record their own (hi)stories. For instance, the works of art lost in the conflagration—"ravishing paintings by Bellini and by Titian, and the ceiling murals" in addition to architectural damage, as he narrates—bring Rini to a distinctive lamentation.[65] Rini could never hope to afford a painting by one of these great masters, but he wanted to record his appreciation of their loss.

Beyond his journals, Rini might have written letters detailing even more extensively his life and the life of his mind that have simply not survived. Vocational and avocational exigencies would have demanded that Rini, like other professionals (let alone ones with such a voracious appetite for intellectual exchange), would have written letters constantly. At the same time, it is not difficult to imagine why the letters Rini surely wrote seem not to have survived: he was not Erasmus, nor was he Galileo. Beyond letters directly regarding financial transactions, his heirs might not have seen the value in the old doctor's correspondence. As we know from Paula Findlen's research, even the heirs of renowned humanists such as Pietro Bembo dismembered, sold off, and effectively destroyed the integrity of painstakingly curated collections of cultural artifacts.[66]

Rini was a member of and donor to Venice's most prestigious confraternity, the Scuola Grande of San Marco. As a result, even if his letters ended up in the trash or found themselves repurposed, his account books at least demanded preservation. Luckily for the cultural and intellectual historian, the old physician accounted and recounted the literary transactions we crave to see alongside the financial ones that interested the brethren in his own time.

Conclusion

The glimpses offered here of the literary lives of medical practitioners, from the verbose epistles of physicians to the laconic book inventories of apothecaries, reinforce the increasing pluralism of the Cinquecento *respublica litterarum*. This chapter has concentrated on the tangents and discrepancies between the republics of medicine and humanism. Even those like Nicolò Massa, whose university degrees suggest their insider status, sometimes reveal a more complex reality. His case raises the issue of disciplinary *habitus*, or professional deformity. As we have seen, for all his degrees, even Massa struggled a bit when he tried to make treatises on surgery or letters concerning practical medicine speak to wider learned audiences.

Attending to the literary lives of health workers, in short, contributes to the current scholarly project of mapping the different "cultural zones" within the larger territory of the Republic of Letters.[67] Membership in the late Renaissance *respublica* required displaying humanistic learning, ideally in Latin. Starting with Petrarch, it also helped to package one's erudition in the genre of the letter. Many medical practitioners enjoyed full literacy, and university-trained physicians unquestionably had command of Latin, but most of them did not have the luxury of spending years refining their literary craft.

Yet letters, even if imperfectly crafted by Petrarchan standards, offered distinctive possibilities for gaining respect. As we have seen, earning residency even in a confined sector of the humanistic *respublica litterarum* enhanced the cultural standing of those who worked in the field of health and, by extension, their profession. After all, the humanist Francesco Sansovino announced his decision to mention the medical doctor Nicolò Massa not because of his skill as a surgeon or his contributions to anatomy but because Massa had published voluminously and on topics of more general interest: philosophy and logic.[68] By the late sixteenth century it should have gone without saying that a physician had command of these subjects. Yet the point evidently still required emphasis. The ghost of Petrarch lurked in the conceptual machinery of the Cinquecento *respublica litterarum*. Exorcising his acerbic spirit required wielding his own preferred weapons: literary texts and, best of all, letters.

Notes

1 I would like to thank Paula Findlen and Suzanne Sutherland for organizing in 2016 a colloquium at Stanford University on the "The Renaissance of Letters: Knowledge and Community, 1300–1650," as well as all the events' participants—but especially Paula, Suzanne, Brian Brege, Meredith Ray, and Filippo de Vivo—for their stimulating work and for their thoughts and questions concerning mine. And yet more thanks to Paula and to my writing group at Boston College, the redoubtable

"WWC," for their invaluable comments on and criticisms of this essay, which have helped enormously in writing and revising.

2 Petrarch, *Invectives*, trans. David Marsh (Cambridge, MA: Harvard University Press, 2008), 73. See also George McClure, *Culture of Profession*, 8.

3 Nancy Siraisi, "The Physician's Task: Medical Reputations in Humanist Collective Biographies," in *The Rational Arts of Living* (Northampton, MA: Smith College Library, 1987), 105–133; esp. 120; McClure, *Culture of Profession*, 7–9, 110–115, and 195–200. See also McClure, "The *Artes* and the *Ars moriendi* in Late Renaissance Venice: The Professions in Fabio Glissenti's *Discorsi Morali contra il dispiacer del morire, detto Athanatophilia* (1596)," *Renaissance Quarterly* 51/1 (1998): 92–127.

4 See especially Teodoro Katinis, *Medicina e filosofia in Marsilio Ficino: Il Consilio contro la pestilentia* (Rome: Edizioni di storia e letteratura, 2007) and, more recently, "A Humanist Confronts the Plague: Ficino's Consilio contro la Pestilentia," *Modern Language Notes* 125/1 (January 2010): 72–83.

5 Moderata Fonte, *The Worth of Women, Wherein Is Clearly Revealed Their Nobility and Their Superiority to Men*, ed. and trans. Virginia Cox (Chicago, IL: The University of Chicago Press, 1997), 180–185.

6 On the interaction of these different bodies of knowledge, see especially Pamela Smith, *The Body of the Artisan: Art and Experience in the Scientific Revolution* (Chicago, IL: The University of Chicago Press, 2004), especially Chapters 5 and 6, and Pamela O. Long, *Artisan/Practitioners and the Rise of the New Sciences 1400–1600* (Corvallis, OR: Oregon State University Press, 2011).

7 Tommaso Garzoni, *Piazza universale di tutte le professioni del mondo* (Venice, 1605), 152–161.

8 Fabio Glissenti, *Discorsi morali contra il dispiacere di morire, detto Athanatophilia* (Venice: Domenico Farri, 1596), 196r.

9 For one case study, see Sarah Gwyneth Ross, *Everyday Renaissances: The Quest for Cultural Legitimacy in Venice* (Cambridge, MA: Harvard University Press, 2016), Chapter 4. More generally on the fraught boundary between medical work as a "civil profession" and as manual labor, with attendant issues of social hierarchy and family origins, see Elena Brambilla, "La medicina del Settecento: dal monopolio dogmatico alla professione medica," in *Storia d'Italia*, Annali 7 (Malattia e Medicina), ed. Franco della Paruta (Turin: Einaudi, 1984), 6–10, 33–39, 137, and 145.

10 See Joanna Kostylo, "Pharmacy as a Centre for Protestant Reform in Renaissance Venice," *Renaissance Studies* 30/2 (2015): 244.

11 Siraisi, *Medieval and Early Renaissance Medicine*, 26.

12 Richard Palmer, *The Studio of Venice and Its Graduates in the Sixteenth Century* (Padua and Trieste: Edizioni Lint, 1983), 31–34.

13 Palmer, *Studio*, 31–34. For discussion of Alderotti, see Siraisi, *Medieval and Early Renaissance Medicine*, 26.

14 See Ross, *Everyday Renaissances*, especially Chapters 3 and 4.

15 Pierre Bourdieu, *Distinction: A Social Critique of the Judgement of Taste*, trans. Richard Nice (Cambridge, MA: Harvard University Press, 1984), 84.

16 Francesco Sansovino, *Delle cose notabili*, 2 Vols. (Venice: Agostin Zopini & Nepoti, 1596), Vol. II, 124.

17 Ibid., 132.

18 The summary of Massa's career derives largely from the immensely rich and helpful study of Richard Palmer, "Nicolò Massa, His Family and His Fortune," *Medical History* 25/4 (October, 1981): 385–410, esp. 390–394.

19 Palmer, "Nicolò Massa," 401.

20 Ibid., 394 and 396.

21 Ibid., esp. 386 and 389.

22 Nancy Siraisi, *Communities of Learned Experience: Epistolary Medicine in the Renaissance* (Baltimore, MD: The Johns Hopkins University Press, 2013), 17–20 for discussion of Massa's letters; 62–84 for Augenio's.

23 Nicolò Massa, *Liber introductorius anatomiae* (Venice: Francesco Bindoni and Maphei Pasini, 1536), sig. A2r.

24 Ibid.

25 Letter of Pietro Bembo to Pope Paul III, quoted in Carol Kidwell, *Pietro Bembo: Lover, Linguist, Cardinal* (Toronto: McGill Queen's Press, 2004), 303; I have adjusted the translation slightly.

26 Draft will of Nicolò Massa (1562), Archivio IRE, Venice, ZIT E, B.30, n.4, fol. 23v. Discussed in Ross, *Everyday Renaissances*, 80.

27 Candice Delisle's most extensive work appears in "Establishing the Facts: Conrad Gessner's *Epistolae Medicinales* between the Particular and the General," PhD Dissertation, University College London (2008); for letters as a form of self-presentation as a learned physician, 53–69, and more generally as a form of writing by medical practitioners, 264–286. See also Delisle's "The Letter: Private Text or Public Place? The Mattioli-Gessner Controversy about the *aconitum primum*," *Gesnerus* 61 (2004): 161–176; and "Spices of Our Art," from Dirk van Miert, ed., *Communicating Observations in Early Modern Letters (1500–1675): Epistolography and Epistemology in the Age of the Scientific Revolution* (London and Turin: The Warburg Institute and Nino Aragno Editore, 2013), 27–42.

28 On popular interest in medical literature, Andrew Pettegree, *The Book in the Renaissance* (New Haven, CT and London: Yale University Press, 2010), 313. On letters as "fashionable," see Meredith Ray, *Writing Gender in Women's Letter Collections of the Italian Renaissance* (Toronto: University of Toronto Press, 2009), and Cecil Clough, "The Cult of Antiquity: Letters and Letter Collections," in Clough, ed., *Cultural Aspects of the Italian Renaissance: Essays in Honour of Paul Oskar Kristeller* (New York: Manchester University Press, 1976). See also Delisle, "Establishing the Facts," 265–269.

29 Delisle, "Establishing the Facts," 268.

30 An elegant translation of Petrarch's "Letter to Posterity" appears in Francesco Petrarch, *Letters on Old Age/Rerum senilium libri*, trans. Aldo S. Bernardo, Saul Levin, and Reta A. Bernardo (New York: Italica Press, 2005): I: 672–680. For the Ciceronian conception of reputational posterity in letters, see Andrew Lintott, *Cicero as Evidence: A Historian's Companion* (Oxford: Oxford University Press, 2011), 215–424.

31 Siraisi, *Communities of Knowledge*, Chapter 3.

32 Massa, *Epistolarum*, Vol. 2, sig. A1v.

33 Ibid., sig. A2r.

34 Pietro Aretino, *Cortigiana*, trans. J. Douglas Campbell and Leonard G. Sbrocchi (Ottawa, Canada: Dovehouse Editions, 2003).

35 Niccolò Machiavelli, *Mandragola*, trans. Mera J. Flaumenhaft (Prospect Heights, IL: Waveland Press, 1981).

36 Palmer, "Nicolò Massa," 398. Nancy Siraisi doubts that Apollonio had Lutheran tendencies, but the fact remains that his uncle was very worried about public perception, whatever the realities. See Siraisi, *Communities*, 17–19.

37 Joanna Kostylo, "Commonwealth of All Faiths: Republican Myth and the Italian Diaspora in Sixteenth-Century Poland-Lithuania," in Karin Friedrich and Barbara M. Pendzich, eds., *Citizenship and Identity in a Multinational Commonwealth: Poland-Lithuania in Context, 1550–1772* (Leiden: Brill, 2008), 176n22. See also Palmer, *Studio*, 3–14.

38 Petrocchi, "Bona Sforza," 326–330; for anti-courtly rhetoric, see Paola Ugolini, "The Satirist's Purgatory: 'Il Purgatorio delle Cortigiane' and the Writer's Discontent," *Italian Studies*, Vol. 64 No. 1, (Spring 2009): 1–19.

39 Meredith Ray, *Daughters of Alchemy: Women and Scientific Culture in Early Modern Italy*, I Tatti Studies in Italian Renaissance History (Cambridge, MA: Harvard University Press, 2015), Chapter 1; Diana Robin and Lynn Westwater, eds. and transls., *Ippolita Maria Sforza, Duchess and Hostage in Renaissance Naples: Letters and Orations*, The Other Voice in Early Modern Europe (Toronto: The University of Toronto Press, 2017).

40 On Cristoforo de Brugora, see Ray, *Daughters of Alchemy*, 172n19.

41 On Brugora and Guarico, Ray, *Daughters of Alchemy*, 18 and 118. Concerning ben Meshullam, see Gianfranco Miletto and Giuseppe Veltri, eds., *Judah Moscato Sermons* (Leiden: Brill, 2010), 324.

42 Kostylo, "Commonwealth," 188. By 1558, the same year as the second edition of Massa's *Epistolarum*, Biandrata had brought to Poland two fellow physicians and Antitrinitarians, Giovanni Valentino Gentile and Giovanni Paolo Alciati (ibid.).

43 Massa, *Epistolarum*, vol 1, sig.*2r.

44 Ibid., sig. *2v.

45 Ibid., vol. 2, sigs. *iiir–vr.

46 Ibid, vol. 1, sig.*2r: "Nicolaus Massa salutem plurimam *nestoriamque vitam* & foelicitatem exoptat" (italics mine).

47 Siraisi, *Communities*, 18. See also Palmer, "Nicolò Massa," 391–394.

48 Siraisi, *Communities*, 20. Two outstanding digital resources emanating from teams at Stanford University are now shedding new light on the scope and significance of Galileo's letters. See the "Galileo Correspondence Project" (http://galileo.stanford. edu); and "Mapping Galileo," one case study in "Mapping the Republic of Letters" (http://republicofletters.stanford.edu/casestudies/galileo.html).

49 On a physician's arrangement of letters to create an intellectual self-portrait or portfolio, see Candice Delisle, "Establishing the Facts," esp. 53–55, 60–69, and 264–286.

50 Vettore Trincavella, *Opera omnia* (London: Paulo Guitti, 1586).

51 For the full breadth of Erasmus's letters, see the ongoing publication project, *The Collected Works of Erasmus*, coming out in a steady trickle from the University of Toronto Press. On Erasmus's strategies of self-promotion, see Lisa Jardine, *Erasmus, Man of Letters: The Construction of Charisma in Print* (Princeton, NJ: Princeton University Press, 1994).

52 Alvise Luisin *Dialogo intitolato la cecità* (Venice: Giorgio de' Cavalli, 1569). Discussed in Ross, *Everyday Renaissances*, 89–91.

53 Ross, *Everyday Renaissances*, 36–45. For a similar pattern, see Albert Labarre, *Le livre dans la vie amiénoise du seizième siècle: L'enseignement des inventaires après décès, 1503–1576* (Paris: Nauwelaerts, 1971) and Marino Zorzi, "La circolazione del libro a Venezia nel Cinquecento: biblioteche private e pubbliche," *Ateneo veneto* 177 (1990): 117–120.

54 Household inventory of Adrian Vidal, Archivio di Stato di Venezia (ASV), CI, B.42, n.6 and n.6bis. Some of the names appear in the inventory, but others in the 1591 autograph will of Letizia (or Cecilia) Vidal, ASV, Notarile Testamenti, B.222, n.1193; and still others emerge in the 1582 will of Lelio Vidal, ASV, Notarile Testamenti, B.222, n.1167.

55 Filippo de Vivo, "Pharmacies as Centres of Communication in Early Modern Venice," in *Spaces, Objects and Identities in Early Modern Italian Medicine*, eds. Sandra Cavallo and David Gentilcore (Oxford, UK: Blackwell Publishing, 2008).

56 See especially the seminal article by Robert Darnton, "In Search of Enlightenment: Recent Attempts to Create a Social History of Ideas," *Journal of Modern History* 43/1 (1971): 113–132.

57 James Grubb, "Memory and Identity: Why Venetians Didn't Keep *Ricordanze*," *Renaissance Studies* 8/4 (1994): 375–387.

58 Alberto Rini[o], "Giornali," Archivio di Stato di Venezia, Scuola Grande di S. Marco, B.112, fasc.1; Giornale A covers the years 1557–1574 and Giornale

B those from 1574–1599. My thanks to Beth and Jonathan Glixon for putting me onto these remarkable documents.

59 William Eamon, *Science and the Secrets of Nature: Books of Secrets in Medieval and Early Modern Culture* (Princeton, NJ: Princeton University Press, 1996); Tara Nummedal, *Alchemy and Authority in the Holy Roman Empire* (Chicago, IL: University of Chicago Press, 2007), 23, 35, and 70 on books of secrets as such, and Chapter 5 on the concept of secrecy.

60 Rini, Giornale B, ASV, Scuola Grande di San Marco, B.112, fasc. 1, fols. 49r–51v.

61 Brian Maxson, *The Humanist World of Renaissance Florence* (Cambridge: Cambridge University Press, 2013).

62 Rini, Giornale B, fol. 20v.

63 Nancy Siraisi, *History, Medicine, and the Traditions of Renaissance Learning* (Ann Arbor, MI: University of Michigan Press, 2007), especially 42–46, 63–64, and 183–187 on Mercuriale's *De arte gymnastica*.

64 Hannah Florence Marcus, "Banned Books: Medicine, Readers, and Censors in Early Modern Italy, 1559–1664," PhD diss., Stanford University, 2016; especially 107–132 for a vivid case in point, Girolamo Rossi's career as historian, physician, and censor.

65 Rini, Giornale B, fol. 20v.

66 Paula Findlen, "Ereditare un museo: Collezionismo, strategie familiari e pratiche culturali nell'Italia del XVI secolo," *Quaderni Storici* 115 (2004): 45–81.

67 Dan Edelstein, Paula Findlen et al., "Historical Research in a Digital Age: Reflections from the Mapping the Republic of Letters Project," *AHR* Forum (April 2017), 422 for "cultural zones."

68 Francesco Sansovino, *Delle cose notabili*, Vol. II, 124.

10

A FLORENTINE HUMANIST IN INDIA

Filippo Sassetti, Medici agent by annual letter

Brian Brege

In Goa in 1586, amidst the cosmopolitan swirl of peoples from around the Indian Ocean and beyond, stood a garden. Here, in the tropical heat and humidity, where a nearly infinite supply of water and abundant sun made nature particularly fecund, a Florentine merchant named Filippo Sassetti (1540–1588) set out to pursue one of the most exciting and politically cherished sciences of the late Renaissance: botany. This presented a daunting challenge since, "On the earth are represented all new things, as much the plants as the animals and men. The plants are all different from ours," as Sassetti explained in a letter to Cardinal Ferdinando de' Medici.[1] The cardinal and his brother, Grand Duke Francesco I de' Medici (r. 1574–1587), valued Sassetti's botanical correspondence precisely because of its newness, of the exciting prospects opened by India's striking difference with Tuscany. Sassetti, his garden, and his house in Goa, in the heart of the Portuguese Empire, offer an entry point into the world of Tuscan global activity and the correspondence that bound it together.

Today, slightly inland from the Arabian sea, on the south bank of the Mandovi River stand vast churches, nearly alone, the eerie remnants of a great city long abandoned. In the 1580s, near its peak, these ecclesiastical edifices stood amidst a bustling metropolis, its docks bringing together people and goods from ports thousands of miles apart.[2] Mirroring its exemplar, Lisbon, even in its riverine position by the sea, late sixteenth-century Goa was the Lisbon and the Rome of the East. Goa concentrated Portuguese commercial activity, military power, and political administration even as it served as the eastern center of the *Padroado Real*.[3]

Sheer distance and the monsoon sharply constrained the Cape of Good Hope route binding Lisbon and Goa. Although rare and urgent correspondence could cross the Middle East, most correspondence traveled on the annual *Carreira da Índia*.[4] This voyage from Lisbon around the Cape of Good Hope along East

Africa to Western India and back operated according to the strongly prevailing winds of the monsoon and their subsequent reversal. Fittingly, volumes containing correspondence with Lisbon in the Historical Archives of Goa are known as the Monsoon Books of the Kingdom (*Livros das Monções do Reino*).[5] The hard, practical limit imposed by the monsoon meant that Europeans in India could expect to write a letter to and receive one from Europe just once a year, regardless of a correspondent's status. Filippo Sassetti's correspondence, a fine exemplar of Italian literary letters and long published as such, needs to be understood as shaped both by this seasonal limit and the broader context of his network.[6] The published letters remain fragments of a larger conversation shaped by long-distance travel, temporary expatriatism, and oral communication.

Born in 1540, Filippo Sassetti had originally been trained as a merchant, as befit his prominent Florentine family's tradition, before renouncing the commercial life in his early twenties.[7] He then became, like other privileged young men of his generation, a university-educated literary figure and academician. Immersed in the literary and intellectual milieu of Florence, Sassetti wrote on Aristotle, Dante, and Ariosto.[8] Then, in September 1577, Sassetti dedicated his treatise advocating trade links to the Ottoman world, *On Commerce between Tuscany and the Levantine Nations*, to a gentleman of the Medici court; it was timely.[9] That year, the Medici had asked for open and reciprocal trade and diplomatic relations with the Ottoman Empire, an effort that foundered on Tuscan bad faith.[10] Now in his late thirties, Sassetti resumed work as a merchant. He joined the politically connected firm of the Capponi – a major Florentine family – in Lisbon and Spain, before taking up a senior post with one of the pepper contractors, Giovan Battista Rovellasco. From 1582, Sassetti was to be Rovellasco's chief purchasing agent in India.[11]

During Sassetti's stay on the Iberian Peninsula, he embedded himself in the overlapping commercial networks that tied Tuscans to other Italians, Portuguese, and Spaniards in global trade networks. The Florentines in Lisbon continued a commercial tradition dating back more than a century.[12] Yet, their presence in 1580 was especially significant. While Sassetti worked for the Capponi firm in Lisbon, war clouds were lowering. Specifically, after the dynastic succession crisis sparked by the death of the childless king Dom Sebastian I in the disastrous defeat of the Portuguese army at the Battle of Alcácer Quibir in Morocco in 1578, King Philip II of Spain decided to vindicate his claim to the Portuguese Crown by force of arms. In 1580, the Spanish army invaded, bringing Portugal into an Iberian Union; this composite monarchy lasted until 1640.

Grand Duke Francesco I of Tuscany financed the invasion.[13] In 1579, Philip II had borrowed 400,000 crowns from the Grand Duke of Tuscany as part of his campaign of rearmament in preparation for the invasion of Portugal.[14] The next year, the costs of thousands of guns, ammunition, raising troops, and financing part of the fleet were billed directly to the Grand Duke of Tuscany.[15] Over the whole period 1579–1583, the Medici and the Averona and Caccia, Carnesecchi, and Strozzi banks of Tuscany advanced Philip II a total of 1,414,667 scudi.[16] This proved to be the apogee of Tuscan lending to the prudent king. With the return of the Genoese and South Germans bankers to center stage, the pressure on the Tuscans receded, but only slightly, as Philip II's borrowing continued to spiral. The king borrowed 600,000 crowns from the Florentines in 1589, for instance.[17] In these critical years, then, the Medici stood at the heart of Spanish Habsburg finance. It has been argued that, during his time in Lisbon, Sassetti played a role in this, acting effectively as a front for the investments of Grand Duke Francesco I.[18]

Whatever his prior role, when Filippo Sassetti left Lisbon, he was an agent both of the pepper monopoly contractors and of the Medici. As it happened, he had to leave twice. In 1582, he set out for India only to be foiled when his first ship, having been held up off Guinea and then in sandbanks off Brazil, missed the monsoon and returned to Lisbon in 1582.[19] The following year, Sassetti successfully launched for India. He did not go alone, traveling with his friends and collaborators Orazio Neretti and Giovanni Buondelmonti, both of whom received far lower salaries. In his brief return to business, Sassetti had managed to secure the senior role. Sassetti's work for the pepper consortium involved sailing his small ship up and down the Malabar Coast, purchasing pepper from the small producers and the minor kings. The pepper was often grown in the Ghat mountains and then taken to the coast for sale. Both Neretti and Buondelmonti would later play important roles in Sassetti's relationship with Florentines and the Medici.[20]

While his work for the pepper consortium constituted Sassetti's primary official employment, his role as a Medici agent was simultaneous. As an annual correspondent of the Medici brothers, Sassetti interpreted his duties as including the supply of commercial and strategic information, rare and exotic goods, and botanical samples and analysis.[21] This seems to have been a role that he relished. Sassetti wrote annual letters of literary quality to various members of the Florentine elite, including especially Grand Duke Francesco I and his brother (and successor as Grand Duke) Cardinal Ferdinando (r. 1587–1609). These letters were meant to – and did – circulate. For instance, a fair copy of one of Sassetti's letters from India, to Piero Vettori in Florence, can be found in a collection of documents on various Tuscan subjects probably made in the 1590s (Figure 10.1). Sassetti seems to have counted on this manuscript circulation; as a result, he generally avoided repeating information and analyses.[22] His letters read like private correspondence, albeit with a measure of formality that recognized the recipient's status. In these letters, Sassetti commented on anthropological, botanical, geographic, and linguistic subjects; he noted a linguistic connection between Sanskrit and Greek and Latin.[23]

Sassetti's correspondence presents a typically early modern puzzle. The body of published letters is substantial, yet quite incomplete.[24] The high degree of polish that most of the letters display, and the internal commentaries in his letters noting, for instance, that the first part of a letter was written in a different place than the second, point to the limited usefulness of the letters' written dates. An extreme case may demonstrate the point. The exigencies of the monsoons – which made it possible to travel long distances in only one direction for several months before reversing – certainly explain the months of composition. Still, it seems unlikely that he wrote five letters in full on 27 January 1585.[25]

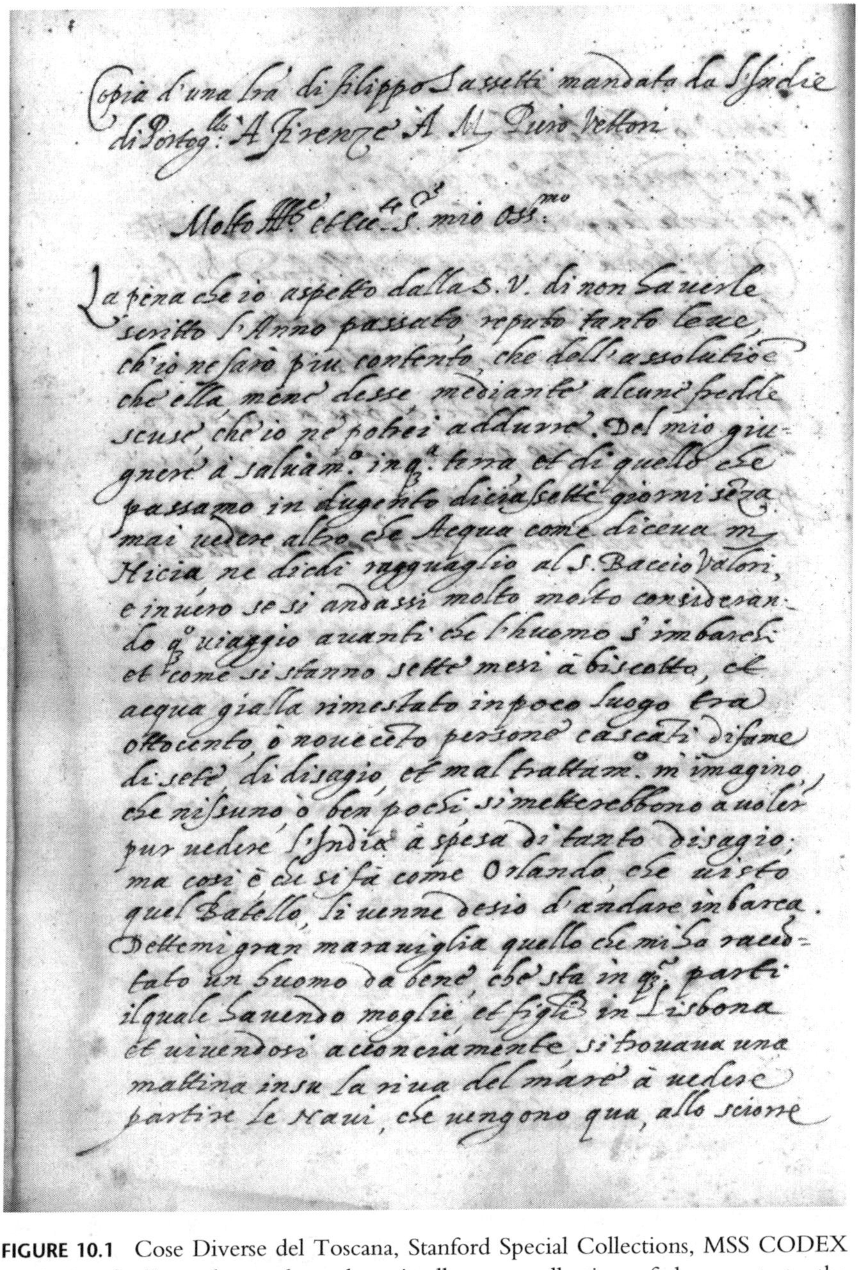

Copia d'una lra di Filippo Sassetti mandata da l'Indie
di Portog.llo A Firenze A M. Piero Vettori

Molto Ill.re et Ecc.te S.r mio Oss.mo

La pena che io aspetto dalla S.V. di non hauerle
scritto l'Anno passato reputo tanto leue,
ch'io ne sarò più contento, che dell'assolutiõe
che ella mene desse mediante alcune fredde
scuse che io ne potrei addurre. Del mio giu-
gnere à saluam.to in q.ta terra et di quello che
passamo in dugento diciasette giorni sẽza
mai uedere altro che Acqua come diceua m.
Nicia, ne diedi ragguaglio al S. Baccio Valori,
e inuero se si andassi molto molto consideran-
do q.o uiaggio auanti che l'huomo s'imbarchi
et come si stanno sette mesi à biscotto, et
acqua gialla rimestato in poco luogo tra
ottocento, ò nouecẽto persone cascati di fame
di sete di disagio, et mal trattam.to m'imagino,
che nissuno ò ben pochi si metterebbono à uoler
pur uedere l'India à spesa di tanto disagio;
ma così è chi si fà come Orlando, che uisto
quel Batello, li uenne desio d'andare in barca.
Dettemi gran marauiglia quello che mi ha racco-
tato un huomo da bene, che sta in q.e parti
ilquale hauendo moglie, et figli in Lisbona
et uiuendosi acconciamente si trouaua una
mattina insu la riua del mare à uedere
partire le naui, che uengono qua, allo sciorre

FIGURE 10.1 Cose Diverse del Toscana, Stanford Special Collections, MSS CODEX 0462. Stanford's catalogue dates the miscellaneous collection of documents to the 1590s. Image courtesy of Stanford University's Special Collections

Literary and scientific, performative and practical, public and private, Sassetti's letters operate in different registers and address multiple audiences. This befits the circumstances of their transmission and reception. To make the journey, letters and accompanying items were forwarded repeatedly before reaching Tuscany. The transmission of the letters to Francesco I, for instance, relied on the official diplomatic network. This has made it possible to follow the ripples of receipt and retransmission as Sassetti's correspondence moved. A 1584 letter from Ambassador to Spain Bongianni Gianfigliazzi gave news of Filippo Sassetti's arrival in India.[26] Gianfigliazzi reported that he had received a packet of letters for Francesco I from Sassetti.[27] Likewise, on 28 July 1584 Giulio Battaglini in Madrid wrote to Pietro di Francesco Usimbardi in Rome mentioning, among other matters, the arrival of Sassetti's letters in Lisbon.[28] Once Sassetti's packet arrived, Francesco I responded to Gianfigliazzi, acknowledging that he had received things from Sassetti.[29] Early practitioners of centralized bureaucracy, the Grand Ducal government carefully filed away their agents' correspondence.[30]

In his capacity as purchasing agent, Sassetti reported on his progress in spending the 800 ducats entrusted to him in Lisbon by the Medici.[31] In his first letter to the Grand Duke from India, Sassetti closed with a list of items purchased with the money entrusted to him,

> A cape of Bengal embroidered with hunting scenes as described, with pearls and certain rubies cost ... 100 *serafini*
> Two capes of iridescent silk from China embroidered with hunting scenes with gold and silk ... 100 *serafini*
> A little porcupine stone ... 40 *serafini*
> A piece of Maldive coconut marrow (two ounces) ... 20 *serafini*
> The total cost of these ... 200 *serafini*
> It remains to me to spend on Your Highness's account 736 *serafini*, 2 *tanghe* and 16 *basalucchi*.[32]

As the Grand Duke's agent, Sassetti provided his prince with a direct supply of extraordinary items. Just as with the letters, the items moved through the Iberian Peninsula. In the middle of February 1585, for instance, Sassetti sent three letters in quick succession to the Medici. In his letter of 10 February to Cardinal Ferdinando, Sassetti mentioned that he had remitted items to Andrea Migliorati in Lisbon the previous year and that he would be sending the textiles and coins the same way this year, and excused himself for failing to send seeds. Sassetti used the same transmission mechanism for the two swords from Malabar sent to Francesco I, as Sassetti explained at the end of his letter to the Grand Duke of the following day. A week later, in what appears to be an addendum to his previous letter, Sassetti explained that a ship from Malacca and three from China had arrived and that he expected to find something for the Grand Duke. The secure transportation from Lisbon to Florence of items sent by Sassetti was still being discussed in 1588, the year of Sassetti's death. Taking a step back from the details to consider the structure of this enterprise, Sassetti functioned in Goa and Cochin much as the Medici agents in Lisbon and elsewhere on the Iberian Peninsula; he secured both local materials and items from much further afield.[33]

The same handful of ships that carried objects and letters back from India also brought other Tuscans, some of whom would see the Grand Duke in person. This started with Sassetti's inner circle, his friend Giovanni Buondelmonti, who had traveled to Goa with him and whose return to Florence helped Sassetti complete a core commission for the Medici.[34] In a 1585 letter to the Grand Duke, Sassetti recalled that he had been commissioned to collect seeds for the Medici. Primarily engaged in the pepper business, Sassetti could not devote his whole time to this pursuit and employed a "pagan physician" – that is, probably a Hindu – to tend to it when he left Goa for Cochin. Even so, Sassetti wrote to explain that,

> Of the diverse domestic fruit of the land, Giovanni Buondelmonti, who returns there with this armada, brings nuts and seeds. Conducting himself safely, he will kiss the hand of Your Highness and, if they are conserved on the road, he will give them to you. That which I can assemble, I will send for the coming year.[35]

While Sassetti was confined by the patterns of the monsoon to writing an annual letter, Buondelmonti provided a stronger link. He had been Sassetti's companion since their departure from Portugal and might be expected to deliver an extensive report to the Grand Duke, including on matters not suitable for inclusion in a letter likely to circulate.

Following the establishment of one of the first botanical gardens in Europe in Pisa, the Medici had made a project of acquiring seeds from around the world. Under Cosimo I's (r. 1537–1574) son and successor, Francesco I, Grand Ducal Tuscany relied on a network of prosperous merchants, intellectuals, and diplomats to provide seeds and samples from their global travels. These were shared with the Medici court and the linked networks of correspondents and institutions engaged in the botanical enterprise in Tuscany and neighboring parts of central Italy. Although almost none of these figures operated as full-time botanical collectors, their engagement with the project was often substantial.[36] Tuscan world traveler Francesco Carletti, for instance, sent citrus seeds from Japan and attempted to bring back lychee from China.[37]

Sassetti, however, engaged with the botanical project at an altogether different level. His letters offer general comments on local plants and animals, discuss the collection and transportation of plants and seeds, and contain an extended analysis of cinnamon in which he concluded that the ancients had been poorly informed.[38] In 1586, the year after Buondelmonti's departure, Sassetti wrote to Baccio Valori, a jurist, Grand Ducal official, and brother of Sassetti's friend Francesco Valori,[39]

> I put one of these pagan physicians in the mind to recognize and breed simples. I went this year and saw a few plants and medicines, of which I send seeds to His Highness, with what little that, in little time, I could find out. I have purchased to this effect a garden in Goa, where I plan to put up to a hundred of the most identified plants in these parts.[40]

Sassetti had a fraught relationship with the local experts on whom he depended. He complained about the Portuguese and *mestizo* apothecaries' lack of curiosity and knowledgeable Indian experts' secrecy.[41] Access to the secrets of Indian nature was socially mediated. Sassetti's letters offer a glimpse of the social interactions that both impeded and made possible this botanical enterprise.

As a humanist intellectual, Sassetti deployed his textual skills on the samples provided by local suppliers. This can be seen most clearly in his more extended effort to understand cinnamon. In his "Discourse on Cinnamon," included in a letter sent to Baccio Valori in Florence from Cochin in January 1587, Sassetti laid out the views of various authors on the correspondence between the ancient *cinnamomo* and modern plants.[42] Since the two terms used to describe cinnamon – *cannella* and *cinnamomo* – both translate to cinnamon in English and Sassetti's whole point rests on the difference in Italian, I give them in the original.[43] Sassetti wrote,

> Taking myself to India, I saw this *cannella* plant many times in the land of Malabar, Canara, and Goa. They call it *di mattos*, emphasizing the making and the quality of all the root, as above the green earth how it is cut and dried. By observing the white sprigs, the black, and the various [colors], I judged that it cannot be other *cinnamomo*. This is the same plant found on the island of Ceylon. There, they remove the husk for the *canella*, cut from its shrub with all its parts, and carried to our country. For two years, I continually paid people who went to that island to bring me *cannella* plants of that land in order to test my theory. The second time I did so, they brought me two large bundles of trees or roots of the said plant, with all the branches, leaves, bark, and other parts, just as they had grown in nature. After analyzing these, I assured myself that the *cinnamomo* of the ancients was no other than the stalk of the *cannella* plucked from its bush just as nature created it. It matched up with all the qualities that the ancients attributed to it.[44]

Sassetti's description and analysis continue, but the essentials are here. He relied on agents to gather samples from the point of origin and used the evidence of those samples to evaluate and explain the opinions of the ancients. In his enclosing letter for the "Discourse on Cinnamon," Sassetti wrote to Valori,

> Last year, I was working on understanding what the *cinnamomo* of the ancients actually was. I wrote to Your Lordship that I would send that plant I believed it to be ... I sent a plant of my *cinnamomo* in a case. It is in transit to Lisbon to my cousin, Carlo Velluti, and he will send it to Pisa.[45]

If the story were to end here, there would be a clear narrative of observation and botanical collecting. Unfortunately, the case seems to have met with ill-fortune. A year later Sassetti sent a follow-up letter to Baccio Valori,

Last year, I sent to Your Lordship my concept of *cinnamomo*, such as it was. Alas, the case it was in was sent on a ship that capsized. Since the island of Ceylon is now at war, I do not know when I will return there to acquire another specimen. It would have been better, perhaps, if my writing had never come to your hands (if this could have been, saving the other things), because it is necessary to correct some faults about the fruit. That can be subject to the amount of faith one can give those who report on the state of things in India. I have been left deceived, despite having observed the specimen with my own eyes. Having left Cochin, when I returned to Goa the year before, they were asked to make me a large vase of this fruit to conserve. I aimed to give it to whoever might wish to view it, because the flavor is aromatic and good and drawn from the resin of pistachio. However, I ought not to have believed these simpletons diligent enough to be trusted with this task. It turned out to be an idiocy, and they did not serve at all. They tried my patience, asking me questions like "what good was that seed?" That is the reason that these people give to the things that are not to their humor. I have not had occasion to converse with men of science where I might have been able to portray something worthy of coming to your knowledge.[46]

Sassetti regretted his letter's survival, as it had proved unreliable, an artifact of failures of communication and understanding in India. The sample, on the other hand, would have been accurate, though Sassetti's observation of it in India had been insufficient to protect him from error. Nor, for that matter, were the samples he sent to Tuscany unmediated natural objects, depending as they did on his suppliers in India, local experts, and the friends and relatives with whom they traveled.

The letters that bound Sassetti to Florence were capacious enough to allow Sassetti to play many roles. To his roles as botanical analyst and collector, Sassetti added that of provider of strategic information. This ranged from discussion of the construction of a new Portuguese fortress near Cochin[47] to critical commentary on Portuguese grand strategy in the Indian Ocean.[48] In 1585 he wrote,

In these parts, there are planned three undertakings of great importance. One is the discovery of a silver mine, that they say the mineral keeps the *** of Plata in a river called Cuamo near Sofala and Mozambique, where there remains a band of Portuguese who went to discover it. The second undertaking is the conquest of the island of Ceylon. That island is possessed by a pagan prince called *Ragiù* who is a very great enemy of the Portuguese. Faced with almost continuous travail, they have maintained a fortress called Colombo, located on the western part of Ceylon. Each year, they spend a great deal of money on it for both maintenance and defense. The third undertaking is the conquest of a port on the island of Sumatra that they call Dacem. Today, it is controlled by Moors, although the island itself is controlled by diverse pagan kings. But these dogs enter through dissimulation and are honored by the pagans. In this port, they load three quarters of the ships that carry spices to Mecca and Suez, because from that place they ship pepper that we call *gauro*, which comes from the island of Java and from a place they call Sunda.[49]

Fittingly, for an agent of the spice monopoly, the third enterprise against a Sumatran port reappeared as a suggestion Sassetti made the next year.[50] The problem of Sumatra serves as a reminder that, even at the height of Portuguese power, vibrant trading networks run by Arab, Gujarati, Malay, Acehnese, Javanese, Chinese, and Japanese merchants remained.[51] While the scope of Portuguese activity was astonishingly broad and the *Estado da Índia* and the corresponding informal empire played a large commercial role, the Portuguese were minor political players in most of Asia and Africa. The titanic efforts of the great Mughal Emperor Akbar dominated India in Sassetti's day.[52] Sassetti had the good sense to understand, carefully reporting Mughal conquests. Consistent with his sound strategic judgment, Sassetti feared the Mughals as a threat of a much higher order of magnitude than that posed by the rulers of Cochin, Calicut, Ceylon, or Ternate. By 1586, Sassetti issued quite a clear warning that the Mughals planned to conquer "all of India."[53] This they very nearly did in the following century.

Whether as a supplier of botanical samples or strategic analysis, Sassetti relied on informants and collaborators to address his correspondents' diverse interests. He did this in the expectation that his actions partook of a wider set of social interactions, both present and future, the most important of which would take place in person. While Sassetti's ultimate social reward might reasonably be assumed to be an honored place at the Medici court in Florence, in-person contact with Medici projects started in India. To see this, let us return to Sassetti's house and garden in Goa. There, Sassetti hosted a pair of agents, operating on behalf of the Papacy and of the Medici, engaged in work for the Medici Oriental Press (*Tipografia Medicea Orientale*). Led by the remarkable scholar Giovanni Battista Raimondi and jointly patronized by the Papacy and the Medici, the Press was dedicated to printing works of scientific and religious value in the languages of the greater Middle East.[54]

In 1584, Giovanni Battista Vecchietti and Giovanni Battista Britti set out for Alexandria. It was the first stop on their respective missions to gather information about the various routes across the Middle East; this was part of a project to distribute the books printed by the Press.[55] Both Giovanni Battistas were from Cosenza; the Vecchietti of Cosenza, however, were by origin an important Florentine family.[56] Britti was charged with going to Ethiopia on behalf of the Press and Pope Gregory XIII, but he chose a rather circuitous route from Alexandria, going via Tripoli in Syria, Aleppo, Baghdad, Basra, and Hormuz. He ran into trouble with pirates aboard a ship from Hormuz headed toward Ethiopia and ended up in Goa, where Sassetti wrote about him on 23 January 1586; Britti's story peters out here.[57] Giovanni Battista Vecchietti fared rather better on his voyage. Beyond the search for manuscripts for the Press to print, he had two diplomatic missions. He was to hold discussions about reunion with the Coptic

Church. Then, he was to travel to Iran to meet with the Shah to discuss anti-Turkish alliances. Vecchietti traveled from Egypt via Antioch, Damascus, and Aleppo, eventually reaching Tabriz. He reappeared in Hormuz in 1587 and was with Sassetti in Goa and Cochin in 1588, returning thence to Europe; Vecchietti would honor his host in Goa with a funeral oration for Sassetti in Florence.[58] Back in Europe, Vecchietti would present a well-received report on Safavid Iran to King Philip II. At the behest of Grand Duke Ferdinando I, Vecchietti explained what had been negotiated in Iran. Vecchietti's subsequent plan for Tuscany to send artillery and fortification experts to the Shah were met with Grand Ducal interest, but skepticism about Philip II's receptiveness to the idea from the Tuscan ambassador in Madrid.[59]

We can look at all this through multiple lenses. Through one we see a papal ambassador who stayed with the agent of the holders of a Portuguese government contract in the Portuguese viceregal capital of Goa. Through this lens, we see close cooperation between the Papacy and the Portuguese state – now under Spanish Habsburg management – in the Indian Ocean world, continuing an almost century-old tradition. Seen through a different lens, we have a scion of a family with old Tuscan roots – Vecchietti[60] – staying with the scion of an old Florentine house – Sassetti – both of whom worked on behalf of the Medici dynasty to serve its interests. Both lenses show a true picture, but neither shows the whole story. There is one further parallel. Both Britti and Vecchietti were supposed to send seeds and rare plants to Cardinal Ferdinando de' Medici's garden.[61]

Just as Filippo Sassetti's friends, traveling companions, and guests substantially supplemented the web of connections constituted by his letters, so also Sassetti's personal travels were designed to complement the letters. To move beyond the limits of an annual correspondence, though, Sassetti needed to go home to Florence. This he sought to do spectacularly, surpassing Marco Polo and cementing his reputation as a great traveler. In his last surviving letter to the Medici, to Cardinal Ferdinando in 1586, Sassetti proposed to continue in Medici service for at least another eight years.[62] His plan was to circumnavigate the globe, taking seven or eight years to travel to Malacca, the Moluccas, China, Manila, on the Manila Galleon to Acapulco, two years throughout the Americas, and finally to return to Tuscany.[63]

Sassetti pointed out that imperial officials were quite hostile to the presence of foreigners within their domains, being suspicious of the information they might gain.[64] Indeed, the Castilians prohibited travel by foreigners through the Indies without a license.[65] While the Iberian Union of 1580 that the Medici had financed made circumnavigation through the Iberian Empires seem eminently possible, the title of a copy of a March 1594 letter from Philip II to the Viceroy in Goa, held in the Historical Archives of Goa, "about not having commerce between East India and the West Indies"[66] conveys the extent to which the Iberian monarchies remained composite structures with strong internal barriers. To circumvent this obstacle, Sassetti requested the Medici

Cardinal's intercession on his behalf to enter Philip II's service and to gain extensive special privileges to permit the circumnavigation through Philip II's empires.[67] Unfortunately, application for permission proved irrelevant, for Sassetti died in India in 1588.[68]

Orazio Neretti, who we met earlier as Sassetti's friend who had traveled with him to India, wrote this Latin epitaph for Sassetti, placed at his grave in the Church of the Company of Mercy:[69]

> Filippo Sassetti Florentine citizen
> Overseer of office for spice exports
> Distinguished in the study of nature and mathematics
> Renowned for eloquence in Greek Latin and Etruscan
> To study new things
> Rather than for gain
> Traversed the empty African Ocean
> Stayed in Goa in India
> Nearly all of Europe
> Was enriched by his most excellent observations
> Of the treasures of India
> Orazio Neretti Florentine
> Perpetual dear companion
> With many tears set down
> His dear life and yet still abroad at 46 years
> died in Goa in the year 1588.[70]

Sassetti's set of mathematical instruments and Greek and Latin texts were left to the Jesuits in general, while a couple of framed globes were given to Father Gaspare Stuiven, SJ.[71]

Despite his untimely end, Sassetti seems to have inspired emulation. While the evidence is circumstantial, Sassetti's fame in Florence and the memory of him carried by Orazio Neretti appear to have combined to inspire a young Florentine merchant adventurer, Francesco Carletti (1573/1574–1636), to carry Sassetti's ambitions to fruition.[72] Carletti's experience offers a guide to how Sassetti may have expected to have been received by his patrons and correspondents upon returning to Europe.

Completing an adventurous, picaresque circumnavigation (1591–1606) that involved imprisonment in Cartagena and Macao, long stays in Lima, Mexico City, Nagasaki, Macao, and Goa, and capture by the Dutch in a naval battle off Saint Helena, Carletti returned to Florence on 12 July 1606.[73] Having received extensive support from the Medici, especially during his legal action against the VOC, Carletti was taken to see the Grand Duke the day he arrived. The result was eventually Carletti's *Ragionamenti*, his account of his circumnavigation, ostensibly presented as twelve daily presentations to the Grand Duke of Tuscany.[74]

Like Sassetti, Carletti was a prolific source of information about the early modern world; he brought both physical objects from his travels and useful knowledge. For instance, Carletti made a demonstration of some Bengali textiles and taught the Grand Duke's physicians how to properly use bezoar stones. We may imagine that a similar request for information and demonstrations would have been made of Sassetti had he returned from his voyage sometime in the mid-1590s and that Sassetti would have expected this.[75]

Carletti did not merely continue Sassetti's project. Rather, his life interleaved with the legacy of Sassetti's network. Carletti sent citrus seeds from Japan to the Medici in Tuscany and mentioned that only Francesco Capponi's plant had grown; Sassetti had worked for a Capponi firm.[76] Smuggling goods into Macao from Japan, Carletti consigned his goods to Jesuits, who also subsequently helped him buy Ming porcelain.[77] Sassetti had not only left his goods to the Jesuits, but had commented, in a letter of 1587, on the return journey through India of the four young Japanese boys who Alessandro Valignano, SJ had sent to Rome in 1581; they had arrived in Livorno in 1585 and had been received by Grand Duke Francesco I in Pisa.[78] Carletti, in turn, had had a conversation with Valignano about the expenses of the Catholic religious establishment in East Asia. Finally, shortly after the loss of his father in Macao in July 1598, Carletti met and relied on Orazio Neretti, Sassetti's old travel companion.[79] These parallels and connections give a sense of what Sassetti might have done. While Sassetti envisioned his journey as extending longer than it ultimately did, he did not envision his time away from Florence as permanent; he fully intended to return home.

Sassetti's intended return and Carletti's successful, if belated, one point to an essential feature of Tuscan engagement with the wider world. Precluded by geopolitics from securing an independent empire and facing few of the social, religious, and demographic pressures for colonial settlement, Tuscans shunned mass emigration. Instead, they continued to pursue old patterns of travel, albeit at vastly greater distances, linked to trade, political exile, religious calling, warfare, and state service. Many, perhaps most, of those who did leave Tuscany sought to maintain connections to Florence and especially to the Medici. The Medici continued their long family tradition of brokering favors using their political position and connections to Rome and powerful foreign courts, simply on a larger scale than they could have dreamed in the fifteenth century.[80] The expectation of return, Medici munificence and connections, and a shared sense of identity as Florentines contributed to Medici affiliates' striking propensity to constitute themselves as an interconnected network. This allowed a small number of travelers to weave a globe-spanning web of connections that became more useful to all involved as it grew. Figure 10.2 shows how just four of these Tuscan affiliates traveled through the Ottoman and Safavid Empires and spanned the furthest limits of Iberian Empire. They constituted but a small part of the Medici affiliates abroad, linked by letters and travel, who together opened Florence to the possibilities of the First Global Age.

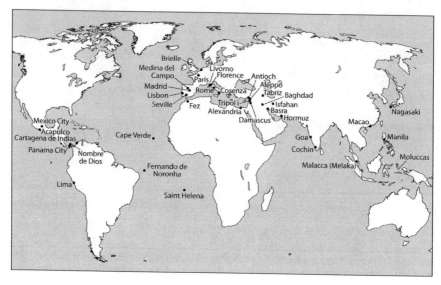

FIGURE 10.2 Selected sites of Tuscan-affiliated travel: the marked places indicate locations Filippo Sassetti, Giovanni Battista Britti, Giovanni Battista Vecchietti, and Francesco Carletti traveled, with one exception. Sassetti planned to visit the Moluccas but died before he could make the journey.[81] Map credit: Bill Nelson

Notes

1 I am particularly grateful for comments on the original version of this chapter given at Stanford's Renaissance of Letters Conference. I have shared research on Sassetti and benefitted from comments at Boston College, Penn State, and Syracuse University and at the RSA and Scientiae conferences. On the images, thanks go to John Mustain, Curator of Rare Books at Stanford University's Special Collection, for his generous assistance. Ettore Marcucci, ed., *Lettere edite e inedite di Filippo Sassetti* (Firenze: Felice Le Monnier, 1855), 262. The letter to Cardinal Ferdinando I (261–265) was sent from Cochin in January 1584 (265).

2 For population figures see Teotonio R. De Souza, ed., *Goa Through the Ages: An Economic History*, vol. 2, Goa University Publications Series No. 6 (New Delhi: Concept Publishing, 1990).

3 This was the arrangement with the Papacy that granted the Portuguese Crown extensive rights of patronage and control over the Church in the Portuguese Empire. A. R. Disney, *A History of Portugal and the Portuguese Empire: From Beginnings to 1807*, 2 vols., I: *Portugal*; II: *The Portuguese Empire* (New York: Cambridge University Press, 2009), vol. II, 67–68, 163, and 201.

4 Sanjay Subrahmanyam, *The Portuguese Empire in Asia, 1500–1700: A Political and Economic History* (New York: Longman, 1993), 142 and Table 5.5. James C. Boyajian, *Portuguese Trade in Asia under the Habsburgs, 1580–1640* (Baltimore, MD: The Johns Hopkins University Press, 1993), 124–127.

5 See, for example, Historical Archives of Goa, Archive Number 7, Livros das Monções do Reino, no. 5, 44r–45r. This appears to be a clean copy of a letter received and recorded in the register of royal correspondence.

6 Marcucci, ed., *Lettere*.

7 Milanesi, *Filippo Sassetti*, 56.
8 Marica Milanesi, *Filippo Sassetti*, Publicazioni della Facoltà di Lettere e Filosofia dell'Università di Milano (Firenze, Italia: La Nuova Italia Editrice, 1973), 23–31 and 52–77.
9 Milanesi, *Filippo Sassetti*, 23–31. Medici Archive Project (MAP) Person ID 1240. The original title is: *Sul commercio tra la Toscana e le Nazioni levantine*. For a recent analysis of this text in the context of Livorno see Corey Tazzara, *The Free Port of Livorno and the Transformation of the Mediterranean World, 1574–1790* (New York: Oxford University Press, 2017), 32–37.
10 Riguccio Galluzzi, *Storia del Granducato di Toscana*, 11 vols., vols. 3 and 4 bound together, Nuova Edizione (Firenze: Leonardo Marchini, 1822), Vol. 4, Lib. IV, Cap. III, 66–71, years 1577 and 1578. Caroline Finkel, *Osman's Dream: The Story of the Ottoman Empire 1300–1923*, 2005, paperback ed. (New York: Basic Books, 2007), 562; Özden Mercan, "Medici–Ottoman Diplomatic Relations (1574–1578): What Went Wrong?" in Arfaioli and Caroscio, eds., *The Grand Ducal Medici and the Levant: Material Culture, Diplomacy, and Imagery in the Eastern Mediterranean*, The Medici Archive Project Series (London: Harvey Miller Publishers, 2016), 19–31.
11 Milanesi, *Filippo Sassetti*, 23, 33–34, 38–46, and 69. Filippo Sassetti, *Lettere dall'India (1583–1588)*, ed. Adele Dei (Roma, Italia: Salerno Editrice, 1995), Letter 20, 157 n. 6. On the pepper contracts, see Ernst van Veen, *Decay or Defeat? An Inquiry into the Portuguese Decline in Asia, 1580–1645*, Studies in Overseas History (Leiden, Netherlands: Research School CNWS, Leiden University, 2000), Appendix 3.2 – The Carreira pepper contracts, 252–253. Nunziatella Alessandrini, "Images of India through the Eyes of Filippo Sassetti, a Florentine Humanist Merchant in the Sixteenth Century," in *Sights and Insights: Interactive Images of Europe and the Wider World*, eds. Mary N. Harris and Csaba Lévai (Pisa: Pisa University Press, 2007), 46.
12 Nunziatella Alessandrini, "Images of India," 46.
13 Richard A. Goldthwaite, *The Economy of Renaissance Florence* (Baltimore, MD: The Johns Hopkins University Press, 2009), 123–124. Milanesi, *Filippo Sassetti*, 23, 33–34, and 42–46. Alessandrini, "Images of India," 46. Fernand Braudel, *The Mediterranean and the Mediterranean World in the Age of Philip II*, 2 vols., 2nd revised ed., 1966, trans. Siân Reynolds (Berkeley, CA: University of California Press, 1995), vol. II, 1181. Henry Kamen, *Empire: How Spain Became a World Power 1492–1763* (New York: Harper Collins, 2003), 302.
14 Braudel, *The Mediterranean and the Mediterranean World in the Age of Philip II*, vol. II, 1181.
15 Kamen, *Empire*, 302.
16 Eladi Romero García, *El imperialismo hispanico en la Toscana durante el siglo XVI* (Lleida: Dilagro, 1986), 120, gives a slightly higher 1,1416,667 than Eric Cochrane, *Florence in the Forgotten Centuries 1527–1800: A History of Florence and the Florentines in the Age of the Grand Dukes* (Chicago, IL: The University of Chicago Press, 1973), 113 and Milanesi, *Filippo Sassetti*, 39–40.
17 Braudel, *The Mediterranean and the Mediterranean World in the Age of Philip II*, vol. I, 492 and 492 n. 213–214.
18 Milanesi, *Filippo Sassetti*, 38–40.
19 This left Sassetti five months of an ultimately fruitless voyage. Adele Dei, "Nota biografica" in Sassetti, *Lettere dall'India*, 22.
20 For Sassetti's task in India and the roles of Buondelmonti and Neretti, see Milanesi, *Filippo Sassetti*, 42–46 and 49. On India and Europeans see Meera Juncu, *India in the Italian Renaissance: Visions of a Contemporary Pagan World 1300–1600* (New York: Routledge, 2016); Sanjay Subrahmanyam, *Explorations in Connected History: From the Tagus to the Ganges, 2005* (New Delhi: Oxford India Paperbacks, 2011); Sanjay Subrahmanyam, *Europe's India: Words, People, Empires, 1500–1800* (Cambridge, MA: Harvard University Press, 2017); and Jonathan Gil Harris, *The First Firangis:*

Remarkable Stories of Heroes, Healers, Charlatans, Courtesans and Other Foreigners who Become Indian (New Delhi: Aleph, 2015).

21 Dei, ed., Sassetti, *Lettere dall'India*, Letter 1, 31–32 n. 16, 34–35, and 34 n. 24 and Letter 4, 22 January 1584, 45–47. Milanesi, *Filippo Sassetti*, 42–46, 49, and 67. Cochrane, *Florence in the Forgotten Centuries 1527–1800*, 262. Jean-Claude Waquet, *Corruption: Ethics and Power in Florence, 1600–1770*, 1984, trans. Linda McCall (University Park, PA: The Pennsylvania State University Press, 1992). Boyajian, *Portuguese Trade in Asia under the Habsburgs, 1580–1640*, 124–127.

22 See Figure 10.2, Stanford University Libraries, Special Collections, MSS M462 *Cose Diverse del Toscana M.S.* Dei, ed., Sassetti, *Lettere dall'India*, Letter 4, 54 and Letter 14, 113. It has been convincingly claimed that Sassetti's letters were open to a privileged Florentine public and that they may have been intended for publication, Milanesi, *Filippo Sassetti*, 1–2.

23 For one of Sassetti's botanical reports see Dei, ed., Sassetti, *Lettere dall'India*, Letter 4, 48–49. For Sassetti's discovery of the connection between Greek, Latin, and Sanskrit see Dei, ed., Sassetti, *Lettere dall'India*, Letter, 22, 179–180 and 180 n. 52. For grudging recognition of Sassetti's role see Jarl Charpentier, "The Original Home of the Indo-Europeans: Two Lectures Delivered at the School of Oriental Studies, London, on 10th and 17 June 1925," *Bulletin of the School of Oriental Studies, University of London* 4, no. 1 (1926), 149. For Sassetti's connection with Mercator and Ortelius see Dei, ed., Sassetti, *Lettere dall'India*, Letter 19, 147 n. 17 and Letter 31, 239n. 7 and Letter 19, 147 n. 18 respectively. See also Milanesi, *Filippo Sassetti*, 2. For Sassetti's role as a member of the *Accademia degli Alterati*, see Dei, ed., *Lettere dall'India*, "Nota biografica," 21 and Cochrane, *Florence in the Forgotten Centuries 1527–1800*, 108 and 116–121. Many of Sassetti's correspondents were also members of the Alterati: Dei, ed., *Lettere dall'India*, Sassetti, Letter 17, 122–123 n. 13; Letter 18, 132 n. 1; and Letter 21, 161 n. 4. For more on Sassetti in India see, Joan-Pau Rubiés, *Travel and Ethnology in the Renaissance: South India Through European Eyes, 1250–1625* (New York: Cambridge University Press, 2000), 381–383 and Sanjay Subrahmanyam, *Explorations in Connected History: Mughals and Franks, 2005* (New Delhi: Oxford India Paperbacks, 2011), 83.

24 Marcucci, ed., *Lettere*. The "Discorso sopra il Cinnamomo" was included in the letter to Baccio Valori. The letter to Valori (382–384); the "Discourse on Cinnamon" (384–398).

25 Milanesi, *Filippo Sassetti*, 73 n. 102 and Dei, ed., Sassetti, *Lettere dall'India*, Letter 25, 208.

26 Archivio di Stato di Firenze (ASF), Mediceo del Principato (MdP), 5046, 56v–57r. From Bongianni di Piero Gianfigliazzi in Madrid to Grand Duke Francesco I de' Medici, 9 July 1584 (57r). Medici Archive Project (MAP) Doc ID 16081. MAP Person ID 430 for Gianfigliazzi gives his role as Medici ambassador in Spain at this point.

27 ASF, MdP 5046, 58v–60v. MAP Doc ID 14540. From Bongianni di Piero (Fra) Gianfigliazzi in Madrid to Francesco I de' Medici in Florence on 28 July 1584.

28 MAP Doc ID 15682. MAP entry for ASF, MdP 5113, Insert 1, 217. From Giulio Battaglini in Madrid to Pietro di Francesco Usimbardi in Rome on 28 July 1584. On Battaglini see MAP Person ID 256. On Usimbardi, see MAP Person ID 469.

29 ASF, MdP 5046, 385r–386v.

30 MAP Doc ID 22796. MAP entry for ASF, MdP 5037, 508. From Filippo Sassetti in Kochi to Francesco I de' Medici in Florence on 20 January 1584. MAP Doc ID 15581. MAP entry for ASF, MdP 5113, Insert 1, 354. From Filippo Sassetti in Kochi to Ferdinando I de' Medici in Rome on 10 February 1585. MAP Doc ID 22813. MAP entry for ASF, MdP 5037, 523. From Filippo Sassetti in Kochi to Francesco I de' Medici in Florence on 11 February 1585. See Andréa Doré, "Cristãos na Ìndia no século XVI: a presença portuguesa e os viajantes italianos,"

Revista Brasileira de História 22 no. 44 (2002): 311–339. Subrahmanyam, *The Portuguese Empire in Asia, 1500–1700*, esp. 113–117. See also Cochrane, *Florence in the Forgotten Centuries 1527–1800*, 108. On Lorenzo Strozzi, Sassetti, *Lettere dall'India*, Letter 1, 30 n. 8.

31 Marcucci, ed., *Lettere*, 235–236, Letter LXXVII, to the Grand Duke of Tuscany, Francesco I (235) from Lisbon 7 February 1583 (236).

32 Dei, ed., Sassetti, *Lettere dall'India*, Letter 4, 22 January 1584, from Filippo Sassetti in Cochin to Grand Duke Francesco I in Florence, 55.

33 See ASF, MDP 4919, P. I, 281r–284v, 21 May 1588 from Carlo Velluti in Lisbon to Grand Duke Ferdinando I in Florence, MAP Doc ID 8256. Dei, ed., Sassetti, *Lettere dall'India*, Letter 13, 102–107; Letter 14, 113; Letter 15, 114. On Sassetti's description on goods available and his purchases for the Medici, see R.W. Lightbown, "Oriental Art and the Orient in Late Renaissance and Baroque Italy," *Journal of the Warburg and Courtauld Institutes* 32 (1969): 235–238.

34 Milanesi, *Filippo Sassetti*, 42–46.

35 Marcucci, ed., *Lettere*, 301. This passage appears in Sassetti's letter to Grand Duke Francesco I (299–303) sent from the city of Santa Croce of Cochin on 11 February 1585 (303). On colonial bioprospecting, see Londa Schiebinger, *Plants and Empire: Colonial Bioprospecting in the Atlantic World* (Cambridge, MA: Harvard University Press, 2004).

36 Lucia Tongiorgi Tomasi, "The Flowering of Florence: Botanical Art for the Medici" in Lucia Tongiorgi Tomasi and Gretchen A. Hirschauer, *The Flowering of Florence: Botanical Art for the Medici*, Catalog of an exhibition held at the National Gallery of Art, Washington, D.C. 3 Mar.–27 May 2002 (Burlington, VT: Lund Humphries, 2002), 38. See also, Milanesi, *Filippo Sassetti*, 69; Dei, ed., Sassetti, *Lettere dall'India*, Letter 4, 50 n. 17; and Cochrane, *Florence in the Forgotten Centuries 1527–1800*, 129. On Tuscany, botany, exotica, and collecting see Cristina Bellorini, *The World of Plants in Renaissance Tuscany: Medicine and Botany* (Burlington, VT: Ashgate, 2016); Francisco Zamora Rodríguez, "Interest and Curiosity: American Products, Information, and Exotica in Tuscany," in Aram and Yun-Casalilla, eds. *Global Goods and the Spanish Empire, 1492–1824: Circulation, Resistance and Diversity* (New York: Palgrave Macmillan, 2014), 174–193; and William Eamon, *Science and the Secrets of Nature: Books of Secrets in Medieval and Early Modern Culture* (Princeton, NJ: Princeton University Press, 1994), 270.

37 Carletti, *My Voyage Around the World*, 108–109, 170–171, 170 n., and 171 n.

38 In one of his letters to Cardinal Ferdinando de' Medici, Sassetti discussed the use of elephants to load and unload boats. Marcucci, ed., *Lettere*, 262–263. For cinnamon see idem, 389–390.

39 Dei, ed., Sassetti, *Lettere dall'India*, Letter 3, 42 n. 1.

40 Marcucci, ed., *Lettere*, 338–339. This passage appears in Sassetti's letter to Baccio Valori in Florence (338–341) sent from Cochin on 22 January 1586.

41 Marcucci, ed., *Lettere*, 301–302. Sassetti's comments appear in a letter written to Grand Duke Francesco I (299–303), dated from the city of "Santa Croce di Coccino," on 11 February 1585. See also Mark Harrison, *Climates and Constitutions: Health, Race, Environment and British Imperialism in India, 1600–1800*, 1999, Oxford India Paperbacks (New Delhi: Oxford University Press, 2002).

42 Since the two terms used to describe cinnamon – *cannella* and *cinnamomo* – both translate to cinnamon in English, I have left them in the original. Marcucci, ed., *Lettere*, 384–385. The "Discorso sopra il Cinnamomo" (384–398) was included in the letter to Baccio Valori (382–384).

43 For "Cannella" John Florio, "*Queen Anna's New World of Words, or Dictionarie of the Italian and English tongues*" (London: "Printed by *Melch. Bradwood*, for *Edw. Blount* and *William Barret*," 1611), gives, "a little cane, reede or pipe. Also a flute or recorder. Also a tap or spiggot. Also the arme-bone of a man. Also the spice Cinnamond." Florio defines "Cinamómo" as "the spice Cinamond," "Cinamomíno" as

"the oyle of Cinamond," and "Cinnamológo" as "a bird that buildeth her nest of Cynamond twigges."

44 Marcucci, ed., *Lettere*, 393–394.

45 Marcucci, ed., *Lettere*, 383.

46 Marcucci, ed., *Lettere*, 409. The quotation appears in a letter to Baccio Valori (407–410) sent from Cochin on 11 January 1588 (410).

47 Dei, ed., Sassetti, *Lettere dall'India*, Letter 25, 197–198 and 197 n. 11.

48 Subrahmanyam, *The Portuguese Empire in Asia, 1500–1700*, 62–74. Frederic C. Lane, *Venice: A Maritime Republic* (Baltimore, MD: The Johns Hopkins University Press, 1973), 284–294. Sassetti, *Lettere dall'India*, Letter 14, 110 and 110n9.

49 Dei, ed. Sassetti, *Lettere dall'India*, Letter 14, 109–110. The translation of "gauro" is taken directly from the Salvatore Battaglia, *Grande Dizionario della Lingua Italiana* 21 vols. vol. 6 FIO~GRAU (Torino, Italia: Unione Tipografico-Editrice Torino, begun in 1961), which, circularly, cites this passage from Sassetti for one of its definitions.

50 Sassetti, *Lettere dall'India*, Letter 25, 212. It may be the same port. Sassetti used the word "Dacen," but perhaps he meant "Dacem."

51 Anthony Reid, *Southeast Asia in the Age of Commerce: 1450–1680*, 2 vols. (New Haven, CT: Yale University Press, 1988 and 1993): Volume 1: *Southeast Asia in the Age of Commerce: 1450–1680: Volume One: The Lands Below the Winds* (New Haven, CT: Yale University Press, 1988); Volume 2: *Southeast Asia in the Age of Commerce: 1450–1680: Volume Two: Expansion and Crisis* (New Haven, CT: Yale University Press, 1993).

52 John F. Richards, *The Mughal Empire*, The New Cambridge History of India, Paperback Edition (Cambridge: Cambridge University Press, 1993). Sanjay Subrahmanyam, *The Political Economy of Commerce: Southern India, 1500–1650*, 1990, South Asian Studies 45, paperback edition (New York: Cambridge University Press, 2002).

53 Dei, ed., Sassetti, *Lettere dall'India*, Letter 25, 202–203.

54 Margherita Farina, "La nascita della Tipografia Medicea: personaggi e idee," in Sara Fani and Margherita Farina, eds. *le vie delle lettere: la Tipografia Medicea tra Roma e l'Oriente*, Catalogue and essays for an exhibition at the Biblioteca Medicea Laurenziana from 10/26/12–6/22/13 (Firenze: Mandragora, 2012), especially 43–56. On Egypt and Renaissance Italians, Alan Mikhail, *Under Osman's Tree: The Ottoman Empire, Egypt, and Environmental History* (Chicago, IL: The University of Chicago Press, 2017); Brian Curran, *The Egyptian Renaissance: The Afterlife of Ancient Egypt in Early Modern Italy* (Chicago, IL: The University of Chicago Press, 2007); and Margaret Meserve, *Empires of Islam in Renaissance Historical Thought* (Cambridge, MA: Harvard University Press, 2008).

55 Farina, "La nascita della Tipografia Medicea: personaggi e idee," 48–49.

56 Farina, "La nascita della Tipografia Medicea: personaggi e idee," 60 and 63.

57 Farina, "La nascita della Tipografia Medicea: personaggi e idee," 60–63. Farina suggests that he may have died in Goa.

58 Farina, "La nascita della Tipografia Medicea: personaggi e idee," 63–65. Angelo De Gubernatis, ed., *Storia dei Viaggiatori Italiani nelle Indie Orientali*, Pubblicata in Occasione del Congresso Geografico di Parigi (Livorno: Franc. Vigo, 1875), 25 and 25 n. 1. On the Ottoman Empire against which the Tuscans plotted see Palmira Brummett, *Mapping the Ottomans: Sovereignty, Territory, and Identity in Early Modern Mediterranean* (New York: Cambridge University Press, 2015); Suraiya Faroqhi, *The Ottoman Empire and the World Around It* (New York: I.B. Tauris, 2006); Daniel Goffman, *The Ottoman Empire and Early Modern Europe* (New York: Cambridge University Press, 2002); Baki Tezcan, *The Second Ottoman Empire: Political and Social Transformation in the Early Modern World* (New York: Cambridge University Press, 2010); and Noel Malcolm, *Agents of Empire: Knights, Corsairs, Jesuits, and Spies in the Sixteenth Century Mediterranean World* (New York: Oxford University Press, 2015). See also my "Making a New Prince: Tuscany, the Pasha of Aleppo, and the Dream of a New Levant" in Francesco Freddolini and Marco Musillo, eds. *Eurasian Tuscany: Art, Mobility, and Exchange, c. 1500–1750* [Forthcoming] and "The Advantages of Stability:

Medici Tuscany's Ambitions in the Eastern Mediterranean" in Brian Maxson and Nicholas Baker, eds., *Florence in the Early Modern World* [Forthcoming].

59 ASF, MdP 4919, P. II, 602r–603v, 10 December 1588, from Giovanni Battista Vecchietti in Madrid to Ferdinando I de' Medici in Florence. MAP Doc ID 16228. ASF MdP 4919, 602. From Giovanni Battista Vecchietti in Madrid to Ferdinando I de' Medici in Florence on 10 December 1588. ASF, MdP 4919, P. II, 612r–615v, 10 December 1588, from Vicenzo di Andrea Alamanni in Madrid to Ferdinando I de' Medici in Florence. MAP Doc ID 8446. ASF, MdP 4818, 612. ASF MdP 4919, 568. From Giovanni Battista Vecchietti in Madrid to Ferdinando I in Firenze on 12 November 1588. MAP Doc ID 2718. ASF, MdP 4920, 23r–25v, 27 May 1589 from Ambassador Vicenzo di Andrea Alamanni in Madrid to Pietro di Francesco Usimbardi in Florence. MAP Doc ID 949. ASF, MdP 4920, 23. On Iran, see Rudolph P. Mathee, *The Politics of Trade in Safavid Iran: Silk for Silver, 1600–1730* (New York: Cambridge University Press, 1999); Rudi Matthee and Jorge Flores, eds., *Acta Iranica: Portugal, the Persian Gulf and Safavid Persia*, Iran Heritage Foundation and Freer Gallery of Art and Arthur M. Sackler Gallery, Smithsonian Institution (Leuven, Belgium: Peeters, 2011); Willem Floor and Edmund Herzig, eds., *Iran and the World in the Safavid Age* (New York: I.B. Tauris, 2012).

60 Farina, "La nascita della Tipografia Medicea: personaggi e idee," 63. The name Vecchietti was certainly a historically important one in Florence. John M. Najemy, *A History of Florence: 1200–1575*, 2006, Paperback ed. (Malden, MA: Blackwell Publishing, 2008), 22 and 271–272 shows the Vecchietti as politically active in Florence in both the thirteenth and fifteenth centuries. See the *Dizionario Biografico degli Italiani* entry for "Vecchiétti, Giambattista e Girolamo," www.treccani.it/enciclopedia/giambattista-e-girolamo-vecchietti.

61 Farina, "La nascita della Tipografia Medicea: personaggi e idee," 50.

62 Dei, ed., Sassetti, *Lettere dall'India*, Letter 26, 213–214.

63 Dei, ed., Sassetti, *Lettere dall'India*, Letter 26, 213–214.

64 Dei, ed., Sassetti, *Lettere dall'India*, Letter 26, 215.

65 Dei, ed., Sassetti, *Lettere dall'India*, Letter 26, 215.

66 Historical Archives of Goa, Archive Number 7, Livros das Monções do Reino, no. 5, 44r–45r.

67 Dei, ed., Sassetti, *Lettere dall'India*, Letter 26, 213–218.

68 Gubernatis, ed. *Storia dei Viaggiatori Italiani nelle Indie Orientali*, 26–27.

69 Carletti, *My Voyage Around the World*, 142–144 and 143nn. The translator's notes on 143 point out that Neretti was a friend of Sassetti's, had been present at Sassetti's death, and had served as his executor. Gubernatis, ed. *Storia dei Viaggiatori Italiani nelle Indie Orientali*, 26–27.

70 Gubernatis, ed. *Storia dei Viaggiatori Italiani nelle Indie Orientali*, 26–27. A. Werner; G. A. Grierson; Stephen Jones; Barnarsi Das Jain; and T. Grahame Bailey, "Notes and Queries," *Bulletin of the School of Oriental Studies, University of London* 4, no. 1 (1926), 207 (letter from Giuseppina Maranca).

71 I rely here on the letter of a Florentine university student – Giuseppina Maranca – of 14 July 1924 and the 1925 reply, printed in the Bulletin of the School of Oriental Studies, University of London in 1926. A. Werner, G.A. Grierson, Stephen Jones, Barnarsi Das Jain, and T. Grahame Bailey, "Notes and Queries," *Bulletin of the School of Oriental Studies, University of London* 4, no. 1 (1926), 207–211.

72 "Carletti, Francesco," *Dizionario Biografico degli Italiani*, vol. 20, 1977, online version: www.treccani.it/enciclopedia/francesco-carletti_(Dizionario-Biografico).

73 Francesco Carletti, *My Voyage Around the World: The Chronicles of a Sixteenth Century Florentine Merchant*, trans. Herbert Weinstock (New York: Pantheon Books, 1964), 229–243. Carletti's adventurous circumnavigation and his collection and extended discussion of things match recent historiography on the period quite well; see Timothy Brook, *Vermeer's Hat* (New York: Bloomsbury Press, 2008); Paula Findlen, ed. *Early Modern Things: Objects and their Histories, 1500–1800* (New York: Routledge, 2012); Anne Gerritsen and Giorgio Riello, eds. *The Global Lives of Things: The*

Material Culture of Connections in the Early Modern World (New York: Routledge, 2016); and Charles C. Mann, *1493: Uncovering the New World Columbus Created* (New York: Vintage Books, 2011), among many others.

74 The text of Carletti's account of his travels was first published in a heavily edited edition in 1701 as Francesco Carletti, *Ragionamenti di Francesco Carletti Fiorentino sopra le cose da lui Vedute ne' suoi viaggi: Si dell'Indie Occidentali, e Orientali Come d'altri Paesi* (Firenze: Giuseppe Manni, 1701). To avoid these editorial distortions, the Weinstock translation of the seventeenth-century manuscript version held in Rome has been used. See the translator's note in Carletti, *My Voyage*, xiv. For the dates of Carletti's journey, see Carletti, *My Voyage*, 3–4, 243–244, and 270. Carletti's presentations to the Grand Duke (3 and 11) were from memory as his notes had been lost (95–96 and 124). The Medici Archive Project entry for "Carletti, Francesco," (MAP Person ID 4431) notes that Carletti was "Maestro di Casa" from "1609–" and that he was "Salariato di Cosimo II de'Medici" from 1609–1613.

75 Carletti, *My Voyage*, 196 (on bezoars) and 217 (on Bengali textiles). On Carletti's role as a consultant see "Carletti, Francesco," *Dizionario Biografico degli Italiani*, vol. 20, 1977, online version: www.treccani.it/enciclopedia/francesco-carletti_(Dizionario-Biografico). On the cultural freighting of products Europeans adopted see Marcy Norton, *Sacred Gifts, Profane Pleasures: A History of Tobacco and Chocolate in the Atlantic World* (Ithaca, NY: Cornell University Press, 2008). On the issue of reception, see Detlef Heikamp with contributions by Ferdinand Anders, *Mexico and the Medici*, Quaderni d'Arte (Florence: Edam, 1972); Lia Markey, *Imagining the Americas in Medici Florence* (University Park, PA: The Pennsylvania State University Press, 2016) and Elizabeth Horodowich and Lia Markey, eds., *The New World in Early Modern Italy, 1492–1750* (New York: Cambridge University Press, 2017).

76 Carletti, *My Voyage*, 108–109.

77 Carletti, *My Voyage*, 141 and 150.

78 This was the Tenshō embassy. Lightbown, "Oriental Art and the Orient in Late Renaissance and Baroque Italy," 233 and 235. On this journey, Michael Cooper, *The Japanese Mission to Europe, 1582–1590: The Journey of Four Samurai Boys Through Portugal, Spain, and Italy* (Kent, UK: Global Oriental, 2005). On Livorno, see Tazzara, *The Free Port of Livorno*.

79 Carletti, *My Voyage*, 142–144.

80 See Anthony Molho, "Cosimo de' Medici: *Pater Patriae* or *Padrino?*" *Stanford Italian Review*, 1 (1979), 5–33.

81 Filippo Sassetti's Travels, 1577–1583: Florence, Medina del Campo, Lisbon, Cochin, and Goa. Giovanni Battista Britti's Travels, 1584–1586: Alexandria, Tripoli, Aleppo, Baghdad, Basra, Hormuz, and Goa. Giovanni Battista Vecchietti's Travels, 1584–1588: Alexandria, Antioch, Aleppo, Damascus, Tabriz, Hormuz, Goa, Cochin, Madrid, and Florence. Filippo Sassetti's Planned travels, 1586: Goa, Malacca (Melaka), Moluccas (Maluku), Macao, Manila, *Acapulco, Mexico City, Lima, Panama City, Cartagena*, Seville, and Florence. Sassetti described his plans in his letter to Ferdinando de' Medici (from Cochin, 2/10/1586), using sometimes generic language, especially about spending two years seeing the "other Indies." Based on the standard itineraries determined by the major imperial routes, I infer that he would have seen at least the two viceregal capitals and the key maritime transit points; these sites are labeled in italics. In Asia, I take Sassetti's reference to "China" as being to the Portuguese outpost of Macao. Francesco Carletti, 1591–1606: Florence, Seville, São Tiago Island (Cape Verde), Cartagena, Nombre de Dios, Panama City, Lima, Acapulco, Mexico City, Acapulco, Manila, Nagasaki, Macao, Malacca (Melaka), Cochin, Goa, Saint Helena, Fernando de Noronha, Brielle, Paris, and Florence. For Sassetti, see Dei, ed., Sassetti, *Lettere dall'India* and Marica Milanesi, *Filippo Sassetti*; for his planned journey see Dei, ed., Sassetti, *Lettere dall'India*, Letter 26, 213–217. For Britti and Vecchietti see Farina, "La nascita della Tipografia Medicea: personaggi e idee," 60–65. For Carletti, see Francesco Carletti, *My Voyage*, 3–6, 16, 24–39, 48, 51–57, 69–71, 78–81, 90–91, 99, 135–142, 183–187, 196–200, 226–243, 249, 267–268, 270.

11

"LA VERITÀ DELLE STELLE"

Margherita Sarrocchi's letters to Galileo[1]

Meredith K. Ray

The Neapolitan polymath Margherita Sarrocchi (1560–1617) was a seventeenth-century celebrity, linked to some of the most well-known figures of her time and praised in letters and verse by her contemporaries. Deeply integrated into the intellectual fabric of her adopted city of Rome, Sarrocchi was renowned not only for her *Scanderbeide* (Figure 11.1), the ambitious epic poem with which she is most associated today, but also for her brilliance in natural philosophy and, in particular, her interest in mathematics, astrology, and astronomy.[2] These pursuits, together with her activities as the host of a highly regarded salon in her home, rendered Sarrocchi well situated to participate in the debates over Galileo's telescopic discoveries that unfolded in the early part of the century. Indeed, Sarrocchi's correspondence with Galileo in the period from 1611–1612 demonstrates that her reputation in both scientific and literary circles, together with her ties to various academies and her status as the former ward of an important cardinal, made her a particularly attractive ally for Galileo during his early efforts to secure Roman support. In turn, Galileo's status as a rising star in the world of astronomy and a man of letters who privileged the Tuscan model in his vernacular writings made him a desirable connection for Sarrocchi, who was intent on seeking higher-profile patronage for her epic poem from the environs of Florence. Sarrocchi's extant correspondence with Galileo is bounded by the publication of his *Sidereus nuncius* (*Starry Messenger*) on one end and by the *Istoria e dimonstrazioni intorno alle macchie solari* (*Letters on Sunspots*) on the other, rippling out to include members of the wider scientific community in Rome. Composed of eight letters,[3] the *carteggio* attests to the complex entanglement of literature and science in early modern Italy and to the crucial role of epistolary partnerships in building scientific networks that were more diverse than is often thought. Undertaken at a pivotal moment in the careers of each, the Sarrocchi–Galileo correspondence highlights the engagement of women with intellectual circles and their participation, through the republic of letters, in scientific debate.

FIGURE 11.1   Margherita Sarrocchi, *Scanderbeide* (Rome: Per Andrea Fei, 1623), title page. Beinecke Rare Books and Manuscript Library, Yale University

Scholars increasingly have recognized the centrality of epistolary exchange to the circulation of scientific knowledge and the building, expansion, and maintenance of intellectual networks. Correspondence served to establish connections between individuals and forge relationships across social, geographic, and linguistic boundaries. To an even greater extent than printed scientific texts, which by the seventeenth century had begun to function as the "keystone of a new model of sociability" for young scientific academies such as the Accademia dei Lincei (to which both Galileo and Sarrocchi had ties), letters allowed writers to engage in a strategic quest for support and credibility on a more immediate level than that permitted by other genres.[4] Theorized in antiquity as "one half of a spoken dialogue," letters – much like that related form, which Galileo famously employed in his *Dialogo sui due massimi sistemi del mondo* (*Dialogue on the Two Chief World Systems*) – offered a malleable medium in which to present ideas, respond to critique, and navigate conflict.[5] Letters establish nuanced relationships between sender and recipient(s), evoking a concentric series of readers both internal (the explicit addressee) and external (others who might be exposed to the broader circulation of a letter): each one engages with a letter's contents on varying levels and from different perspectives, supplying it with meaning and amplifying its impact.[6] Whether sent privately to a specific individual or published as polished compositions (printed *epistolari* remained popular well into the seventeenth century), early modern letters were "sociotexts": their tone, style, and content always conditioned by the identity of the interlocutor and by the goals of the letter writer.[7]

A copious writer of letters, Galileo understood the myriad functions they could serve: letters formed a central element of his arsenal of patronage, persuasion, and promotion. Antonio Favaro was the first to catalogue Galileo's extensive personal correspondence, from his earliest surviving letter – addressed to Cristopher Clavius in 1588 – to the missives dating to the later part of his life, when the parameters of his epistolary network altered radically, as Paula Findlen and Hannah Marcus demonstrate in a recent study.[8] Galileo tended to use unpublished letters as a tool for "negotiating a position," reserving publication for those that instead made "bold declarations" about the implications of his observations of nature.[9] Galileo adopted the epistolary form in his *Letters on Sunspots* (Figure 11.2), for example (a work he sent to Sarrocchi and her circle), to respond in kind to the claims of Christoph Scheiner and argue that sunspots were contiguous to the sun's surface and thus indicative of its corruptibility. In this case, the epistolary form exploits the authority of print, lending important weight to Galileo's public debate with a Jesuit interlocutor.[10] Galileo's manuscript letters seek rather to establish a more direct connection with his interlocutors, in order to arrive, through the back-and-forth of epistolary conversation, at a desired result. Though they may assume a less formal tone, such unpublished exchanges, too, are carefully constructed. The correspondence of Galileo and Sarrocchi, for example, reveals a clear awareness that these documents will be shared with others (particularly with their mutual friend Luca Valerio, the mathematician and Lincean who is a constant background presence in the Sarrocchi–Galileo *carteggio*). No letter, even unpublished, is truly "private," but instead assumes varied layers of meaning depending on the circumstances and company in which it is consumed.

Letters also offered a way to bridge the boundaries of gender: as Mario Biagioli writes, it would indeed be difficult to conceive of a republic of letters "without the virtual renegotiations of social and gender boundaries

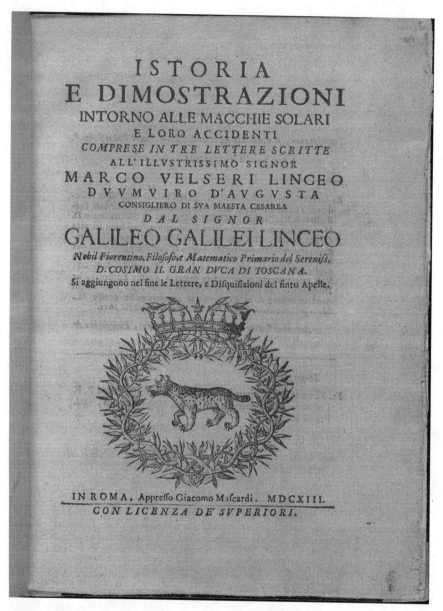

FIGURE 11.2 Galileo Galilei, *Istoria e dimonstrazioni intorno alle macchie solari* (Rome: Appresso Giacamo Mascardi, 1613), title page. Beinecke Rare Books and Manuscript Library, Yale University

allowed by letter writing."[11] Often composed in the vernacular, familiar letters (like those exchanged between Sarrocchi and Galileo) were more accessible to women than scientific treatises written in Latin. Although Sarrocchi read Latin, most women did not have access to a formal humanist education:

the use of the vernacular thus facilitated the circulation of ideas at a broader variety of social and educational levels.[12] That there was interest on the part of women in access to scientific discussion in the vernacular is also reflected in the increasing efforts to engage them as an audience, for example by translating Latin works on natural philosophy into Italian, frequently with dedications to women.[13] Letter writing itself, moreover, was widely perceived in early modern Italy as a suitable medium for women: a "natural" and unmediated form of writing that stemmed from emotion rather than formal training (unlike ostensibly "masculine" literary genres such as epic, which Sarrocchi – unusual among early modern women writers in this respect – also employed).[14] A genre familiar to women, letter writing allowed the writer to assert authority even while demonstrating deference and respect toward the recipient: thus women could circumvent the criticism they often faced for participating in public literary discourse. In seeking out the traces of women's participation in early modern scientific discourse, therefore, it is useful to turn to letters as a key source of evidence, for they offered a uniquely powerful platform for the negotiation of gender and power. More than a simple vehicle for the exchange of information, early modern letters were a venue for careful self-fashioning and the navigation of social and intellectual prestige.

At least sixteen women numbered among Galileo's correspondents. Galileo's epistolary relationship with his daughter, Virginia (Suor Maria Celeste), a nun in the convent of San Matteo near Florence, was the most extensive, followed by that with Sarrocchi in Rome.[15] These *carteggi* reveal the interplay between concerns related specifically to Galileo's efforts to publicize and promote his scientific discoveries, on the one hand, and a host of other topics from the literary to the quotidian, on the other. The letters of Galileo and Maria Celeste, for example, range from discussion of his works to the foodstuffs and medicines she prepared for him.[16] Analyzing the metadata of Galileo's correspondence collected by Favaro, Findlen and Marcus show that in the early part of the seventeenth century the center of Galileo's republic of letters was Rome; following the collapse of his Roman network after 1633 it shifted to other cities such as Paris.[17] The correspondence between Sarrocchi and Galileo falls squarely within the former period, when Galileo was seeking to establish support in Rome and journeyed there twice to build in person upon the relationships he had begun to establish through the exchange of letters.

Embedded in Galileo's epistolary exchanges with Sarrocchi is the story of his efforts to promote and publicize the *Starry Messenger* while laying the groundwork for the publication and, he hoped, positive reception of his *Letters of Sunspots*. Galileo mentioned both works in exchanges with Sarrocchi and her circle. Beginning in 1610, Galileo began focusing on Rome as the key to obtaining authorization from curial channels as well as support from literary and scientific avenues. He reached out to celebrated writers such as Sarrocchi and established a relationship with the Accademia dei Lincei, which welcomed him as a member in 1611. Members of this academy constitute a significant percentage of his correspondents in these years: Sarrocchi's former tutor Valerio, for example, occupies thirteenth place in a list of Galileo's top twenty correspondents between 1589 and 1642.[18] Galileo's relations with the Jesuits at this juncture were also positive. Like him, they were interested in making observations of the heavens and had not yet moved toward an explicit condemnation of heliocentrism. Indeed, an important factor in Galileo's success in this period was the active intellectual exchange between Church figures and laypeople, censors, and academicians. As Sabina Brevaglieri notes, the climate of papal Rome in this period was one of "institutional and cultural polycentrism" – an environment in which members of the Lincean Academy and the Roman Curia could find themselves connected through a shared interest in scientific observation and study.[19] At the same time, so many of these figures were employed on behalf of the Church as consultants that they found themselves simultaneously engaged in both "the cultural sphere and in the institutions which attempted to regulate it," resulting in various forms not just of censorship, but also self-censorship.[20]

This climate of uneasy collaboration serves as a useful lens through which to interpret the tensions that appear in Sarrocchi's epistolary interactions with Galileo, which appear to break off after 1612. However, just as epistolary interactions give us only half of a conversation, they are also marked by gaps and absences, by what is missing as well as what is preserved. Despite the vast corpus of letters assembled by Favaro, the record of Galileo's epistolary exchanges remains necessarily incomplete. We cannot always be sure when a correspondence began or when it ended; when there are holes in a *carteggio*, we cannot always know with certainty whether this is due to some motivating factor (illness, a disagreement, other obstacles to communication) or simply to a lack of extant documents. Galileo's trial in 1632 would have drastic consequences on the preservation of materials related to him, including letters.[21] Even without such a dramatic external event, however, letters could and did encounter delays in delivery or went astray entirely. The problem of assessing completeness is especially delicate in the case of the Sarrocchi–Galileo correspondence, given both the question of gender (the archives are notoriously incomplete when it comes to female figures, even well-known ones like Sarrocchi) and that of Galileo's increasing trouble with the Church. Scholars have pointed to its seemingly abrupt conclusion as evidence of a rift caused between the two, stemming from Sarrocchi's discomfort with Galileo's Copernican views. Perhaps the break is part of a larger pattern noted by Findlen and Marcus, who note the "virtual disappearance" of any correspondence from 1615–1616 – the period in which Galileo returned to Rome amid intensifying debate, culminating in the condemnation of heliocentrism by Cardinal Bellarmine in 1616.[22] This may be the case; however, it seems certain that the pair exchanged additional letters that have been lost.

This essay examines the surviving Sarrocchi–Galileo correspondence within the broader context of early modern epistolary relationships by focusing on three principal areas: first, Sarrocchi's request that Galileo help her to revise her epic poem, which she was attempting to streamline (and what this tells us about Galileo's engagement with the ongoing discussions about epic poetry and literary language); second, Galileo's expectation that Sarrocchi would promote his discoveries to a broad community (and what this suggests about women's involvement with scientific culture); and finally, their mutual interest in astrology and what this reveals about contested aspects of astrological praxis in the early decades of the seventeenth century. We begin with a brief overview of Sarrocchi's cultural environment and a description of her epic poem, *Scanderbeide*, before moving into a closer analysis of the letters themselves and the function of epistolarity in this series of exchanges.

*

Born in Naples in 1560, Margherita Sarrocchi came to Rome after the death of her parents under the protection of the erudite cardinal Guglielmo Sirleto (1514–1585).[23] Here, she resided for a time in the convent of Santa Cecilia in Trastevere. Sarrocchi developed powerful connections in her adopted city, not only to her guardian the Cardinal, but also to the powerful Colonna family, which boasted the poet Vittoria Colonna among its line and was an important player in the political landscape of both Rome and Naples. Sarrocchi was a guest of Marcantonio Colonna and his wife Felice Orsini, and traveled with the Colonna household to Naples on at least one occasion. Bartolomeo Sereno recalls in his *Trattato de l'uso della lancia* (1610) how "there shines in the residence of the *signori* Colonna the exquisite intelligence of Margherita Sarrocchi, who has reached such heights of knowledge"; Giulio Cesare Capaccio likewise notes that "a good poet has arrived in Naples with Donna Felice Orsini ... she is called Margherita."[24] It is against this backdrop of connections that we can contextualize Sarrocchi's earliest published composition: a sonnet in praise of Felice Orsini in Muzio Manfredi's anthology, *Componimenti raccolti da diversi per Dame Romane* [Compositions for Roman Ladies, 1575].[25] Sarrocchi's inclusion at age fifteen in the volume – one of only five female contributors among dozens of male poets – was an early imprimatur by literary society; some years later, Manfredi, the volume's editor, would write to Sarrocchi recalling her sonnet and comparing her to the admired Vittoria Colonna.[26]

Sarrocchi soon began working on other compositions: in addition to poetry, she composed a commentary on the work of Giovanni Della Casa, a Latin treatise on pre-destination, and an essay on Euclid – all documented by her contemporaries, although no longer extant.[27] The last of these works was perhaps inspired by Sarrocchi's studies with her tutor, the mathematician Luca Valerio – also from Naples – who corresponded with Galileo about Euclid's theorems and remained Sarrocchi's long-time intellectual partner and companion; it was Valerio who first introduced Sarrocchi to Galileo in a letter dating to 1609.[28]

Sarrocchi thus had an early interest in scientific as well as literary questions. Her presence in a 1588 work on balneology by Giulio Iasolino of Monteleone attests to her growing reputation in matters pertaining to natural philosophy as well as her ties to Naples and to the Colonna family. Dedicated to Geronima Colonna, duchess of Monteleone, Iasolini's *De' remedi naturali* offers a detailed analysis of Ischia's numerous thermal springs, hot sands, and other marvels, describing their properties by using famous patients (primarily women) as case studies.[29] A sonnet by Sarrocchi in praise of the author appears in the apparatus of the book, situating her alongside a cast of male medical writers who offer support for Iasolino.[30] In a work that positions itself as exceeding all prior discussions on this topic, Sarrocchi's presence is telling. She, now twenty-eight, is a writer with a reputation for excellence in natural philosophy as well as strong connections to the Colonna family, making her advocacy of a work celebrating Ischia – which, in addition to its *bagni*, had a tradition of literary community centered around the Colonna women – especially evocative.[31]

Sarrocchi continued to establish herself within literary networks, exchanging letters and poems with Torquato Tasso, Giambattista Marino (with whom she was closely linked until a falling out, seemingly over differences in poetic taste), and others, including Luigi di Heredia, Roberto Ubaldino, and Pietro Strozzi.[32] She hosted a well-attended salon in her home – described by one contemporary as "the refuge and academy of the best minds in Rome"[33] – through which she cultivated relationships with a wide array of writers, scientists, and mathematicians (including Galileo himself, who would later warmly recall the time he spent there);[34] and she was deeply integrated into Rome's academic culture as a member of the Accademia degli Umoristi and subsequently the Accademia degli Ordinati.[35] The historian Giuseppe Gabrieli has suggested that Federico Cesi may at one time have considered Sarrocchi for admission to the influential Accademia dei Lincei.[36] Praise for the lectures and orations Sarrocchi offered in these academic contexts abounded.[37] Cristofano Bronzini, for example, recalls a debate between Sarrocchi and Galileo in which Sarrocchi delighted her listeners with her discussion of "the movements of the heavens and other truly productive and celestial things";[38] his observation offers a glimpse into one of the ways – in addition to letter writing – in which women like Sarrocchi were able to take an active and public role in the evaluation and circulation of scientific knowledge. Likewise, in Naples – a cultural milieu at once vibrantly diverse and deeply orthodox[39] – Sarrocchi was the sole female member of the Neapolitan Accademia degli Oziosi, whose agenda stipulated that lectures should revolve around "la Poetica, [la] Retorica, [le] Discipline Matematiche, et tutte le parti della Filosofia," neatly reflecting the wide umbrella of topics at which she excelled.[40] The Oziosi forbade, however, discussion of "alcuna materia di Teologia, e della Sacra Scrittura" as well as "cose appartenenti al Publico

Governo."[41] Sarrocchi would seek to navigate such tensions in her own work, balancing her clear interest in new ideas — for example, Galileo's celestial discoveries — against a carefully orthodox public and literary persona. Such tensions would come to the fore by 1616, as the controversy over Galileo's Copernicanism intensified. When the Accademia dei Lincei, which counted both Galileo and Sarrocchi's friend Valerio among its members,[42] continued to stand by its most famous associate, both Sarrocchi and Valerio began to distance themselves from the Academy. Valerio, evidently fearing the consequences of continued association with the Linceans, attempted to resign his membership, a step that was met with shock and disdain by the Academy, which was founded on the ideals of loyal brotherhood and philosophical freedom.[43] Unable or unwilling to account for Valerio's action, some members attributed Valerio's decision to Sarrocchi's influence, reflecting the deep-seated distrust she faced as a female intellectual despite her standing in Roman academic society.[44]

By the early 1600s, however, well before the blossoming of Galileo's conflict with the Church, Sarrocchi was deeply immersed in the composition of her *Scanderbeide*, an ambitious work that would eventually stretch to twenty-three cantos. Although Sarrocchi was admired in both Roman and Neapolitan academic society,[45] she was also subject to the kinds of criticism typically faced by women writers in this period — denigrations of her literary worth, aspersions on her chastity — and it is clear she was concerned about the reception of her epic poem. Seeking a female figure of authority as protector, Sarrocchi turned again to Naples, and to the Colonna: this time, Costanza Colonna, duchess of Caravaggio — great-niece of Vittoria Colonna, daughter of Sarrocchi's previous patron Felice Orsini, and favored niece of Geronima of Monteleone, the dedicatee of Iasolino's work. Indeed, it is likely that Sarrocchi capitalized on these indirect connections to approach Costanza, though she would have also had the opportunity to meet her in Rome in 1600 when the widowed duchess stopped there on pilgrimage to Loreto. Costanza was a sensible initial choice for Sarrocchi: despite a tumultuous period early in her marriage to Francesco I Sforza di Caravaggio, the duchess had become a widely admired example of devout Counter-Reformation womanhood.[46] She frequently expressed her desire to live as a nun; as one Colonna agent wrote of her, "she is an angel from heaven … so far removed from the things of the world that it is a miracle to see a woman her age so mortified in spirit."[47] Sarrocchi, who believed that a broad understanding of natural philosophy was critical to the writing of epic and intended to fill her *Scanderbeide* with digressions on astrology and astronomy, but was deeply concerned that her work not stray from the bounds of Catholic orthodoxy, needed the aura of spiritual rectitude that Costanza could provide. In the two sonnets to Costanza included in the 1606 *Scanderbeide*, Sarrocchi underscores not only Costanza's regal origins, but also her purity, virtue, and moral uprightness. Costanza is a "regal woman/within whose chaste breast/reigns only the thought of eternal honor," and a lady whose very visage shines with divine light.[48] So concerned was Sarrocchi about the implications of her poem that, in addition to choosing an irreproachable female dedicatee, she also included a letter to the reader distancing her own views from certain episodes represented in the book (these chiefly involve astrology), stating that these "appear only in pleasurable imitation of other poets, and not out of any meaning and power they might have in a world imagined and recounted by the poet."[49]

Following the 1606 printing of the *Scanderbeide* (a partial edition of only eleven cantos, which Sarrocchi claimed – probably disingenuously – not to have authorized), Sarrocchi began working to polish the poem and publish a complete edition. She wanted, among other things, to streamline the narrative around a single bellic storyline, eliminating the problematic episodes referenced in her earlier letter to the reader, and to make the language of the poem more Tuscan. She also wished – perhaps because of an apparent falling out with at least one member of the Colonna family[50] – to secure a new patron for the poem. It was during this period of revision that Sarrocchi encountered Galileo, who was in Rome to seek support for the discoveries detailed in his *Starry Messenger*, and to whom Sarrocchi would turn for advice in these matters.

*

When Galileo arrived in Rome in the spring of 1611, five years before the Church's warning to cease teaching and writing about Copernicanism, Sarrocchi's admiration for him was at its zenith. Galileo's observations of the moon's uneven surface, carried out with the help of his improved telescope and detailed in his *Starry Messenger*,[51] had upended the traditional ontological distinctions between heaven and earth, while his discovery of four "wandering stars" orbiting Jupiter – which earned him a place at the Medici court – offered the first direct evidence that the heavenly bodies did not all orbit the earth as their common center.[52] Printed in Venice in March 1610, *The Starry Messenger* was an instant bestseller, although its contents were not immediately accepted by all. In an effort to persuade key figures of the work's validity, Galileo traveled south to meet with the Jesuits and others in Rome. There, he gave demonstrations with the telescope, which Sarrocchi likely attended.[53] Received several times at the Collegio Romano and celebrated there publicly on May 13, Galileo extended his successful sojourn, remaining in Rome until June 4.

Galileo's celestial observations – and their astrological implications – immediately drew the attention of Sarrocchi, who regularly incorporated the language of natural philosophy into her own literary works. The dedicatory letter to the 1606 edition of her *Scanderbeide* makes clear that knowledge of natural philosophy is, in fact, a prerequisite for writing epic,[54] and explains that the new cantos of the poem, not included in the present, still incomplete, edition, will contain additional material regarding "the heavens, astrological knowledge, [and] a study of very curious natural things, all appropriately and poetically explained."[55] The modifiers *appropriately* and *poetically* are important, for – whatever her views on the cosmos – Sarrocchi was prudently orthodox in matters of theology, and careful to categorize her discussions of such matters as belonging to the realm of poetic invention (at least, in her written work). In fact, virtually all the material dealing with astrology and the movements of the planets in the *Scanderbeide* would actually be cut from the later edition of her poem.

Sarrocchi's *Scanderbeide*, and her concerns about revising it for a second edition, figure prominently in her letters to Galileo. Sarrocchi very clearly saw Galileo not only as an astronomer but also as a *letterato*. Galileo composed sonnets and works of literary criticism – including an analysis of the geography of Dante's Hell and a critique of Tasso – and would later structure his major work, the *Dialogue Concerning the Two Chief World Systems*, not as a treatise, but as an accessible vernacular dialogue. Sarrocchi, along with many others, considered Galileo to be a well-placed admirer and protector of writers, one who understood, from his own successful efforts to secure a position at the Medici court, the patronage system and could help others navigate it.

Determined to publish a polished work that adheres to appropriate models of language, style, and structure, Sarrocchi repeatedly asks Galileo to assess the poem critically, writing,

> The principal favor I desire of you is that you should review my poem with the greatest diligence and with an enemy eye, so that you may note every little error, and believe me that I say this truly, and I will take all the criticism you give me as a sign of great goodness and great affection.[56]

Sarrocchi hoped not only for Galileo's input, but also for that of others in his circle and indicated that he should share her poem with his friends in Florence so that they might critique it together.[57] Although Sarrocchi does not highlight her own position as a woman writer, her profound concerns about errors in the *Scanderbeide* suggest that she – well aware of the pitfalls of print – wished to preempt any criticism she might face in publishing a work of epic poetry.[58] Marino had ridiculed Sarrocchi in print as a "chattering magpie," and even some who wrote admiringly of her accused her, in gendered terms, of being difficult and attention-seeking.[59] If Galileo were to read her manuscript with an "enemy eye," then perhaps Sarrocchi could anticipate and avoid the mistakes on which her critics might focus. Employing the language of legal argument – thereby reiterating the gravity of the problem – Sarrocchi explains to Galileo that "just as print can display one's erudition, so it sometimes displays one's poor judgment. For this reason, not wishing to commit such a mistake, *in propria causa advocatum quero* [I seek an advocate on my behalf]."[60] In Galileo, therefore, Sarrocchi sought a literary advisor who could make concrete corrections and improvements to her text, one with an influential network of friends capable of deflecting and discouraging her detractors.

Despite Galileo's well-known preference for Ariosto over Tasso, Sarrocchi's preferred model, their literary philosophies converged in their mutual privileging of Tuscan Italian as the most appropriate language for epic poetry.[61]

Thus Sarrocchi also asks Galileo to aid her in her revisions by "looking over and correcting the language, because I wish it to be as Tuscan as possible, at least in the expressions – so long as it does not diminish the exalted style, being that Tuscan sounds so sweet."[62] She also requests that Galileo look for errors in orthography, and asks his assistance in appropriately restructuring the cantos.[63] In return for Galileo's editorial expertise, as well as his advice in helping to identify an appropriate patron for her work from the environs of the Medici court, Sarrocchi offers to insert his name, and those of his relatives, into her poem.[64] Her completed *Scanderbeide* will contain a passage listing the names of all the various Italians who come to the aid of the work's hero. As she explains, she has left much of this list blank (or rather, inserted temporary names as placeholders) in order to revise it at a later date by inserting the names of her friends and supporters:

> It is true that I have not finished the list of the Italians who have to go to Scanderbeg's aid; I have not finished it because I have not fully deter- mined all those I will wish to send, and also in order to leave space to praise some prince; such that if Your Lordship will send me some of your own relatives, I will honor my pages with the name of your family and, what's more, given the right occasion, I will make mention of Your Lord- ship as one who is to come along in the future.[65]

As Sarrocchi assures Galileo, this is quick work, and can happen later in the revision process: "Waiting to finish such a list doesn't matter, since for someone as experienced in such things as I am, it will take only fifteen or twenty days [to complete it]."[66] The delicate balance here between Sarrocchi's confidence, even bravura, as an experienced and capable writer sure of her ability to deliver on a tight timetable, and her deference to Galileo as a literary authority, is striking. In this moment of their epistolary exchange, it is clearly Sarrocchi who seeks the protection of Galileo, offering the highest form of payment she can: recog- nition in print. Implicit in this agreement is the acknowledgment that Sarroc- chi's words have weight: the poetic memorial she is offering the astronomer has intrinsic value – not unlike the celestial monument Galileo offered to his Medici patron with the *Starry Messenger*. Despite Sarrocchi's promise, however, her cor- respondent's name does not appear in the 1623 edition of the *Scanderbeide*, likely a casualty of Galileo's conflict with the Church.

Sarrocchi's offer to write Galileo into the *Scanderbeide* was not the only way she could repay him for his help. Her letters reveal that Galileo, for his part, also sought protection of a sort from Sarrocchi. Five of Sarrocchi's seven letters to Galileo refer to her efforts to defend him against those who doubted his discov- eries, as well as to her offers to read and promote his works. In these endeavors Sarrocchi was aided by Valerio, an equally fervent supporter of Galileo.[67] That Sarrocchi and Valerio were connected to several of the most important scientific and literary academies in Rome was surely not lost on their Tuscan correspondent. However, it was not only their stature in the scientific disciplines, but also their capabilities as writers, that made Sarrocchi and Valerio such important allies for Galileo. As much as Galileo required Rome's confirmation of his scientific discoveries, he likewise needed the literary arena to legitimize them in a broader courtly context.[68] Indeed Valerio was a key element of this strategy. Galileo solicited Valerio, for example, to contribute verses to a planned (but never-executed) second edition of *Sidereus nuncius*, and Valerio would go on to produce sonnets for Galileo's *Letters on Sunspots*, a work he was instrumental in helping bring to press.[69] If Valerio was promoting and supporting Galileo's discoveries in verse, we can imagine that Galileo hoped Sarrocchi – who was more celebrated in the literary world than Valerio – would use her pen to support him in similar fashion.

Sarrocchi made good on her offer to promote Galileo's findings, at least for a time. As debate churned over whether the observations recorded in Galileo's *Starry Messenger* were accurate, Sarrocchi – in a testament to her reputation and influence – found herself called upon to vouch for them. In a letter to Sarrocchi dated June 4, 1611, Guido Bettoli of the University of Perugia begs her to weigh in on the question, praising her knowledge in this arena and stressing the credibility of her account:

> The marvelous effects one continues to hear of concerning the scope, or if we wish to say, spyglass, of Signor Galileo Galilei, and which continue to drive everyone to give their opinion, have made me presumptuous to take up my pen to greet Your Ladyship and beg you to favor me with your opinion; you being so perfectly skilled in every science, I hope for a perfect account of the truth, since by now you, too, must have tried it a thousand times.[70]

Bettoli goes on to explain the controversy over Galileo's findings, anxious that Sarrocchi should know it does not reflect the views of the Studio di Perugia and noting that it has caused "more than a little commotion."[71] Bettoli's letter, which asks Sarrocchi to intervene with Galileo, conveys the importance of her standing in Rome's scientific community, while also highlighting the degree to which her connection to Galileo was widely recognized and suggesting that they likely shared an even more extensive – and more public – relationship than what is known from their letters.

In a series of missives to Bettoli and to Galileo himself, Sarrocchi dives into the debate herself, strenuously defending Galileo. Insisting on her own empirical testimony, Sarrocchi describes how she wielded the telescope and confirmed Galileo's observations for herself:

> all that is said about the discovery of the stars by Signor Galileo is true: that is, that with Jupiter there are four wandering stars with their own motion, always equally distant from Jupiter, but not from each other; and

I saw them with my own eyes through Signor Galileo's spyglass, and showed them to several friends, which the whole world knows. With Saturn there are two stars, one on one side and one on the other, that almost touch it. Venus, when it joins itself to the sun, can already be seen to become illuminated and, like the moon, horned, until it can then be seen completely full; and as it becomes full, it appears smaller, a clear sign – indeed, a geometric proof – that it revolves around the sun; and when it is full, it is above it, and because of the great distance it appears smaller: this, I say, is known by geometric proof, since it cannot appear full because of the opposition it has to the sun.[72]

Sarrocchi had likely tested Galileo's *cannocchiale* at one of his demonstrations during his visit to Rome, and makes this direct experience the cornerstone of her statement of support. While she does not – here or elsewhere – explicitly follow the implications of Galileo's discoveries through to their full Copernican conclusions, she writes knowledgeably and with detail about her own observations of them and their significance. Sarrocchi goes on to refer to the reversals in position of the Jesuits Cristopher Clavius and Cristoph Grienberger, who first denied, and then accepted, Galileo's findings, demonstrating that she is aware of the latest developments in the controversy and that she is part of the network of scientific community through which such news is transmitted.[73]

Following this exchange, Sarrocchi sent Galileo a copy of her letter to Bettoli so that he might know "everything that is going on," as well as copies of her correspondence with a friar from Perugia who engaged her in debate on the same subject.[74] In this latter exchange, one of the most interesting – and cryptic – of the Sarrocchi–Galileo *carteggio*, we see how the common interests of these two figures encompass not just epic poetry and astronomy, but also judicial astrology and, in particular, the casting of horoscopes and nativities, or natal charts. As Sarrocchi explains to Galileo, an Augustinian friar at Santa Maria Novella in Perugia called Padre Innocenzio had asked her opinion regarding the Medicean stars. She writes that she readily confirmed the discovery, only to be offended by her interlocutor's response:

I had also written to him regarding the truth of [your discovery of] the stars, and praised the genius of Your Lordship ... [Innocenzio] responded to me with a letter that offended me greatly; and so I replied as I saw fit ... he replied, as Your Lordship will be able to see, as I am also sending you both of his latest letters.[75]

In Sarrocchi's description of her epistolary "battle" with Innocenzio, which continues in a second letter to Galileo (Figure 11.3), we see the question of gender intertwine with Sarrocchi's study of astrology, as she writes:

FIGURE 11.3 Letter of Margherita Sarrocchi to Galileo Galilei, October 12, 1611. Biblioteca Nazionale Centrale di Firenze, Ms. Gal. 23, cc. 12r–v. By permission of the Ministero dei Beni e delle attività culturali e del turismo/Biblioteca Nazionale Centrale di Firenze

It is quite true that the friar seems to have it in for me, and wants to bicker with me over words by asking me the meaning of certain terms, as I was trying to apply astrology to the newly discovered stars, as if to say that the discovery of these stars is not real; but I have set other people straight besides him, and I hope to do the same with him, even though I am a woman and he is a learned friar.[76]

In this encounter, Sarrocchi's particular interest in astrology, attested to in positive terms by many seventeenth-century sources, is manipulated by the friar in an attempt to diminish both the branch of scientific inquiry and Sarrocchi as a practitioner of it. Implicit in Innocenzio's words, in fact, is an innate, and negative, linkage of female gender and astrology as an inferior discipline with respect to astronomy.[77] Alert to the undertones of the friar's comments, Sarrocchi promptly accuses him of challenging her solely in order to establish masculine authority, and notes that she will soon correct his error.[78] This is one of few moments in Sarrocchi's writing – epistolary or poetic – in which she explicitly identifies herself as a female intellectual and adopts a protofeminist tone. It is also an instance in which we see astrology co-existing alongside the new science, with Sarrocchi making use of it to defend Galileo's astronomical discoveries.

Innocenzio's dismissive view of Sarrocchi's interest in astrology takes on added significance in light of an earlier letter from Sarrocchi to Galileo regarding this same exchange. There, we find not only that Sarrocchi openly practiced judicial astrology by casting natal charts, but that her detractor had approached her for her help in this very area (and even engaged in it himself).[79] Sarrocchi tells Galileo how this same Innocenzio had also asked her to examine his own natal chart (*natività*). Despite any potentially problematic implications, genitures were commonplace in early modern Italy, often sought out by the elite, given as gifts, or offered in exchange for patronage.[80] As Sarrocchi explains, Innocenzio's request accompanies that for her opinion on Galileo's Medicean stars, merging the two subjects together in a single invitation:

> Father Innocenzio had written to a servant of mine, saying he wanted me to see a certain natal chart of his; and at the same time he begged me, on behalf of the Studio di Perugia, to tell him my opinion about the new stars discovered by Your Lordship.[81]

Sarrocchi agreed to these favors, and also to a third: to examine a second natal chart of a young girl who had been the victim of a horrible trauma in Perugia.[82] In other letters, Innocenzio elaborates on this incident, identifying the mother of the child and referring to a horoscope and astrological judgment the family had requested from him (and which he had subsequently sent to Sarrocchi for her interpretation).[83] Innocenzio also mentions the natal chart produced for himself by Sarrocchi, referring disparagingly to "those extravagant opinions predicted by the Signora [Sarrocchi] in my geniture."[84]

Sarrocchi had good reason to believe that Galileo might be interested in this episode, which she recounts in some detail. Galileo, too, calculated horoscopes, including charts for his two daughters, certain friends and acquaintances, and his patrons.[85] One of two nativities sketched out in a manuscript copy of *Sidereus nuncius* at the Biblioteca Nazionale di Firenze, for example, was drawn by Galileo for Cosimo II de' Medici. Galileo also made several others, including for himself and for Giovanfrancesco Sagredo, the Venetian nobleman depicted in his *Dialogue*.[86] Such documents reveal the depth of Galileo's engagement with astrology. Indeed, documents located by Antonino Poppi show that in 1604, less than a decade before his correspondence with Sarrocchi commenced, Galileo's astrological activities had earned him attention from the Venetian Inquisition. At the heart of the inquiry was suspicion about the degree of astrological determinism that accompanied Galileo's horoscopes and judgments.[87] Questioned about the nativities his employer cast, Galileo's former amanuensis Silvestro Pagnoni indicated that the astronomer presented his predictions as "certain and indubitable" (*fermo e indubitato*), prompting the interrogator to respond: "You said before that in the nativities this Galileo makes, he calls his predictions certain; this is heresy."[88] While Pagnoni professed not to have understood this distinction, such fatalism marked – as Sarrocchi seems to have known – a line that was not to be crossed.[89]

If, in the wake of this episode, Galileo became more cautious about the nativities he drew, his interest in astrology was not a secret. In later years he would be described in a Roman newsletter as "the astrologer," and he was on familiar terms with established astrologers such as Orazio Morandi, who had the misfortune to have prematurely predicted the death of Pope Urban VIII.[90] Galileo himself was briefly embroiled in the Morandi scandal, named as an associate and co-conspirator of the accused.[91] As Brendan Dooley notes, Galileo was assuredly not a "categorical opponent of the ideas that stood at the foundations of astrology."[92]

The episode of the nativity recounted by Sarrocchi to Galileo, opaque as it is, reveals something of the complexity of astrological activity – widely practiced, yet in some aspects officially condemned – in early modern Rome. The lines between orthodoxy and heresy were far from clear when it came to judicial astrology. Similarly, the boundaries between astrology and astronomy were by no means impermeable. Innocenzio, an ecclesiastical figure, belittles astrology as inferior to astronomy while simultaneously seeking to apply it to illuminate a personal matter. At the same time, Sarrocchi's decision to recount the exchange to Galileo, alongside discussion of the controversy over his stars, not only suggests that she knew he would find it of interest, but further illustrates how astrology continued to meld with the new science.

*

Despite the shared literary and scientific interests described here, the correspondence between Sarrocchi and Galileo seems to have ended in 1612. Some scholars have argued that Sarrocchi was offended by Galileo's delay in attending to her manuscript and thus broke off their exchange.[93] However, in Sarrocchi's final extant letter to Galileo, not only does she intimate that she will send more work for him to read, but she also promises to review a treatise he has sent her (the *Discourse on Floating Bodies*; a letter from Valerio to Galileo the following year states that she has also read Galileo's *Letters on Sunspots* with enthusiasm).[94] Sarrocchi's appreciative thanks to Galileo for the treatise and her warm expression of "heartfelt affection" do not suggest a rift.[95] On the contrary, Sarrocchi was aware that Galileo was unwell in this period, and goes to great lengths to express concern and to assure him that the editing of her manuscript can wait. For his part, Galileo openly acknowledges the difficult circumstances in his own surviving letter to Sarrocchi, in which he catalogues his bodily ailments in detail and bemoans the insalubrious effects of Florence's winter air. Noting that he is fighting "many pains in the chest and kidneys with great discharge of blood, by which I have nearly emptied my veins," Galileo asks Sarrocchi to therefore "excuse my impotence, which does not allow me to exercise the mind, let alone the pen, without the greatest harm."[96] At the same time, he thanks Sarrocchi for sending the poem and assures her of his continued service to her.[97] A letter from Valerio to Galileo, written more than a year later, updating Galileo on the status of Sarrocchi's completed revisions to her poem, suggests that Galileo continued to take an interest in Sarrocchi's literary career.[98]

More plausible than a falling out over Galileo's failure to follow through with his promise of editorial help is the possibility that Sarrocchi, like Valerio, began to distance herself from Galileo in 1612 or at least by 1616, when heliocentrism was officially declared to be heretical and Galileo cautioned against teaching it. The agenda of the Accademia dei Lincei, to which Sarrocchi was connected via Valerio, had to this point revolved around publishing and circulating new scientific ideas while remaining in cooperation with ecclesiastical authority. However, as Galileo's claims began to push the boundaries of this fragile partnership, Valerio – who had been a crucial intermediary for Galileo – became uncomfortable.[99] For Sarrocchi, too, who had taken care to highlight her own orthodoxy when publishing *Scanderbeide*, the tensions may have grown too pronounced to continue the relationship, or she may have simply deemed it unlikely to prove fruitful for her own literary aims any longer. It is also possible, of course, that Sarrocchi's correspondence with Galileo did continue, and that the remaining letters have not yet been found (Valerio's letters to Galileo, for instance, continue up to at least 1614[100]).

Sarrocchi died in 1617, with the new edition of her poem still unpublished (it was printed posthumously in 1623). The later events of Galileo's life are of course well known; his trial in 1633 marks, in many respects, the apex of the Counter-Reformation's constrictive effects on intellectual expression in seventeenth-century Italy. Yet in the early years of the seventeenth century, as revealed by the letters of Sarrocchi and Galileo, Rome was a city in which scientific and literary debate thrived and men and women of diverse social status and background collaborated in intellectual partnership even as they vied to achieve individual recognition and acclaim. In this vibrant, heterogeneous cultural climate, boundaries of discipline as well as gender were blurred: the literary and the scientific were deeply enmeshed, and learned women, such as Sarrocchi, engaged – as men did – in the dissemination of new knowledge. The epistolary relationship of Sarrocchi and Galileo is thus a brief but important interlude, one that illuminates the nature of intellectual networks in seventeenth-century Italy and highlights the engagement of women with the discoveries and controversies of the Scientific Revolution. If letter writing constituted a fundamental tool for the creation of scientific community, connecting the republic of letters throughout Italy and across Europe, its importance to women as a medium of communication was especially critical. Letters offered an accessible and acceptable means by which women could participate in conversation and debate outside the world of print. Ostensibly private in nature, letter writing allowed female writers to engage their interlocutors without incurring the criticism so often encountered by women writers who sought a broader public audience through print. Though even unpublished letters were rarely wholly private documents, and were often as carefully attentive as their published counterparts to self-positioning, audience, and objective, epistolary communication remained a vital vehicle for women who wished to engage in intellectual discourse. By scouring the epistolary record for traces of such women, we can hope better to understand those who, like Sarrocchi, offered their judgments about the rapidly evolving understanding of the cosmos.

Notes

1 Portions of this essay appear in Meredith K. Ray, *Margherita Sarrocchi's Letters to Galileo: Astronomy, Astrology, and Poetics in Seventeenth-Century Italy* (New York: Palgrave Macmillan Press, 2016) (hereafter RMS). The phrase *la verità delle stelle,* or "the truth of the stars," stems from Sarrocchi's letter to Galileo of September 10, 1611, in which she describes having defended Galileo's observations to others ("havendogli ancora scritta io la verità delle stelle"); see Antonio Favaro, ed., *Edizione nazionale delle opere di Galileo Galilei* (OG) (Florence: Barbera, 20 vols, 1890–1909, XI:579; translated in RMS, 71). All translations are my own unless otherwise noted.

2 Sarrocchi's *Scanderbeide* was first published in Rome, 1606, in an abbreviated edition; the longer, complete version was published posthumously (Rome, 1623). A modern edition and English translation is edited by Rinaldina Russell (Chicago, IL: The University of Chicago Press, 2006). Sarrocchi's narrative is based on a historical episode that circulated in numerous iterations; her principal source was Marinus Barletius, *Historia de vita et gestis Scandebegi,* published around 1506 (see B. B. Ashcom, "Notes on the Development of the Scanderbeg Theme," *Comparative Literature* 5.1 [1953]: 16–29; Serena Pezzini, "Ideologia della conquista, ideologia dell'accoglienza: La "Scanderbeide" di Margherita Sarrocchi [1623], *MLN* 120.1 [2005]: 190–222).

3 Sarrocchi's letters to Galileo are in the Biblioteca Nazionale Centrale di Firenze, Manoscritti Galileiani, busta 23, carte 8, 10, 12, 14, 16, 18, and 20 (cf. OG, XI:563, 579, 593, 596, 636, 647, 696; references are to the online edition at the "Archivio Integrato Galileo" [http://moro.imss.fi.it:9000/struts-aig/sceltoArchivio.do?key=SUBJ], by volume and document number). Galileo's extant letter to Sarrocchi in the Archivio di Stato, Mantua is published in Gilberto Govi, *Tre lettere di Galileo Galilei* (Rome: Tipografia delle scienze matematiche e fisiche, 1870, 9–10). Internal references in surviving letters make clear that Sarrocchi and Galileo exchanged additional letters, now lost.

4 Sabina Brevaglieri, "Science, Books and Censorship in The Academy of the Lincei: Johannes Faber as Cultural Mediator," in *Conflicting Duties: Science, Medicine, and Religion in Rome, 1500–1750,* Warburg Institute Colloquia 15 (2009): 133–157, 137.

5 Meredith K. Ray, *Writing Gender in Women's Letter Collections of the Italian Renaissance* (Toronto: University of Toronto Press, 2010), 6.

6 Janet Gurkin Altman, *Epistolarity: Approaches to a Form* (Columbus, OH: Ohio State University Press, 1982), 88.

7 Gary Schneider, *The Culture of Epistolarity: Vernacular Letters and Letter Writing in Early Modern England, 1500–1700* (Newark, DE: University of Delaware Press, 2005), 22.

8 Paula Findlen and Hannah Marcus, "The Breakdown of Galileo's Roman Network: Crisis and Community, ca. 1633," in *Social Studies of Science* 47.3 (2017): 326–352.

9 Findlen and Marcus, "The Breakdown of Galileo's Roman Network," 338.

10 Findlen and Marcus suggest that Galileo shifted away from engaging the Jesuits in direct correspondence after 1615, preferring instead to address them in print (see

Findlen and Marcus, "The Breakdown of Galileo's Roman Network," 336; see also Mario Biagioli, *Galileo Courtier: The Practice of Science in the Culture of Absolutism* [Chicago, IL: The University of Chicago Press, 1993], 267–311).

11 Mario Biagioli, *Galileo's Instruments of Credit: Telescopes, Images, Secrecy* (Chicago, IL: University of Chicago Press, 2006), 70–71.

12 An interesting contrast is offered by Galileo's *Letters on Sunspots*, composed in Italian in response to Scheiner's Latin letters; in this case the use of the vernacular functioned as an obstacle to accessibility.

13 Ray, *Daughters of Alchemy: Women and Scientific Culture in Early Modern Italy* (Cambridge, MA: Harvard University Press, 2015), 112–113.

14 Ray, *Writing Gender*, 3–15. Few early modern women ventured into the arena of epic: Lucrezia Marinella's *L'Enrico, overo Bisantio acquistato*, published in 1635, suggests the influence of Sarrocchi's text.

15 Dava Sobel, *Galileo's Daughter: A Memoir of Science, Faith, and Love* (New York: Walker, 1999); *Letters to Father: Suor Maria Celeste to Galileo, 1623–1633* (New York: Walker, 2001). Other female figures with whom Galileo corresponded include Caterina Riccardi Niccolini, wife of the Tuscan ambassador in Rome, and the artist Artemisa Gentileschi.

16 Ibid.

17 Findlen and Marcus, "Galileo's Roman Network," 344.

18 Findlen and Marcus, "Galileo's Roman Network," 333.

19 Brevaglieri, "Science, Books and Censorship," 134.

20 Brevaglieri, "Science, Books and Censorship," 135.

21 Mario Bucciantini, "Celebration and Conservation: The Galilean Collection of the National Library of Florence," in M. Hunter, ed., *Archives of the Scientific Revolution: The Formation and Exchange of Ideas in Seventeenth-Century Europe* (Woodbridge: Boydell Press, 1998), 21–34.

22 Findlen and Marcus, "Galileo's Roman Network," 338.

23 Bartolomeo Chioccarelli, *De illustribus scriptoribus Regni Neapolitani* (ms. XIV.A.28, cc. 67v–68r). For Sarrocchi's biography see also Nadia Verdile, "Contributi alla biografia di Margherita Sarrocchi," *Rendiconti dell'Accademia di Archeologia, Lettere, e Belle Arti di Napoli* 61 (1989–1990): 165–206, and Russell, ed., *Scanderbeide*, 1–17.

24 Bartolomeo Sereno, *Trattato de l'uso della lancia* (Naples, 1610), cited in Russell, ed. 9, n15; Giulio Cesare Capaccio, *Illustrium mulierum ét illustrium litteris virorum elogia* (Naples, 1608), in Verdile, "Contributi," 180.

25 Sarrocchi's sonnet compares Felice to her namesake constellation, *Orsa*, or the "Bear" ("Orsa nostra,/de la celeste assai più vaga"): see Muzio Manfredi, *Per donne romane: Rime di diversi raccolte e dedicate al Signor Giacomo Buoncampagni* (Bologna, 1585), 126.

26 Muzio Manfredi, *Lettere brevissime* (Venice, 1606), 142.

27 Sarrocchi's work on Euclid focused on the applications of Valerio's ideas regarding the problem of the volume and gravity of solids (see Russell, ed., *Scanderbeide*, 8). These works by Sarrocchi have been lost, but there are references to them by Sarrocchi's contemporaries and in early biographies (see Ray, *Daughters of Alchemy*, 98).

28 Luca Valerio to Galileo Galilei, April 4, 1609 [OG: 10.239]. On Valerio, see Ugo Baldini and Pier Daniele Napolitani, "Per una biografia di Luca Valerio: Fonti edite e inedite per un riscostruzione della sua carriera scientifica" in *Bollettino di storia delle scienze matematiche/Unione matematica italiana* 11, no. 2 (1991): 3–157.

29 Among these women is Donna Geronima, the dedicatee of the work, whom Iasolino claims was cured by the Ischian waters of a bothersome ulcer in her abdomen (Giulio Iasolino, *De remedi naturali che sono nell'isola di Pithecusa: hoggi detta Ischia* [Naples, 1588]). On this work, see Ilia Delizia, "Giulio Iasolino: Un viaggiatore

scientifico nell'Isola di Ischia," in *Souvenir d'Italie: il viaggio in Italia nelle memorie scritte e figuative tra il XVI secolo e l'età contemporanea: atti del Convegno, Genova, 6–8 Novembre 2007* (Genoa: De Ferrari, 2008), 139–150.

30 Sarrocchi's contribution sonnet praises Iasolino for uncovering and revealing earth's hidden secrets: "Quinci al tuo gran saver la terra, e l'onde/Cedon l'occulta lor maggior virtute/E n'ha vita, e sostegno il secol nostro" (ibid., GGr–v).

31 On the *cenacolo* presided over by Costanza d'Avalos and Vittoria Colonna at Ischia, see for example Diana Robin, *Publishing Women: Salons, the Presses, and the Counter-Reformation* (Chicago, IL: The University of Chicago Press, 2007).

32 See Russell, ed., *Scanderbeide*, 9n17. For Tasso's sonnets on Sarrocchi, see *Le Rime*, ed. Bruno Basile (Rome: Salerno, 1994), I:899 and 900; 2:1846. The poet also mentions her in two letters (see in Verdile, "Contributi," 172).

33 Guido Bettoli to Margherita Sarrocchi, June 4, 1611; OG, XI:537. Translations of letters here and throughout from RMS.

34 Aldus Manutius the Younger fondly remembers his time at Sarrocchi's salon (Aldus Manutius the Younger to Margherita Sarrocchi, December 18, 1585, in *Lettere volgari al molto ill. Sign. Lodovico Riccio* (Rome, 1592), 26–28. Sarrocchi makes reference to Galileo's presence in her home in a letter offering greetings from herself and Valerio. (Galileo to Margherita Sarrocchi, January 21, 1612, OG XI:647; trans. in RMS, 75–76). In his *Della dignità e nobiltà delle donne* (Florence, 1625), Cristofano Bronzini describes Sarrocchi's home as an "honorata habitazione, continuamente piena dei più nobili, e virtuosi spiriti, che habitino, e capitino in Roma d'ogni tempo" (130).

35 RMS, 4. On early modern women and academy membership see Virginia Cox, "Members, Muses, and Mascots: Women and Italian Academies," in *The Italian Academies 1525–1700: Networks of Culture, Innovation, Dissent,* ed. Jane E. Everson, Denis V. Reidy, and Lisa Sampson (Oxford: Legenda, 2015), 130–167.

36 Giuseppe Gabrieli speculates that Cesi's willingness to entertain female membership among the Lynceans, noted in a document from the Academy's archives (Ms. Linceo 4), stemmed from the case of Sarrocchi; Giuseppe Gabrieli, "Contributi alla storia dell'accademia dei Lincei" (Rome: Accademia Nazionale dei Lincei, 1939, v. 1, 474.

37 See for example the praise issued by Bronzini in his *Della dignità* (131); F.A. della Chiesa in *Theatro delle donne letterate* (Modovi, 1620, 253–254); and Gian Vittorio Rossi [Janus Nicius Erythraeus], *Pinacoteca imaginum illustrium doctrinae vel ingenii laude virorum* (Wolfenbuttel, 1729]).

38 In *Della dignità*, 135, Bronzini recounts: "This singular woman was heard to treat with such excellence on nature and on the movements of the heavens and other truly productive and celestial things, that just as she nearly paralyzed the minds of those who listened to her by the movement of her tongue, so it was that everyone began to regard her intently with the greatest admiration, and then to interrogate her loftily; among these Galileo of Tuscany, to whose questions the wise woman responded not only readily, but prudently, with lofty and well founded conclusions; she raised such deep and lofty questions in him that it gave him something to think about for a good while."

39 See Lorenza Ginanfrancesco, "From Propaganda to Science: Looking at the World of Academies in Early Seventeenth-Century Naples," *California Italian Studies* 3.1 (2012): 1–31.

40 Ibid., 11–12; also Carlo Padiglione, *Le Leggi dell'Accademia degli Oziozi in Napoli* (Naples, Giannini, 1878, 19). This academy also included Giovan Battista Manso, like Sarrocchi an admirer of Galileo, among its members (see Gianfrancesco, "From Propaganda to Science," 11, n43).

41 Ibid.

42 Galileo was inducted into the Lincei in 1611; Valerio the next year.
43 Mario Biagioli, "Knowledge, Freedom, and Brotherly Love: Homosociality and the Accademia dei Lincei" in *Configurations* 3.2 (1995): 139–166.
44 Once an admirer of Sarrocchi, Cesi came to perceive Sarrocchi as a negative influence on Valerio; see Baldini and Napoletani, "Per una biografia di Luca Valerio," 121. On Valerio's attempts to withdraw from the academy, see Giuseppe Gabrieli, Luca Valerio Linceo e un episodio memorabile della vecchia academia, *Rendiconti della Classe di scienze morali, storiche, e filologiche* (ser. VI, vol. IX, fasc. 11–12 (1934), 691–728).
45 Capaccio, for example, praises Sarrocchi specifically as a fellow Neapolitan writer; Verdile, "Contributi," 201.
46 Renèe Bearnstein, "In My Own Hand": Costanza Colonna and the Art of the Letter in Sixteenth-Century Italy, *Renaissance Quarterly* 66 (2013): 130–168.
47 Bearnstein, "In My Own Hand," 149.
48 Sarrocchi, *Scanderbeide*, 1606. These sonnets are included, together with her sonnet for Felice Orsini, in Luisa Bergalli, *Componimenti poetici delle più illustre rimatrici d'ogni secolo, parte seconda* (Venice, 1776), 111–112. Along with Costanza's devoutness, her independence – having taken responsibility for her husband's estates after his death in 1583 – would have made her an attractive prospect for Sarrocchi, who populated her poem with self-sufficient, powerful female characters. Additionally, Costanza, like her female relatives Felice Orsini and Geronima Colonna, had ties to literary society, as suggested by her presence as a dedicatee of works such as Giovanni Talentone's *Discorso ... sopra la maraviglia* (Milan, 1597), a treatise on the nature of the marvelous. Talentone, a philosopher at Pavia, praises Costanza effusively as "the most illustrious woman alive today," adding that she emulates her relative, the celebrated Vittoria Colonna, and declaring her his "patron and protector" (dedication).
49 *Scanderbeide*, 1606, "A benigni lettori." Sarrocchi refers specifically to the episodes centered on the sorceress Calidora, removed from the 1623 edition.
50 A January 19, 1613 letter by Sarrocchi to Ferdinando Gonzaga, Duke of Mantua in the Archivio di Stato, Mantua, seeks support in litigation against Filippo Colonna; Angelo Borzelli, *Note intorno a Margherita Sarrocchi ed al suo poema La Scanderbeide* (Naples: Artigianelli, 1935), 56–57.
51 The work's Latin title, *Sidereus nuncius*, may be translated as either "sidereal message" or "sidereal messenger"; it is generally agreed that Galileo intended the former (William R. Shea and Tiziana Bascelli, trans., *Galileo's Sidereus nuncius, or a Sidereal Message* [Sagamore Beach, MA: Science History Publications, 2009], 93n2).
52 Mario Bucciantini, Michele Camerota, and Franco Giudice, *Galileo's Telescope: A European Story*, trans. Catherine Bolton (Cambridge, MA: Harvard University Press, 2015), 7. See also David Wootton, "New Light on the Composition and Publication of the *Sidereus Nuncius*," *Galileiana* 6 (2009): 123–140, p. 129, who argues that only after securing Medici patronage was Galileo confident enough to add Copernican ideas to the manuscript (133).
53 For the *avviso* detailing this event, see in Bucciantini et al., *Galileo's Telescope*, 215.
54 Sarrocchi, *Scanderbeide* [1606], 2v. This sentiment is echoed in the preface to the 1701 edition of the *Scanderbeide*, which states that epic requires a nearly universal understanding of the most important sciences and all the good arts, not to mention the mechanical arts, a perfect and sublime eloquence, and that marvelous and wide-ranging wisdom to which all our study is directed, the most holy philosophy, that which is commonly called the understanding of nature (*scienza del mondo*) (Sarrocchi, *Scanderbeide poema eroico* [Naples, 1701], 209).
55 Sarrocchi, *Scanderbeide* [1606], unnumbered but 3r.
56 Margherita Sarrocchi to Galileo Galilei, July 29, 1611; OG, XI:563. In another letter, she reiterates her desire for Galileo's opinion of the work; Margherita Sarrocchi to Galileo Galilei, September 10, 1611; OG, XI:579.

57 Margherita Sarrocchi to Galileo Galilei, October 12, 1611; OG, XI:593. Sarrocchi chooses a forceful word, *censurare* – literally, to censure – to render the degree of scrupulousness she wishes her readers to apply to their critique.

58 As Sarrocchi cautions, "just as print displays men's learning, so it also exposes ignorance"; Margherita Sarrocchi to Galileo Galilei, January 13, 1612; OG, XI:643.

59 Giambattista Marino, *Adone,* IX, 187 (*Adone,* ed. Marzio Pieri. Rome and Bari: Laterza, 1975–1977); see also Rossi, *Pinachoteca,* 259–261.

60 Margherita Sarrocchi to Galileo Galilei, July 29, 1611; OG, XI:563.

61 Galileo worked diligently to make sure his vernacular works reached such a literary standard: see for example Cesi's letter to Galileo regarding the *Letters on Sunspots,* which complains of printers unfamiliar with the Tuscan language: "nor should you marvel if the printers are not very Tuscan, because, even though they are supervised and the proofreader reads everything twice and sometimes three times, they still make mistakes" (Federico Cesi to Galileo Galilei, December 28, 1612; OG, XI:815). Sarrocchi, for her part, was praised by Muzio Manfredi for her skill in employing the Tuscan model: "so far had [Sarrocchi] advanced in the composition of Tuscan verse that now our own era will have no need to envy those before us the valor of their Victoria Colonnas, Veronica Gambaras, and any other famous female poets"; Muzio Manfredi to Margherita Sarrocchi, June 22, 1591, in *Lettere brevissime* (Venice, 1606, 142).

62 Margherita Sarrocchi to Galileo Galilei, January 13, 1612; OG, XI: 643.

63 Sarrocchi writes, "I would also like you to look it over with respect to orthography. You will also find many changes and many verses that have been altered." Ibid.

64 Margherita Sarrocchi to Galileo Galilei, July 29, 1611; OG, XI:563.

65 Ibid.

66 Ibid. In another letter, Sarrocchi says the list will take only eight or ten days to complete. "The poem is complete, except for the list of those who came to Scanderbeg's aid, which I left incomplete so that I could insert the names of my friends and patrons, as you will see by many of the names, which I chose randomly, and then changed to the names of my friends; and the list will take me eight, or maybe ten, days"; Margherita Sarrocchi to Galileo Galilei, January 13, 1612; OG, XI:643.

67 In a letter dated June 9, 1612, for example, Sarrocchi makes reference to reading Galileo's *Discourse on Floating Bodies* with Valerio; Margherita Sarrocchi to Galileo Galilei, June 9, 1612; OG, XI:696.

68 Biagioli, *Galileo Courtier,* 138.

69 Valerio was involved with Cesi in printing the *Letters on Sunspots*: David Freedberg, *The Eye of the Lynx: Galileo, His Friends, and the Beginnings of Modern Natural History* (Chicago, IL: The University of Chicago Press), 124. On the planned Florentine edition of the *Sidereus nuncius* see Biagioli, *Galileo Courtier,* 45–56; for the poetic contributions solicited for it by Galileo see Nuzio Vaccalluzzo, *Galileo Galilei nella poesia del suo secolo* (Milan: R. Sandron, 1910), i–lxx.

70 Guido Bettoli to Margherita Sarrocchi, June 4, 1611; OG, XI:537.

71 Ibid. Bettoli refers to the controversy over Galileo's findings described in a letter by Cosimo Sassetti of Perugia to Monsignor Piero Dini in Rome (May 14, 1611: OG, XI:530).

72 Margherita Sarrocchi to Guido Bettoli, August 27, 1611; OG, XI:574.

73 Ibid.

74 Margherita Sarrocchi to Galileo Galilei, September 10, 1611; OG, XI:579. Galileo kept a copy of this letter, marking it with a note that reads: "Regards the telescope and the new discoveries."

75 Ibid.

76 Margherita Sarrocchi to Galileo Galilei, October 12, 1611; OG, XI:593.

77 For example, Bronzini, *Della dignità e nobiltà delle donne,* 134–135.

78   In another letter to a colleague in Perugia, Innocenzio continues to speak dismissively of Sarrocchi, attributing her defense of Galileo's discoveries to the affection she has for him rather than to her scientific opinion (Fra Innocenzio Perugino to Girolamo Perugini, July 20, 1611, cited in Favaro, *Amici e corrispondenti di Galileo* [Venice: Officine Grafiche C. Ferrari, 1894], 26).

79   In another letter, Innocenzio says he possesses a "smattering of astrological knowledge" and discusses his interest in horoscopes (Fra Innocenzio Perugino to Girolamo Perugino, August 28, 1611; cited in Favaro, *Amici e corrispondenti*, 28).

80   See Monica Azzolini, *The Duke and the Stars: Astrology and Politics in Renaissance Milan* (Cambridge, MA: Harvard University Press, 2013, 17). Despite papal bulls against judicial astrology in 1586 and 1631, it was widely practiced (see Ugo Baldini, "The Roman Inquisition's Condemnation of Astrology: Antecedents, Reasons, and Consequences," in *Church Censorship and Culture in Early Modern Italy*, ed. Gigiola Fragnito [Cambridge: Cambridge University Press, 2001], 107). For an overview of astrology and astrological practice in the period, see Brendan Dooley, ed., *A Companion to Astrology in the Renaissance* (Leiden: Brill, 2014).

81   Margherita Sarrocchi to Galileo Galilei, September 10, 1611; OG, XI:579.

82   Ibid. Darrel H. Rutkin notes this letter as evidence of Galileo's astrological interest, but does not discuss it further (see "Galileo Astrologer: Astrology and Mathematical Practice in the Late-Sixteenth and Early-Seventeenth Centuries" *Galileiana* (2005): 8–143, 124).

83   "I stopped to procure the nativity of that child born to Cassandra's daughter, as you wrote me the signora desired, and I am enclosing it here, so that the signora may have less bother, and I drew up a judgment about it for you." [Fra Innocenzo Perugino to Girolamo Perugino, July 20, 1611, in Favaro, *Amici e corrispondenti*, 26]).

84   August 28, 1611, in ibid., 28.

85   Guglielmo Righini, "L'oroscopo Galileiano di Cosimo II De' Medici," *Annali dell'Istituto e Museo di Storia di Scienza di Firenze* I (1976): 29–56, at pp. 29–33; Rutkin, "Galileo Astrologer," 117–121.

86   On this figure, see Nick Wilding, *Galileo's Idol: Gianfrancesco Sagredo and the Politics of Knowledge* (Chicago, IL: The University of Chicago Press, 2015).

87   Poppi ties Galileo's astrological praxis specifically to his financial straits. See Antonino Poppi, *Cremonini e Galilei inquisiti a Padova nel 1604: Nuovi documenti d'archivio* [Padua: Antenore], 1992, 41–49, at p. 56 n3; see also Favaro, *Galileo e lo Studio di Padova*, I: 146–147.

88   Quoted in Poppi, *Cremonini e Galilei*, 54; also discussed in Rutkin, Galileo Astrologer, 126–128. The charge against Galileo was eventually dismissed.

89   In his response, Pagnoni stated, "I know that he said this and that he renders a firm judgment in the nativities he produces, but I [did not] know that this had been declared heresy," cited in Poppi, *Cremonini e Galilei*, 60.

90   Brendan Dooley, *Science and the Marketplace in Renaissance Italy* (Lanham, MD: Lexington Books, 2001), 59; ibid., "The Morandi Affair and Seventeenth-Century Rome," in *A Renaissance of Conflicts: Visions and Revisions of Law and Society in Italy and Spain*, ed. John A. Marino and Thomas Kuhn, 395–420 (Toronto: Centre for Reformation and Renaissance Studies, 2004), 400–401.

91   On this episode, see Dooley, *Morandi's Last Prophecy and the End of Renaissance Politics* (Princeton, NJ: Princeton University Press, 2002); Rutkin, "Galileo Astrologer," 136–143.

92   Dooley, "The Morandi Affair," 397.

93   See, for example, Baldini and Napolitani, "Per una biografia," 68.

94   "As for my poem, as I wrote before, *Vostra Signoria* will do me the favor of returning it to me, because I have made many changes, such that your copy is no longer good. I will have it copied again, and I will send it to *Vostra Signoria*" (Margherita Sarrocchi to Galileo Galilei, June 9, 1612, OG, XI:696]). Despite Sarrocchi's

"La verità delle stelle" **251**

promise to send Galileo a new copy of her poem, Favaro's extensive inventory of Galileo's library does not show that he held any works by Sarrocchi (whether the *Scanderbeide* or her poetry; cf. Favaro, "La libreria di Galileo Galilei," *Bullettino di bibliografia e di storia delle scienze matematiche e fisiche*, XIX, 1886). However, we know that Galileo possessed books that, for one reason or another, were no longer present in his library when the inventory was made (Poppi, *Cremonini e Galilei inquisiti*, 59 n12).

95 Sarrocchi to Galilei, June 9, 1612.

96 The letter is reproduced in Gilberto Govi, *Tre Lettere di Galileo*, 14–15.

97 Galileo Galilei to Margherita Sarrocchi, January 21, 1612 (see Letter 7 here); in OG, XI:647.

98 "She has finished looking over and revising her poem to her satisfaction and that of other men very talented in this art, with the idea of giving it over, if it please God, to be published this coming year" (Luca Valerio to Galileo Galilei, Agosto 31, 1613 [see Letter 11 here], OG, XI:919). Despite Valerio's words, it would be another ten years before the *Scanderbeide* was published in its revised format, six years after Sarrocchi's death.

99 Brevaglieri, "Science, Books, and Censorship," 137.

100 Baldini and Napoletani, "Per una biografia," 65.

PART V
Information, politics, and war

12

PUBLISHING THE BAROQUE POST

The postal itinerary and the mailbag novel

Rachel Midura

The sixteenth and seventeenth centuries were key for the development of a shared European communication infrastructure and common habits of its use. The renaissance of letters developed alongside a renaissance of the post, meaning the establishment of official waystations for the pick-up and distribution of mail across Europe. The semi-public "ordinary" messengers, run on a regularized route and schedule, were soon followed by the innovations of the postal inn and post coach. Published letter collections and letter-writing manuals frequently took these technologies for granted; however, two earlier genres of publication articulated fascination with the radical potential of the post: the postal itinerary and the "mailbag" novel. The first advocated top-down information control, while the latter delighted in the violent liberation of the mail from state agents. Together, they represented competing visions of the role of the post in contemporary society.

Two works epitomize Northern Italy's key contributions to the development of pan-European postal culture. In 1608, Milanese lieutenant postmaster Ottavio Codogno published *A New Itinerary of the Posts Throughout the World,*[1] which instructed users in the address and postage of mail through the imperial, Venetian, and French systems. It provided routes to and from many European destinations, and as far as the Indies and Ottoman Empire, with glossed lists of stops along each route. Today the itinerary is most used by postal historians for determining the times and costs of exchange.[2] Yet Codogno also presented a history of the post from antiquity forward with anecdotes from his own institutional experience within the Spanish post of Milan. Codogno praised the last century's postal development as providing speed, security, and regularity of service with a strong professional culture.

In 1641, Venetian satirist Ferrante Pallavicino published *The Courier Waylaid,* a satirical novel that instead emphasized the susceptibility of the post. Robbing the courier thwarted delivery and removed any veil of secrecy.[3] Pallavicino's work and several of its imitators precede the epistolary novel, but merit consideration as a separate genre: the "mailbag" novel.[4] Rather than following a single plotline involving multiple parties, the genre instead fictionalized the jumbled contents of the courier's bag.[5] It created a cacophony of voices to obscure the satirist as a hidden conductor. This early mailbag novel represents Pallavicino's ventriloquism at its finest, while also offering insight as to the contents of the contemporary post, especially missives decidedly outside the scholarly Republic of Letters. Only in the courier's valet, Pallavicino seemed to suggest, could we find the governor rubbing elbows with the executioner.

The sixteenth century had seen the establishment of official posts and their opening to public use. The tumult of the seventeenth century put much of that infrastructure in jeopardy; Codogno and Pallavicino stood on either side of the start of the Thirty Years' War (1618–1648). Their works address the definition of a "public service" and its relation to the state—a central issue of their time. Codogno wrote as a postmaster historian, arguing for the deep roots of a pan-European communication system. He denounced the recent plague of courier assaults as attacks on the common good. He emphasized the responsibility of civil servants to protect the vital information that passed through their hands. Pallavicino's *Courier*, by contrast, featured the fight against censorship and hypocrisy, especially among public figures, from statesmen to clergy.[6] Pallavicino invited the reader to voyeuristically sit alongside the despoilers of the courier, applauding their curious impulse. Publishing the post in both genres advanced new ethical principles for communication, such as privacy, publicity, and the right to know.

Codogno's itinerary

Since the late Middle Ages, Northern Italy had a number of early mail services. Universities, banks, and cities often ran messengers on foot (*pedoni*) or horseback (*cavallari*). A postal system depended upon the establishment of staffed waystations (*poste*) for couriers to change horses or pick up or distribute mail. The Tassis (also Tasso or Taxis) family of Bergamo worked as postmasters and key developers of postal lines for the Venetian, papal, imperial, and Spanish posts. By 1608, the Tassis family monopoly had weakened from its mid-sixteenth-century apex. Following the abdication of Charles V in 1556, the imperial post fractured into Spanish and Austrian branches, and Philip II of Spain took possession of the Habsburg Italian posts. Upon the death of postmaster Ruggero Tassis in 1588, his widow Lucina Cataneo Tassis negotiated with Spanish cousin-in-law, Juan de Tassis y Acuña, Count of Villamediana, to lease the office. Ottavio Codogno (c.1570–1630) served her as a capable deputy until her death in 1619, and as procurator for her sons until his own death in 1630.[7]

Codogno was partially responsible for overseeing one of the largest hubs in Europe. We know little for sure of Codogno's background, but a Venetian ambassador believed him to be lowborn and possibly originating from the Spanish Netherlands.[8] His publication of the itinerary in 1608 was driven by a combination of career ambitions and social aspirations. Codogno was an outsider to both the Tassis family and the Spanish gentry that dominated Milan. The itinerary showcased his greatest asset: his expert professional knowledge and training. While never becoming the official officeholder, Codogno wielded substantial authority, and was frequently addressed as the de facto postmaster (*corriero maggiore*) until his death in 1630 (Figures 12.1 and 12.2).[9]

After 1608, Codogno's *Nuovo itinerario* appeared in at least six more editions published in Milan and Venice across the next century.[10] The itinerary was a publishing success for several reasons: first, there was its sheer utility as a reference guide for route tables for couriers and travelers. Second, Codogno wrote from a uniquely informed perspective on the postal system's historical development from both experience and study. He demonstrated his humanist education with frequent references to Livy, Pliny, and Plutarch.[11] He expanded the 1616 edition of the itinerary to include citations from the most recent works, engaging on the scholarly question of the origin of the postal system.[12] Finally, Codogno provided unprecedented administrative guidance for postmasters, such as templates for noting the arrival and departure of couriers.[13]

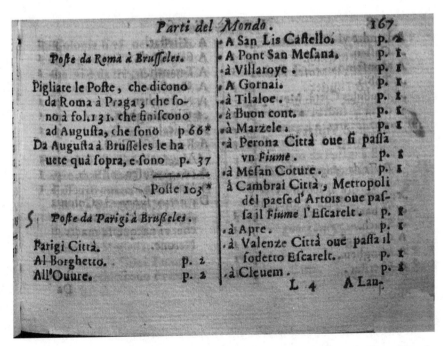

FIGURE 12.1 Example of routes from Rome and Paris to Brussels from Ottavio Codogno, *Nuovo itinerario*, 1608. Bayerische Staatsbibliothek München, Res/Geo.u. 86, p. 167

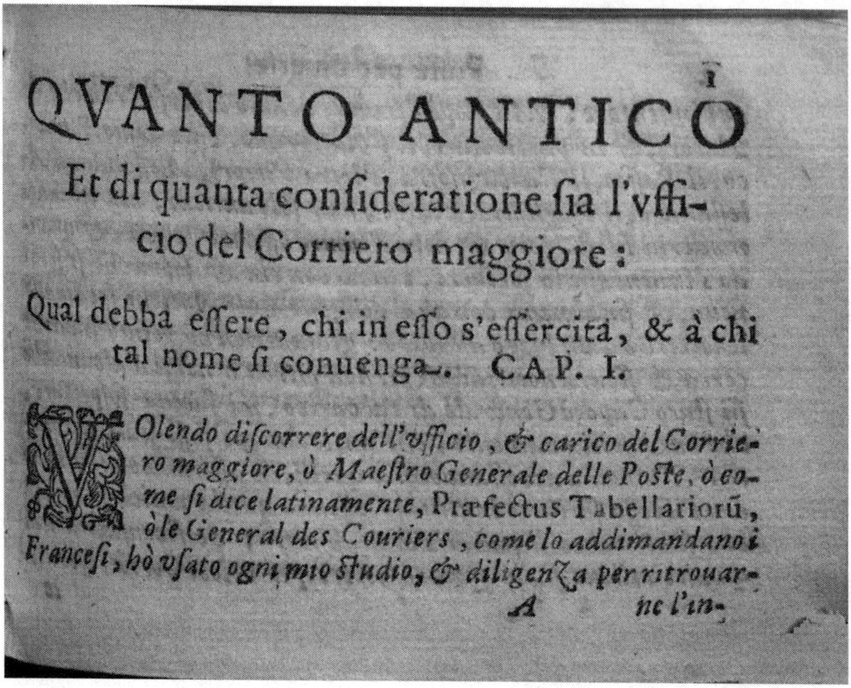

1

QVANTO ANTICO
Et di quanta conſideratione ſia l'vfficio del Corriero maggiore:
Qual debba eſſere, chi in eſſo s'eſſercita, & à chi
tal nome ſi conuenga. CAP. I.

VOlendo diſcorrere dell'vfficio, & carico del Corriero maggiore, ò Maeſtro Generale delle Poſte, ò come ſi dice latinamente, Præfectus Tabellariorũ,
ò le General des Couriers, come lo addimandano i
Franceſi, hò vſato ogni mio ſtudio, & diligenza per ritrouar-
A ne l'in-

FIGURE 12.2 Chapter heading, "How Ancient and Important Is the Office of Postmaster," from Ottavio Codogno, *Nuovo itinerario*, 1608. Bayerische Staatsbibliothek München, Res/Geo.u. 86, p. 1

A late seventeenth-century Venetian author praised him as "the best author, who had distilled the finest matters of governing the posts and couriers."[14] The book's palm-sized format was ideal for a busy administrator, but also a courier, clerk, or even traveling merchant.

The first book of the itinerary instructed the reader not only in the use of the post, but also its history and internal logic.[15] Within the hundred-some dense prose pages of this otherwise reference work, Codogno demonstrated the ethical professionalism of the post, posing a convincing case for its ability to encompass every interest in its tightly sealed mailbag. He also established comprehensive guidelines for postal officials, from couriers to administrators. For Codogno, service both to the prince and public were mutually affirming.[16]

Codogno's itinerary was a guide, but also an effective advertisement for the official post. He frequently compared the regular couriers (*ordinari*) to unlicensed messengers (*procacci*), warning of the dangers of trusting freelancers. While they might casually delay or misplace the mail, Codogno related his own great efforts to correctly deliver "a pearl worth thirty scudi, which had been sent to jeweler Battista Parisi in Venice, and through inattention, had been posted without the name of the city."[17] Codogno presented the official post as the pinnacle of administrative achievement, from its illustrious Roman origins, to the dedication of public servants like himself.[18]

The handling of public mail was always a necessary evil from the perspective of the state: it distracted messengers, caused delays, and attracted thieves and newsmongers. Codogno instead emphasized the public utility of the post, describing postmasters as: "not only very important, useful, and convenient to particular private persons, but also the *public*." He compared the choice of a postmaster to that of elected rulers and popes, in that "how, and who they are, concerns the interests of all." Over the past century, the Tassis had linked Europe from Spain to Burgundy "not just for the convenience of their princes and lords, but also for the common good (*commune utilità*) of all men of business (*negotianti*)."[19] Codogno's use of print to put the itinerary into public hands further underscored his belief in public service. In his depiction, the post was "public" in both its service to the state, as well as society, consisting of many civilian letter writers.[20] At times, Codogno addressed the beneficiaries of the public service directly, reminding stingy merchants that they must "render unto Caesar" and take responsibility for their own mailing errors.[21]

While his position in Milan no doubt shaped Codogno's overall perspective of the European postal web, the *Nuovo itinerario* was remarkably egalitarian in many ways. Codogno remained equivocal about any state's claims to invent the post, to such a degree that his *Nuovo itinerario* did not even include the local history of the Visconti and Sforza post.[22] Given the delicate political situation of now Spanish-governed Milan, he likely opted for discretion on the matter. Codogno appeared to advocate a neo-Roman *cursus publicus*: national and regional distinctions such as local currencies and postage practices were relegated to a minor inconvenience. Codogno did not address questions of a hierarchy among postmasters based on their locales—a particularly interesting omission given several embarrassing historical incidents caused by internal power jockeying treated in the following section.[23] Codogno's history of the post always had propagandizing purpose; Codogno opened the post to public view, but presented the post as the provider of mutually beneficial ties between state and society, tending toward harmony rather than conflict.

Codogno's silence on certain contentious points in the history of the post was in keeping with the neutral disposition he encouraged the postmaster to cultivate toward his clients. He repeatedly instructed the postmaster to be "wise, prudent and a friend of equity."[24] The postmaster had to be circumspect at all times; this was especially (but not exclusively) true around foreigners and the enemies of one's clients, when matters had to be kept *occultissimo*.[25] The itinerary avoided distinguishing patrons by status or class: "this secrecy and diligence is not just necessary in the affairs of Princes, or similar persons, but also in the affairs of the clerics, gentlemen, businessmen, and others."[26] By doing so, the post would facilitate communications across borders without being a partisan, judge, or publisher. Codogno's careful framing likely helped the itinerary's export outside of Milan; with the removal of the dedication to the Spanish governor, it was easily translated to Venice and beyond.[27]

Yet the connections between the itinerary and the Spanish Habsburg state ran deeper than the paratextual material. Information management, although a modern term, is useful as an analytical category to consider a constellation of related responsibilities of the post.[28] The first duty of the postal official was the *reporting* of information. This was of course the basic function of the system—to carry correspondence from place to place—but reporting could also mean carrying information to someone other than the intended recipient. The second duty was the *protection* of information, primarily through resisting pressure toward publication, and therefore partisanship and poor business practice. The reward was honor, the punishment dishonor. These two duties alone were occasionally contradictory, and the ethical waters were further muddied by a third responsibility: the *gathering* of information. The role of a postal official as an "intelligencer" for the prince was an important qualification upon Codogno's ideal of universal equity and secrecy.

The itinerary makes clear that the postmaster was always expected to facilitate a prince's access to news. While Codogno scolded the postmaster who told news to the public, he encouraged him to race to the prince when an item of interest passed through his hands.[29] The contracts of Tassis postmastership frequently specified the need for in-person access for the court at all times—this meaning the Spanish governor in the case of Milan.[30] Codogno reiterated the need for proximity to the local authority in order to minimize the time between the arrival of news and its delivery. The ideal postmaster delivered mail to the prince first, before any client, usually in person. The postmaster also provided the prince with regular opportunities to intervene, including informing him of every dispatch, in case he wished to add his own letters, or hold the courier for some time. Codogno specifically addressed those periods of highest demand from the clergy, such as during a *sede vacante*, or from businessmen during an important fair: while the postmaster would face a great deal of outside pressure, the "public" must always come second to the prince.[31] The rhetorical ideal may have been universal equity, but we actually see two distinct classes of treatment in the practice of the post.

Codogno took it for granted that news would pass through his hands in unsealed form, either textually or orally. Posts, often located at postal inns, were natural information hubs. The first European "Black Chambers"—systematic intelligence-gathering operations—were frequently established in conjunction with post offices.[32] Codogno did not address such operations, although he did provide guidance suggesting that the postmaster walked a dangerous line. Codogno recommended that the postmaster avoid "being a prattler, newsteller, or trying to appear smart," and above all, the suspicion that he was the source for foreign news:

> because if some new strange thing is divulged, and spread through the city, the opinion will be that the postmaster is a newsteller (*novellista*), and soon everyone will say that it came from the post; even if it is in fact false, the Prince will nonetheless easily believe that he is the author of it.

Codogno then invoked both Cassandra's unheeded warning and Aesop's boy who cried wolf as cautionary tales.[33] A postmaster's failure to keep information from public knowledge was directly connected to his ability to convey vital information to his prince.

In fact, Codogno precisely described the sorts of tricks that individuals might employ to learn secrets from the post, describing those who "come to the post, with the pretense of having something to mail ... pretending to want to deliver, or carry something, demanding something of theirs (although nothing has been sent), demanding something of their adversary" as a ruse for gathering information. Such men might even bribe or threaten officials, but as Codogno sternly reminded, "pay them no mind, because honor carries more value than fear." Codogno scolded those who violated the post, accusing them of "committing grave errors against the interests of the public and the Prince," and also the courier, who would "bear the dishonor henceforth."[34] Concerns with "dishonor" (*dishonore*) and "shame" (*vergogna*) appear throughout Codogno's treatment, suggesting that there was a code of ethics to information management: the postal official who failed in his responsibility was personally, in addition to professionally, culpable.

Espionage and counter-espionage became increasingly pertinent as political tensions increased on the eve of the Thirty Years' War. Contemporaries were preparing for conflict long before the 1618 Bohemian revolt. The Netherlands remained in an uneasy truce, and the newly enthroned Louis XIII (r. 1610–1643) was openly antagonistic toward his Habsburg rival, Philip III of Spain (r. 1598–1621).[35] Lombardy was ripe with intelligence given its centrality to Habsburg communications, and the proximity of politically and religiously disputed territories such as the Valtellina. A collection of printed edicts from the period conveys the threats faced by the post: within a seven-year period, five decrees addressed specific assaults on couriers.[36] Each followed a similar format, providing the details of the recent crime, then offering impunity for a conspirator, should he provide sufficient evidence against others. As the assaults continued, the promised rewards increased: by a 1611 assault on a Venetian courier, the accomplice-turned-informer could also request the release of two bandits of his choice, while his conspirators faced torture and hanging.[37]

Codogno saw trickery, not violence, as the more insidious threat to the postal enterprise. He treated "murderers and thieves" glancingly compared to the number of stories of spies.[38] Codogno cited a 1556 incident that landed the unfortunate Roman postmaster in prison when incriminating letters were planted in the valise while a courier slept. Once, he reported, a postmaster of Piacenza sought news from a courier en route to Brussels with "flattery and caresses," later delaying him with "food and drink" so that the courier would arrive late, depriving the next postmaster of the ability to deliver news in a timely fashion.[39] The courier needed to be vigilant about such false friends, who might even present themselves as traveling companions for the duration of the journey, but "sleep like the crocodile."[40] Many malicious parties could benefit from slowing or seizing the post, whether rival postmasters or enemies to one's prince.

Given these threats, how else could information be protected? This was the question that preoccupied a broad collection of texts outside of Codogno's itinerary, including the particularly sophisticated development of cipher literature.[41] The itinerary did evolve to address the changing conditions of Northern Italy: the majority of additions to the 1616 edition relate to information management, from the first mention of ciphers (*zifre*),[42] to lessons learned from recent travails in war-torn Piedmont.[43] Ciphers accomplished the information-control function of protection, but frustrated information gathering and reporting. They were in fact prohibited in Spain, and ciphered letters could be legally seized.[44] Nonetheless, capture and publication of the post was so common as to be a cultural trope by the mid-seventeenth century. The most famous incidents caused crises in contemporary politics: the letters incriminating Charles II's favorite, the Duke of Buckingham, or the published letters of the Spanish chancellery, abandoned in the chaos of retreat from battle.[45]

Codogno's itinerary demonstrates how an ideology of state control girded the postal itinerary as a genre. He went beyond a reference book to provide a comprehensive vision of the postal service as an information administration, with a professional culture of idealized equity and impartiality. However, the proscriptive elements, and additions to the 1616 edition, suggest a growing divergence between ideal and reality in a challenging political climate.

Pallavicino's novel

Where Codogno saw only bandits and spies, Pallavicino developed another vision entirely of the combatants in the battle for information control. As many historians of espionage, illicit publishing, and smuggling have found, writing an institutional history from official documents often provides an incomplete picture at best.[46] By turning to the mailbag novel, we can glimpse a strong vein of resistance to state information management, as well as the contents of the contemporary post.

Pallavicino's *Corriero svaligiato* can be linked to many Italian imitators such as *Il postiglione* (Venice, 1666) and *Avanzi delle poste* (Venice, 1677), as well as books published in France and England, including a popular reworking of Pallavicino's letters by Charles Gildon as *The Post-boy Robbed of his Bag* (London, 1706). Authorship of another mailbag novel, *Mercurio postiglione* (1667), has even been attributed to Pallavicino, although there is little evidence for this attribution beyond stylistic similarity.[47] Pallavicino appears to have inspired this brief flowering of mailbag novels, and we may draw some generalizations about how the genre functioned from his work.

First, the seizure itself often had the excitement of war, but little of the true violence. Tricks, traps, and elaborate backstories predominated rather than brute force, evoking late medieval literary antecedents like Boccaccio and Chaucer. The embarrassment of the courier and his clients through the publication of their letters was performative humor, similar to the ritualized punishment of the cuckold's horns. See, for example, the frontispiece of a German edition of *Mercurio* which depicted the pagan gods rifling through Mercury's mail between the worlds of the living and dead (Figure 12.3). The image is amiably social—Mercury is cornered by the others, but the drawn sword and grabbing hands seem positioned to hold him still rather than cause harm, and their postures are relaxed. The inclusion of Momus, a god of satire and mockery from outside the usual pantheon, further underscores the novel's theme. In *Corriero svaligiato* as well, the guilt of the assailants was softened as they "only took what suited their intent, in this interest of politics."[48] Pallavicino indicated that the courier's inability to perceive the trickery was partially to blame for his own predicament.[49]

The second trait of the "mailbag novel" was its dependence on verisimilitude as a literary *trompe l'oeil*. In *Corriero*, the (fictional) publisher Gironfaccio Spironcini explained to the reader that the letters had been carried by the ordinary messenger of Milan, who had wandered from his journey and been seized by the German baron "Hochenberg."[50] The baron discarded the letters that did not interest him, which were then reassembled by various court wits (*ingegni vivaci*). "Spironcini" explained that it was these wits who supplied additional letters and a framing narrative of another (fictionalized) court and waylaid courier, then delivered the completed manuscript to him. Within this narrative, the letters are explained as having been seized instead by an Italian prince seeking to spy on the Spanish Governor of Milan. The letters were accompanied by snippets from a discussion carried out by different set of court wits, including the (fictional) Marchese di Salsas, Baron di Moinpier, Conte di Sineda, and Cavalier Sinibaldi. The convoluted premise of *Corriero* simulated the murky process by which letters traveled and mutated once untethered from the official courier.

Pallavicino represented the exposure of the contents of the mailbag not as an attack on the public, but rather as a benefit to the public, aimed at revealing the true nature of society. The premise absolved "Spironcini" from all responsibility by obscuring the identities of contributors as well as the line between the fictional and real. In fact, the publisher even declared the book decidedly not satirical, but instead a "game" (*gioco*), "jokes" (*scherzi*), and "for fun" (*fatto per gioco*).[51] Because it did not seek to uphold virtue, or condemn vice, it was too impartial to be a satire, seeking instead to turn the reader's eyes to the world as it was, particularly the "deformity of the great." The publisher declared it safe for all to read, except, perhaps, for those who send their own packages by the post—for them, it would perhaps be "too painful."[52] In fact, the novel presented a variety of potential justifications, from the Italian prince, who ordered the assault "hoping to be able to disperse his own suspicions, or clarify the news that he desired,"[53] to the joking wits who protested that they had no purpose at

FIGURE 12.3 Frontispiece image from the German translation of *Mercurio postiglione*, some-
times attributed to Ferrante Pallavicino. The gods are shown discussing the contents of
Mercury's mailbag. *Der auff der Post angehaltene Mercurius: bey welchem unterschiedene Staats-
Sachen und Schreiben gefunden worden: aus dem Italienischen in unsere Mutter-Sprache übersetzt
und eines und das andere mit eingerückt* (Meissen, 1668). Courtesy of Department of Special
Collections, Stanford University Libraries

all. The mailbag novel subverted the logic of the itinerary, arguing that it was the control of the mailbag that prevented, rather than aided, the post in public service.

The contents of *Corriero* vary widely in tone, and—much like the false story of its piecemeal assembly—also vary from edition to edition. The first versions appeared in the early 1640s and were viciously polemical: in the letters, an executioner sought a soon-to-be-vacated office in Rome, a Jesuit priest confessed the misdeeds of his order, and anonymous writers railed against the censorship of books, Spanish tyranny in Italy, and sodomy in the monasteries. The wits provided minimal commentary, usually echoing the points made within letters. By the 1646 edition, the addition of another thirty-seven letters to the original thirteen and the significant expansion of the witty commentary made for a very different novel. *Corriero* now included many letters from secretaries, merchants, scholars, and young (and mature) lovers. The religious and political polemic was now diluted by the amorous, misogynistic, mundane, and absurd; in short, the full range of everyday behavior that might end up in a letter. Many of these additions seemed intended to heighten the verisimilitude, including the Viceroy of Naple's order for glasses, a creditor's dispute of debt, and a receipt for a cardinal's shipment of soap.[54] Each provided the wits with metaphors for further satire, but also made the whole seem more like a mailbag in truth. These additional letters, occasionally distributed under the title of *Continuazione del Corriero svaligiato*, seem to have been supplied in response to the unpredicted popularity of these more quotidian elements.[55] The novel increasingly appealed to readers who didn't seek to know the secrets of state and church, but rather to experience the mailbag as a mirror of society and invaluable source on the human condition.

Pallavicino embraced the perverse curiosity of the readers of the mailbag, whose opening of the mail inverted status and power. The wits pounced on the letters "with the vivacity of courtiers, ready at the occasion of gossip." They "busied themselves with opening the letters and satisfying their curiosity regarding those who live in a sleepy idleness in the shadow of their betters."[56] Each reader of the mailbag finds something enlightening about the mysterious other. The most striking lesson is that of shared humanity: the most erudite letters, such as that from a troubled Jesuit father, are followed by the most salacious, such as a young man seeking to escape the sodomitical intent of a cardinal in Rome.[57] When the baron announced, "'while you have been talking … I have found a love letter with a seal already broken,'" the wits quickly dropped their lackluster discussion of an erudite letter based on the trope of Parnassus, "attentive for him to begin reading." Similarly, the wits approved of a burlesque of fantastical pagan symbolism, but bemoaned the single letter written in Latin as being too serious and erudite.[58] They made no secret of their gossipy desire to learn from letters and the mailbag provided ample material.

The success of the mailbag novel depended upon an already well-developed postal culture. Pallavicino assumed familiarity with the post on the part of his popular print reading audience. In many cases, the humor and titillation derived from the divergence between the ideal post and his depiction, from the unfortunate wandering courier to the pompous letters and broken seals. In one letter, a writer told a fantastical story of how a snail arrived as courier for the King of Transylvania, carrying "a valise full of shadows and chimeras," perhaps a reference to the phenomenon of fake war news.[59] In discussing another, the wits addressed the "cryptic" style of a secretary's requests:

> "It is from some great man," added the Marquis, "because like princes, he uses signs in order to not be understood, like ciphers."
>
> "Oh," responded the Baron, "What a nice sight these letters would make atop a spice box (*scatola di Speciaria*)."
>
> Perhaps whoever was to receive this letter had such a box, in which they would find aromatics to discover his ambitious designs.[60]

Here the humor depends upon a reference to the use of invisible ink—and methods of its discovery. Finally, in a particularly pointed parallel, a letter relates how an old man, driven by paranoia, sought to steal the mail to prevent his enemies from discussing him. In reading about his trial, the wits mock the man, and agree with the judge's verdict of insanity. The irony of their own waylaying of the courier, ordered by their suspicious patron, is completely lost on them.[61] Pallavicino's mailbag represented postal culture as deeply ingrained in contemporary life. The hunger for news that it both stirred and fed was shared across gender, class, and status.

Codogno instructed postal officers to demonstrate polite neutrality to clients, neither censoring nor judging the contents of their mailbags. His ideal public service was keeping sensitive information from the eyes and ears of a news-hungry public, while delivering it to serve the appetites of the state. The satirical author, fictional publisher, and conjured wits served a directly opposing purpose: they served a patron, took advantage of the courier, and judged and mocked every letter-writer, particularly public figures. Their jocularity contrasted with Codogno's grim sense of "dishonor and shame." And yet the wits also described their work in terms of a public service, making the previously invisible visible to the "eyes of the world" and "public light" for "universal satisfaction."[62] Pallavicino's own career frustrations lent strength to a letter railing against limitations on "public knowledge" (*publica notizia*). Count Spineda sympathized with the anonymous letter-writer, describing how information control was the resort of corrupted states hoping to keep certain truths secret, particularly the Spanish regime.[63]

Despite Codogno's insistence on seeing the early modern post as a reinvention of an idealized Roman imperial system of communication, both books were grounded in a Northern Italian context in which French, Spanish, Italian, Papal, and German interests were frequently at odds. The debate about the correct interpretation of "public service" and the post was carried out in front of a readership with a vested interest, as they too sought to communicate by letters, transfer goods, or avoid violent robbery—Pallavicino's dig at those who might not wish to read the book because of empathetic pangs makes that clear. Both books offer insight into just what the public was and how it should be served. Whereas Codogno saw the Spanish Habsburgs and Tassis postmasters as continuing the Roman *cursus publicus*, by the 1640s, Pallavicino saw Spanish tyranny threatening to destroy the free flow of information. The integrity of Codogno's post depended upon the guarantee of secrecy to princes, but the integrity of Pallavicino's post demanded occasional violent intervention to redress the balance in favor of a broader public.

Mercury's mailbag

While *Corriero* briefly landed Pallavicino in Venetian prison, he continued to write and publish abroad and under pseudonyms during his imprisonment and after his release. In 1643, after months of staying just ahead of pursuant authorities, the Roman Inquisition captured Pallavicino in France. Despite the intercession of many powerful friends—including the imperial postmaster in Venice, Ruggero Tassis—Pallavicino was executed in Avignon in 1644.[64] In 1667, another mailbag novel appeared in print and manuscript miscellanies, posthumously attributed to the unfortunate satirist. In *Mercurio postiglione*, Jupiter, although admitting apathy toward the behavior of impious tyrants, nonetheless encouraged Mercury to share the letters. Mercury initially expressed qualms, but his scruples were quickly overcome, as Jupiter assured him that he would be in good company breaking professional secrecy. The surveillance of "private" communication, after all, was a hallowed tenet of "World Politicians" (*Politici del Mondo*)—why else would Jesuits invent the ritual of confession, if not to spy for a prince?[65]

Like *Corriero*, *Mercurio* displays an in-depth understanding of and cultural engagement with postal culture. It suggested important answers to the questions of who used the post and to what purpose, licit or illicit. The popularity of these mailbag novels indicated an informed contemporary audience who sought out the subversion of one of the most powerful symbols of government information control. The targeted mockery of the mailbag novel was to the disadvantage of the letter writers, but also depicted a re-engagement with politics on the part of the public, much like Jupiter's hesitant interest. The curiosity of the Gods, and by extension the reader, was not contemptible, or to the dishonor of Mercury, but rather a natural and even healthy alternative to stoic disillusionment. Despite the threats to postal infrastructure posed by war and espionage, we see that its cultural habits had taken deep roots in the imagination of an increasingly literate Europe.

Codogno's itinerary sought to advertise the official post as offering a public service that both historical precedents and contemporary rivals could not. His desire to demonstrate the public utility of the post, to show the impartiality and neutrality of its officers, and to reach a wide audience of potential clients conflicted with the exclusionary information management of the state. Pallavicino and other contemporaries appear to have shared Codogno's view of postal information as a precious commodity. However, whereas Codogno saw the publication of the post as an attack on society and an obstacle to public service, Pallavicino defended such a violation on the basis of public information. The mailbag novel presents itself as yet another "Mirror for Society," teaching the lessons that lust, avarice, and ignorance crossed borders as much as letters. Waylaying the courier was an act of reclamation, performed with ritual festivity. Pallavicino did not seek to undermine, let alone collapse, the system of the post, but rather to expose the hypocrisy of surveilling authorities.

The postal itinerary and the mailbag novel demonstrated the constellation of relations forming the postal culture of the early seventeenth century. The technology of the postal service and its supporting infrastructure influenced the lives and habits of contemporaries, but were shaped by their concerns in turn, particularly with regards to the role of the state vis-à-vis a news-hungry public. By supplementing administrative documents with the products of the popular press, we might better understand the history of the early modern post and the epistolary society it served.

Notes

1 With thanks to Paula Findlen, Suzanne Sutherland, Filippo de Vivo, and the Stanford Center for Early Modern and Medieval Studies workshop. Ottavio Codogno, *Nuovo itinerario delle poste per tutto il mondo* (Milano: Girolamo Bordone, 1608). For sixteenth-century examples of itinerary books, see those by Charles Estienne (Paris, 1553), Giovanni Dall'Erba (Rome, 1563), Cherubino de Stella (Venice, 1564), and Alessandro Beccaria (Rome, 1591).
2 Clemente Fedele, Marco Gerosa, and Armando Serra, eds, *Europa Postale: L'Opera di Ottavio Codogno luogotenente dei Tasso nella Milano settecentesca* (Camerata Cornello: Museo dei Tasso e della Storia Postale, 2014). For overviews of early modern postal history, see Bruno Caizzi, *Dalla posta dei re alla posta di tutti : territorio e comunicazioni in Italia dal XVI secolo all'Unità* (Milano: Franco Angeli, 1993) and Wolfgang Behringer, *Im Zeichen des Merkur: Reichspost und Kommunikationsrevolution in der Frühen Neuzeit* (Göttingen: Vandenhoeck & Ruprecht, 2003).
3 Ferrante Pallavicino, *Il corriero svaligiato* (Villafranca: G. Gibaldo, 1644). Unless otherwise noted, excerpts have been taken from Armando Marchi ed., "Il corriero svaligiato," in *Il corriero svaligiato con la Lettera dalla prigionia, aggiuntavi La semplicità ingannata di suor Arcangela Tarabotti*, Archivio Barocco (Parma: Università di Parma, 1984).
4 The genre name is my own, but draws from the work of Thomas O. Beebee, *Epistolary Fiction in Europe: 1500–1850* (Cambridge, UK: Cambridge University Press, 1999); Bernhard Siegert, *Relays: Literature as an Epoch of the Postal System* (Stanford, CA: Stanford University Press, 1999); and Charles E. Kany, *The Beginnings of the Epistolary Novel in France, Italy and Spain* (Berkeley, CA: University of California Press, 1937).
5 Contrast with the perhaps most famous example of the epistolary novel, Charles de Secondat Montesquieu, *Lettres Persanes* (Cologne, 1721).
6 Pallavicino's motivation may be best understood in the context of the Venetian "Academy of the Unknowns" (*Accademia degli Incogniti*) who delighted in obfuscation

and espoused many tenets of libertinage. See Edward Muir, *The Culture Wars of the Late Renaissance Skeptics, Libertines, and Opera* (Cambridge, MA: Harvard University Press, 2007) as well as Gunter S. Berger, "Italienische Studien: Der Corriero svaligiato Ferrante Pallavicinos– ein libertinistischer Briefroman?"in *Italienische Studien*, N. 17 1996, 8–19.

7 The development of the post in Northern Italy will be the subject of my dissertation, "Masters of the Post: Northern Italy and the European Communication Network, 1530–1730." Simone Tassis (d.1563), the subject of a recent monograph, served as a particularly powerful imperial postmaster general in Milan. Tarcisio Bottani, Giorgio Migliavacca eds, *Simone Tasso e Le Poste di Milano nel Rinascimento* (Camerata Cornello: Museo dei Tasso e della storia postale, 2008). The period following Ruggero Tassis' death is best addressed by Marco Gerosa, "Per una biografia di Ottavio Codogno luogotenente delle poste di Milano e autore di guide postali," in *Europa postale: L'opera di Ottavio Codogno luogotenente dei Tassis nella Milano seicentesca* (Camerata Cornello: Museo dei Tassis e della storia postale, 2014) and Marco Gerosa, *La famiglia Tasso e le poste dello Stato di Milano in età Spagnola (1556–1650)* (Camerata Cornello: Museo dei Tassis e della storia postale, 2019); however, it also generated a vast number of documents held at the Archivo Generale de Simancas to be treated in my forthcoming work.

8 Ciphered letter from Antonio Pauluzzi (Milan: May 6, 1607) in Archivio di Stato di Venezia, *Inquisitori di Stato*, 449.

9 See a letter of appeal from Ottavio Codogno (Milan: April 4, 1621) in Archivio di Stato di Milano, *Dispacci Real*, 57.

10 In addition to the 1608, 1616, and 1623 editions in Milan, there were three Venetian editions of the *Nuovo itinerario* (Venice: Lucio Spineda, 1611; 1620); (Venice: Giacomo Zattoni, 1666); (Venice: Stefano Curti, 1676).

11 Codogno, *Nuovo itinerario* (1608), 1–2.

12 On this question he refers to "Sign. d'Argentone," likely Filippo Di Comines, author of *Le memorie intorno alle azzion principali de' due Rè di Francia Ludovico Undicesimo* (Brescia, 1613). He also referenced Caesar's account of a postal system existing in Spain. Codogno, *Nuovo itinerario* (Milan: Girolamo Bordone, 1616), 1, 53.

13 Codogno, *Nuovo itinerario* (1608), 43–48.

14 Biblioteca del Museo Correr, MS. Cicogna 2532. The volume is simply labeled "Scritture, Lettere e Affari," but the document in question likely dates to the 1670s.

15 Several editions held at Bavarian, British, and Italian libraries have marginalia within the prose as well as reference sections, suggesting reader interest.

16 For more on the development of Renaissance and Baroque professionalism, see George McClure, *The Culture of Profession in Late Renaissance Italy* (Toronto: University of Toronto Press, 2004) and Douglas Biow, *Doctors, Ambassadors, Secretaries: Humanism and Professions in Renaissance Italy* (Chicago, IL: University of Chicago Press, 2002).

17 Codogno, *Nuovo itinerario* (1608), 38.

18 Codogno compared the journey time by contemporary couriers favorably against their ancient predecessors in ibid., 70.

19 Ibid., 15.

20 The term "public service" (*servigio publico*) appears a handful of times; see an example in ibid., 57.

21 Ibid., 100.

22 The Sforza and Visconti established some of the earliest postal networks. Giovan Battista Bidelli, Codogno's second Milanese publisher, also noticeably published histories of both families: Paolo Giovio et al., *Le vite de i dodeci Visconti che signoreggiarono Milano* (Milan: Gio. Battista Bidelli, 1645). Paolo Giovio, Lodovico Domenichi, and *La vita di Sforza, valorosissimo capitano, che fu padre del conte Francesco Sforza duca di Milano* (Milan: Gio. Battista Bidelli, 1630).

23 Simone Tassis frequently battled with other postmasters about the right of appointment to local offices and was involved in court battles with former employees. Bottani and Migliavacca, *Simone Tasso*.

24 Codogno, *Nuovo itinerario* (1608), 12.

25 Ibid., 15–16.

26 Ibid., 9.

27 I have found little direct proof of Codogno's involvement with the 1611 Venetian edition published before his death, but he does label the 1616 Milan edition as "the third time my book has gone to press." Ibid., "A chi legge."

28 The editors endorse its early modern use in Joad Raymond and Noah Moxham, *News Networks in Early Modern Europe* (Leiden and Boston, MA: Brill Academic Publishers, 2016).

29 Codogno, *Nuovo itinerario* (1608), 9.

30 Bottani and Migliavacca, *Simone Tasso*, 52.

31 The following was added to the 1616 edition: "Qualunque haverà tal carico, dovera stare assistente appresso alla persona del Prencipe, o Governatore più vicino di casa, che sia possibile, per puor meno intervallo fra l'arrivo del Corriero, o Staffetta, & l'avviso da farsi al Prencipe." Codogno, *Nuovo itinerario* (1616), 11.

32 Nadine Akkerman, "The Postmistress, the Diplomat, and a Black Chamber? Alexandrine of Taxis, Sir Balthazar Gerbier and the Power of Postal Control," in *Diplomacy and Early Modern Culture*, ed. Robyn Adams and Rosanna Cox (New York, NY: Palgrave Macmillan, 2011).

33 Codogno, *Nuovo itinerario* (1608), 12–13.

34 Ibid., 78.

35 Cicely Veronica Wedgwood, *The Thirty Years War* (London: J. Cape, 1964).

36 "Grida sopra i svaligiamenti, o assasinamenti de' corrieri" (1604), "Grida contra quelli, che hanno svaligiato il Corriero di Roma" (1604), "Grida contra quelli, che hanno svaliggiato il Corriero di Venetia" (1604), "Grida contra quelli, che hanno svaliggiato il Corriero da Lione" (1605), "Grida d'impunita per scoprire lo svaliggiamento fatto al Corriero di Venetia" (1611), "Grida per il svaliggiamento del Corriero di Venetia" (1611) in *Compendio di tutte le gride et ordini publicati nella città & stato di Milano* (Milan: Malatesti, 1612).

37 Ibid.

38 These points are particularly fascinating given preliminary evidence that Codogno was himself involved in spying, first for the Spanish Governor, then later potentially the Venetian Representative in Milan. See ciphered letter from Pier Antonio Marinoni (Aug 21, 1630) in ASVe, *Senato, Dispacci, Milano*, 71. See also Midura, "Masters of the Post."

39 Codogno, *Nuovo itinerario* (1616), 44; (1608), 79–80.

40 Codogno, *Nuovo itinerario* (1616), 46.

41 For more, see Katherine Ellison and Susan Kim eds, *A Material History of Medieval and Early Modern Ciphers* (New York: Routledge, 2017).

42 Codogno, *Nuovo itinerario* (1616).

43 Ibid., 11.

44 Ibid., 52.

45 See for example Thomas Alured, *The Coppie of a Letter Written to the Duke of Buckingham Concerning the Match with Spaine* … (Printed at London: For George Tomlinson, 1642); Wilhelm Jocher and Raphael Sulpicius a Munscrod, *Secreta Principis Anhaltini Cancellaria* (Halle, Saale: Universitäts- und Landesbibliothek Sachsen-Anhalt, 1621); Ludwig Camerarius, *Der Röm: Spanischen Cantzley Nachtrab* (1624); Ludwig Camerarius, *Mysterium Iniquitatis, sive Secreta Secretorum Turco-Papistica Secreta* (Justinopoli, 1625). For a good overview of the genre see Noel Malcolm, *Reason of State, Propaganda, and the Thirty Years' War* (Oxford: Oxford University Press, 2007).

46 See for example Rachel Weil, *A Plague of Informers: Conspiracy and Political Trust in William III's England* (New Haven, CT: Yale University Press, 2013).

47 We should add to this list an anomalously early English example, Nicholas Breton, *A Poste with a madde packet of letters* (London: [Thomas Creede] for John Smethicke, 1602).
48 Marchi ed., *Corriero*, 5.
49 Ibid., 3.
50 This could be read as a veiled reference to the Habsburg family name.
51 Marchi ed., *Corriero*, "A chi legge."
52 Ibid., 3–4.
53 Marchi ed., *Corriero*, 5.
54 Ibid., "Lettera d'uno che invia due dozine d'occhiali al Vice Re di Napoli," 21–23, "Lettera d'un balordo lasciato da un mercante alla cura de' suoi negozi," 78–81, "Lettera di chi manda balle per lavar macchie ad un Cardinale," 38–39.
55 The strange publication history of *Corriero*, rife with variations and false imprints, makes traditional citation difficult. Several editions were attributed to the pseudonymous Spironcini and were likely produced in Geneva; many carried a false location of Villafranca.
56 Marchi ed., *Corriero*, 5.
57 Ibid., "Lettera latina d'un Padre Giesuita, che confessa gli errori della propria Religione," 18–21; "Lettera d'accidente occorso ad un giovane in Roma, fatto amorosa preda d'un Cardinale," 21–23.
58 Ibid., "Lettera burlesca," 35–36, "Lettera latina d'un Padre Giesuita ... " 43–46.
59 Ibid., "Lettera di spropositi a proposito," 39–41.
60 Ibid., "Lettera alla Repubblica di S. Marino," 16–18.
61 Ibid., "Lettera contro d'un tale vecchi," 70–72.
62 Ibid., "a chi legge," 3–4.
63 Ibid., "Lettera contri chi proibisce li libri," 95–100.
64 Infelise, Mario, "Pallavicino, Ferrante," *Dizionario Biografico degli Italiani*, Vol. 80 (2014). Available at www.treccani.it/enciclopedia/ferrante-pallavicino_%28Dizionario-Biografico%29.
65 *Il Mercurio Postiglione, di questo e l'altro mondo* (Villa-Franc [Amsterdam?]: Appresso Claudio del Monte, 1667). A manuscript version also appears in a Strozzi family miscellany held at the Folger Shakespeare Library, *Discorsi Satirici in forma di Dialoghi sopra i correnti avenimenti d'Europa*, Parte 2a., W.b.132 (158), no. 3.

13

WAR, MOBILITY, AND LETTERS AT THE START OF THE THIRTY YEARS' WAR (1621–23)

Suzanne Sutherland

In the summer of 1621, the Roman nobleman Pietro Aldobrandini received instructions from the papal court to recruit 3,000 Germans, organized into ten companies "for the assistance of His Majesty the Emperor in the wars against the rebels or other enemy heretics."[1] Aldobrandini was already in Central Europe fighting for the allied Catholic forces supporting the Habsburg emperor, Ferdinand II (r. 1619–37) in the Thirty Years' War (1618–48), after starting his military career as an independent adventurer. At the time, the Catholics were empowered by their resounding defeat of the usurper King of Bohemia, Frederick V, the Elector Palatine, at White Mountain (1620) and the rapid disintegration of Protestant power that followed. Frederick V was placed under the imperial ban and lost his territory and electoral title. Nonetheless, the war continued, as Frederick V's opportunistic allies, including the voyvode of Transylvania, Gábor Bethlen, and the margrave of Jägerndorf skirmished with Habsburg-allied troops in Central and Eastern Europe. By directly funding ten companies, a new pope, Gregory XV (r. 1621–23), attempted to project a forceful Roman presence onto the Central European battleground in the hopes that, as one cardinal wrote, "it would be seen and perceived in these victories that the armies of the Apostolic Seat yet have their part."[2] Gregory and his energetic nephew, Cardinal Ludovico Ludovisi (1595–1632), were convinced that the moment for total Catholic victory—cultural, diplomatic, and military—had arrived.

Gregory was in ill-health from the start and died just two and a half years after his election. However brief, the Ludovisi papacy's focus on Central European issues represented an important departure from the policies of Paul V. Emperor Ferdinand II welcomed the shift. He had been seeking a Catholic alliance ever since he was Archduke of Inner Austria when he started implementing Counter Reformation measures and faced off against the Ottoman army in the Long Turkish War (1593–1606).[3] Roman–imperial relations would decline after Gregory's death during the papacy of Urban VIII (r. 1623–44). In 1621, however, Central Europe became a Roman stage, the prime setting for a new assertion of Catholic universalism.[4]

Aldobrandini was in the right place at the right time. He would become the papal general at the head of a crusading force directed against heretics as a militant energy radiated out from Rome. He was the son of a former papal general, Gian Francesco Aldobrandini, and the scion of an illustrious family that held the papacy under Clement VIII (r. 1592–1605). Aldobrandini and his short-lived papal forces have become a footnote of the Thirty Years' War, overshadowed by the problematic relations between Vienna and Rome during Urban's reign and nearly lost in the bewildering mire of troop movements that Moravia and Hungary witnessed during these years. What remains, however, is a series of letters Aldobrandini wrote to Cardinal Ludovisi during the time he was papal general, which provide insight into what happened on the ground when Aldobrandini attempted to set papal vision in motion.

Aldobrandini's instructions stated that his military mission should not only serve the Austrian Habsburg ruler's needs, but be undertaken "with the reputation and dignity of this Holy Seat and with Your Most Illustrious Lordship's military glory, which one hopes for greatly and expects from your valor."[5] As the twenty-three surviving letters from Aldobrandini reveal, he strove to fulfill his patrons' expectations from afar and gain the experience at war important for a noble career. Travel was a necessary part of military education as warfare reached new geographic dimensions with armies marching back and forth across the continent on a near-continuous basis. During these years, Aldobrandini moved between Prague, Vienna, Brünn (Brno), Nikolsberg (Mikulov), several garrisons in Moravia, and Brussels, while he entertained further plans to fight in Hungary and Alsace.[6] In this environment, letters took on a new significance, permitting military men to maintain contact with patrons and build international political networks that facilitated far-ranging careers (Figure 13.1).

Aldobrandini's ambition to see battlefield action was quickly thwarted by Habsburg orders to garrison his troops, while the disappearance of soldiers and lack of provisions presented an ongoing struggle. He continued to seek out ways to serve his papal patrons, turning his letters into a testament to the kind of papal servant he aspired to be. The Thirty Years' War has long been seen as a site for the development of standing armies and the more efficient strategies, tactics, and methods of organization that characterized the military revolution and contributed to state-building.[7] Letters, however, reveal the war as a vast and evolving landscape of opportunity and limitation, shaped primarily by scarce resources, convoluted political relationships, and the challenges of distance.

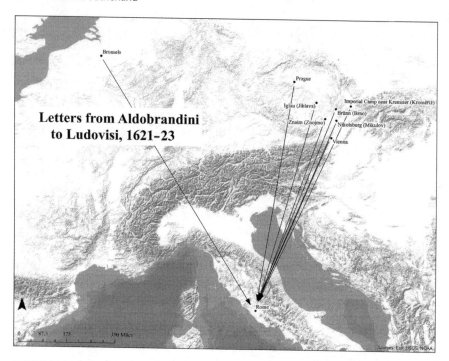

FIGURE 13.1   Map showing places from which Aldobandini sent letters to Ludovisi in Rome, 1621–23. Map by Andrew Fialka

Roman ambitions, long-distance war, and letters

On August 3, 1621, Aldobrandini reported to Ludovisi from Znaim (Znojmo), a town overlooking the Dyje River in southwestern Moravia that housed some of his troops. He had only been there for four days and boasted of progress. The cavalry, Aldobrandini explained, "grows larger every day." He continued, "the end corresponding to a good beginning, I hope that it will be a very good, fine regiment." He promised to set off for infantry quarters in Iglau (Jihlava) the following day, approximately 75 kilometers northwest. Quarters were uncomfortable. Aldobrandini was ready to muster his troops in order to enter battle. Aldobrandini explained that he wrote to Ludovisi "so that you know that time is not lost."[8] Despite formidable distances and insecure lines of communication, Aldobrandini's letters served as assurances that his patrons' investment in a war halfway across Europe was put to quick and effective use.

While Aldobrandini strove to provide a sense of precision in his reports, the letters themselves were never accurate or timely reflections of battlefield realities. The ballooning numbers of letters written by military men during the Thirty Years' War were stamped with particular moments and perspectives, conveying diverse and often confusing experiences in a piecemeal yet steady fashion to courts and castles across Europe. Letters continuously revised and reshaped the war, becoming actors themselves. Aldobrandini's correspondence was part of a larger discussion of the increasingly common Italian experience of military service abroad and Rome's role in shaping politics beyond the peninsula, which had been taking place ever since news of the initial Bohemian rebellion broke. The Roman public avidly followed developments thanks to correspondence as well as an influx of manuscript newssheets (*avvisi*).[9] Paul V held a special jubilee and sent financial support to Emperor Ferdinand II,[10] while Roman noblemen took their own initiative and volunteered for war. The same newssheets reported the comings and goings of adventurers "with good bands of captains and men practiced in war" who sought permission to join the forces of one of Emperor Ferdinand II's generals once they arrived in Central Europe and often successfully negotiated for titles and ownership of imperial regiments.[11]

After White Mountain, Paul V's successor, Gregory XV, intensified papal efforts in what appeared to be a restoration of the Aldobrandini pope, Clement VIII's, broader vision of the place of the "world's theatre" in international politics.[12] Gregory XV also intervened in the Valtelline conflict between Spain and France and founded the Congregation for the Propagation of the Faith, all while suffering a severe grain shortage at home. After some Catholic soldiers claimed Teresa of Avila had appeared to them in a vision prior to the Battle of White Mountain, he canonized the Spanish saint, along with Ignatius of Loyola, Francis Xavier, Philip Neri, and Peter of Alcántara.[13] In 1623 he helped secure Frederick's electoral title for Maximilian of Bavaria, shoring up the Catholic majority among the imperial electors.[14] In a magnificent expression of gratitude, Maximilian donated the Palatine Library, which his troops had seized from Frederick during the 1622 Siege of Heidelberg, to the papacy.[15]

Gregory XV nearly doubled subsidies sent to Central Europe, including the payments for Aldobrandini's troops.[16] A few months before Aldobrandini's appointment, the Protestant Union had dissolved. As his instructions to his new imperial nuncio, Carlo Caraffa, reveal, Gregory believed that God had energized all Catholics to join together to extinguish heresy in Central Europe once and for all. Caraffa should direct his diplomatic mission towards

> harvesting as much fruit as one can from this happy change and victorious state of things, moving forward with securing the Empire for Catholics, the propagation of the Catholic religion, the raising up of the suppressed ecclesiastical jurisdiction and discipline, not leaving behind the thought of returning the persecuted authority of the Apostolic Seat to that place.[17]

Caraffa built a conspicuous and influential position in Vienna to carry out these instructions, a crusader who ultimately butted heads with the court's Jesuit faction, including Ferdinand II's influential confessor William Lamormaini.[18] Despite disagreements about how to implement the Counter Reformation, Catholics were dominant throughout the period: Catholicism was equated to political loyalty, Protestant properties were confiscated, and missionaries flooded the region.[19] Ferdinand's 1629 Edict of Restitution, which demanded the return of all church lands seized by Protestants since 1555, seemed like a natural culmination of the triumphs of the 1620s.

Gregory XV's military support for Habsburg efforts echoed Clement VIII's contributions to the Habsburg cause during the Long Turkish War (1593–1606), which then-Archduke Ferdinand had requested after the 1600 Fall of Kanisza in Lower Hungary left his territory in the path of attack. In 1601 Ferdinand personally led troops into battle for the first and only time in his life with his general Vincenzo Gonzaga, as well as Pietro Aldobrandini's father, Gian Francesco, resulting in a disastrous retreat.[20] Gian Francesco fell ill and died in Hungary, his body sent back to Rome for burial.[21] Pietro Aldobrandini must have felt the enormity of the moment when he followed in his father's footsteps as papal general and prepared to lead troops into the same battlegrounds where his father had died.

The Ludovisi and Aldobrandini families shared a vision of Roman militancy, as well as a long history of patronage ties that transformed into a "formidable alliance" during Gregory XV's rule.[22] Decades before he became Pope Gregory XV, Alessandro Ludovisi built his career under Clement VIII, holding various administrative and judicial positions and traveling in Clement's entourage on at least two occasions.[23] Pietro Aldobrandini's uncle, Cardinal Pietro Aldobrandini (1571–1621), was a powerful Roman figure who campaigned for Ludovisi's election as pope in 1621. After Cardinal Aldobrandini's February 1621 death, the Aldobrandini and Ludovisi political factions merged. Gregory promoted Aldobrandini's clients as his own, including two of Pietro Aldobrandini's brothers: Cardinal Ippolito Aldobrandini, who became *camerlengo*, and Giovanni Giorgio Aldobrandini, who married Gregory's niece, Ippolita Ludovisi.[24]

Pietro Aldobrandini's appointment emerged out of a distinctive Roman political universe anchored by these families. As he selected captains and major officers for his troops in Central Europe, Aldobrandini often turned to Italians: Pietro Cesarini, who served as captain, and the Florentine Antonio Miniati, whom he placed in charge of his cavalry regiment.[25] The selection of Italians for these positions suggest that as papal general, Aldobrandini was a cog in a larger wheel of patronage that moved men between the Italian peninsula and Central Europe at a time when many Italian families sent their sons to war across the Alps. Although they fought on battlefields far from home, Italian officers were aware that they continued to operate within an Italian courtly network.

Aldobrandini's letters were thus important tools for shaping perceptions in Rome among a wider group of political elites. His patrons demanded regular reports and Aldobrandini took those demands seriously, writing letters even when there was no news to report.[26] On January 5, 1622, Aldobrandini arrived at quarters in Iglau (Jihlava), where he found a letter from Ludovisi dated November 27 waiting for him. Aldobrandini's response is now damaged and mostly illegible save for the first lines, which reported the receipt of Ludovisi's letter. Aldobrandini then noted that Ludovisi did not ask for "anything particular" but simple desired "another response."[27]

Ludovisi did not expect much more from his correspondence with Aldobrandini than to remain loosely informed about events. This attitude made sense, considering the daunting obstacles to long-distance communication. Aldobrandini's January 5 response to Ludovisi's November 27 letter would have arrived in Rome around January 19 at the earliest. Ludovisi would have had to wait at least eight weeks from sending a letter to receiving a response, while some letters were undoubtedly lost.[28] The "struggle against distance" that Braudel described for the late sixteenth century continued to shape the basic conditions of long-distance communication in the seventeenth century.[29] War made matters worse. Aldobrandini complained that Hungarian raids prevented the movements of couriers, while his own mobility between cities and garrisons caused additional delays.[30]

Delays as well as the receipt of other, often contradictory, reports created confusion. In between sending his November 27 letter and receiving Aldobrandini's January 6 response, Ludovisi received two other letters Aldobrandini had written in December that addressed outdated issues such as an early December reform of regiments and Aldobrandini's latest desire to see battle.[31] Ludovisi had to interpret Aldobrandini's outdated letters alongside reports on the Peace of Nikolsberg, which was successfully concluded at the end of December, putting a temporary halt to fighting. All of these different reports might have created a larger picture of accuracy, but all too often led to an information overload that incapacitated government.[32] Despite Aldobrandini's desire to demonstrate that "time is not being lost," a great deal of time was indeed lost in the transmission of information. Letters generated an excruciating awareness of delay and, to use an anachronistic term, crossed wires.

Because of communication problems as well as the fact that rulers contracted out military services to powerful and resourceful nobles, generals operated in a semi-autonomous capacity. Even if rulers promised funding, powerful noblemen relied on their own wealth and credit for the initial recruitment of men and to participate in the conspicuous consumption necessary for maintaining reputation. Numerous other circumstances on campaign might force a nobleman to tap into his own resources, including the need to supplement funds in order to attract higher-quality recruits, pay the ransoms of captive officers, or even make up for fluctuations in exchange rates.[33] Rulers who expected noblemen to rely heavily on their own resources also expected them to pursue private goals, turning early modern armies into vehicles of aristocratic ambition.[34] Shared political goals among the ruling elite gradually emerged, especially in the case of closely allied families like the Ludovisi and Aldobrandini, and yet the international dimensions of the war resulted in inevitable collisions of power between families. The variety of independent and semi-independent commands generated turmoil—a "most pernicious matter" according to the contemporary military theorist Raimondo Montecuccoli—that reached far beyond the control of any single state.[35] Adding to the confusion of the early 1620s was the fact that the leader of the allied Catholic forces, Charles Bonaventure de Longueval, Count of Bucquoy, died the month before Aldobrandini began organizing his troops and was not formally replaced by Geronimo Carafa for half a year.[36]

Aldobrandini learned to navigate politically contentious circumstances. His letters were not accurate observations of reality, but represented an evolving set of arguments about his position as a Roman general and nobleman within a transregional military-political network that drew together an often confusing array of aristocratic interests.

On the ground in Moravia

After his initial letter to Ludovisi in early August, Aldobrandini sent an update from Iglau (Jihlava) at the end of the month. He explained, "I do not fail to use every diligence to put these troops together in order to be put into service as soon as possible." The cavalry, he wrote, "is very well completed and can be mustered in five or six days"—a prelude to putting troops into action.[37] The infantry, which had 1,000 men, "is not yet complete" and he continued to wait for weapons. Nevertheless, he was optimistic, announcing, "soldiers arrive every day." Once he received the weapons, he planned to hold a general muster, "according to the pleasure of His Imperial Majesty."[38] Although the correspondence was positioned around service to the papacy, Emperor Ferdinand II and other Habsburg patrons shaped Aldobrandini's mission.

Aldobrandini labored to fulfill his official instructions, which demanded that he work quickly in order to join "the present expedition in Hungary."[39] This campaign was a response to Bethlen's ongoing attacks, despite the dissolution of the Protestant Union. In the months leading up to White Mountain, the Transylvanian ruler attacked Royal Hungary and seized the Habsburg-claimed Hungarian crown as part of a bid to ally Transylvania to Protestant powers and gain a stable foothold within the European system of alliances.[40] After Frederick's 1620 loss, Bethlen and the Habsburgs started peace talks, but they dissolved because Bethlen demanded the inclusion of his Bohemian allies. Throughout the talks, he and the margrave of Jägerndorf continued to fight against the Habsburgs, aided by Moravian rebels who refused to submit such as Count Matthis von Thurn. Habsburg authority was soon contested throughout eastern Moravia. In the months leading up to Bucquoy's death, Habsburg forces included 20,000 men under Bucquoy and a further 5,000 under Rambaldo Collalto, facing off against Bethlen's 17,000 light horse and 4,000 infantrymen.[41] The numbers indicate the seriousness of this relatively understudied phase of the war.

Since he was already in Central Europe at the time of his appointment, Aldobrandini could act fast. Ideally, Caraffa would receive and monitor the funds for Aldobrandini's troops, inspecting the army in person and disbursing funds to an experienced paymaster, Matteo Pini.[42] The papal nuncio also served as Aldobrandini's advocate at court.[43] However, Pini would not arrive in time and so Aldobrandini's instructions stated that "in order to pay out the initial money, which there befalls, Your Most Illustrious Lordship will substitute some other way of provisioning."[44] Aldobrandini shouldered financial burdens from the outset. He would have relied on his family's eminent name and international connections to raise credit and to persuade subcontracting colonels and captains to invest in regiments and companies.[45]

Aldobrandini had a family friend in Moravia to whom he could turn for help: the Moravian magnate and governor of the region, Cardinal Franz Dietrichstein (1570–1636). Dietrichstein helped Aldobrandini obtain a company of cavalry in 1619 when he was still an independent adventurer. The relationship was mediated by Cardinal Aldobrandini, who effused to Dietrichstein that "everything should be attributed to (you), who has been the primary motor of his fortune."[46] Like Gregory XV and Cardinal Ludovisi, Dietrichstein studied at the Collegium Germanicum in Rome and became a client of Clement VIII's, who elevated him to the cardinalate in 1599. He was an important though distant member of the Ludovisi–Aldobrandini nexus of power with its special focus on German issues. Dietrichstein's wealth and power grew exponentially during the early years of the Thirty Years' War. He directed a process similar to the Prague commission overseen by Karl Liechtenstein, which resulted in the 1621 Blood Court, at which the rebels lost ownership of their properties and twenty-seven were executed.[47] Native families were the greatest beneficiaries of the confiscations, expanding their possessions and consolidating power.[48] In June Emperor Ferdinand II had alerted Dietrichstein to Aldobrandini's appointment and anticipated arrival in Moravia.[49] Dietrichstein responded that he would endeavor to accommodate Aldobrandini's troops, but that Moravia was already "completely ruined, burned, and plundered."[50] Multiple companies of Spanish-backed Neapolitan and Walloon troops also traversed Moravia, demanding scarce resources from inhabitants of the devastated region.

Dietrichstein was friendly to the Ludovisi papacy and Aldobrandini family, but in the complex weave of pro-Habsburg ties that mobilized men and resources across the continent, his primary loyalty was to the Spanish. Born in Madrid, he conducted a significant part of his correspondence in Spanish, and relied on Spanish diplomatic support in Vienna during his rise to power. In the same month that Aldobrandini received his instructions, Dietrichstein congratulated the Count-Duke of Olivares on his promotion to first minister and begged for more aid.[51] Throughout the period of Aldobrandini's service in Moravia, Dietrichstein juggled the needs and ambitions of an international cast of military men. He struck a careful balance, conceding to Spanish allies while attempting to protect the region from what must have seemed like an unending stream of rapacious soldiers, Catholic or otherwise.[52] Aldobrandini was forced to navigate layers of contentious relationships enervated by competition over resources and position that lay beneath the surface of Catholic unity at the start of the war.[53]

Aldobrandini, who wanted to leave for the war zone in Hungary, soon found that Habsburg officials, including Dietrichstein and Emperor Ferdinand II, wanted him to garrison his troops in Moravia.[54] Aldobrandini discerned a Spanish political maneuver, explaining that the Spanish ambassador, Oñate, did not want to keep the Spanish troops in garrisons. To his Habsburg patrons he asserted the desires of his Roman patrons: "the intention of Our Lord and of Your Most Illustrious Lordship is that your troops would be used on occasions where they could acquire honor and reputation and not standing around idly in garrisons." Dietrichstein then apparently threatened Aldobrandini with the possibility that Ferdinand II would revoke his orders. Aldobrandini bristled, begging Ludovisi to convey papal desires directly to Ferdinand II if the emperor followed through, warning that "for the greater reputation of the Apostolic Seat, do not permit your army to remain idle." If Ludovisi wished to "gratify" Ferdinand II and garrison the troops, Aldobrandini expected him to communicate that wish explicitly. He concluded that breaking up the army to enter garrisons on the verge of a muster "would be the greatest inconvenience."[55]

Aldobrandini saw garrisoning as detrimental to the honor and reputation he and the Holy See craved, which demanded that the soldiers of the pope engage the enemies of the faith in battle. Aldobrandini's disdain for garrisoning stemmed in part from its long association with idleness and misbehavior. Leave policies were abused, soldiers might integrate with the local population by marrying or taking on a second job, while paymasters and captains siphoned off official funds for personal use.[56] For Dietrichstein, the maintenance and protection of occupied lands, or quarters, was critical. He needed enough men to hold the land and force the population, from whom the army extracted resources, into compliance. At the same time, Dietrichstein wanted to prevent occupying forces from totally depleting the region. Such an outcome would make Moravia fundamentally incapable of hosting an army, and therefore unable to defend itself in future.[57]

Within days, Aldobrandini received a new set of orders "that I should muster these troops" because the emperor decided to evacuate his Moravian garrisons "in order to refresh his camp in Hungary." Aldobrandini must have been satisfied. Soldiers continued to stream in and once the weapons arrived, he surmised, "I think that everything will be in order." Aldobrandini added, "and as soon as it is I will send a note to Your Most Illustrious Lordship as you command."[58] Aldobrandini moved busily between quarters, eventually summarizing his efforts in a letter from Vienna on September 18. He claimed that he had mustered his cavalry regiment for Caraffa, who was "most satisfied." Aldobrandini felt certain that Caraffa "will provide very good information to Your Most Illustrious Lordship and that His Holiness will have the complete pleasure of understanding that all has happened in this place prosperously" (Figure 13.2).[59]

Nevertheless, Aldobrandini reported that Caraffa returned to Vienna that morning and implored Ferdinand II on behalf of Dietrichstein to garrison Aldobrandini's troops in Moravia during the rapidly approaching winter.[60] Although he had once attempted to escape such an order, Aldobrandini claimed that he now accepted it "willingly." Provisions were low and so remaining in camp would only "destroy the poor army." He admitted that he desired to flee "the difficulties with other heads (*capi*), who presently command, since I, with my reputation, am not able to obey any of those who are now in the field." Aldobrandini continued, "I hope to have the opportunity to toil in the acquisition of reputation for the Apostolic Seat and for myself even in the Province of Moravia" since a recent

Callot inuenit et fecit.   Ifrael excudit cum priuilegio Regis

FIGURE 13.2 Print made by Jacques Callot, military review with, in the foreground at right, officer on horseback, seen from behind. c. 1628 etching, X,4.275. Source: © The Trustees of the British Museum

attack at the border by Bethlen's forces threatened the whole region.[61] Faced with the likelihood of a loss of reputation if he mobilized his troops without provisions and marched into Hungary, Aldobrandini looked for other opportunities. He promised that the troops would not remain "idle."[62]

Throughout October and November, Aldobrandini received orders to muster troops, followed by orders to garrison them. The frequently shifting orders were reactions to rapidly changing battlefield realities. It is also hard not to interpret them as the product of disorganization, especially as Dietrichstein negotiated with numerous allies and tried to figure out how many soldiers could be reasonably maintained in Moravia.[63] Despite the ways his mission changed, Aldobrandini conveyed his dedication to papal service, assuring Ludovisi that "time is not lost here and that one searches to satisfy the desire of you and His Imperial Majesty."[64] Earlier, he reported that he provided the papal nuncio to Poland, Cosimo de Torres, with a 100-horse escort to the border. "And I do this voluntarily," Aldobrandini wrote, "because the aforementioned Monsignor being minister of His Holiness, it seemed to me to be my obligation to secure him in every way possible."[65] He also demonstrated his efforts in the careful selection of officers, a task which Ludovisi's instructions emphasized as crucial. In September, he put Antonio Miniati, "man of experience in the career of arms," in charge of a cavalry unit. After explaining the merits of his choice, he concluded, "I hope that Your Most Illustrious Lordship will rest satisfied with this election and that you will receive good reports of the afore-mentioned Lord Miniati from all sides."[66] On October 28, Aldobrandini was in Brünn (Brno) to inspect his infantry, which he claimed to visit "very often and with greater diligence," making sure they did not lack provisions since they were quartered particularly close to the enemy.[67]

By November, the cold season was taking its toll. Aldobrandini continued to travel back and forth between garrisons and visited the imperial camp. Although he admitted there was no news, he reported on the poor conditions suffered by all.[68] Pini, who was in Vienna, would soon return to the garrisons to perform yet another muster. Aldobrandini was probably feeling desperate and helpless, stranded in a miserable situation. He begged Ludovisi "to conserve me in your good grace" and signed off.[69] By December 1, Aldobrandini had received another letter from Ludovisi, which, he surmised, "does not contain in itself any particularity other than requesting another response." He explained that he had traveled to the imperial camp to deal with a possible reform of regiments and also because he found himself "in a certain faction, which hopes to see the enemy." The troops had orders to follow Bethlen's forces if they retreated into Silesia. "But if another new order to march occurs, I will inform Your Most Illustrious Lordship about it," he promised.[70] Soon after this exchange, peace was struck. In need of a break from garrison life, Aldobrandini traveled to Prague for Christmas.[71]

Aldobrandini's stint as papal general did not involve much more than an exhausting process of mustering and garrisoning soldiers. These experiences testify to the fact that in its opening years the war was waged without strategic vision and was dominated by the problem of troop numbers and provisions, dampening papal plans for crusade and the quest for Aldobrandini family glory. Aldobrandini's letters nonetheless crafted a careful image of prudence in recruiting, organizing, and supplying papal troops and faithfulness to patrons. His request to leave papal service in the spring of 1622 suggests shifting papal priorities and a sense that better opportunities lay elsewhere.

"So that I can send myself where I want"

After the Peace of Nikolsburg, Bethlen abandoned the Hungarian crown, receiving territorial concessions, amnesties for his supporters, and a confirmation of Hungarian religious privileges.[72] He would return to the fray later. Pope Gregory XV's January instructions to his extraordinary nuncio Fabrizio Verospi reflect the same five key objectives he had given Caraffa in May 1621. He stated that they could be accomplished through "the prosperity of the emperor's arms," as well as through the formal transfer of the electoral title to Maximilian, which occurred in 1623.[73] In order to achieve military goals, Gregory urged the appointment of a new supreme head of imperial forces to replace the deceased Bucquoy.[74] When a new campaigning season started in spring, a variety of poorly unified Habsburg opponents—the Protestant Paladins—drew the conflict into western and northern Germany, while conflicts against Bethlen resumed in the east.[75] Ferdinand II requested that the money supporting the papal troops, or in the very least the army itself, be redirected to Alsace where Archduke Leopold was fighting. Gregory XV's attention was soon drawn to the Valtelline conflict, to which he committed papal troops under the command of his brother, Orazio Ludovisi.[76]

Aldobrandini told Ludovisi that he wanted to go to Alsace at the head of papal troops. Perhaps because of conflicts with other officers, he could not imagine remaining in Central Europe without an office.[77] On March 21, he asked Ludovisi for permission to follow Ferdinand II's orders: "I wanted to once again signify to Your Most Illustrious Lordship that to me it is a supreme pleasure to leave from here, where there is nothing more than hard work and where foreigners are not viewed well." He mentioned other reasons for desiring to serve in Alsace, including the benefit of working directly under a prince, Archduke Leopold.[78]

As a foreigner—or outsider—without a record of military successes in Central Europe, Aldobrandini may have found the continuous need to recruit and muster men and compete for resources and position with other generals daunting. At one point he admitted that his Italian officers found it difficult to recruit men "on account of their small experience in this country where they are not well known."[79] Italian noblemen may have had the reputation to earn positions in Aldobrandini's army, but that sense of who they were and why they should lead did not necessarily translate to common soldiers. Inability to speak German and/or ignorance about Central European geography, customs, and history generated skepticism.[80] Nonetheless, some Italian noblemen succeeded. A contemporary of Aldobrandini's who was on the battlefield at White Mountain was the Tuscan nobleman and future *generalissimo* of the imperial army, Ottavio Piccolomini (1599–1656). Piccolomini shared many of Aldobrandini's early Thirty Years' War experiences, but the door to a prosperous, long-term career in Habsburg service was not yet open to either man in 1622. Piccolomini's ascent began during the War of the Mantuan Succession (1627–31) and as the trusted subordinate of Wallenstein, who was essential to Ferdinand II's military operations by the mid-1620s.[81]

In 1622 Aldobrandini probably had no other choice but to move on from the Central European theater. And yet Aldobrandini found himself immobilized as he awaited funds to pay troops he needed to disband. Five months later, on August 27, he reported to Ludovisi that he had successfully paid and released his infantry regiment in Brünn (Brno) and would depart for Alsace "still anticipated by the Most Serene Leopold" as soon as he reached an agreement with Ferdinand II concerning payments for his cavalry regiment, which he planned to take with him to Alsace. Ludovisi approved, urging Aldobrandini to travel at once to Alsace.[82]

In early September, Ferdinand II decided that Aldobrandini's troops were no longer needed in Alsace on account of "the rumors of peace in that region." Aldobrandini therefore decided to disband his cavalry regiment. He explained that

> my departure to that land would be unprofitable since I desire to be
> employed somewhere else where there would be opportunity to toil and
> to learn in order to render myself that much higher with experience in

the service of the Holy Church, of His Holiness, of Your Most Illustrious Lordship, and of all your Most Excellent House.

The desire to gain experience was so strong that Aldobrandini concluded the letter by begging for leave from papal service "so that I can send myself where I want, proffering myself on every occasion as a most devoted vassal of His Holiness and servant of Your Most Illustrious Lordship."[83] Paradoxically, Aldo-brandini wanted to leave papal service in order to become a better papal servant. Noblemen often claimed that the opportunity to serve in another ruler's army provided the experience to equip them for military service under their trad-itional lords. Even as papal general in Moravia, Aldobrandini took orders from another ruler, Emperor Ferdinand II. Ambiguous authority generated fierce dis-putes among officers, but also created opportunities that military men exploited as they moved between armies and the service of multiple rulers.[84]

Aldobrandini wanted to travel to Flanders, which had resumed its position as a military hotspot with the 1621 expiration of the 12 Years' Truce, but he still had not received Ludovisi's approval when October arrived. The day before his sched-uled departure, Aldobrandini wrote once again, explaining that "because I must set myself on that course tomorrow, I deemed it my debt to let you know," emphasiz-ing his "great anxiety to serve Your Most Illustrious Lordship." He begged for "commands."[85] Ludovisi complied, sending requests to nuncios in Madrid and Flanders on Aldobrandini's behalf.[86] The experience of war involved many sudden shifts, but also demanded an extraordinary amount of patience as military men waited in garrisons or at court for letters from patrons and for accounts to be settled. It is no wonder that many often simply acted without orders.

By spring 1623—the same year that the 7,500 Spanish troops under Carac-ciolo marched from Central Europe to Flanders to rejoin Spanish war efforts—Aldobrandini was in Brussels. Ludovisi had recalled him to Rome and then sud-denly withdrew the order since his contacts in Madrid and Flanders had borne fruit. Aldobrandini explained that, in the midst of packing his bags to return to Rome, he had happily received Ludovisi's order to join the Army of Flanders instead. He thanked his Roman patrons for permitting him to leave Roman ser-vice, making him "capable with such an opportunity to acquire greater experi-ence in order to render myself that much higher in the service of Our Lordship, of Your Most Illustrious Lordship, and of your whole Most Excellent House." Aldobrandini would probably continue to operate as a papal client, receiving and recommending other papal clients and sending information home in letters. He added, "I humbly supplicate you to conserve me in your protection."[87] He undoubtedly intended to use that protection when the time was right.

Aldobrandini's letters helped him retain and expand patronage relationships as he traveled, forging a new kind of aristocratic career in an age of interconnected trans-continental conflicts. His Roman patrons tended to follow his lead, affirm-ing his decisions. The main impediments included clashes with Habsburg offi-cials and military officers as well as sporadic and insufficient funding for troops.

Distance was a struggle, but distance navigated by letters allowed Aldobrandini to stay in touch with patrons while maintaining significant autonomy. Although he faced limitations, his letters show that he played an active role in shaping his career, revealing how the transregional political networks that rulers tapped into for military aid during the Thirty Years' War were flexible springboards for aristocratic ambition.

Conclusion

Pope Gregory XV died a few months after Aldobrandini's last letter and was succeeded by Pope Urban VIII, who emphasized protecting and expanding the territory of the Papal States and viewed Habsburg encirclement as a threat. Gregory's renewal of an aggressive Counter Reformation drive to oppose heretics and infidels—a drive that dated as far back as Pius V's establishment of the Holy League—was over. The first major breach between Urban VIII and Ferdinand II occurred when Urban VIII took Cardinal Harrach's side in the ongoing disputes over control of the university in Prague, the return of ecclesiastical lands, and other reform issues.[88] Papal–imperial relations continued to cool during the War of the Mantuan Succession, which brought Spanish, Imperial, and French troops into the Italian peninsula. The geopolitical landscape was also being shaped by the ascent of two new figures, Olivares and Richelieu.[89]

Throughout this period, Aldobrandini continued to cultivate his Roman military career. His years overseeing garrisons may have paid off as he was in command of the strategic presidio at Ferrara during the War of the Mantuan Succession. He died in 1630.[90] Cardinal Ludovisi, meanwhile, attempted to survive Pope Gregory XV's death with dignity intact. In October 1623, he held lavish banquets—one of which was attended by Cardinal Dietrichstein—to mask the setback suffered by the election of Urban. In 1632 Urban banished him to his see in Bologna where he died.[91] When Gustavus Adolphus of Sweden swept down into Germany at the helm of an impressive army and dealt the Habsburgs their first major defeat at the Battle of Breitenfeld (1631), the heady sense of Catholic invincibility of the 1620s disintegrated. By this period, official papal support for Habsburg military efforts was ebbing. Nonetheless, many Roman noblemen, and Italians more generally, continued to serve in the Thirty Years' War. The invasion of Gustavus Adolphus triggered a fresh surge of recruits intent on rescuing Catholicism anew.

Like Aldobrandini, Piccolomini had also traveled to Flanders after serving for a few years in the Moravian/Hungarian region. He returned to imperial service—first in Italy under Pappenheim, also a veteran of White Mountain—and then in Central Europe where he became head of Wallenstein's personal guard during the period in which Wallenstein personally raised and commanded an entire army for Ferdinand II. Piccolomini was one of several generals who led imperial forces in the War of the Mantuan Succession, a position which greatly enhanced his stature and enriched him. After plotting Wallenstein's 1634 assassination at the order of

Ferdinand II, Piccolomini joined the ranks of the most powerful men in Habsburg Central Europe (although he continued to look for advancement in other armies, including the Army of Flanders).[92] Aldobrandini had followed a common enough career trajectory for Roman noblemen: serve in wars abroad and return home in a stronger position as a military expert. And yet fortune truly shone on men like Piccolomini, who achieved a higher status under the Habsburgs than what he could have attained under his natural lord, the Grand Duke of Tuscany.

The 1634 Habsburg victory at Nördlingen, overseen by another Italian general who had plotted against Wallenstein, Matthias Gallas, again fueled the (ultimately fruitless) hope that the war would end in favor of the Habsburgs. Aldobrandini's brother Aldobrandino Aldobrandini, a Knight of Malta serving as an imperial colonel, died on the battlefield. Nördlingen helped the Habsburgs negotiate the Peace of Prague (1635) with the German princes, but France officially entered the war, openly pitting Catholic power against Catholic power. War continued for thirteen more years. If he had not died, perhaps Aldobrandino would have continued in a lucrative Habsburg career, benefiting from connections to Piccolomini and Gallas.[93] The future imperial *generalissimo* Raimondo Montecuccoli (1609–80) built the foundations of his career in this milieu. The final years of the war and the decades that followed saw him emerge as one of the greatest battlefield commanders and military theorists of the century. Montecuccoli built an effective reputation in Central Europe, married into the Dietrichstein clan, and led Habsburg forces in a celebrated victory over the Ottoman army in 1664. He fully realized the possibilities of the Habsburg career Aldobrandini momentarily brushed past.

Aldobrandini may not have achieved Piccolomini's or Montecuccoli's levels of success, but his letters provide a glimpse of the way that the opening years of the Thirty Years' War galvanized Catholic nobles across Europe. The Habsburg alliance reached a climax of international cohesion as many Catholic rulers and subjects found common cause in the war. And while the decision to finance regiments demonstrated renewed papal commitment to military intervention abroad, Aldobrandini's letters remind us of how important the war was to the aristocracy itself. His role as papal general was short-lived. Aldobrandini quickly moved on, seeking out further opportunities in a vast, evolving web of conflicts that flared up from Hungary to Flanders, which he must have seen as exciting arenas for family advancement.

Ultimately, Aldobrandini's letters are artifacts of a political, social, and physical landscape continuously re-created by war.[94] Letters were practical tools for moving men and resources across large distances, key pieces of infrastructure in a war fueled by transregional support networks. As physical objects, the letters traveled new routes, suffering delay, capture, or destruction, as well as creating connections. By linking the movements and activities of warriors to myriad political relationships and rewards, letters played a fundamental role in making Central Europe into a new political landscape of risk and opportunity in which battlefields, garrisons, border regions, and the routes that linked them became defining features of its topography.

Aldobrandini's letters also symbolized an emerging identity among mobile warriors exploiting this landscape. While he labored to recruit, organize, prepare, and maintain his regiments and manage the diverse, competing interests of an unfamiliar region, Aldobrandini created an image of personal diligence, competence, order, and efficiency. By the end of the seventeenth century, a new ethos of military expertise and professionalism, which was consolidated in treatises such as Montecuccoli's *Treatise on War* (1641) and *On Battle* (1645), had become an essential component of the military revolution.[95] By studying military letters, we can understand the dynamic, international environment in which these ideas took shape as warriors with close ties to distant courts and experiences on far-flung battlefields consciously redefined their places beyond their homelands.

Notes

1 Research for this essay was initially supported by a Fulbright IIE dissertation fellowship and later by a Faculty Research and Creative Activity Committee (FRCAC) award from Middle Tennessee State University. I would like to thank Giampiero Brunelli, Filippo de Vivo, Paula Findlen, and Molly Taylor-Poleskey for reading and commenting on this essay. *Instruttione a VS Illma Sigre D. Pietro Aldobrandini Tnte Gnale di N Sre per la levata da farsi in Germania di un Reggimento di fanti catholici che S. Sta. da per aiuto alla Maestà dell'Imperatore Ferdinando*. Rome, June 1, 1621, Archivio Segreto Vaticano (hereafter ASV), Miscellanea Armadio II (hereafter Misc., Arm. II), V. 177, f. 86r. A copy of these instructions has been published in Klaus Jaitner (ed.), *Die Hauptinstruktionen Gregors XV. für die Nuntien und Gesandten an den europäischen Fürstenhöfen, 1621–1623*. V. 2 (Tübingen: M. Niemeyer, 1997), 737–40.
2 Cardinal B. Cesi to Cardinal L. Ludovisi, "from home," May 24, 1621. Cited in Giampiero Brunelli, *Soldati del papa: politica militare e nobiltà nello Stato della Chiesa: 1560–1644* (Roma: Carocci, 2003), 190. Gregory simultaneously dispatched a new group of nuncios to important courts across Europe. See Mario Rosa, "The 'World's Theatre': The Court of Rome and Politics in the First Half of the Seventeenth Century" in *Court and Politics in Papal Rome, 1492–1700* eds. Gianvittorio Signorotto and Maria Antonietta Visceglia (Cambridge: Cambridge University Press, 2002), 80–81.
3 In 1609 the Catholic polemicist Caspar Shoppe further shaped his vision, arguing (without success) on behalf of Ferdinand in Rome for a new alliance to defeat Protestantism. See Robert Bireley, *Ferdinand II, Counter-Reformation Emperor, 1578–1637* (New York: Cambridge University Press, 2014), 62–63.
4 Brunelli, *Soldati*, 202.
5 *Instruttione*, ASV, Misc., Arm. II, V. 177, f. 88r.
6 I use the German names for towns with the corresponding Czech names in parentheses.
7 Michael Roberts originally defined the military revolution and identified it with the Thirty Years' War, although his definitions and chronology have been contested. See Michael Roberts, "The Military Revolution, 1560–1660" in Clifford J. Rogers, ed., *The Military Revolution Debate: Readings on the Military Transformation of Early Modern Europe* (Boulder, CO: Westview Press, 1995), 13–36, as well as other essays in the volume. The best current synthesis of the Thirty Years' War is Peter Wilson, *Europe's Tragedy: A History of the Thirty Years War* (London: Allen Lane, 2009).
8 Aldobrandini to Ludovisi, Znaim (Znojmo), August 3, 1621, Biblioteca Vaticana (hereafter BV), Barberini latino (hereafter Barb. lat.), 7058, f.1r.
9 Mario Infelise, "Roman Avvisi: Information and Politics in the Seventeenth Century" in *Court and Politics in Papal Rome, 1400–1800*, eds. Gianvittorio Signorotto and Maria Antonietta Visceglia (Cambridge: Cambridge University Press, 2002), 212–28.

10 Abbott Alfonso Pico to Ferdinand II, Rome, January 21, 1620, Haus-, Hof- und Staatsarchiv, Vienna, AT (hereafter HHStA), Rom Korrespondenz 49, ff.1–2.

11 Roman newssheet of April 13, 1619. Cited in Brunelli, *Soldati,* 200. See also Carla Sodini, *L'Ercole Terreno: Guerra e dinastia medicea nella prima metà del'600* (Leo S. Olschki Editore, 2001), 262.

12 Rosa, "'World's Theatre'," 79–81.

13 See Klaus Jaitner, "Einleitung" in Jaitner (ed.), *Die Hauptinstruktionen Gregors XV. für die Nuntien und Gesandten an den europäischen Fürstenhöfen, 1621–1623.* V. 1. (Tübingen: M. Niemeyer, 1997), 9–13 and Dieter Albrecht, *Die deutsche Politik Papst Gregors XV. Die Einwirkung der päpstlichen Diplomatie auf die Politik der Häuser Habsburg und Wittelsbach, 1621–1623* (Munich, 1956).

14 Bireley, *Ferdinand II,* 151–57; D. Albrecht, "Der Heilige Stuhl und die Kurübertragung von 1623" in *Quellen und Forschungen aus italienischen Archiven und Bibliotheken* 34 (1954): 236–49; and Alessandro Catalano, "La politica della curia romana in Boemia" in Richard Bösel, Grete Klingenstein, and Alexander Koller, eds., *Kaiserhof-Papsthof (16.–18. Jahrhundert)* (Vienna: Verlag der österreichischen akademie der wissenshaften, 2006), 105–21.

15 Gregory's librarian, Leone Allacci, arranged the transfer of books. See "Instruktion für Leone Allacci," Rome, October 23, 1622 in Jaitner (eds.), *Hauptinstruktionen,* V. 2, no. 28, 889–96; Elmar Mittler, ed., *Bibliotheca Palatina: Katalog zur Asstellung vom 8. Juli bis 2. Nov. 1986, Heiliggeistkirche Heidelberg* (Heidelberg: Braus, 1986); and Dieter Albrecht, "Maximilian I. von Bayern und die Entführung der Bibliotheca Palatina nach Rom," in *Archiv für Geschichte des Buchwesens* XIX (1978): 1401–46. Besides appropriating books, Gregory instructed Allacci to remove accounts of the construction and growth of the library building and collections, revealing a deep desire to obliterate the cultural and intellectual foundations of Protestantism. See Jill Bepler, "Vicissitudo Temporum: Some Sidelights on Book Collecting in the Thirty Years' War," *The Sixteenth Century Journal* vol. 32, no. 4 (Winter 2001): 955–56.

16 Georg Lutz, "Roma e il mondo germanico nel period della Guerra dei Trent-anni" in *La corte di Roma tra Cinque e Seicento: teatro della politica europea,* eds. Gianvittorio Signorotto and Maria Antonietta Visceglia (Roma: Bulzoni, 2005), 432. See also Albrecht, "Zur Finanzierung," 541–45.

17 "Instruktion für Carlo Caraffa," Rome, April 12, 1621 in Jaitner (ed.), *Hauptinstruktionen,* V. 2, no. 6, 606–7. Quote on 607.

18 Bireley, *Ferdinand II,* 145–50; Alessandro Catalano, *La Boemia e la rinconquista delle coscienze: Ernst Adalbert von Harrach e la controriforma in Europa Centrale (1620–1667)* (Rome: Edizioni di storia e letteratura, 2008), 64. Caraffa's reports to Ludovisi have been printed in Ignatius Kollmann (ed.), *Acta sacrae congregationis de propaganda fide res gestas Bohemicas illustrantia,* V. I/1 (Prague: Typis Gregerianis, 1923–55) and are analyzed in Catalano, *La Boemia* and Guido Braun, "Kaiserhof, Kaiser und Reich in der 'Relazione' des Nuntius Carlo Carafa (1628)" in Richard Bösel, Grete Klingenstein, and Alexander Koller, eds., *Kaiserhof-Papsthof (16.–18. Jahrhundert)* (Vienna: Verlag der österreichischen akademie der wissenshaften, 2006), 77–104.

19 Catalano, *La Boemia,* 58–66 and Robert Evans, *The Making of the Habsburg Monarchy, 1550–1700* (New York: Oxford University Press, 1979).

20 Bireley, *Ferdinand II,* 43–44.

21 Hanlon, *Twilight,* 84–85 and Giampiero Brunelli, *La santa impresa. Le crociate del papa in Ungheria. 1595–1601* (Rome: Salerno Editrice, 2018).

22 Maria Antonietta Visceglia, "Fazioni e lotta politica nel Sacro Romano Collegio nella prima metà del Seicento" in *La corte di Roma tra Cinque e Seicento: "Teatro" della politica europea,* eds. Gianvittorio Signorotto and Maria Antonietta Visceglia (Rome: Bulzoni, 1998), 78.

23 Jaitner (ed.), *Hauptinstruktionen,* 75–76.

24 R. Lefevre, "Il patrimonio romano degli Aldobrandini nel Seicento" in *Archivio della Società romana di Storia patria*, LXXXII (1959), 18 and Jaitner (ed.), *Hauptinstruktionen*, 106–12. For the Aldobrandini family tree, see Christoph Weber, *Genealogien zur Papstgeschichte*, I (Stuttgart: Hiersemann, 1999), 30.

25 He originally wanted to put the Roman nobleman Torquato Conti in charge of the regiment, but Conti had been captured. Conti and Miniati are mentioned in: Aldobrandini to Ludovisi, Vienna, September 18, 1621, f.7r. Cesarini is mentioned in: Aldobrandini to Ludovisi, Iglau (Jihlava), November 4, 1621, BV, Barb. lat., 7058, f.14v.

26 For an example, see Aldobrandini to Ludovisi, Prague, December 30, 1621, BV, Barb. lat., 7058, f.18r.

27 Aldobrandini to Ludovisi, Iglau (Jihlava), January 5, 1622, BV, Barb. lat., 7058, f.19.

28 Vienna lies 1,121 kilometers northeast of Rome, while Prague—the most distant city from which Aldobrandini sent a letter at this time—is an additional 182 kilometers further north. A century after the Thirty Years' War, a letter sent from Rome to Vienna via Venice took two weeks to complete its journey, encountering unreliable postmasters along the way. See Bruno Caizzi, *Dalla posta dei rei alla posta di tutti: Territorio e comunicazioni in Italia dal XVI secolo all'Unità* (Milan: FrancoAngeli Saggi di Storia, 1993), 133. Letter carriers might get lost since roads were not consistently marked while even an experienced traveler could become confused or simply stuck because of rain, snow, or ice, especially when crossing the Alps, where snow lingered into the summer months. On these issues, see Antoni Mączak, *Travel in Early Modern Europe* (Cambridge, MA: Polity Press, 1995), 8 and E. John B. Allen, *Post and Courier Service in the Diplomacy of Early Modern Europe* (Martinus Nijhoff: The Hague, 1972).

29 Fernand Braudel, *The Mediterranean and the Mediterranean World in the Age of Philip II*, V. 1 (Berkeley and Los Angeles, CA: University of California Press, 1995), 355–74.

30 Aldobrandini to Ludovisi, Iglau (Jihlava), August 26, 1621, BV, Barb. lat., 7058, f.2r. The popularity of the mailbag novel, a genre in which authors wrote fictionalized letters purported to have been seized from couriers, is a fascinating example of how the common military reality of mailbag seizure inspired the popular imagination. See Rachel Midura's essay in this volume, Chapter 12.

31 Aldobrandini to Ludovisi, Tobician, December 1, 1621, BV, Barb. lat., 7058, f.16r.

32 Geoffrey Parker has examined communication difficulties encountered by Philip II. See Parker, *The Army of Flanders and the Spanish Road, 1567–1659: The Logistics of Spanish Victory and Defeat in the Low Countries' Wars*. 2nd ed. (New York: Cambridge University Press, 2004), especially 52–54 and 267–68 and Parker, *The Grand Strategy of Philip II* (New Haven, CT: Yale University Press, 1998). On the attempts of Italian administrators to construct and efficiently use archival systems to manage an influx of information, see Filippo de Vivo, "Archival Intelligence: Diplomatic Correspondence and Information Management in Italy, 1450–1650" in *Archives & Information in the Early Modern World*, edited by Liesbeth Corens, Kate Peters, and Alexandra Walsham. *Proceedings of the British Academy*, vol. 212 (Oxford: Oxford University Press, 2018), 53–85.

33 John Lynn, *Giant of the Grand Siècle: The French Army, 1610–1715* (Cambridge: Cambridge University Press, 1997), 30, 234–41. See also David Parrott, *The Business of War: Military Enterprise and Military Revolution in Early Modern Europe* (Cambridge; New York: Cambridge University Press, 2012).

34 Guy Rowlands, *The Dynastic State and the Army Under Louis XIV: Royal Service and Private Interest, 1661–1701* (Cambridge; New York: Cambridge University Press, 2002).

35 Raimondo Montecuccoli, *Le opere di Raimondo Montecuccoli*, V. I, 2a ed., Raimondo Luraghi and Andrea Testa, eds. (Rome: Stato maggiore dell'esercito, Ufficio storico, 2000), 193.

36 Bucquoy's absence was felt until 1625 when a figure with comparable prominence, Wallenstein, finally filled the leadership vacuum. After Bucquoy's death, Maximillian Liechtenstein assumed command of imperial troops while Spanish

forces remained under the Neapolitan nobleman Tommaso Caracciolo. Wilson, *Tragedy*, 324.

37 Aldobrandini to Ludovisi, Iglau (Jihlava), August 26, 1621, BV, Barb. lat., 7058, f.2r. J.R. Hale refers to the muster as a "positive initiation rite." See J.R. Hale, *War and Society in Renaissance Europe, 1450–1620* (Baltimore, MD: Johns Hopkins University Press, 1985), 150–51.

38 Aldobrandini to Ludovisi, Iglau (Jihlava), August 26, 1621, BV, Barb. lat., 7058, f.2r.

39 *Instruttione*, ASV, Misc., Arm. II, V. 177, f.87v.

40 Ágnes R. Várkonyi, "Gábor Bethlen and His European Presence" in *Hungarian Historical Review*, 2, no. 4 (2013): 695–732.

41 Wilson, *Tragedy*, 323–25.

42 Avvisi di Roma, June 5, 1621, in BV, *Urb. lat.* 1089, f. 410r. See also *Instruttione*, ASV, Misc., Arm. II, V. 177, f. 87r. Pini was nominated collaterale generale in 1607. See Brunelli, *Soldati*, 232, n. 144. Albrecht, "Zur Finanzierung," 541. On Caraffa's nunciature, see Braun, "Kaiserhof," 77–104.

43 On this role as played by the nuncio Malatesta Baglioni for others, see Rotraut Becker, "Aus dem Alltag des Nuntius Malatesta Baglioni. Nichtdiplomatische Aufgaben der Wiener Nuntiatur um 1635" in *Quellen und Forschungen aus italienischen Archiven und Bibliotheken* 65 (1985): 328–40.

44 *Instruttione*, ASV, Misc., Arm. II, V. 177, f.87v.

45 Aldobrandini might have relied on an "aristocratic credit system" in which he received loans from other noblemen. See Redlich, *Enterpriser*, V. 1, 31.

46 Cardinal Aldobrandini to Cardinal Dietrichstein, Rome, September 7, 1619, Moravský zemský archiv v Brně (hereafter MZA), Brno, CZ, Rodinný Archiv Ditrichstejnů (hereafter RAD), Franz Dietrichstein correspondence, 427.

47 Josef Válka, *Dějiny Moravy díl 2: Morava Reformace Renesance a Baroka. Vlastivěda moravská země a lid nová řada svazek 6.* (Brno: Muzejní a vlastivědná společnost, 1995), 98–114, especially 101 and 106 and Tomáš Parma, *František kardinál Dietrichstein a jeho vztahy k římské kurii: Prostředky a metody politické komunikace ve službách moravské cíkve* (Brno: Matice Moravská, 2011).

48 Catalano, *La Boemia*, 52–58 and Vaclav Bůzek and Petr Maťa, "Wandlungen des Adels in Böhmen und Mähren im Zeitalter des 'Absolutismus' (1620–1740)" in Ronald G. Asch, *Der europäische Adel in der Frühen Neuzeit: eine Einführung* (Köln: Böhlau, 2008), 303–07. See also Thomas Winkelbauer's erudite study of Liechtenstein: Thomas Winkelbauer, *Fürst und Fürstendiener. Gundaker von Liechtenstein, ein österreichischer Aristokrat des konfessionellen Zeitalters* (Vienna/Munich, 1999), 24–46.

49 Ferdinand II to Cardinal Dietrichstein, Vienna, June 28, 1621 in *Documenta Bohemica Bellum Tricennale Illustrantia Tomus III: Der Kampf des Hauses Habsburg gegen die Niederlande und ihre Verbündeten. Quellen zur Geschichte des Pfälzisch-Niederländisch-Ungarischen Krieges 1621–25*, eds. Miloš Kouřil et al. (Prague: Academia, nakladatelství Československé akademie věd, 1976), no. 85, 50.

50 Cardinal Dietrichstein to Ferdinand II, Brünn, July 4, 1621 in *Documenta Bohemica*, V. 3, eds. Miloš Kouřil et al., no. 102, 54.

51 Cardinal Dietrichstein to Olivares, Olmütz (Olomouc), circa June 22, 1621 in *Documenta Bohemica*, V. 3, eds. Miloš Kouřil et al., no. 71, 47.

52 Josef Polišenský and Frederick Snider, *War and Society in Europe, 1618–1648* (Cambridge; New York: Cambridge University Press, 1978), 84, 87–88. For information on Dietrichstein's correspondence with these figures, see *Documenta Bohemica*, V. 3, eds. Miloš Kouřil et al., passim.

53 As Filippo de Vivo's essay in this volume shows, Habsburg opponents like Fulgenzio Micanzio and his network of English contacts interpreted the Habsburg political alliance as more uniform than it really was. See Chapter 14 of this volume.

54 Aldobrandini to Ludovisi, Iglau (Jihlava), August 26, 1621, BV, Barb. lat., 7058, f.2v. Days earlier, Ferdinand II mentioned the plan in a letter to Wallenstein. See

Ferdinand II to Albrecht Wallenstein, Vienna, August 22, 1621 in *Documenta Bohemica*, V. 3, eds. Miloš Kouřil et al., no. 196, 78.

55 Aldobrandini to Ludovisi, Iglau (Jihlava), August 26, 1621, BV, Barb. lat., 7058, f.2v. Count Oñate was the Spanish ambassador in Vienna who played an important role in negotiating military support.
56 These views of garrison life were longstanding. Hale, *War and Society*, 133.
57 For this problem see Tryntje Helferrich, "A Levy in Liège for Mazarin's Army: Practical and Strategic Difficulties in Raising and Supporting Troops in the Thirty Years War" in *JEMH* 11:6 (2007): 475–500.
58 Aldobrandini to Ludovisi, Iglau (Jihlava), September 1, 1621, BV, Barb. lat., 7058, f.4r.
59 Aldobrandini to Ludovisi, Vienna, September 18, 1621, BV, Barb. lat., 7058, f.6r.
60 Ibid. See also Cardinal Dietrichstein to Ferdinand II, Brünn (Brno), September 17, 1621 in *Documenta Bohemica*, V. 3, eds. Miloš Kouřil et al., no. 221, 85.
61 Aldobrandini to Ludovisi, Vienna, September 18, 1621, BV, Barb. lat., 7058, f.6rv.
62 Aldobrandini to Ludovisi, Vienna, September 25, 1621, BV, Barb. lat., 7058, f.8.
63 For Habsburg officials' correspondence, see Ferdinand II to Cardinal Dietrichstein, Vienna, 2September 1, 1621; Cardinal Dietrichstein to Ferdinand II, Brünn (Brno), September 23, 1621; and Ferdinand II to Wallenstein, Vienna, September 29, 1621 in *Documenta Bohemica*, V. 3, eds. Miloš Kouřil, et. al., nos. 230, 233, and 237, 87–88.
64 Aldobrandini to Ludovisi, Iglau (Jihlava), October 23, 1621, BV, Barb. lat., 7058, f.11rv.
65 Aldobrandini to Ludovisi, Vienna, September 18, 1621, BV, Barb. lat., 7058, f.6v.
66 Aldobrandini to Ludovisi, Vienna September 18, 1621, BV, Barb. lat., 7058, f.7r. On Miniati, see Eugenio Gamurrini, *Istoria geneaologica delle famiglie nobili Toscane, et Umbre*, V. I, in Fiorenza, nella stamperia di Francesco Onofri, 1668, 138–140.
67 Aldobrandini to Ludovisi, Brünn (Brno), October 28, 1621, BV, Barb. lat., 7058, f.13rv.
68 Aldobrandini to Ludovisi, Iglau (Jihlava), November 4, 1621, BV, Barb. lat., 7058, f.14rv.
69 He added a postscript with last-minute news about the siege of Tabor. Aldobrandini to Ludovisi, Iglau (Jihlava), November 18, 1621, f.15r.
70 Aldobrandini to Ludovisi, Tobician, December 1, 1621, BV, Barb. lat., 7058, f.16r. At the time, Aldobrandini was visiting the Imperial Camp near Kremsier (Kroměříž), which is the location included on the map in Figure 13.1.
71 Aldobrandini to Ludovisi, Prague, December 30, 1631, BV, Barb. lat., 7058, f.18r.
72 Wilson, *Tragedy*, 324.
73 Jaitner, *Hauptinstruktionen*, V. 2, no. 20, 828.
74 Geronimo Caraffa won the position in May 1622. See Jaitner, *Hauptinstruktionen*, V. 2, 833.
75 Wilson, *Tragedy*, 325–31.
76 Brunelli, *Soldati*, 190.
77 Aldobrandini to Ludovisi, Vienna March 19, 1622, BV, Barb. lat., 7058, f.21r.
78 Aldobrandini to Ludovisi, Vienna, March 21, 1622, BV, Barb. lat., 7058, f.25r.
79 Aldobrandini to Ludovisi, Iglau (Jihlava), October 6, 1621. BV, Barb. lat., 7058, f.10r.
80 Sodini, *L'ercole terreno*, 264–66.
81 On Piccolomini, see Thomas Barker, "Ottavio Piccolomini (1599–1659): A Fair Historical Judgment?" in *Army, Aristocracy, Monarchy: Essays on War, Society, and Government in Austria, 1618–1780* (Boulder, CO: Social Science Monographs, 1982), 61–111.
82 Aldobrandini to Ludovisi, Vienna, August 27, 1622, BV, Barb. lat., 7058, ff.35rv. Ludovico Ludovisi, Rome, September 17, 1622, BV, Barb. lat., 7058, f.36r.
83 Aldobrandini to Ludovisi, Vienna, September 9, 1622, BV, Barb. lat., 7058, f.38r.

84 Giampiero Brunelli, "*Prima maestro, che scolare*'. *Nobiltà romana e carriere militari nel Cinque e Seicento*," in Maria Antonietta Visceglia (ed.), in *La nobiltà romana in età moderna. Profili istituzionali e pratiche sociali* (Roma: Carocci, 2001), 89–132 and Suzanne Sutherland, "Warfare, Entrepreneurship, and Politics" in William Caferro ed., *The Routledge History of the Renaissance* (Abingdon and New York: Routledge, 2017), 302–18.

85 Aldobrandini to Ludovisi, Vienna, October 26, 1622, BV, Barb. lat., 7058, f.39r. This is the last letter until April 1623, when he writes from Brussels.

86 BV, Barb. lat., 7058, f.41r.

87 Aldobrandini to Ludovisi, Brussels, April 1, 1623, BV, Barb. lat., 7058, f.40r.

88 Bireley, *Ferdinand II*, 146–47.

89 Bireley, *Ferdinand II*, 158.

90 Aldobrandini's position in Ferrara and his death are mentioned in the following documents: Carlo Barberini to Tarquinio Capizucchi, Rome, April 26, 1628, BAV, Barb. lat. 6168, f.5rv; Taddeo Barberini to Alessandro Sacchetti, Rome September 14, 1630, BAV, Barb. lat. 6313, f.5rv; and Taddeo Barberini to Guido San Giorgio, Rome, November 9, 1630, BAV, Barb. lat. 9317, f.13r. I am grateful to Giampiero Brunelli for this information and for sharing unpublished research on Aldobrandini.

91 Rosa, "'World's Theatre,'" 96–97.

92 Golo Mann, *Wallenstein, His Life Narrated* (New York: Holt, Rinehart, and Winston, 1976).

93 Weber, *Genealogien*, 30.

94 Mary Lindemann has called for more attention to the impact of war on the seventeenth-century Central European landscape. Mary Lindemann, "Picking Up the Pieces: Rebuilding Brandenburg after the Thirty Years War," Plenary Session Keynote Speech, Frühe Neuzeit Interdisziplinär Conference, March 10, 2018. I would like to thank Dr. Lindemann for providing me with a copy of her unpublished paper.

95 Fernando Gonzalez de Leon, "'Doctors of Military Discipline': Technical Expertise and the Paradigm of the Spanish Soldier in the Early Modern Period," *Sixteenth Century Journal* 27:1 (Spring 1996): 61–85. Montecuccoli's treatises have been published in Luraghi and Testa (eds.), *Le opere*, V. I–III.

14

MAKING SENSE OF THE NEWS

Micanzio's letters, Cavendish, Bacon, and the Thirty Years' War

Filippo de Vivo

In his 1625 essay describing travel as 'in the younger Sort … a Part of Education; In the Elder, a Part of Experience', Francis Bacon advised the traveller to
continue acquiring knowledge after returning home: 'let him not leave the
Countries, where he hath *Travailed*, altogether behind him; But maintain
a Correspondence, by letters, with those of his Acquaintance, which are of most
worth'.[1] His suggestion elaborated on a double trope: travel as a source of first-
hand knowledge, derived from manuals on travelling or *ars apodemica*; and letters
as a means of long-distance conversation, from treatises on *ars epistolica*.[2] A firm
believer in intellectual exchange, Bacon could have cited many famous cases in
Europe's Republic of Letters of brief personal encounters occasioning protracted
correspondences about philosophical reflections, natural experiments, or antiquarian discoveries. But could he also have been thinking of letters of news,
concerning not enduring institutions or abstract concepts, but haphazard and
ephemeral affairs? Today these letters tend to be studied for their contents, but
do they also have an interest in themselves, as means for the formulation and
the circulation of ideas and knowledge?

I propose to answer these questions by considering a case that may have been
high in Bacon's mind when he wrote his essay: the letters by friar Fulgenzio
Micanzio (1570–1654), legal-theological advisor of the Republic of Venice, to
Sir William, later Lord Cavendish (1590–1628), an extremely well-connected
courtier (from 1626 second earl of Devonshire) and an admirer of Bacon.[3]
Between 1615 and 1628, they corresponded at length: Micanzio's 75 letters
alone amount to a total of around 100,000 words. On the background of war in
Northern Italy first, and then of the entangled conflicts that would later be
known as the Thirty Years' War, the letters discuss Bacon's works and verge
especially on political and military affairs: from factional politics in Italian courts
to the negotiations for a dynastic alliance between England and Spain (the

'Spanish match'), from battles in the Valtelline, Bohemia, and the Palatinate, to upheavals in the Ottoman empire.[4] Cavendish's side of the correspondence is lost, as are Micanzio's originals. But Micanzio's letters survive in the English translation by Thomas Hobbes, Cavendish's secretary. This was prepared for circulation in late 1624 (as we shall see): a turning point in English foreign policy, and the period when Bacon — who wrote to Micanzio thanks to Cavendish's introduction — prepared his essays for a new edition, with secretarial help by Hobbes.[5]

One interest of Micanzio's letters lies in what they tell us about that remarkable transnational network, deeply embedded in long-distance political conversation stretching across territorial and confessional boundaries over years of dire European crisis. At times of war and religious strife, many members of the Republic of Letters focused on the 'Letters' as a way not of avoiding, but of engaging with pressing issues. Some tried to overcome divisions by cultivating an irenic ideal of universal peace through shared erudition aloof from the harshness of real events.[6] Others, like Micanzio and Sarpi, saw historical and philosophical learning as tools of militant engagement, participated in the events, and saw letter-writing as itself an extension of civic engagement.[7] In the face of overwhelming open and covert aggression by the Spanish and Austrian Habsburgs acting in union with each other and with the papacy, Micanzio regarded peace as impossible and hoped that England would abandon James I's preferred appeasement to join the fight alongside Venice and Savoy, and later the Calvinist Elector Palatine.[8] This was Micanzio's *strategic* aim. But to achieve it, his letters employed a number of *tactics*: demonstrating the broader implications of individual events, drawing durable teachings from contingencies, and formulating conjectures in a shared language. The relations between political goals and intellectual arguments, news and ideas, could not be closer.

My broader point, then, is that to make sense of early modern letters of news we need to take seriously the ways in which their authors and recipients themselves made sense of the news: the reasons why and the ways in which they selected, understood, presented, or mis-represented information. This is crucial for the history of letter-writing and information more generally. The letter was since ancient times the main carrier of news, and recent historians have underlined its increasing importance even in the age of the press: merchants wrote to inform commercial decisions; diplomats, to solicit instructions; courtly intelligencers, to cultivate patrons; missionaries, to edify and encourage.[9] Since the sixteenth century in Italy and Germany and then in the rest of Europe, professionals also began producing regular manuscript newsletters for paying subscribers, which in the seventeenth fed and inspired the first printed periodicals.[10] Letters and periodicals shared style and logistics.[11] But while all the cases just mentioned had obvious professional aims, this cannot be said of private or 'familiar' letters, a genre that famously expanded in the Renaissance yet involved no economic gain.[12] The increase of information enabled letter-writers to mix personal matters with large quantities of detailed news, but this complicates rather than clarifies the letters' uses. Was informing even the primary function of personal letters of news in the age of professional newsletters, when information would become obsolete before reaching its destination? Of course, many occasional letters reported extraordinary events to surprise, awe, or endear, and for this reason they sometimes circulated in print. But why correspond about the news regularly and over many years?[13]

Some answers can be found in epistolographies: printed manuals of letter-writing and collections of letters that thrived in the sixteenth century. Montaigne famously owned a hundred such books published in Italy.[14] They treated news with ambivalence, perhaps in line with the earlier humanists' conflicted reaction to the discovery of Cicero's letters, full of political news.[15] Unlike the medieval *ars dictaminis* – confined to official letters – early modern epistolographies included private correspondence about public affairs, but mostly relegated the *littera nunciatoria* to a secondary position, after thanks, petitions, congratulations, and so on. For Erasmus, this was an unconventional genre because it escaped the three branches of rhetoric.[16] Juan Luis Vives and Justus Lipsius took it more seriously, but focused on private news, perhaps because they considered political affairs too sensitive or controversial.[17] A collection of letters printed only a few years before the Micanzio–Cavendish correspondence stood out by proposing for the first time a special category of *lettere di ragguaglio*: but again, the news was personal rather than political.[18] More substantial discussions can be found in manuals for secretaries. For example, Sansovino recommended that they cover six points when reporting a 'notitia': who, what, when, where, how, and why.[19] But even as they expanded massively in early modern Europe, personal letters of political news tended to escape abstract discussions at the time. To understand their uses we need to turn from theory to cases of actual practice.

'Frendly commerce': spirit and style

Cavendish met Micanzio in Venice in 1615 towards the end of a year-long trip that he (and/or Hobbes) may later have recounted to Bacon. Just as Bacon's essay suggested 10 years later, Cavendish travelled with a tutor, Hobbes himself; practised the local language, partly by translating some of Bacon's early essays into Italian; recorded his observations in his own Baconian essay; and as Bacon advised, did not just study ancient and modern sites, but also went to 'see and visit eminent persons in all kinds'.[20] Even on his way back home, then, Cavendish wrote to Micanzio, to continue a conversation initiated in person.

Micanzio was born in 1570 near Brescia, close to the Venetian republic's border with Spanish Milan; having entered the Servite order, he moved to the capital in 1590, where he became the disciple of Paolo Sarpi.[21] He then taught theology in Mantua, Bologna, and Florence, thereby extending his experience beyond republican and independent Venice, to Spanish-leaning, princely, and papal Italy. He returned in 1606 on the eve of the interdict struggle with the papacy, and became one of Venice's official theologians and a staunch member of the anti-papal and anti-Spanish faction. His subsequent status is unclear, but he received an annual stipend and essentially assisted Sarpi as secretary, until succeeding him as the Republic's legal-theological advisor in 1623. He wrote nearly 2,000 briefs for the government and retained the post until his death in 1654. Today he has been overshadowed by Sarpi, but this was partly his own choice: his most famous work was an anonymous biography of Sarpi that intentionally cast himself in the role of loyal pupil and also, incidentally, attributed to Sarpi the authorship of the only work printed, during the Interdict, under his name.[22]

If Micanzio published little, he was a prolific letter writer.[23] He corresponded at length with Galileo Galilei: in 150 extant letters, mostly from 1630–42, Micanzio remembered their time in Venice, described astronomical observations, enquired about the astronomer's work, offered consolation after the trial, and mediated with publishers like the Elzeviers. On receiving the *Dialogue Concerning the Two Chief World Systems*, he wrote that he had 'stolen hours from annoying business to devour it'.[24] Later, when Galileo's works were prohibited, Micanzio consoled him:

> Let your Lordship fret not: a friend of yours, who is in Heaven, wrote a *History of the Council of Trent*. Rome prohibited it: yet all the copies that arrive to Italy circulate even in Rome. I have it in Italian, Latin, English, French: rest assured the same will happen to your *Dialogues*.[25]

The same hope that the circulation of ideas would defeat dogmatism, but accompanied by a more pronounced political force, animated Micanzio's earlier letters to a network of Englishmen and Italians in England, including ambassador Dudley Carleton, lawyer and later college head Nathanael Brent (with whom he arranged the shipping of Sarpi's *History* for publication in England), apostate archbishop Marc'Antonio De Dominis, Protestant exile Giovan Francesco Biondi, and Venetian ambassador Alvise Vallaresso. Micanzio mentioned these correspondents in his letters to Cavendish (though he politely added that 'your Lo^ps letters are ye welcomest of all that I receaue').[26]

Micanzio's correspondence was functional to creating a network of contacts useful to Venice's aggressively anti-Spanish and anti-papal faction. Since critics would have been ready to jump on him for corresponding with heretics, he took precautions to cover his traces. He wrote in cypher to Carleton, and mostly under false names to both him and Cavendish, with whom he also used fictive locations from Italy and Venetian Dalmatia.[27] He clearly wanted to be able to deny authorship in case the letters went astray, as some did. For the letters' delivery he relied on the Flemish merchant Daniel Nijs, and in 1622–24 on the intermediary of ambassador Vallaresso.[28] On the whole, his tone is remarkably free, as he cast aspersions on Venice and also voiced thinly veiled criticisms of James I. Many in England at the time viewed Micanzio, rightly or wrongly, as more enthusiastic than Sarpi in not just opposing Rome but positively embracing Protestantism. Although we are far from ascertaining the truth of these claims, he had particular familiarity with Anglican debates and, when he met Cavendish, had been learning English for some time (Figure 14.1).[29]

A certain congeniality transpires from Micanzio's first letter – in reply to one we have lost:

> By what you aduise by your most welcome letter from Paris, this of mine will arriue to doe you humble reuerence about the time of your being back att Court. And although in these parts we haue no newes, wherewith to requite those you haue sent vnto mee, yet I will not omit to write, as well for to giue you thankes for the honour you doe me in keeping your seruant in remembrance, as also because my letters may perhaps giue you the content of a good occasion to exercise the Italian language you haue learned in your trauell. But aboue all, to giue you a testimony of my reuerent affection, and to recompense in this kind the misfortune of not hauing [>sooner] knowne you in this citty. In Italye the affaires are in good way to a peace, notwith-stand[>inge] that the eyes of all men are now vpon France.[30]

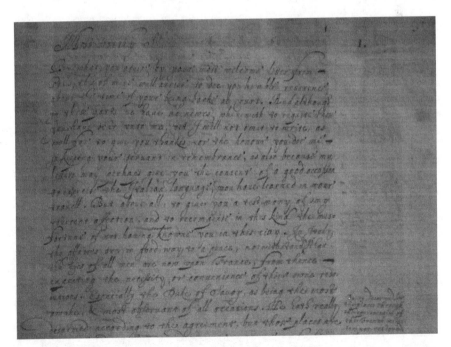

FIGURE 14.1 Thomas Hobbes' translation of Fulgenzio Micanzio's first letter to William Cavendish dated 30 October 1615, with Cavendish's annotations in the margins; small correction in Hobbes' hand on line 14. Hobbes manuscripts, unnumbered, translation of Italian letters, Chatsworth, Bakewell, Derbyshire, fol. 1 (detail). By permission of the Chatsworth Settlement Trustees

A long letter followed, entirely devoted to recent news. Before addressing this aspect, it is worth considering the spirit of the correspondence encapsulated in this passage. According to letter-writing manuals of the time, the letter's *exordium* was designed to put the reader in the proper frame of mind for considering the request(s) that followed.[31] Micanzio was keen to share a sense of intimacy, deriving from an enjoyable if prematurely interrupted acquaintance, but made no requests – in fact he agreed to Cavendish's request to continue their conversation. This by itself marks Micanzio off from both professional newswriters, who wrote for a fee yet avoided personal references, and from clients who reported news to serve a patron and obtain favours in return.

Intimacy was perhaps possible because geographical distance alleviated social difference. While junior in age, Cavendish was by far superior in status – Micanzio was closer to Hobbes both by origin and profession; moreover, when the correspondence began, he lacked an established position. But he expressed his deference in moderate terms, avoided the flourishes that were usual in letters at the time, and kept salutation formulas to a minimum. Perhaps he shared Cavendish's antipathy for flattery or the objection to excessive honorifics that was common in epistolographies at the time – as formulated, for example, in the first letter of the often-reprinted collection by Bernardo Tasso, which Micanzio may have read in Sarpi's copy.[32] From Micanzio's acknowledgements, we know that Cavendish described their exchange as a 'frendly commerce' – to which Micanzio replied with equal politeness that his letters constituted an act of 'service' whereby he gave 'reverence' and received 'honour' as well as 'content'.[33] But, it was a service that Micanzio offered *gratis*: he was under no obligation to write and could expect no tangible benefits in return. Cavendish was a useful contact at the English court – Micanzio, for example, recommended two Venetian ambassadors to him, thereby no doubt gaining social capital for himself and political capital for the faction to which he and they belonged. And as Micanzio knew, Cavendish initiated the correspondence, solicited it when it lagged, and asked him to share his letters with other readers. Clearly, this 'commerce of letters' – a common expression in this and other personal correspondences at the time – was equally valuable to both. What, then, did they trade?

Philosophy and politics: contents

Two main interests drove the correspondence and, in different proportions, occupy almost the entirety of the letters: Francis Bacon and politics. Micanzio almost always sent greetings for Bacon and devoted a brief section at the beginning or the end of many letters to Bacon's works. These are the best-known parts of the letters because they give precious indications about Bacon's fortune in Italy.[34] Micanzio and Cavendish may have talked about him in Venice, at a time when Cavendish was translating Bacon's *Essays*. Micanzio's letters expressed genuine admiration. In a typical instance, in 1621 he asked Cavendish 'to remember my humble & reuerend salutations to y^t great Personnage, whom

I obserue & reuerence as a diuine thinge of our age, & a testimony that our age is not so barren of Vertue, that it doeth [>not] produce men comparable to ye wisest & best qualified of ancient Memory'. He expressed the wish that *The Advancement of Learning* be translated into Italian, and asked for a copy of the recently published *Novum Organum*: 'that printed worke of naturall Philosophy, hoping that it will be answerable to his other of Morall [the *Essays*], the which Mirabiliter excellit'.[35] Micanzio evidently had an overview of Bacon's multifaceted project, which Bacon himself later summed up for him in his one extant letter (1625).[36] Micanzio also played an active role in the circulation of Bacon's ideas. He reported reading 'some peeces' of the *Advancement* 'to some Virtuosi here', probably in an impromptu translation, and asked Cavendish for a Latin edition.[37] He encouraged Cavendish to publish his Italian translation of the *Essays*, suggested to his friend De Dominis that he translate *De Sapientia veterum*, and translated six essays himself.[38] This aspect of Micanzio's letters is typical of the Republic of Letters, where the discussion and circulation of ideas with like-minded people sometimes led to their further publication.

However, it was a shared interest in current affairs that dominated the letters. Micanzio devoted the largest part of *all* letters to reporting and commenting recent events. His first letter (above, Figure 14.1) lamented that 'in these parts we haue no newes', but then went on to report a whole string: the difficulties of the armistice between Spain and Savoy; the rise of the *dévot* party in France; the imminent creation of new cardinals in Rome; and skirmishes between Venice and the Archduke of Inner Austria, who as Emperor Ferdinand II was soon to become a protagonist of the Thirty Years' War. Like other private correspondents at the time, Micanzio downplayed the amount of information he had.[39] But it was feigned modesty, after which he advertised himself as one who knew both the news and what *made* news: what, in his words, attracted 'the eyes of all men'. We know indirectly that Cavendish replied with more news that helped Micanzio, as he once wrote, 'better to make a Judgement, if at all it be possible to make any judgement in this period'.[40]

Intellectual and political themes interlaced in both a narrow and a broad sense. First, until his dramatic fall in 1621, Bacon of course played a prominent role in English politics, as Micanzio underlined, writing that 'God preserue' Bacon 'for ye good of learning and of ye state'.[41] Micanzio may have relished the contact because he believed, or was told by Cavendish, that his anti-Spanish stance could find sympathy with Bacon – a hope that, as we shall see, may have come true in Bacon's later years. Long after Bacon's fall, Micanzio continued to praise his works as containing a warning against the dogmatism he associated with papal and Spanish theologians. He lamented that the essays 'Of Religion' and 'Of Superstition' were expunged from the Italian edition because they attacked the political uses of Catholicism.[42] Micanzio the dissenting friar and anti-Habsburg activist held Bacon as a model of anti-dogmatism, in the same light he did Sarpi and Galileo – indeed his letters used very similar words for Sarpi and Bacon.[43]

Nonetheless, Micanzio was aware of the contrast between the two objects of the correspondence, as he revealed in subsequent letters written at a turning point in his career following Sarpi's death in January 1623. In a parallel-lives moment, two years after Bacon fell from power, Micanzio too thought he would be marginalised, or worse, when hostile patricians agitated against him and the papal nuncio tried to have him prosecuted by the Inquisition.[44] 'I haue very much separated myselfe from ye conuersation of ye Piazza, so that I know little or nothing of ye newes current, & therefore for hereafter I could with your Lord^P be content to change ye forme of l[ett]res, & rather write of humanity and things morall, then of matters ciuill'. Just as Bacon's fall forced him to devote himself to his books, so Micanzio intended to 'spend ye next sommer in meditating on ye worke of <u>Instauratio magna</u>'. Yet, having stated that he knew 'nothing of ye affaires current', Micanzio immediately went on to add news from the Grisons, Bavaria, the Palatinate, France, and the Ottoman empire.[45] Clearly unable to stay away from politics, in the following months Micanzio took on Sarpi's old job as Venice's counsellor, and so finally entered official employment. In the next letter, then, he corrected himself:

> I had thought wholly to haue reduced my selfe into a priuate estate, wherein [...] I might haue not only answered the l[ett]res of yo[u]^r Lord^P & My Lord Chancellour Bacon, but also haue obteyned a more frequent commerce of letters in naturall & morall matter, But necessity hath borne me into a contrary course, forcing me into some participation of Publique affaires.[46]

In these passages, Micanzio rehearsed the classic opposition between *vita activa* and *contemplativa* as one that concerned both his personal life, his occupation, and the content his letters, contrasting meditation about moral philosophy with the discussion of public affairs.

Micanzio's reference to the 'chang[ing] ye forme of l[ett]res' suggests that he had in mind the formal distinction between epistolary genres that, as we saw, was discussed in manuals of letter-writing at the time. In some ways, he repeated the dichotomy between serious and learned, philosophical and informatory epistles as proposed by Justus Lipsius, whose *Epistolica institutio* he may have read in the first edition owned by Sarpi.[47] But Micanzio clearly reversed the philologist's order of priorities. They may have shared a Tacitist reading of politics, but Lipsius exercised it on ancient histories and, from his garden, tried to avoid current affairs – a stance that to many came to symbolise the Republic of Letters' ideal attitude to politics.[48] Instead, Micanzio resolutely opted for the news and was keen not just to report and analyse contemporary affairs, but to take an active stance. More than to the Lipsian model, he adhered to the Ciceronian tradition of private letter-writing as a form of civic engagement. Nonetheless, this entails a methodological paradox for historians interested in ideas: while

Lipsius formulated political reflections in abstract and general terms, we must cull Micanzio's thinking from comments contingent on occurrences. Let us try.

Prospect and point of view: the partisan's perspective

Venice offered Micanzio and his correspondents a unique vantage point over developments in Europe and the Mediterranean. Micanzio obtained news through his work as Sarpi's assistant and later as official counsellor: he had indirect then direct access to government information, including dispatches from governors in overseas territories as well as ambassadors and consuls abroad.[49] His letters also referred to newsletters and printed reports, and his allusion to 'the Piazza' indicates that, like Sarpi, he also frequented city centres for the oral exchange of news.[50] His own act of reporting by letter, then, was based on a combination of local sources and reports originating from abroad. This double nature of information is reflected in his own letters, which combined a specific point of view with broader prospect.

Micanzio wrote little about home affairs. For example, he mentioned only one ducal election of five that took place during the correspondence.[51] He avoided some sensitive issues – thus he replied only briefly when Cavendish repeatedly asked him about the alleged Spanish conspiracy against Venice in 1618.[52] But he touched on others with a degree of frankness that the government would hardly have tolerated: disagreements inside the patriciate, military mistakes at the front, or an ambassador's alleged embezzlement of war funds.[53] In January 1621 he denounced Spanish 'intelligence' and 'plotting of treasons' in Verona.[54] In previous months, the Venetian Inquisitors of State had opened a file on this threat, but found nothing.[55] Micanzio himself explained that these were mere 'bragges'. But the government would not have wanted such reports to circulate, and within weeks the Venetian ambassador in London denied rumours of a Spanish plot on Verona – rumours that Micanzio's letter may well have created, or reinforced, via Cavendish.[56] Thus, to foster anti-Spanish opinion, Micanzio was prepared to divulge information which his government would have censored.

Micanzio wrote mostly about international affairs. He reported Venice's war with the Habsburgs in 1615–17, naval operations in the Adriatic in 1618, the alliance with the United Provinces in 1619, and joint intervention with France in the Valtelline in 1624–25. Beyond Venice, he covered the Italian peninsula: dynastic rivalries in Tuscany and Urbino; papal elections and the corruption of the curia; opposition to Spanish government in Naples. And beyond Italy, he reported in detail the troubles in the Grisons, the Bohemian revolt, the invasion of the Palatinate, and the resumption of war in Flanders. Finally, he transcended Europe itself to include the silver fleets from Spanish America, fighting between Cossacks and Tartars on the Black Sea, palace intrigues in Istanbul and rebellions in the Ottoman provinces, from Lebanon to eastern Anatolia, and war between the Ottoman and Persian empires. In each letter, he switched easily from one event to the other, with little by way of discursive transitions. But he underlined constantly the connectedness of all these fronts: in particular, the convergence of Habsburg policies in Spain and the Empire, their consequences for Italy and France, and, of course, the relevance of these developments for England.

While displaying knowledge of large regions of the world, Micanzio was open about his point of view. First, he wanted to report to Cavendish how events involving England were viewed in Italy. For example, he reported that Rome saw the negotiations for the Spanish match as paving the way for the restoration of Catholicism in England.[57] Micanzio ridiculed such self-delusions, but recognised that they would trouble Cavendish and his friends, warn them against Spanish duplicity, and perhaps give them ammunition against the match. More generally, Micanzio was open about taking sides, including both condemnation of the Habsburgs and also criticism of James I. For example, even before the defenestration of Prague, he underlined the urgency of the situation in Italy, possibly in order to solicit English support for Venice's war with the Austrian Habsburgs and Savoy's with the Spanish. On the one hand, he reported Spanish hostilities that made it impossible to maintain the 1615 armistice, partly brokered by England.[58] On the other, he argued that Spain's expansionism had consequences beyond Italy:

> with these aduantages which ye Spaniards haue in Italy, you may joyne those they haue in Germany, France, England, & other places, & then judge, if ye point be not now, if euer, of arriuing to ye Monarchy, they haue so long in hope deuoured.[59]

The letter form enabled him to phrase this point as if in a dialogue, asking his addressee to make the connections for himself. Against this prospect, he stressed that the moment was favourable for others to support Venice and Savoy: 'here I see resolution & courage such, as [>with the lest foment, from such as] may perhaps quickly finde that their owne interest is here treated of, they might be made certaynly to prosecute the cause with all egrenesse'.[60] So the situation in Italy was one of danger, but also of opportunity ... if only his friends in England could see the connections as clearly as he did.

Since Micanzio's wish did not come true, time and again he came back to his predictions to vindicate his argument, thereby underlining connections across time as much as space. 'Of ye affaires of ye world I can say no more to yor Lord^p then w^t I haue written at other times', he wrote once the Habsburgs overran the Palatinate: 'that the fortune of Spayne seemeth such, as if they doe not in a few yeres obteyne ye Monarchy they aspire vnto, it seemes not that they can euer come nerer to it'.[61] Micanzio frequently evoked the predictions he had ventured in earlier letters: for example, about the rise of the Spanish faction in the Grisons ('that which at other times I remember I haue deuined to your Lo^p'); about De Dominis' volteface ('I haue not ben deceaued in my prognostique'); about the self-defeating implications of appeasement in the Palatinate (namely to achieve 'y^t effect, which I remember I haue often written to your Lord^P, which is, to put Germany into ye full power of Spayne'); about French duplicity ('They begin to declare the[m]selues to be such as I haue alwayes to your Lord^P foretold').[62] Thus, he rested his argument not just on individual pieces of news, but on cross-referencing between his interpretations of past events and his comments on present circumstances.

To understand Micanzio's perspective, it is useful to compare his letters with the professional newsletters known in Italy as *avvisi*, which constituted the principal medium for the distribution of news at the time. Strictly periodical, they were mostly anonymous and devoid of personal references to recipients – which enabled their authors to duplicate copies for different subscribers. By contrast, Micanzio commented on events in Cavendish's life, was keen to relate his reports to Cavendish's travelling or activity in Parliament, and only wrote when he was written to.[63] The authors of *avvisi* collated the news they received from other newsletters to offer information as complete as possible. Instead, Micanzio wrote no bulletins: he did not aim at completeness, but rather dwelled upon those events that were relevant to his cause. Above all, unlike *avvisi*, Micanzio enriched each report with commentaries about their connections with other events. In other words, he wanted to demonstrate the significance of the events, to show not just wealth of information, but clarity of interpretation. Arguably, Cavendish – who could easily have had access to professional newsletters – appreciated the letters precisely because he valued Micanzio's point of view, whether or not he agreed with it.[64]

Ottoman news: connections and comparisons

Micanzio was partisan but not parochial. His reports about the Ottoman empire demonstrate the breadth of his perspective. Just like global historians today, so Micanzio highlighted both comparisons and connections between developments in the Balkans, Anatolia, and the Near East and other parts of Europe. To some extent his analysis was self-centred. Like the Bohemian rebels, Micanzio too hoped the Ottomans would enter war against the emperor.[65] In 1620–21 he welcomed the sultan's victory against the Christian Poles, because it would undermine the Habsburgs.[66] Conversely in 1622–23 he lamented that unrest in the Ottoman empire forced peace with Poland, and correctly saw that this would free the Cossacks to march against the Palatinate and undermine Gabor Bethlen, the prince of Transylvania who had until then fought against the Habsburgs with Ottoman support. But Micanzio was also alert to connections that evaded his own interests. Thus, he explained Ottoman unrest as the result of a combination of wider and increasingly distant factors: factional conflict and military ambitions in the capital; separate provincial rebellions in Erzurum, Baghdad, and Lebanon; and mounting hostilities with Persia, which culminated in Shah Abbas' invasion.[67]

Micanzio avoided the anti–Ottoman stereotypes shared by many of his con-temporaries. For example, most European observers blamed the Ottoman tur-moil of 1620–24 on the *valides*, the mothers of the sultans who combined the despotism, intrigue, and reversal of gender hierarchies that they saw as both typ-ical of and responsible for Ottoman corruption and decline.[68] Of course, Mican-zio was not alien to the sexism of the time – he certainly criticised the Bourbons and the Medici for relying on pro-Spanish female regents during the minority of rulers.[69] But unlike his contemporaries, he had no contempt for the *valides* as women, and in fact he wrote of Kösem – who in 1622 conspired in Osman II's downfall, and as the mother of two successive sultans soon emerged as the most influential personality in Istanbul – that she was 'a woman of great knowledge & gouerment' – almost an oxymoron for men at the time.[70]

Rather than insisting on Ottoman otherness, he resorted to comparison as a tool of analysis and established parallels between developments in the empire and in the rest of Europe. Thus, in 1620 he wrote that:

> The affaires of Constantinople are continually in change, Whether it arrise because ye Gran Sig^r now rouseth himselfe & purposeth to vnderstand ye staté himself, or else that they of ye Serraglio which haue power, do (according to ye fashion of all greate Courtes) sometimes one & some times another gett ye vpper hand.[71]

As modern historians agree, Osman II's reign was indeed marked by the attempt to centralise authority, resisted by the judicial-theological elites and the army cadres in the capital.[72] Contemporaries of Louis XIII and Richelieu would easily have understood this struggle, and Micanzio's explicit allusion to 'all great Courtes' shows that he tried to make sense of distant events by analogy to those at home.

Even more strikingly, he was ready to extend the analogy to religion. When Osman II was deposed in 1622, Micanzio commented that 'the raysers of this tumult were ye Santoni, which wee would call ye Cardinalls or Ecclesiastical men'.[73] This served a double purpose: to explain the unknown in terms of the known but also, since Micanzio abhorred clerical interference in state affairs, to denounce the power of the clergy in Europe. He used the parallel to familiarise his reader with the alien, and in turn to redefine the familiar as noxious. The word *santoni* indicated Muslim holy men or hermits in contemporary descrip-tions; the fact that Hobbes chose to leave it in the original suggests either that he was not familiar with it or, if he was, that he appreciated its capacity to orientalise the Catholic clergy.[74] Micanzio did not claim he could explain the specificities of Muslim policy. As he reported, Osman's plans to marry and go on pilgrimage to Mecca incurred criticisms as dangerous innovations meant 'for a purpose to change ye Religion': 'which – Micanzio commented – wee vnder-stand not here wherein it consisteth, as perhaps they also would not vnderstand vs'.[75] For critical purposes, then, Micanzio displayed empathy with different religious viewpoints – of a kind that later in the century would form the back-bone of Marana's fictional 'letters of a Turkish spy', themselves a model for Montesquieu's *Persian Letters*.[76]

Occasionally Micanzio's comparisons implied criticisms of European rulers. Thus in January 1623, he described the courage with which the Janissaries threatened war against Poland even in the middle of their rebellion, 'protesting all of them rather to lose their liues then see ye dishon^r of y^t Monarchy': 'an accident, wch shewes how much they whom we call Barbarous haue more Spirit & Vertue the[n] haue our vanters of wisedome'.[77] Who the latter may have been, Micanzio left unsaid, but in the previous letter he had criticised 'wise' King James for earning the 'infamy' of the Spanish and failing to defend his 'honor' on the Palatinate.[78] Instead, he now invited Cavendish to conclude the comparison: 'What says yo[u]r Lo^p to these generous Spirits in compariso[n] of others of our time?'[79] Cavendish's answer is lost, but Micanzio's question shows that the epistolary form turned comparative remarks into dialectical tools to stimulate thought.

Current affairs, ancient histories, general maxims

Micanzio also drew broader conclusions from the news through citations and aphorisms. Anthony Grafton and Lisa Jardine showed that humanistically trained scholars studied classical texts for pragmatic purposes, as a commentary on polit-ics that would help their patrons to take active part in politics.[80] Micanzio too kept a small commonplace book of annotations and thoughts including a long section of excerpts from the classics as well as more recent authors (especially theologians and canon lawyers, as was appropriate to a friar and doctor *utriusque*).[81] But he was no humanist scholar. None of the sources cited in his letters was particularly recondite: Livy and Tacitus dominate, alongside Virgil, Cicero, Suetonius, Homer, and Thucydides. And he often took liberty with the wording: the effectiveness of the quotations rested not on philological accuracy but on their suitability to the events. He used ancient history less as a set of examples to imitate than as tools to stimulate thinking: to draw timeless moral or political teachings from the news and so, he must have hoped, to persuade his correspondent to interpret events in the way he did.

For example, a passage recurred three times in which Tacitus explained the Roman defeat of – appropriately – the Britons in terms of lack of unity: *dum singuli pugnant, universi vincuntur*, 'while they fight separately, they are all beaten', a warning and a rallying cry which Micanzio addressed to anti-Habsburg forces throughout Europe.[82] Another reference that Micanzio used repeatedly to the same effect came from the Odyssey, again to preach unity against the Habsburgs: lest the latter reserve their enemies 'ye fauo^r of Polyphemus, that one shall be sooner, another later deuoured'.[83] Ancient histories could even be invoked to demonstrate the urgency of present situations. For example, in commenting on different factions at the French court debating opposite policies on 'the businesse of the Valteline' – the strategic Alpine pass seized by the Spanish at the beginning of the war – Micanzio wrote that 'it is just *Dum Romæ consulitur, Saguntum expugnatur*'.[84] This adapted a famous passage from Livy: while in Rome senators wasted time debating the appropriate response to the Carthaginian advance, Hannibal captured the Iberian city and so opened the Second Punic War that eventually menaced Rome itself. There was no need to explain further: Micanzio knew Cavendish would immediately recognise the sentence as a timeless warning against inaction.

Classical learning could help make sense of the news even without resorting to direct quotations. Ancient precedents inserted current events into general rules. Thus, the revolt of armies in the Ottoman provinces that followed that of the Janissaries in the capital, confirmed 'ye old prognostique, or example, that when ye infection crept once into ye Pretorian soldjers, it soone passed also into the legionary'.[85] Or they could provide powerful warnings, as with the archbishop of Spalato's triumphal return to Rome which, Micanzio correctly foresaw, 'put vs in mind of ye Institution of ye ancient barbarous people, who with flowers, songes, & shewes were led to the gallowes'.[86]

Often Micanzio condensed his thought into aphorisms of his own, meant to highlight general comments from particular circumstances. Sometimes, he made puns: 'with reasonnable fortune (if those termes may stand together)'.[87] Sometimes, he paused a report to express general points: on De Dominis's increasing opposition to the Church of England, that it entailed rebellion, since 'I call euery mans contry that wherein he leades his life';[88] on the dissolution of Parliament (bad news for Micanzio, since it prevented intervention on the Continent,) that 'Kingdomes & Gouerments imitate naturall bodyes, which being once ill habituate receaue harme from all things'.[89] In a remarkable passage Micanzio summed up his vision of the entanglement of international affairs with a striking metaphor:

> States are like vnto great trees, which though they seeme outwardly far a sunder, yet are nere one another in ye rootes, So ye mischiefe that befalls one, concernes another, & ye supplanting of one draws with it very often ye eradication of another, that one would little thinke.[90]

Such aphorisms were more than flourishes: they helped Micanzio to judge recent news, and to do so in general terms which, he must have hoped, would appeal to his reader. Cavendish highlighted the passage and summarised it as 'States depend on one another'.

Other times, reverse-wise, Micanzio opposed principle on the basis of practice. Thus, after Prague's surrender following the Protestants' defeat at the White Mountain 1620, he reported that the Bavarian–Imperial army plundered the city in breach of the promised amnesty:

> those Cittizens haue vpon their promises ben deceaued, pillaged, spoyled & euill entreated. You may perhaps say that it is an ordinary fault in Ciuill

warres, for ye soldjer to haue more licenze then ye Captaynes, but this cannot be alleadged by such as know that those that are so ill handled are none of them of ye Roman Religion.[91]

Once again, the dialogic nature of letter-writing is obvious even in the absence of Cavendish's replies. Having reported a disturbing piece of news, Micanzio pre-empted a possible objection based on a general point – the inevitable violence of troops against civilians – with specific information. Then, adding one more general remark, he tried to sound a more optimistic message: 'I neuer yet obserued that in people by nature fierce such courses did euer put ye victor in peaceable possession, but rather renewed the warres & tumults'.[92] The desperate hope that persecution might yet incite resistance was echoed at the time on the Palatine front.[93] Here it took a universal aura: that the rulers' excessive violence will lead to rebellion, a point which Cavendish marked with a manicule in the margin, and which Hobbes may well have pondered about.

From contingencies to conclusions: writing and reading hidden knowledge

Micanzio's letters embodied a specific point of view while also transcending it to establish sophisticated connections and comparisons over time and space. Corresponding as a protracted form of communication enabled him, like other writers of news in this period, to refer to the past in order to interpret the present, and to cite his previous interpretations as proofs of his future forecasts.[94] In turn, by ranging widely geographically, he pointed out comparisons and entanglements between remote countries including, in true Venetian spirit, both Christian states and the Ottoman empire. While many members of Europe's Republic of Letters championed war against Muslims as a way of overcoming infra-Christian divisions, Micanzio saw the Ottomans as an equal element in the anti-Spanish alliance he advocated. He wove politics and philosophy together in different measures, and rather than abstract ideas, he offered commentaries on specific circumstances. But from contingencies he evidently wanted to infer broader conclusions: not least because this, in turn, helped him advance his cause. He offered not just wide-ranging information – this was so obvious that, as we saw, he could afford a rhetoric of modesty about it – but insight in dissecting the news, uncovering a reality hidden behind appearances. This was essential to inspiring a change in policy against a consensus that seemed overwhelming.

In doing so Micanzio appealed to broader ideas of hidden knowledge. First, his attacks on Spain and the Papacy as selfishly pursuing worldly power 'cloaked' under religious principles echoed the language of Tacitism and reason of state.[95] Moreover, he turned political realism to positive use by insisting on the idea of underlying, concealed 'interests', a notion which was gaining favour at the time.[96] By pursuing the Spanish alliance, the king of England failed to act in his 'proper interest';[97] he and others would choose to fight the Habsburgs, 'if it please God to giue resolution & a heart to such as haue interest in this just cause'.[98] By discerning their underlying common interest, Micanzio argued, England, the German Protestants, Venice, France, even the Ottomans could all overcome their outward religious differences and focus on their real, common enemy. In the same years, the Dutch ambassador made the same argument to propose an alliance in Venice: and ultimately this idea triumphed when France joined Sweden against the Habsburgs in 1635.[99] Finally, Micanzio turned the news into evidence that Spain's potential enemies could take action because, like many anti-Spanish authors at the time, he showed that Spain was strong on the surface but not in substance.[100] Even while condemning Spanish expansionism, he pointed to its hidden 'defects'.[101] Huge military expenditures brought 'ruyne & destruction'.[102] Spanish forces were more over-stretched than ever, he pointed out by referring to recent history: 'Philip the second made warre in Flanders & was in other places quiet, but now ye Spaniards warre in Italy, Hungary, Bohemia, Germany, ye low contrys, & where not?'[103] Employing a dialogic mixture of statements and questions, as in the last example, enabled Micanzio to point out the news' relevance to his recipient and, since he allowed Cavendish to circulate his letters, to wider networks of readers, as a form of targeted propaganda.

What, then, about the letters' readers? Even in the absence of Cavendish's replies, we know of his interest indirectly, because he started the correspondence and solicited it when it lagged. Like many of his peers at the time, he avidly sought the news.[104] The very timing of Micanzio's letters, almost always responding to those by Cavendish, reflects peaks in Cavendish's attention, generally coinciding with periods at court or in Parliament.[105] The letters must have been useful socially, because they demonstrated Cavendish' connections. Inextricably, they were also a means of political activity, because they gave him precious insight. He summed up their contents in marginal annotations and inscribed manicules in the margins of passages he found particularly significant. They show that he enjoyed citations from ancient histories – after all, just like Gabriel Harvey, Cavendish too extolled the reading of history that 'applying those accidents which then past to the present occasions, must needs be the greatest helpe to inable vs for action, or councell'.[106] He also highlighted maxims and unexpected parallels. These were exactly the aspects (as we have seen) that Micanzio wanted to highlight. The two did not always agree, as we know from Cavendish's annotations and Micanzio's replies.[107] But Cavendish clearly embraced the letters' overall goal. For this reason he maintained the correspondence over many years and at various points asked Micanzio for permission to share his letters.[108] Since Cavendish read the letters in Italian, it was for the purpose of circulation that he had Hobbes translate them, either as they arrived or, possibly, nine years after the correspondence began, in late 1624. It was certainly then that a scribe transcribed the translation of the first 64 letters (up to July 1624) into a continuous volume, and it was then that Hobbes corrected the volume in his own hand.[109]

The dating suggests an aim that Micanzio would have appreciated. The failure of the Spanish match occasioned a veer against the Habsburgs and in favour of France. It was a brief and ultimately short-lived moment described as a 'blessed revolution' by Protestants at the time; Parliament was summoned, and widespread anti-Spanish opinion coalesced around pamphlets and plays like Thomas Middleton's *Game of Chess*, which featured many of the people discussed by Micanzio.[110] After the fall of Bohemia and the Palatinate, anti-Habsburg hopes finally revived on the Continent too, when Richelieu rose to power, France marched alongside Savoy and Venice in Italy and in the Valtelline, and Christian of Denmark prepared to enter the fray.[111] Cavendish wanted to seize the moment. As a member of the 1624 House of Lords, he was instrumental in the impeachment of pro-Spanish Lord Treasurer Cranfield and agitated for intervention in the Continent.[112] He must have seen Micanzio's letters as a timely read to inspire a sense of the opportunities and urgency that were ripe in Europe. By circulating the letters at this moment, Cavendish was less interested in the news as news (after all, the letters stretched back to 1615) than in their overall insight in European politics, all the more authoritative because they came from inside Italy and close to the Spanish dominions.

In this moment of information growth, personal letters of news responded to a demand not just for information but also for interpretation. In a Baconian essay 'Of Affectation' (1620), Cavendish stigmatised 'one sort of affectate Trauellers ... the seeming Statesmen of the time' who bragged about meeting important people abroad, showed off the letters they received, or translated foreign gazettes into English.[113] One would think that he was describing himself, but in fact his essay contrasted such affectation with real knowledge. The braggard only obtained 'the most ordinarie and vncertaine newes in the World', 'not vnderstanding, or not knowing how to apply' political observations 'to the bettering of our iudgement, and manners, [which is] the right vse of all we find either in reading, or trauell'.[114] By contrast, Micanzio's letters enabled Cavendish to get to the essence of things – to discuss (as any educated English gentleman knew Philip Sidney had recommended) not just 'concerning what happened, but about the qualities and circumstances of what happened'.[115]

The same desire inspired the collection, translation, and transcription of letters, as readers continued to see significance even in old news. Noah Millstone and James Daybell have pointed to the practice of gathering or transcribing letters and other news media into collections or compilations complete with paratexts long after the events – exactly in line with Cavendish's treatment of Micanzio's letters.[116] Scribally reproduced letters constituted one of many genres of manuscript pamphleteering that grew in use throughout the 1620s – incidentally as much in Venice as in England.[117] One aspect we are now able to appreciate is that this was envisaged by the letter-writers themselves. Given Micanzio's strategic combination of news with more enduring comments, it was only appropriate that his letters continued to be consulted. The afterlife of his letters shows that readers enjoyed them for a long time. Of the two extant copies, the one prepared in 1624 was enlarged in or after 1628 to include all the rest of the letters (in a different hand but on paper also used in the Cavendish household). Another copy was done probably by a professional scribe later in the century.[118] The owner of the latter read the letters less as news than as a guidebook to European politics at a particular juncture: for this reason he made a list of people and notable things in alphabetical order, for ease of reference. In this way, the letters could turn into commonplace books of sorts, for readers to adapt, summarise, or simply use for inspiration in other letters and works (Figure 14.2).[119]

One of them was Bacon's chaplain and secretary William Rawley, who cited a passage from Hobbes' translation of the letters in his biography of Bacon.[120] As for Bacon himself, he may have taken up Micanzio's suggestions in two different writings both composed in 1624–25, when the letters' translation was transcribed and when he was trying to seize Buckingham's U-turn in foreign policy and regain royal favour.[121] His 'Considerations touching a war with Spain' echoed many points made in Micanzio's letters, including Spain's aspiration to universal monarchy and intrinsic weakness. Of course, Bacon may have derived these insights from countless other texts – though a direct borrowing may be found in his reference to 'Polyphemus' courtesy, to be the last that shall be eaten up'.[122] So Micanzio's hope of influencing English policy was being vindicated at the highest levels of power, even if only briefly. The other text that may contain an echo of Micanzio's ideas comes from the 1625 enlarged edition of the *Essays* from which we started. Bacon partly dictated it to Hobbes – who worked for him occasionally in the same months as he was revising the translation of Micanzio's letters. Micanzio had praised the essay 'On Religion' for condemning 'that doctrine which vnder ye cloake of piety teacheth massacres'.[123] Bacon may have noticed this and combined it with Micanzio's emphasis on 'interests', since the new version of that essay ended by referring to 'a notable Observation of a wise Father, and no lesse ingenuously confessed, That those, which held and perswaded, pressure of Consciences, were commonly interested therin, themselves, for their owne ends'.[124] The reference has never been traced but it would not be unreasonable to see Micanzio behind these words.

Whether or not he really was thinking of Micanzio and Cavendish when he wrote the essay on travel with which we began, Bacon may indeed have seen letters of news as a means for the circulation of ideas, knowledge, and education. From information, both the writers and the readers of these letters – including their immediate recipients and wider groups beyond them – drew ideas that were relevant to immediate political engagements as well as to more enduring philosophical reflections. They hungered not just for news but also for analysis that would help them play a role in the very events they wrote or read about. Ultimately, personal letters of news continued to thrive in the age of professional newsletters because they were not just means of information, but tools for the interpretation of politics and means of political action.

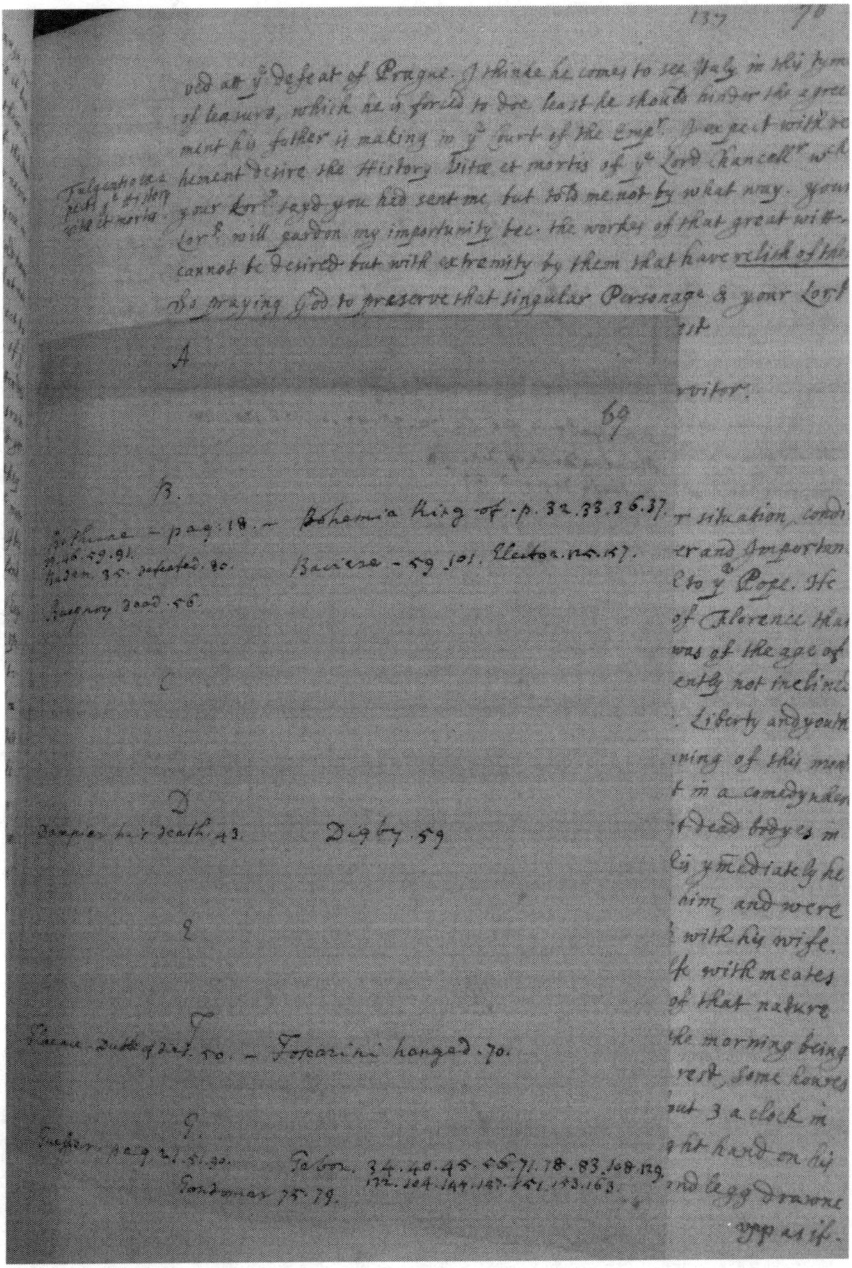

FIGURE 14.2 Alphabetical list of notable names and places in Micanzio's letters, written on a small slip of paper (19 × 15cm) inserted in a scribal copy; the list, clearly an incomplete work in progress, continues overleaf to the letter W. © The British Library Board. Add. Ms 11309, fol. 69[r]

Notes

1 For their comments and help I would like to thank Paula Findlen and Suzanne Sutherland, and Antonella Barzazi and Noel Malcolm. Francis Bacon, *The Essayes or Counsels, Civill and Morall*, ed. Michael Kiernan (Oxford: Clarendon, 1985), 56–58.

2 On the former: Justin Stagl, *A History of Curiosity: The Theory of Travel, 1550–1800* (London: Routledge, 1995); on the latter: Giles Constable, *Letters and Letter-Collections* (Turnhout: Brepols, 1976) and for Italy, Amedeo Quondam, ed. *Le 'carte messaggiere'. Retorica e modelli di comunicazione epistolare: per un indice dei libri di lettere del Cinquecento* (Rome: Bulzoni, 1981), and Lodovica Braida, *Libri di lettere. Le raccolte epistolari del Cinquecento tra inquietudini religiose e 'buon volgare'* (Bari: Laterza, 2009).

3 The letters are published without apparatus in Fulgenzio Micanzio, *Lettere a William Cavendish, nella versione inglese di Thomas Hobbes*, ed. R. Ferrini (Rome: Marianum, 1987) on the basis of a manuscript copy in the British Library; I am currently finalising a critical edition on the basis of the other extant copy, in Chatsworth, with interpolations in Hobbes' hand for the *Clarendon Edition of the Works of Thomas Hobbes*; the citations are drawn from this forthcoming edition.

4 The letters were first presented in Vittorio Gabrieli, 'Bacone, la Riforma e Roma nella versione hobbesiana di un carteggio di Fulgenzio Micanzio', *English Miscellany* 8 (1957): 195–250. While well known to specialists, they have not attracted other studies in their own right, but have been used extensively especially to trace Bacon's reception in Italy: Noel Malcolm, *De Dominis (1560–1624): Venetian, Anglican, Ecumenist and Relapsed Heretic* (London: Strickland & Scott, 1984), 49–54; Richard Tuck, *Philosophy and Government, 1572–1651* (Cambridge: Cambridge University Press, 1993), 93–118.

5 Bacon's only extant letter to Micanzio dates to 1625: Bacon, *Letters and Life*, ed. James Spedding (London: Longman, 1861–74), vol. 7, 531–532, but Micanzio mentioned several other exchanges to Cavendish. On Hobbes' activities in this period, including another translation related to the Thirty Years' War, see Noel Malcolm, *Reason of State, Propaganda, and the Thirty Years' War: An Unknown Translation by Thomas Hobbes* (Oxford: Clarendon, 2007).

6 Hans Bots and Françoise Waquet, *La République des Lettres* (Paris: Belin, 1997), 34–40.

7 Antonella Barzazi, 'Si quid e Gallia afferatur, avide lego. Reti intellettuali, libri e politica tra Venezia e la Francia nella prima metà del Seicento', in A. Tallon and G. Fragnito, eds. *Hétérodoxies croisées. Catholicismes pluriels entre France et Italie, XVIe–XVIIe siècles* (Rome: Ecole française de Rome, 2015), 374–417; cf. Cozzi, 'Nota introduttiva', in Sarpi *Opere*, ed. G. and L. Cozzi (Milan-Naples: Ricciardi, 1969), 635–642.

8 On the first phase of the war, see Peter Wilson, *Europe's Tragedy: A New History of the Thirty Years War* (London: Penguin, 2009), 269–361. On papal support for the Habsburgs in central Europe, see Suzanne Sutherland's essay in this collection, Chapter 13.

9 Francisco Bethencourt and Florike Egmond, eds. *Correspondence and Cultural Exchange in Europe 1400–1700* (Cambridge: Cambridge University Press, 2007); on politics and letter writing, see: Christina Antenhofer and Mario Müller, eds. *Briefe in politischer Kommunikation vom Alten Orient bis ins 20. Jahrhundert* (Göttingen: Vandenhoeck & Ruprecht, 2008); Jean Boutier, Sandro Landi, and Olivier Rouchon, eds. *La Politique par correspondance. Les usages politiques de la lettre en italie (XIVe–XVIIIe siècle)* (Rennes: Presses Universitaires de Rennes, 2009).

10 Mario Infelise, *Prima dei giornali. Alle origini della pubblica informazione (secoli XVI e XVII)* (Bari: Laterza, 2002) and Paola Molino, 'Connected News: German *Zeitungen* and Italian *Avvisi* in the Fugger Collection (1568–1604)', *Media History* 22 (2016): 267–295.

11 Wolfgang Behringer, 'Communications Revolution: A Historiographical Concept', *German History* 24 (2006): 333–374; David Randall, 'Epistolary Rhetoric, the Newspaper, and the Public Sphere', *Past and Present* 198 (2008): 4–32; Joad Raymond and Noah Moxham, eds. *News Networks in Early Modern Europe* (Leiden and Boston, MA: Brill, 2016).

12 Armando Petrucci, *Scrivere lettere. Una storia plurimillenaria* (Bari: Laterza, 2008).

13 Eg. Ottavia Niccoli, 'Visioni e racconti di visioni nell'Italia del primo Cinquecento', *Società e storia* 28 (1985), 253–273.

14 Amedeo Quondam, 'Dal "formulario" al "formulario": cento anni di "libri di lettere"', in Id., ed. *Le 'carte messaggiere'*, 13.

15 Annabel Patterson, *Censorship and Interpretation: Writing and Reading in Early Modern England* (Madison, WI: University of Wisconsin Press, 1984), 203–210.

16 Erasmus, 'On the Writing of Letters/De conscribendis epistolis', ed. Charles Fantazzi, in *Collected Works of Erasmus*, vol. 25 (Toronto: University of Toronto Press, 1985), 225–229.

17 Juan Luis Vives, *De Conscribendis Epistolis*, ed. Charles Fantazzi (Leiden: Brill, 1989), 25; Justus Lipsius, *Principles of Letter-Writing*, ed. R. V. Young and M. Thomas Hester (Carbondale, IL: Library of Renaissance humanism, 1996), ch. 5.

18 Angelo Grillo, *Delle lettere* (Venice: Deuchino, 1612). I wish to thank Virginia Cox for drawing my attention to this point.

19 Francesco Sansovino, *Del secretario* (Venice: Rampazetto, 1564), 22, and cf. Elena Bonora, *Ricerche su Francesco Sansovino imprenditore librario e letterato* (Venice: Istituto Veneto di Scienze, Lettere ed Arti, 1994), ch. 4.

20 Noel Malcolm, 'A Summary Biography of Hobbes', in *Aspects of Hobbes* (Oxford: Clarendon, 2002), 5–8.

21 Antonella Barzazi, 'Micanzio, Fulgenzio', in *Dizionario biografico degli Italiani* (Rome: Istituto della Encicliopedia italiana, 2010), s.v.

22 Antonella Barzazi, 'Fulgenzio Micanzio, *Vita Del Padre Paolo*', in *L'incipit e la tradizione letteraria italiana*, ed. Pasquale Guaragnella, Rossella Abbaticchio and Giancarlo De Marinis Gallo (Lecce: Pensa, 2011), 27–36.

23 Antonella Barzazi, '*Si quid e Gallia afferatur*'; cf. Filippo de Vivo, 'Paolo Sarpi and the Uses of Information in Seventeenth-Century Venice', *Media History* 11 (2005): 37–51.

24 Letter of 15 May 1632, in Galilei, *Opere – Carteggio*, ed. A. Favaro (Florence: Barbera, 1890–1909), vol. 14, 349–350.

25 Letter of 5 August 1634, ibid., vol. 16, 120.

26 Letter 26, 11 February 1622.

27 The letters to Cavendish do not seem to have used cypher – this would disappear in Hobbes' translation, but its use is never even mentioned. Micanzio referred to 'troublesome lets' incurred because of the correspondence: letter 15, 27 December 1619.

28 Letter 5 (24 February 1617); letter 69 (undated, June 1625?).

29 For a recent evaluation of Micanzio's attitude to England and the Anglican Church, see Stefano Villani, 'Uno scisma mancato: Paolo Sarpi, William Bedell e la prima traduzione in italiano del *Book of Common Prayer*', *Rivista di storia e letteratura religiosa* 53 (2017): 64–112.

30 Letter 1, 30 October 1615.

31 Constable, *Letters and Letter-Collections*, 16.

32 [Cavendish], *A Discourse Against Flatterie* (London: Will. Stansby for Walter Burr, 1611); for Tasso's collection, see Gian Ludovico Masetti Zannini, 'Libri di Fra Paolo Sarpi e notizie di altre biblioteche dei Servi (1599–1600)', *Studi storici dell'ordine dei Servi di Maria* 20 (1970).

33 Letter 21, 1 January 1621: 'The desire you shew to haue of mine, is indeed a reprehension of my negligence, but joyned with a great deale of content in y^t you are pleased to continue this commerce, which your Lo^p call[s *deleted*]eth frendly,

But I acknowledge to be of small seruice to your Lo^P to whom I desire to doe much, & full of respect'. Cf. also letter 7, 10 November 1617.

34 Malcolm, *De Dominis*, 49–54.

35 Letter 21, 1 January 1621; *Novum Organum* was published only few weeks before this letter, on 12/22 October 1620: *Letters and Life*, vol. 7, 119–120.

36 *Letters and Life*, vol. 7, 531–532.

37 Letter 5, 24 February 1617.

38 Bacon, *Sette saggi morali non più veduti e tradotti nell'italiano, con trentaquattro esplicationi d'altretante sentenze di Salomone* (Venice, Piuti, 1626), cf. Malcolm, *De Dominis*, 120n.

39 For a near-contemporary example, cf. C. R. Manning, 'News-Letters from Sir Edmund Mounderford, Knt., M.P., to Framlingham Gawdy, Esq., 1627–1633. In the Possession of Daniel Gurney Esq'., *Norfolk Archaeology* 5 (Norwich, 1859), 60, 69.

40 Letter 13, 17 April 1619; cf. also letter 28, 24 February 1622.

41 Letter 5, 24 February 1617.

42 Letter 8, 12 December 1618.

43 Cf. letters 46 (27 January 1623, on Sarpi) and 55 (17 November 1623, on Bacon). On Galileo's correspondence and fame, see Meredith K. Ray's essay in this collection, Chapter 11.

44 Nuncio's correspondence, in Archivio Segreto, Vatican City, *Segreteria di stato, Venezia*, reg. 43, foll. 48r–v.

45 Letter 46, 27.1.1623.

46 Letter 47, 17.3.1623. In *Considerations touching a war with Spain* (see also here, 310), Bacon wrote 'I had wholly sequestered my thoughts from civil affairs' before, like Micanzio, plunging into them.

47 Masetti Zannini, 'Libri'; cf. above, p. X.

48 Anthony Grafton, *Bring Out Your Dead: The Past as Revelation* (Cambridge, MA: Harvard University Press, 2001), 227–243.

49 For an example of epistolary networks stretching Venice's Mediterranean territories, cf. Demetrius C. Loufas' essay in this collection, Chapter 8.

50 On his and Sarpi's sources see Filippo de Vivo, 'Sarpi and the Uses of Information'; on frequenting public spaces as a means of gathering information, see de Vivo, *Information and Communication in Venice: Rethinking Early Modern Politics* (Oxford: Oxford University Press 2007): ch. 3 and 'Walking in Sixteenth-Century Venice: Mobilizing the Early Modern City', *I Tatti Studies in the Italian Renaissance*, 19 (2016): 115–141.

51 Letter 1, 30 October 1615.

52 Letters 9, 12 July 1618, and 13, 17 April 1619.

53 Letter 14, 21 June 1619.

54 Letter 21, 1 January 1621.

55 ASV, *Inquisitori di stato*, b. 357, cc. nn.: dispatch of 31 August 1620.

56 *Calendar of State Papers and Manuscripts Relating to English Affairs Existing in the Archives and Collections of Venice, and in Other Libraries of Northern Italy*, ed. H. R. Brown and A. B. Hinds (London: HM Stationery Office, 1864–1940), vol. 16, 565.

57 Eg. Letters 24 (1621), 45 (1622), 53 (1623).

58 Letter 1, 30 October 1615 and Letter 2, 15 January 1616.

59 Letter 8, 12 January 1618; cf. also letter 7, 10 November 1617: 'it is to be wondred at, that men doe not see, that ye encrease of ye Spanish power in Italy sets them in ye stirrop to sway & doe in other places much more'.

60 Letter 3, 31 March 1616.

61 Letter 48, 26 May 1623.

62 Letter 24, 10 September 1621; letter 33, 27 May 1622; letter 39, 19 August 1622; letter 47, 17 March 1623.

63 Eg., letters 3, 31 March 1616, and 5, 24 February 1617.

64 See below, 307 and 308.

65 A recent assessment and bibliography in Maria Baramova, 'Non-Splendid Isolation: The Ottoman Empire and the Thirty Years' War', *The Ashgate Research Companion to the Thirty Years' War*, ed. Olaf Asbach and Peter Schröder (Farnham: Ashgate, 2014), 115–124.

66 Letters 17, 24 April 1620 and 21, 1 January 1621.

67 Letter 49, 8 June 1623; the rebel governors did go on to join forces as Micanzio reported later in the summer: letter 52 of 2 August 1623. For an introduction to this period of Ottoman history, Caroline Finkel, *Osman's Dream: The Story of the Ottoman Empire 1300–1923* (London: John Murray, 2005), 196–212.

68 References to contemporaries' interpretations in Leslie P. Peirce, *The Imperial Harem: Women and Sovereignty in the Ottoman Empire* (Oxford: Oxford University Press, 1993) and Gabriel Piterberg, *An Ottoman Tragedy: History and Historiography at Play* (Berkeley, CA and London: University of California Press, 2003).

69 Eg. Letter 17, 24 April 1620.

70 Letter 37, 15 July 1622.

71 Letter 18, 5 June 1620.

72 Baki Tezcan, *The Second Ottoman Empire: Political and Social Transformation in the Early Modern World* (Cambridge: Cambridge University Press, 2010), 115–152.

73 Letter 36, 24 June 1622; on religious opposition to Osman II, see Tezcan, *Second Ottoman Empire*, 164, 166–167 and 171.

74 The term was used in sixteenth-century Venice to indicate Muslim religious men, but Sarpi also used it in his history of the Interdict controversy to describe (negatively) Catholic clergymen; cf. *Grande dizionario della lingua italiana*, ed. S. Battaglia (Turin: UTET, 1961–2002) vol. 17, *s.v.* It is mentioned in neither the seventeenth-century editions of the Crusca dictionary nor in John Florio's Italian-English dictionary, but was used by Hakluyt and Moryson according to the OED.

75 Letter 36, 24 June 1622.

76 Cf. Gian Carlo Roscioni, *Sulle tracce dell'esploratore turco* (Milan: Rizzoli, 1992).

77 Letter 46, 27 January 1623.

78 Letter 45, 30 December 1622.

79 Letter 46, 27 January 1623.

80 Lisa Jardine and Anthony Grafton, '"Studied for Action": How Gabriel Harvey Read His Livy', *Past and Present* 129 (1990): 30–78.

81 BMV Cod. Ital. XI.174–175; a summary description of the first volume (partly in Sarpi's hand) in Giovanni Da Pozzo, 'Dodici pensieri inediti del Sarpi', *Giornale storico della letteratura italiana* 156 (1979): 391–393 and, of the second volume, in Gino Benzoni and Tiziano Zanato (eds.), *Storici e politici veneti del Cinquecento e del Seicento* (Milan-Naples: Ricciardi, 1982), 913–917.

82 Letter 21, 37, 48; cf. Karl Benrath, *Neue Briefe von Paolo Sarpi (1608–1616)* (Leipzig: Haupt, 1909), 81.

83 Letters 50, 53, 55 (all written between June and Nov. 1623) and 72 (undated, spring 1627).

84 Letter 52, 2 August 1623.

85 Letter 41, 16 September 1622.

86 Letter 43, 2 November 1622. One and a half years later De Dominis was indeed tried and later died in prison.

87 Letter 11, 31 October 1618.

88 Letter 25, 10 December 1621.

89 Letter 28, 24 Febr. 1622.

90 Letter 38, 29 July 1622.

91 Letter 21, 1 January 1621.

92 Letter 21, 1 January 1621.

93 Friedrich-Hermann Schubert, *Ludwig Camerarius (1573–1651): eine Biographie* (Münster: Aschendorff, 2013), 96 and 194–195 and Josef V. Polišensky, *The Thirty Years War* (London, Batsford, 1970), 147, 159; for a time it seemed confirmed in rebellions in Moravia: Wilson, *Europe's Tragedy*, 351.

94 On the interrelation between current information and attitudes to the future, see Albert Schirrmeister, ed. *Agir au futur. Attitudes d'attente et actions expectatives*, special issue of *Les dossiers du Grihl* (2017), https://journals.openedition.org/dossiersgrihl/6515 and Kirsty Rolfe, 'Probable Pasts and Possible Futures: Contemporaneity and the Consumption of the News in the 1620s', *Media History* 23 (2017): 159–176.

95 Letter 59, 15 March 1624.

96 Eg. Henri de Rohan, *De l'interet des Princes et des Etats de la Chrétienté*, published in 1638, but written in the 1620s; cf. Tuck, *Philosophy and Government*.

97 Letter 40, 26 August 1622.

98 Letter 16, 21 February 1620; also letter 3, cited above, note 59.

99 Gaetano Cozzi, 'Venezia nello scenario europeo (1517–1699)', in *La Repubblica di Venezia nell'età moderna*, ed. Cozzi, Michael Knapton and Giovanni Scarabello (Turin: UTET, 1992), 93.

100 Franco Barcia, 'La Spagna negli scrittori politici italiani del XVI e XVII secolo', in *Repubblica e virtù: pensiero politico e monarchia cattolica fra XVI e XVII secolo*, ed. Chiara Continisio and Cesare Mozzarelli (Rome: Bulzoni, 1995), 179–206.

101 Letter 5, 24 February 1617.

102 Letter 11, 31 October 1618; cf. also Letter 20, 29 October 1620.

103 Letter 22, 12 March 1621.

104 Barbara Shapiro, *Political Communication and Political Culture in England, 1558–1688* (Stanford, CA: Stanford University Press, 2012), 25–53.

105 E.g. Letter 5 of 24 February 1617; 7 of 10 November 1617; and 9 of 12 July 1618.

106 [William Cavendish], 'Of Reading History', in *Horae subseciuae observations and discourses* (London: Edward Blount, 1620), 199; cf. Jardine and Grafton, 'Studied for Action'.

107 For example, Cavendish annotated one of Micanzio's letters as containing a 'Censure of reasons in my letter for the Kings neutrality in ye matter of Bohemia', Letter 21, 1 January 1621.

108 Letter 17, 24 April 1620; cf. also Letters 3, 31 March 1616, and 19, 3 July 1620.

109 The argument dating the transcript and Hobbes' autograph corrections on the manuscript rests largely on internal evidence and will be made at greater length in the edition of his translation.

110 Thomas Cogswell, *The Blessed Revolution: English Politics and the Coming of War, 1621–24* (Cambridge: Cambridge University Press, 1989).

111 On this phase in the war Wilson, *Europe's Tragedy*, 371–391.

112 Menna Prestwich, *Cranfield: Politics and Profits Under the Stuarts – The Career of Lione Cranfield Earl of Middlesex* (Oxford: Clarendon, 1966), 437, 445.

113 [Cavendish], 'Of Affectation', in *Horae subseciuae*, 40; this was a stock target of satire that also recurred in Bacon, cf. Ron Bedford, Lloyd Davis, Philippa Kelly, *Early Modern English Lives: Autobiography and Self-Representation, 1500–1660* (Abingdon: Routledge, 2016), ch. 3.

114 [Cavendish], 'Of Affectation', 45, 33.

115 Jardine and Grafton, 'Studied for Action', 77.

116 James Daybell, *The Material Letter in Early Modern England: Manuscript Letters and the Culture and Practices of Letter-Writing, 1512–1635* (Basingstoke: Palgrave, 2012), 217–229; Noah Millstone, 'Designed for Collection: Early Modern News and the Production of History', *Media History* 23 (2017): 177–198.

117 Cf. Millstone, *Manuscript Circulation and the Invention of Politics in Early Stuart England* (Cambridge: Cambridge University Press, 2016), and for Venice, de Vivo, *Information and Communication*, ch. 2.

118 In 1628 Cavendish, now Earl of Devonshire, again sat in the House of Lords and circulated copies of speeches he delivered there: Millstone, *Manuscript Circulation*, 106–107.

119 On the association between letter-books and commonplace books, see Daybell, *Material Letter*, 197.

120 In *The Works of Francis Bacon*, ed. J. Spedding, R. L. Ellis, and D. D. Health (London: Longman, 1857–61), vol. 1, 16.

121 Lisa Jardine and Alan Stewart, *Hostage to Fortune: The Troubled Life of Francis Bacon* (London: Gollancz, 1998), 494. For a discussion of Hobbes' role in Bacon's new political stance, see Richard Tuck, 'Hobbes and Tacitus', in G. A. J. Rogers and Tom Sorell eds., *Hobbes and History* (London: Routledge), 99–111.

122 *Letters and Life*, vol. 7, 469–505; see above, 305.

123 Letter 8, 12 January 1618. Sarpi too described his history of the Council of Trent as revealing the 'Arte of government covered with the cloacke of religion', Paolo Sarpi, *The Historie of the Councel of Trent* (London: Robert Barker and John Bill, 1620), 41.

124 Bacon, *The Essayes*, 15–16, 186.

EPILOGUE

Lives full of letters: from Renaissance to Republic of Letters[*]

Suzanne Sutherland

In 1651 the Dutch painter Samuel van Hoogstraten traveled to Vienna where he gained an audience with Emperor Ferdinand III and offered the Habsburg ruler three paintings: a history painting, a portrait, and a still life. The emperor was captivated by the still life, which he claimed had utterly deceived him. Alleging he would punish the artist for his deception, Ferdinand III playfully confiscated the painting, adding it to his collection. In return, he offered Van Hoogstraten an imperial medal on a gold chain.[1] Van Hoogstraten must have been thrilled. After studying under Rembrandt in Amsterdam and then setting off to become a master in his own right, he was now an artist whose work belonged to the imperial collection.

Although Van Hoogstraten did not become an imperial client, he depicted Ferdinand III's gold medal in multiple paintings, a prized possession and symbol of his status.[2] Van Hoogstraten would later become known as a key innovator of the still-life genre and one of the most important Dutch art theorists of the century, as well as a polymath who wrote poetry and studied natural philosophy. He also cultivated international ties: after Vienna, he went to Rome and then London. During his travels, he experimented with a new kind of painting: the letter-rack still life.[3]

Van Hoogstraten included Ferdinand III's medal, along with letters and other objects, in four of his surviving letter-rack paintings.[4] A letter rack was a simple technology familiar to the Romans that had reappeared by the Renaissance. It consisted of a wall or a board affixed with ribbons to hold letters and other objects in place. Paintings of letter racks were experiments in *trompe l'oeil*: the objects they contained appeared to protrude from a flat, neutral background, making the viewer think he or she could reach out and touch them. Since both the letter racks and the letters they held were flat, these still-life paintings were a unique exercise because they required an extremely short perspective.[5]

The emergence of a still-life genre featuring letters and letter racks is a testament to what Peter Burke has referred to as the "quotidianization" or "domestication" of the Renaissance or "its gradual permeation into everyday life."[6] Letter writing became a regular activity for many people during the Renaissance, inspiring the creation of devices for storing and organizing papers, including stationery boxes, *tasche* or *sachetti* (letters tied up in bags), and paper weights. Some busy correspondents threaded their papers together with string and hung them on the wall.[7] The letter rack, a similar kind of object, was common enough by the mid-seventeenth century to be unmistakable in a painting. Artists exploited the fact that they were familiar, even mundane, while still capable of arousing intense curiosity because viewers were eager to imagine what the letters they revealed might contain.

Other artists whose careers emerged at the nexus of commerce, the court, and the expanding Republic of Letters, including Wallerant Vaillant and Cornelis Gijsbrechts, also painted letter racks. In Vaillant's earliest-known letter-rack painting, *A Board with Letters, Penknives and Pen Behind Ribbons* (1658), eleven different letters, some showing addresses and others flipped over to reveal broken wax seals, tempt the viewer with the revelation of their contents. A decade later, Gijsbrechts' *Board Partition with Letter Rack and Music Book* (1668) (Figure 15.1) displayed an even messier and more numerous assortment of letters—some half-opened—alluding to friendships, patronage relationships, and partially spilled secrets. He added a partly drawn curtain, alluding to the private nature of letters, as well as the fact that they were often public documents, exposed on purpose or on accident as they were peered at, copied, and passed from hand to hand.

These artists were travelers who must have written and received many letters as their careers evolved. Their letter-rack images testified to busy lives and rich social networks.[8] They also exhibited the concerns of *vanitas* paintings, especially when objects such as pocket watches or hourglasses—signifying the passage of time—were also on display. As the essays in this volume reveal, letters were the lifeblood of relationships conducted at a distance, essential to the flourishing of business, diplomacy, scholarship, politics, war, and friendship. They were also ephemeral: scraps of paper that could easily blow away if they weren't held down by ribbons—or perhaps disappear in the hands of a thief.[9] Finally, if the letters in *trompe-l'oeil* letter racks deceived the eye by appearing to be actual three-dimensional objects, then perhaps the relationships indicated by letters were also, on some level, illusory. These painters were heirs to a long-standing Renaissance fascination with the manipulation of appearances.

For Van Hoogstraten, the letter rack was highly personal. The letters he depicted were sometimes addressed to him, revealing real or imagined social connections. Van Hoogstraten's racks held personal possessions such as his razor

FIGURE 15.1 Cornelis Gijsbrechts, *Board Partition with Letter Rack and Music Book* (1668). Courtesy of Statens Museum for Kunst/National Gallery of Denmark, www. smk.dk

or comb. While such objects symbolized a general human quality such as vanity, they also belonged to him personally, serving to shape his actual appearance. His undated painting, *Trompe l'oeil of a Framed Necessary-Board* (Figure 15.2), features writing implements, a rosary, a cameo, scissors, a magnifying glass, a comb, playing cards, a book, and keys—all redolent with meaning—as well as a letter addressed to "The honourable Samuel van Hoogstraten, painter of His Holy Imperial Majesty."[10] Because of the sheer variety and often ordinary nature of objects displayed in images such as these, the letter rack became known as

FIGURE 15.2 Samuel van Hoogstraten, *Trompe l'oeil of a Framed Necessary-Board,* CMS_KLA12302, Collections—Public courtesy of © National Trust/Simon Harris

a *quodlibet* ("whatever you wish") board. It contained items that one would want readily at hand, starting with the letter.

In addition to self-referencing objects, Van Hoogstraten's images included items that appealed to specific audiences, prompting Michiel Roscam Abbing to interpret them as personalized gifts or tributes that could have facilitated Van Hoogstraten's entry into elite society when he traveled. *Trompe l'oeil of a Framed Necessary-Board* was probably completed during Van Hoogstraten's stay in London between 1662 and 1666/67. Since the letter rack includes an English play by Abraham Cowley (*The Guardian. A Comedy. Acted before Prince Charles at Trinity College, Cambridge, the 13th of March*, 1641), it may have been intended for Cowley, whom Van Hoogstraten probably met through Thomas Povey. Povey, Cowley, and another member of their circle whom Van Hoogstraten probably also encountered, Samuel Pepys, were members of the Royal Society. Pepys attended a revised version of Cowley's play in 1661 and mentioned Van Hoogstraten's work in his diary in 1662, as well as a letter-rack painting he had seen in 1668, which he claimed was "so well painted that in my whole life I never was so pleased or surprized with any picture."[11] Van Hoogstraten's personal letter-rack paintings offer the glimmerings of long-lost conversations and connections at a moment when the Republic of Letters reached further than ever.

If "a letter was a portrait of an individual by other means," a letter rack was a portrait of an individual as a member of a cosmopolitan circle 20.[12] The study of social, intellectual, and political circles is key to understanding the dissemination of the Renaissance, especially as scholars analyze the creative reception of ideas, practices, values, and art forms.[13] Letters help us perceive how this worked since the pervasive use of letters emerged in close interaction with key Renaissance developments such as the spread of commerce, the study of antiquity, the emergence of new understandings of nature, the development of states, and the frequent outbreak of war.

The essays in this volume reveal that the Renaissance understanding of the relationship between communication and community was complex and multi-faceted, encompassing a surprising geographic range. Letters enrich our understanding of the many different kinds of people who were involved in conversations that shaped the Renaissance world: not only scholars, diplomats, and merchants, but also women, Jewish converts, pirates, servants, soldiers, and physicians. A common insight found in these essays is that the lettered networks of Renaissance men and women seemed to function most effectively when the participants were neither strangers nor mere acquaintances, but individuals who orbited one another within a closer sphere of social ties, institutions, and shared culture. Membership in certain circles, as Van Hoogstraten and other letter writers knew, provided access to power and influence. But even in those communities that crossed into the "borderlands" or "regions" of the polycentric Renaissance of Letters, letter writing helped individuals assert status and shape opportunities.[14] Finally, these essays make clear that letters were not just vessels that conveyed information; the experience of writing and exchanging information played a fundamental role in redefining Renaissance values and attitudes toward knowledge, faith, politics, and society. Letters, which naturally belong to more than one place, de-center these developments from any single person or location, reminding us that the Renaissance was the product of an ongoing dialogue, both "a movement and in movement."[15]

This volume ends around 1650, a date which is generally considered to be the furthest one can stretch the concept of a Renaissance. As Europeans reckoned with a vastly expanded globe that included a previously unknown continent and gradually built a consensus around new scientific ideas and methods, the idea of a re-birth or a return to a more glorious past, which characterized the Renaissance, faded. Perhaps that is why letter-rack paintings belong to an epilogue on Renaissance letters. They pertain to the Renaissance, since the genre emerged at the very end of the period with Netherlandish artists recognized for their skill at adapting Renaissance Italian painting traditions to new contexts.[16] The images hint at a deeper background of letter writing that laid the foundations for new ways of thinking about and using letters, while also revealing the evolving, multi-faceted communities that became defined in part by letters. With the rapid expansion of Dutch commerce and the movement of friends and family on account of business, war, political crisis, and faith, artists of the mid-seventeenth century understood the importance of communicating at a distance. Letters and letter writing were nothing new, but the popularity of letter-rack paintings showed an awareness of the critical role played by letters in a world that often took people and their loved ones far from their places of birth. Although letter-rack paintings were a genre of still life, they were conscious reflections on what it meant to be a member of a diverse, cosmopolitan society that was in constant, even frenetic motion.

Letter-rack paintings trail away into a vastly different era. When the Dutch artist Thomas Collier painted letter racks at the end of the seventeenth century and the beginning of the eighteenth century in England, they were more generic, lacking in personal elements. They included newspapers and other cheap printed materials, reflections on the tumult of a new information age that were intended for a wider public than the group of intimates Van Hoogstraten had in mind.[17] In the nineteenth century, the American artists William Harnett and John Peto, influenced by the Dutch tradition, painted letter racks that appear tattered and worn, evoking nostalgia and curiosity rather than cosmopolitanism. They were no longer primarily about letters. And yet the attraction to what at first glance seems like a rather idiosyncratic subject was impressively long-lived.

Dutch Golden Age artists may have established the letter-rack still life as a genre, with its enduring, evolving fascination, but it is important to remember that the understanding of letters and community that these paintings conveyed had evolved across several centuries. Since the fourteenth century, Renaissance Italian societies grappled with an expansion of commercial, political, and cultural horizons. Letters permitted new kinds of social connections that stretched across the geographical and political boundaries that once limited the range of one's possible relationships, drawing many more individuals into correspondence that profoundly altered the way they thought about and acted in the world. Although these exchanges spanned greater and greater distances, they were intimate enough to be conducted by handwritten letter.

Perhaps it is no surprise, then, that more than a century before the Dutch letter-rack genre emerged, the first *trompe-l'oeil* painting of a letter rack appeared in fifteenth-century Venice around the time of the outbreak of the Italian Wars.[18] Vittore Carpaccio's *Letter Rack* can be found on the verso side of his *Hunting on the Lagoon* (1490–1495) (Figure 15.3), a panel painting that used to be joined to his more famous *Two Venetian Ladies*. *Two Venetian Ladies* features two aristocratic-looking women sitting on the balcony of a *palazzo* surrounded by flowers, birds, and a pet dog, gazing vacantly beyond the left edge of the panel. If the lower and upper panels were reattached, the balcony on which the women sat would have overlooked the hunting scene.[19] Although the original use of the panel is unclear, evidence of hinges indicates that it could have been a window shutter or a door with *Hunting on the Lagoon/Two Venetian Ladies* visible when the shutter/door was closed. If the panel was a shutter, the viewer would have seen the *Letter Rack* image next to the actual view from the window when the shutters were wide open. If it was the door

FIGURE 15.3 Vittore Carpaccio, *Hunting on the Lagoon* (recto); *Letter Rack* (verso), about 1490–1495. Oil on panel, 75.6 × 63.8 cm (29 ¾ × 25 ⅛ in.). Digital images courtesy of the Getty's Open Content Program

to, perhaps, a small study, the letter–rack image would appear to a viewer situated inside of the study with the door closed.[20]

In either case, the hunting/balcony scene was intended to mimic a view from a window. With *trompe-l'oeil* letters nestled into a letter rack on the back side of the same panel, Carpaccio alluded to reading letters in a private space near an open window. This theme became explicit in later Dutch works such as Vermeer's *Girl Reading a Letter at an Open Window* (Figure 15.4). In the Dutch tradition, the women are interpreted as reading love letters. It is possible that Carpaccio's work held similar connotations since *Hunting on the Lagoon / Two Venetian Ladies* contrasted the Renaissance feminine ideal of a passive, domestic life with the masculine ideal of virile action in the public domain and was probably an allegory of courtship and marriage, perhaps intended as a wedding present.[21] While no direct evidence of Carpaccio's influence on these works has been found, the similarities are intriguing.[22]

We may never know exactly what Carpaccio intended or how Italian precedents may have influenced the later genre of Dutch letter-rack still lifes. Perhaps, then, the most we can do is try to imagine what it would have been like to be a member of that fifteenth-century Venetian household pausing at an open *palazzo* window or sitting at a desk in a candle-lit study, the image of *trompe-l'oeil* letters tucked in their rack nearby. Whoever admired Carpaccio's work, whether merchant, politician, scholar, aristocratic lady, or even a servant, had a relationship to letters. The world beneath the *palazzo* windows had grown dramatically interconnected by commerce, diplomacy, war, and scholarship. It offered exciting possibilities and many dangers. With the right friends, resources, and knowledge—as well as a strong dose of *fortuna*—one

FIGURE 15.4 Johannes Vermeer, *Girl Reading a Letter by an Open Window*, ca. 1659. Oil on canvas. Inv. 1336. Bpk Bildagentur/Gemaeldegalerie Alte Meister, Staatliche Kunstsammlungen, Dresden, Germany/Herbert Boswank/Art Resource, New York

could alter one's place in it. At the same time, such a life was potentially full of illusions. Perhaps a glance over at the painted letters elicited ideas about love and courtship. And yet no one knew exactly what was in those letters or who had sent them.[23] Their mystery was part of their allure: the viewer could imagine what he or she wished. Ultimately, Renaissance letters offered many different ways to belong to, understand, and fantasize about the world beyond one's doorstep.

Notes

* I would like to thank Paula Findlen, Rebecca McIntyre, and Laura Cochrane for reading and commenting on this essay.

1 For this anecdote, see Celeste Brusati, *Artifice and Illusion: The Art and Writing of Samuel van Hoogstraten* (Chicago, IL: University of Chicago Press, 1995), 54.

2 On what the medal meant to him, see Brusati, *Artifice*, 162–63 and 167.

3 Brusati, *Artifice* and Celeste Brusati, "Honorable Deceptions and Dubious Distinctions: Self-Imagery in Trompe-l'oeil" in *Gijsbrechts, Royal Master of Deception*, ed. Olaf Koester (Copenhagen: Statens Museum for Kunst, 1999), as well as the essays in Thijs Weststeijn (ed.), *The Universal Art of Samuel van Hoogstraten (1627–1678): Painter, Writer, and Courtier* (Amsterdam: Amsterdam University Press, 2013). On his family, see Gijsbert Rutten, *De Archimedische punten van de taalbbeschouwing: David van Hoogstraten (1658–1724) en de vroegmoderne taalcultuur* (Amsterdam and Münster, 2006).

4 Michiel Roscam Abbing, "Samuel van Hoogstraten's Personal Letter-Rack Paintings: Tributes with a Message" in *The Universal Art of Samuel van Hoogstraten (1627–1678): Painter, Writer, and Courtier*, ed. Thijs Weststeijn (Amsterdam: Amsterdam University Press, 2013), 116.

5 Olaf Koester, "Cornelius Norbertus Gijsbrechts—An Introduction" in *Gijsbrechts, Royal Master of Deception*, ed. Olaf Koester (Copenhagen: Statens Museum for Kunst, 1999), 15–16.

6 Peter Burke, *The European Renaissance: Centres and Peripheries* (Malden, MA and Oxford: Blackwell Publishers, Ltd., 1998), 5.

7 Dora Thornton, *The Scholar in His Study: Ownership and Experience in Renaissance Italy* (New Haven, CT and London: Yale University Press, 1997), 130–33.

8 On Van Hoogstraten as a member of the Republic of Letters, see Thijs Weststeijn, *The Visible World: Samuel van Hoogstraten's Art Theory and the Legitimation of Painting in the Dutch Golden Age* (Amsterdam: Amsterdam University Press, 2008), 25–79.

9 See Rachel Midura's essay in this volume, Chapter 12.

10 The translation of the title belongs to Michiel Roscam Abbing. See Abbing, "Paintings," 125.

11 Pepys assumed the images were painted on a board and was shocked to realize that the board was also part of the painting. Samuel Pepys, *The Diary of Samuel Pepys*, Vol. IX: 1668–1669, eds. Robert Latham and William Matthews (Berkeley and Los Angeles, CA: University of California Press, 1976), 119. This quote is cited in Abbing, "Paintings," n. 60. For the investigation of Van Hoogstraten's relationship to this group as regards this painting, see Abbing, "Paintings," 124–28. For more on Van Hoogstraten's travels, especially in Britain, see Fatma Yalcin, "Van Hoogstraten's Success in Britain" in *The Universal Art of Samuel van Hoogstraten (1627–1678): Painter, Writer, and Courtier*, ed. Thijs Weststeijn (Amsterdam: Amsterdam University Press, 2013), 161–81.

12 Introduction to this volume, p. 20.

13 Burke, *Renaissance*, 10 and Peter Burke, "The Circulation of Knowledge" in *The Renaissance World*, ed. John Jeffries Martin (New York and London: Routledge, 2007), 203–05.

14 See Sarah Gwyneth Ross's essay in this volume, chapter 9, p. 189.

15 John Jeffries Martin, "The Renaissance: A World in Motion" in *The Renaissance World*, ed. Martin (New York and London: Routledge, 2007), 6.

16 Burke, *Renaissance*, 106.

17 Dror Wahrman, *Mr. Collier's Letter Racks: A Tale of Art and Illusion at the Threshold of the Modern Information Age* (Oxford: Oxford University Press, 2012). The personal items that appear in Collier's works—for instance, a comb—were not Collier's but rather objects he adopted from Van Hoogstraten's letter-rack paintings. Abbing, "Paintings," 128–29.

18 Another early depiction of a letter rack occurs in Niccolò Antonio Colantonio's *St Jerome in His Study* (c. 1420–after 1460). The letter rack in Colantonio's *St. Jerome* is nothing more than a single leather strap nailed to the side of his desk, stuffed with a handful of letters and a quill—just some of the many details attesting to Jerome's busy scholarship, but not a central feature of the picture or an experiment in *trompe l'oeil*.

19 *Hunting on the Lagoon* belongs to the J. Paul Getty Museum in Los Angeles and *Two Venetian Ladies* belongs to the Museo Correr in Venice.

20 Paintings on another panel would have completed the larger scene, but have been lost. Yvonne Szafran, "Carpaccio's 'Hunting on the Lagoon': A New Perspective" *The Burlington Magazine* 137, no. 1104 (March 1995): 148–58, especially 151 for her diagram of how the shutter/door would have worked.

21 Lisa Boutin Vitela, "Passive Virtue and Active Valor: Carpaccio's Two Ladies on an Altana above a Hunt" *Comitatus* 43 (2012): 133–46. On the transmission of artistic influences between Venice and the north, see the essays in Bernard Aikema and Beverly Louise Brown (eds.), *Renaissance Venice and the North: Crosscurrents in the Time of Bellini, Dürer, and Titian* (New York: Rizzoli, 1999).

22 For more on this, see Rebecca M. Norris, "Carpaccio's *Hunting on the Lagoon* and *Two Venetian Ladies*: A Vignette of Fifteenth-Century Venetian Life" (Master's Thesis, Kent State University, 2007), 66–68.

23 While now illegible, one of the letters had the name "Mozenigo" written on it, leading scholars to speculate that the patron of the painting was Andrea Mocenigo. See Jan Lauts, *Carpaccio: Paintings and Drawings Complete Edition* (London: Phaidon Press, 1962), 248.

INDEX

Locators in *italics* refer to figures, those containing 'n' refer to notes.